JANE ADDAMS, A WRITER'S LIFE

KATHERINE JOSLIN

Jane Addams,
a Writer's Life

UNIVERSITY OF ILLINOIS PRESS

URBANA AND CHICAGO

Frontispiece: Jane Addams seated in wicker chair, 1915?
(Jane Addams Collection, Swarthmore College Peace Collection)

∞ This book is printed on acid-free paper.

Library of Congress Cataloging-in-Publication Data
Joslin, Katherine, 1947–
Jane Addams : a writer's life / Katherine Joslin.
p.   cm.
Includes bibliographical references and index.
ISBN 0-252-02923-2 (cloth : alk. paper)
1. Addams, Jane, 1860–1935—Criticism and interpretation.
2. Women social workers—United States—Biography.
3. Women social reformers—United States—Biography.
I. Title.
HV40.32.A33J67   2004
361.92—dc22   2003026965

To Harrison Hayford

Contents

Acknowledgments

I am grateful to Harry Hayford, who first introduced me to Jane Addams through her letters at the University of Illinois at Chicago. He taught me that literary arguments ought to begin with things you can put your hands on, books and also letters, manuscript fragments, abandoned drafts, and musings written down and saved. This literary biography rests on the long and careful work of Mary Lynn McCree Bryan, who together with Nancy Slote and Maree de Angury, collected scattered material into a microfilm archive, an ongoing project that Bryan, Slote, and Barbara Bair are publishing in a series of volumes through the University of Illinois Press. I have come to know Jane Addams because of their dedication to scholarship, and I thank them all.

The writing of this book began in earnest in the fall of 2000 during a sabbatical leave when I traveled to Strafford, Vermont, and drifted back to Kalamazoo. The Jane Addams Papers are available, all eighty-two reels, at the Baker Library, Dartmouth College, where I found the staff helpful. I would like to thank Western Michigan University for granting me time to write and Waldo Library for purchasing the Jane Addams Papers that fall. The library staff at Waldo made the reading of the microfilm as comfortable as such reading can be. I especially thank Bettina Meyer for supporting the purchase of the microfilm collection, Regina Buchner for finding space, and Stefan Sarenius for setting up equipment. I am grateful to WMU's President Emeritus Diether Haenicke for ensuring library funds for research and former President Elson Floyd for providing an office in the library for me to work.

Pat Bakunas at the University of Illinois at Chicago Library guided me through Addams photographs, and Wendy Chmielewski at Swarthmore College gave me good advice about holdings in the Peace Collection. David Klaasen and Linnea M. Anderson at the Social Welfare History Archives, University of Minnesota, Bernard Schermetzler and Amy Sabo at the University of Wisconsin, and Jane Westenfeld at Allegheny College were all of great help to me as I gathered images for the book. I thank all of these people for their advice and also for their willingness to talk about archival holdings and scholarly projects still to be done.

My readers at the University of Illinois Press were enormously helpful to me as I worked through drafts of the book. I would like to thank them, and, especially, my editor, Joan Catapano, for her advice along the way and her sense of humor. Barbara Bair has been a perceptive reader, and I thank her for encouragement and suggestions for revision. I am grateful to Stephen Barnett for his skillful eye and good sense in copyediting the manuscript. Two graduate students, Vicky Weibert and Tracy Hall, have been genial and helpful, and I thank them for their work. I would also like to thank my colleagues Donna Campbell, Lisbeth Gant-Britton, Irma Lopez, Mary Papke, Carl Smith, and Deborah Williams for ideas about Addams and other literary figures. Over the years, I have worked closely with Janet Beer and am indebted to her for those days and nights of conversation and libation.

There are many friends and colleagues close to home who make a writer's life agreeable. I am always grateful for the intellect of Ed Galligan and the insight of Clare Goldfarb. I would like to thank Mary Meader and Ed Meader for their unflagging support and for asking questions that I ponder still. I am fortunate to have the friendship of Barbara Liner and our long years of swapping tales. I thank Emily for her indulgence of a mother's eccentricities. Of course, the book would never have been written without Tom Bailey, whose cooking is quite simply the best in Kalamazoo.

Introduction:
The Moral Imagination

Perhaps all of us have had, at certain times, a peculiar sen-
sation of discouragement and distrust come over us, when
we pick up some book which is either pokey or weak, and
find attached to the author's name a long string of scholas-
tic titles, as a F.R.S. or Ph.D. We begin to wonder what is
the earthly use of our ever trying to acquire knowledge
and insight if this poor book is all the splendidly-educated
and hard-working scholar could at last produce; there
seems so much elementary knowledge to be attacked and
cleared away before a discovery can be made, that at the
same time we find that we are half pitying the poor man
and ourselves too. We wonder how we will feel about
things if we should study for twenty years more—not that
we mean to write a book to tell people of our state.

—Jane Addams, 1881

Late in the summer of 2000, I went to a reading at the graceful white clapboard town hall in Strafford, Vermont, a place over the last
two hundred years for New England town meetings. Grace Paley and
Christopher Merrill had come to talk about the interweavings of fiction
and politics in their writing. Merrill, a poet and reporter who witnessed
the chaotic and brutal battles in the provinces of the old Yugoslavia—
places like Bosnia, Croatia, and Kosovo—argued that journalism can rise
to the level of literature and that he may share the stage with a fiction
writer like Paley if we think of writing as more than a decorative art.
Writing can become more than decorative by embracing moral dilemmas
such as the ones he encountered in the Balkans, ethnic struggles that

mirrored the tensions and motivated the wars of the twentieth century. His book *Only the Nails Remain: Scenes from the Balkan Wars* (1999) is a personal narrative that owes as much to the imagination as to history. The violence in Kosovo and Bosnia may be brought into the realm of art, both Merrill and Paley agreed, by a writer's ability to express the insights of a well-tuned moral imagination. Paley, who talked about the tension between social action and literary reflection, read poems that evening from *Begin Again* (2000), conceding that her urge when confronted with a complicated concern is "to slip into fiction."

In talking about the prickly relationship between the idea of justice and the writer's imagination, she echoed her own words in *Just as I Thought* (1998): "But what art is about—and this is what justice is about, although you'll have your own interpretations—is the illumination of what isn't known, the lighting up of what is under a rock, of what has been hidden."[1] The talk about the nature of literature and its relationship to the real world that evening reminded me of no one more than Jane Addams, who, in company with writers like Merrill and Paley, wove politics and fiction into art.

Jane Addams couldn't help but tell stories. She resisted the scholarly impulse to stick to an argument, to verify sources, to limit the imagination to the confines of the rational mind. Her books tell a bold personal story of her move from Cedarville, Illinois, into the confining academic world of Rockford Female Seminary and from college through a long period of neurasthenic doubt and leisurely travel into America's second city, settling along with other migrants and immigrants into the neighborhood of Halsted Street, and from Chicago moving intellectually and politically onto an international stage at The Hague. We might think of her books as imaginative autobiographical arguments, giving us the tale of her own life as though it carried with it the story of America's conscience and consciousness of moral questions. She stitched into her story the experiences of hundreds of Chicagoans, people she met in the street, vivid characters who told their stories to her as though giving her the permission to tell them to us. In these vignettes she plotted fates in ways that fiction writers have always done. She was an intuitive and synthetic thinker, writing at a time when the academic disciplines emerging around her valorized rational, empirical, logical thinking with its philosophical roots in the Enlightenment. Addams admired the scientific mind at the same time that her own mind sought routes around the boundaries of academe, imagining a moral world that transcended, and implicitly defied, scholarly analysis.

Scholars and critics have over the years acknowledged her literary bent. Christopher Lasch, in *The Social Thought of Jane Addams* (1965), says of her stories that they "describe how it felt to stumble upon a whole realm of social existence that the conventions of middle-class culture and education had completely concealed."[2] William O. Douglas, reconsidering her relevance to readers a hundred years after her birth in *A Centennial Reader* (1960), calls her words "a real tonic, even though they were written about conditions that we like to think have passed away" (we might well say the same thing today).[3] Helen Hall goes further in appreciating that Addams's writing "brought the clarity and self-discipline of the artist" to social work.[4] And Ashley Montagu adds to the perception of her as a literary artist by placing her in the company of Emerson and Thoreau as one who wrote "as beautifully as they did, but who felt even more strongly than they, that words must be supported by acts."[5] Working to rescue the real Jane Addams from her image as public saint, Allen F. Davis, in his influential biography *American Heroine: The Life and Legend of Jane Addams* (1973), notes wryly that she used fictional techniques to create the myth herself: "Her motives were not entirely selfish, of course, she did want to promote her reform ideas to publicize Hull House, but what better way to accomplish these goals than to write of herself as a heroine?"[6] Mary Jo Deegan begins her academic book *Jane Addams and the Men of the Chicago School, 1892–1918* (1988) with a disclaimer: Addams "was opposed to academic sociology, elitism, patriarchy, and intellectualism."[7]

Deegan is right that Addams had a midwestern small-town skepticism of the intellectual life, social hierarchy, and pretensions of all sorts. We might think of her as predisciplinary rather than antidisciplinary in her approach to the social and political world in Chicago. In *Jane Addams and the Dream of American Democracy: A Life* (2002), Jean Bethke Elshtain portrays her as a public intellectual. "It is the task of the public intellectual as I understand that vocation to keep the nuances alive. A public intellectual is not a paid publicist, not a spinner, nor in the pocket of a narrowly defined purpose," she explains about her biography.[8]

As a public intellectual with a well-tuned moral imagination, Jane Addams could never bring herself to write an academic book. As she put it to her Rockford classmates, she might curl up with such a book only to "wonder what is the earthly use of our ever trying to acquire knowledge and insight if this poor book is all the splendidly-educated and hardworking scholar could at last produce." We can hear in her declaration the voice of a college student nearing graduation. At the age of twenty-one, she eschewed a literary life, declaring, "not that we mean to write a book to tell people of our state." As she entered middle age, however, she did the very thing she so confidently rejected in her youth.

It may well be that her best reader was Harriet Monroe, the Chicago writer and editor of *Poetry Magazine,* who makes the point that Addams's first book, *Democracy and Social Ethics* (1902), "is as interesting as a novel in spite of its formidable title. It is a condition, not a theory, which she presents in this record of her own experience."[9] Monroe's ear catches the sound of Addams's prose: "And the style is so easy and familiar, so much like gracious talk, that one follows it over the heights and depths of a great subject scarcely conscious of the author's mountaineer venturesomeness." Addams's books about the social settlement in immigrant Chicago have the look and feel of life in the midwestern settlement of Cedarville, Illinois, where she was raised in the 1860s. Later, in Chicago as she walks along Halsted Street, she listens to village gossip, local political wranglings, and tall tales of misery and triumph. In her books, she chats with her middle-class readers, using a polyphony of urban voices to illustrate her arguments.

We might curl up more comfortably with her books, as readers in the twenty-first century, and enjoy them as literature if we think of them as imaginative rather than scholarly. Addams displays an eye and ear for language and, at times, a lyrical sensibility. Her nephew James Weber Linn, who has done more than any other biographer to reveal the vital woman who was his aunt, has a good ear for the sound of her writing. In *Jane Addams: A Biography* (1935) he quotes a passage from her autobiography *Twenty Years at Hull-House* (1910) about childhood play with her stepbrother George Haldeman:

> We had of course our favorite places and trees and birds and flowers. It is hard to reproduce the companionship which children establish with nature, but certainly it is much too unconscious and intimate to come under the head of esthetic appreciation, or anything of the sort. When we said that the purple wind-flowers—the anemone patens, "Looked as if the winds had made them," we thought much more of the fact that they were windborn than that they were beautiful; we clapped our hands in sudden joy over the soft radiance of the rainbow, but its enchantment lay in our half-belief that a pot of gold was to be found at its farther end; we yielded to a soft melancholy when we heard the whippoorwill in the early twilight, but while he aroused in us vague longings of which we spoke solemnly, we felt no beauty in his call.[10]

Her voice is straightforward, pragmatic, juxtaposing the promise of poetic meaning and the practicality of childhood experience. The language she uses is simple, conversational, except for the scientific name "anemone patens" with its subtle music. Had she followed her imagination, she might have ventured into free verse poetry, creating a voice from the Midwest to match the voice she admired in Walt Whitman. Her sentences build in length and complexity of ideas, ending in the long periodic sentence that promises symbolic meaning and then mocks the desire. Not that meaning isn't there. Her line, "we felt no beauty in his call" reminds us of Wallace Stevens's lone figure in "The Snow Man" who beholds "Nothing that is not there and the nothing that is."[11] The prose poetry of the middle land, for Addams, gives no ground to sentimentality.

Her imagination ranged beyond creativity for its own sake into dense moral thickets that confounded her generation and continue to vex us today: the social and economic disparity between rich and poor; the cultural ramifications of migration; the lure of the capitalist marketplace; the politics of fair play, especially in cities; and the strains of nationalism on world peace. We have not come much farther toward easing these tensions as we move into the twenty-first century.

Jane Addams has always been thought of as an intensely public woman, the cofounder of Hull-House, the social settlement in Chicago that opened in 1889, and the first president of the Women's International League for Peace and Freedom and the first female recipient of the Nobel Peace Prize in 1931. Ironically, although she was considered in her day the mother of social work in America, social work programs in universities today focus more on the current culture than on the history of the discipline. Sociology, perhaps always shy of women, has nurtured a decidedly male pantheon of thinkers, and it is only amid the political revisions of the late twentieth century that textbooks have retrieved some of her writings. American history has been her strongest advocate in the university curriculum, although historians have largely moved away from discussions of such primary figures as Addams, a white Anglo-Saxon Protestant, into the experiences of the ethnic and racial communities she depicted in her writing. She has appeared in recent years in literary anthologies that have sought an interdisciplinary range of genres. The book considered her masterwork is *Twenty Years at Hull-House*. Few scholars have read her many other books.

A used bookstore may be the best barometer of literary reputation and the place to see the fate of writers who have slipped between traditional academic disciplines. Ask where to find Jane Addams's books and you will often get a quizzical stare: sociology, perhaps; Midwest or Chicago writers, a good bet; American history, at times; women's or feminist studies, depending on the bookstore. The truth is that her moral and artistic imagination transcends disciplinary boundaries constructed by academe in the late nineteenth and early twentieth centuries. We might place her most accurately, I am arguing, on the shelf among literary writers of her day.

The themes in her books resemble those of other midwestern writers. Hamlin Garland, Sherwood Anderson, and Jane Addams sensed the isolation of rural and small-town life and created characters who yearn to move to Chicago, the enticingly flawed place she described in *The Spirit of Youth and the City Streets* (1909). Her study of what was called the "white slave trade" in *A New Conscience and an Ancient Evil* (1912) explored the movement of daring yet vulnerable young women into the city, women like the Dreiser sisters from Terre Haute, Indiana, whose story their brother Theodore tried to tell in *Sister Carrie* (1900) and *Jennie Gerhardt* (1911). Addams felt an affinity for the prickly Charlotte Perkins Gilman, whose work includes sociological texts as well as fiction, especially "The Yellow Wallpaper," a fictional story based on the S. Weir Mitchell "rest cure" that both women underwent to relieve hysteria, the depression that plagued wealthy, educated women of their day. Her literary coterie included W. E. B. Du Bois, who, like Addams, crossed disciplines and mixes genres in *The Souls of Black Folk* (1903) in a monumental effort to record what he sees and especially what he hears as he travels through the South. The midwestern realist Zona Gale and the muckraker who so unsettled John D. Rockefeller, Ida Tarbell, both friends of hers, created a literature that struggles to be more than decorative and registers a well-tuned moral imagination. The intensely political exposés of lynchings in America attracted Addams to Ida Wells-Barnett.

Midwestern writers surrounded her in Chicago although they were not always as aware as she was of the immigrant communities that made up three-quarters of the population in the late nineteenth century. Her descriptions of the poor caught in the jaws of industry read like the naturalist novels produced by the muckraking interlopers Upton Sinclair and Frank Norris, whose work she admired. Her Chicago looked and sounded much like the literary world of radical younger writers, including James T. Farrell and Richard Wright. Her book *The Long Road of Woman's Memory* (1916) is a modern, even modernist, consideration of female mythology and psychology, themes that Willa Cather worked out in tales of the Midwest and the West. In her most literary book Addams imagined herself and the immigrant women in Chicago partaking in a collective maternal memory, one she depicted as thrusting its "ghostly fingers into the delicate fabric of human experience."

We might think of her alongside writers outside the Midwest, including Henry James, whom she encountered in her youth, and William Dean Howells, whom she called "a charming comrade," and her contemporary Edith Wharton, whose politics often clashed with hers over the years of their writing. Addams's books earned the admiration of William James, who wanted to be sure that copies of *Newer Ideals of Peace* (1907) were sent to H. G. Wells and George Bernard Shaw, whom he called "a fanatic moralist of the new style." Shaw and Wells along with John Galsworthy were literary kin to settlement workers. Hull-House drew the attention of other international writers. In 1896, Addams journeyed to Yásnaya Polyana to talk with Leo Tolstoy and to London to meet with Fabian social thinkers and writers, including Beatrice and Sidney Webb and Eleanor Marx Aveling. She read and admired Virginia Woolf, who questioned the literary value of writers like Galsworthy and Wells.

This study of the literary life of Jane Addams crosses genres in that it borrows from biography, social history, and literary criticism. In a review of biographies about literary figures, Jay Parini considers the difficulty biographers encounter in trying to tell the story of literary lives: "The problem is that most writers, unlike soldiers, politicians, and wilderness explorers, lead outwardly dull lives."[12] "Good biographers" of literary figures, he argues, "therefore, become fiction-makers." The story of a figure like Jane Addams, who had a full active life as a "wilderness explorer" (if the urban terrain of Chicago can be seen as a culturally wild place) can easily move away from her literary work toward the drama of her life. I am deliberately moving in the direction of the literary work she produced with the goal of enhancing our understanding of her moral imagination as she expressed it in artistic form.

Another goal of this study is to try through her writing and her sense of herself as a literary woman to look beyond the popular image of Addams. Telling the story of such a well-known public figure is a difficult task. The recognizable narrative of her life has a predictable and forceful plot, one she did much to construct and preserve, as Davis points out: "The public image of Jane Addams as a gentle angel of mercy, a lady bountiful bent on aiding the lowly had some remote basis in fact, but an accurate picture of her must include the shrewd business woman, the expert fund raiser and publicity agent, as well as the careful compromiser."[13] Based rather loosely on factual details, the popular tale develops from embellishments and arrangement of events into a shape that, despite the work of revisionist biographers, has satisfied American readers for a century.

The story goes something like this. Laura Jane Addams (she called herself Jennie as a child), the daughter of John Huy Addams, a second-generation pioneer, entrepreneur, and political friend of Abraham Lincoln, grew up in a moneyed household in Cedarville, Illinois. Her father owned a sawmill, a gristmill, and the town bank and went on to serve his community in the state legislature. Sarah Addams, her otherwise hardy mother, died pregnant at forty-five when Jane was only two. Naturally the young motherless child looked to her father for moral guidance. Suffering from a congenitally malformed spine, Jane grew to be strong in character and graduated first in her class at Rockford Female Seminary. She survived the machinations of her overbearing (not to say wicked) stepmother, Anna Haldeman Addams. The frail young woman responded to her father's sense of social responsibility and Rockford's Christian mission by moving to Chicago in 1889 with her friend Ellen Gates Starr to live and work among the poor in the settlement they founded at Hull-House in an immigrant neighborhood on Halsted Street. Her decision came after eight years of hysteria and the spinal deformity that put marriage and the rigors of childbearing out of the question. Her settlement work at Hull-House and her subsequent peace work in the Women's International League for Peace and Freedom gave useful expression to her womanly and motherlike qualities in the service of the larger human community, and thus she became a public sage and even saint, creating the profession of social work, largely a woman's field even to this day. Her pacifism developed alongside her social work but came under fire during the First World War, when her lack of political savvy resulted in public disfavor, and yet she continued to nurture and nourish the nation. Before her death in 1935, she became the first woman to receive the Nobel Peace Prize, crowning the many achievements of her long life. Addams distinguished herself as perhaps the best-known public woman in America before Eleanor Roosevelt.

The many versions of the narrative that we have from her as well as from friends, family, and scholars move sluggishly after telling the dramatic story of her early life. The main obstacle appears to be the astonishing number of institutions and organizations that surrounded her life and work. Mary Lynn McCree Bryan, the tenacious editor of the Jane Addams's Papers Project, attaches her to no fewer than 173 organizations in *The Jane Addams Papers: A Comprehensive Guide* (1996). Organizations such as the American Academy of Political and Social Science, the American Civil Liberties Union, the Century of Progress Exposition in Chicago, the Daughters of the American Revolution, the Fortnightly Club of Chicago, the Juvenile Protective Association, the League of Nations, the National Women's Party, the New School for Social Research in New York, Northwestern University, the Save the Children Fund, the Social Workers Country Club, the Socialist Labor Party, the University of Chicago, and the Women's International League for Peace and Freedom all have stories of their own, stories in which Jane Addams is merely an individual with, in many cases, a good deal of authority and influence. The well-known narrative of her early life soon glides away from Jane Addams into the story of her memberships. Here the story has so many parts that it often branches into a listing of her political battles with the bosses of Chicago and Illinois and with the corporate forces surrounding her, the growth of programs at Hull-House, and later, her peace work, the public vilification of her during and after the First World War, and her international activities in the 1920s. Indeed, she herself diverts the reader's attention from her private life in her own telling of the story in *Twenty Years at Hull-House*. Jill Conway has observed in the autobiographies of Progressive Era women, including Addams, that the narratives they tell are flat and not as revealing as their letters. As Carolyn Heilbrun has argued in *Writing a Woman's Life* (1988), women of Addams's generation found telling the private story of their individual lives unnerving and therefore told a story that moved into the shelter of the larger world around them.[14]

Another diversion is the desire to see her life as part of the story of female achievement at the turn into the last century. Feminist scholars in the latter twentieth century, as a rallying project, took up the considerable task of retrieving women writers and placing them on a public rather than a private stage. A group of young women scholars, new to academe, were eager to identify with the history and literature of female writers. McCree Bryan places her reclamation project in this tradition: "With the reawakening of the woman's movement in the mid-part of the 20th century, women began a search for the heroines of the past. What had women accomplished not only on their own behalf, but also for humankind?"[15] The new narratives about the collective female effort in America focused on the public good. The retrieval of heroines encouraged the newly public women of the late twentieth century, the group of female scholars making their own way into professional life, to tell the story of the movement of women into public life in America.

The narrative of female achievement begins with the story of nineteenth-century women living within the private, domestic sphere of activity and influence and then heroically breaking out into the public, social sphere that had been male territory. Addams perhaps more than any woman of her time has come to embody the move from the domestic to the public sphere. Here, too, no one has told the story of her movement across the traditional boundary better than she herself did. Her autobiography takes us on a walk in the public square where John Addams, the dignified banker, tips his hat to his young daughter, who sees herself as ugly and unworthy. As the citizens watch the spectacle, Addams describes the scene from the eye of young Jane:

I imagined that the strangers were filled with admiration for this dignified person, and I prayed with all my heart that the ugly, pigeon-toed little girl, whose crooked back obliged her to walk with her head held very much upon one side, would never be pointed out to these visitors as the daughter of this fine man. . . . One day I met my father coming out of his bank on the main street of the neighboring city which seemed to me a veritable whirlpool of society and commerce. With a playful touch of exaggeration, he lifted his high and shining silk hat and made me an imposing bow.[16]

In the public square, a "veritable whirlpool of society and commerce," the domestic heroine is transformed into a public figure. Addams's tone, like Benjamin Franklin's, is ironic and playful, and yet the point about her identity is clear. She is moving, along with her generation of girls, into public life, and attention is being paid.

The narrative of the frail yet eager young woman from Illinois, the quintessential female success story, moves away from her personal experiences into her larger symbolic meaning in American culture. As a public woman she embodied a cultural icon, as Erwin Panofsky describes the term, the "basic attitude of a nation, a period, a class, a religious or philosophical persuasion—unconsciously qualified by one personality and condensed into one work."[17] To the public, both in the United States and abroad, she became "Saint Jane." The British reformer William T. Stead, who visited her at Hull-House, captures the icon in its most potent form in his 1894 exposé of vice in urban America, *If Christ Came to Chicago!* His view of her is laden with metaphors from the stage. He watches the midwestern city as "an intensely interested spectator of the rapidly unfolding drama of city life in the great city."[18] Christ asks, "Who is My Neighbor?" Stead answers, "The poor." With no sense of irony, Stead points out to Christ that no one has fulfilled the task better than Jane Addams. She embodies "a woman's instinct of natural motherliness," a "gracious and blessed influence," and as a modern-day saint, "Miss Addams, pale and weary, but indomitable to the last, answer[s] with ready helpfulness to every appeal from without." He goes on to make the link between Addams and Christ even stronger: "Miss Addams, like the name of the Lord, is a strong tower, and not the righteous only but all the forlorn and miserable in the neighborhood feel that if they can but run into that stronghold they are safe."

Jane Addams of Hull-House was already, only five years after her move to Chicago, a quasireligious figure, saint and sage, a blending of Mary and Christ, even a strong tower and refuge, indistinguishable from Hull-House itself. Indeed, if the move of American women into professional life were to be symbolized by Addams and social work, who would dare find the move questionable? She was to become over the next two decades a cultural icon beyond reproach.

In reality, of course, she was an odd candidate for Mother Mary. Jane Addams was unmarried, a virginal public figure, perhaps, and never a literal mother, although she helped to care for nieces and nephews. The truth is that Addams preferred the intimate company of women, first in her girlhood attachments to Vallie Beck and Ida Carey, later to her Rockford teacher Sarah Anderson and especially her classmate Ellen Gates Starr, her professional partner at Hull-House. In Chicago she met Mary Rozet Smith, a beautiful and wealthy woman eight years her junior, who would become the long love of her life. Many women of their generation chose to live together. Blanche Weisen Cooke argues that such relationships may be seen as homosocial, if not homosexual, in that women preferred to keep company with each other. Carroll Smith-Rosenberg likewise uses metaphoric language in imagining a "female world of love and ritual."[19] In the most recent portrait of Addams, Jean Bethke Elshtain maintains, somewhat defensively, that such female relationships were celibate in nature: "Celibate lives need not be lonely lives or distorted lives."[20] Kathryn Kish Sklar has discovered that Mary began to pay Jane's bills in the 1890s and, too, became a dominant figure in the funding of social work in Chicago.[21] Henry James referred to couplings among educated, well-to-do women on the East Coast as "Boston marriages." This book will, in part, chronicle the relationship as it developed in the letters between the two women. Jane and Mary called their forty-year relationship, quite simply, a marriage.

Addams's public image melded remnants of the Victorian angel in the house with the newly independent college woman, giving her the sheltering wings of the domestic angel in the city. She readily accepted the maternal public image, writing to her sister Alice Addams Haldeman as early as 1893 after speaking to the Nineteenth-Century Club of New York: "(I find I am considered quite the grandmother of American settlements) and I have spoken at Bryn Mawr, Vassar & Wellesley, and at Smith tonight."[22] In a more personal letter to Mary Smith, she wrote from the Paris Exposition in 1900, "I am regarded as a veteran by all of the Settlement people here and find myself a little amused by it."[23] As her compatriot Henry Adams looked upon the Dynamo and fretted over the fate of the Virgin, Jane Addams joked comfortably about herself as cultural icon.

Icons, of course, can be difficult to control. As Addams struggled to place herself on an international stage amid the outbreak of the First World War, she stumbled when the public turned against her at home.

During time of war, she was to learn, the young soldier becomes the central figure in public life, the symbol of homeland and the icon of manliness and nobility, irresistible to people less involved in warfare. Her womanly image, part angel and part mother, worked against her in the role of capable, rational pacifist; she could not function effectively or even credibly as an expert on war, nor even as a mother of soldiers. During the war years and over the 1920s, she found herself condemned as inexperienced and naïve at best and treasonous at worst. After some time in the wilderness, however, Addams reemerged in old age as a noble figure in the international peace effort, the first president of the Women's International League for Peace and Freedom and first female recipient of the Nobel Peace Prize. The public, in the wake of the Depression, began to revere her again nearly as much as they had vilified her.

Christopher Lasch, among the twentieth-century critics who considered Jane Addams a serious American intellectual, has come the closest to understanding the myth of her saintliness in his introduction to *The Social Thought of Jane Addams* (1965): "Praising her goodness, her saintliness, was a way to avoid answering her questions. The myth of Jane Addams served to render her harmless."[24] By coopting her criticism and by seeing her as cultural icon, the American public blunted her power as a citizen and as a single figure. One need only read the titles of the many biographies of Addams to see how the view of her as a good woman and a useful citizen has endured over the years since her death in 1935: Miriam Gilbert's *Jane Addams: World Neighbor* (1960), John C. Farrell's *Beloved Lady: A History of Jane Addams' Ideas on Reform and Peace* (1967), Cornelia Meigs's *Jane Addams: Pioneer of Social Justice* (1970), Daniel Levine's *Jane Addams and the Liberal Tradition* (1971), Allen F. Davis's *American Heroine: The Life and Legend of Jane Addams* (1973), Mary Jo Deegan's *Jane Addams and the Men of the Chicago School, 1892–1918* (1990), Eleanor J. Stebner's *The Women of Hull House: A Study in Spirituality, Vocation, and Friendship* (1997), Barbara Garland Polikoff's *With One Bold Act: The Story of Jane Addams* (1999), Gioia Diliberto's *A Useful Woman: The Early Life of Jane Addams* (1999), Shannon Jackson's *Lines of Activity: Performance, Historiography, Hull-House Domesticity* (2000) and Jean Bethke Elshtain's *Jane Addams and the Dream of American Democracy: A Life* (2002). She is cast as neighbor and friend, a loved and admired lady, a spiritual guide and a trusted citizen of Chicago, and always as a bold, useful woman in national and international politics.

The Jane Addams outside the public view has remained a little-known figure, and the Jane Addams who lived as a writer is hardly known at all. The private woman lived a long, vigorous life and was given to reflection and sensitive to language. She grasped the ironies of the world around her. She came from the American Midwest and, in so many ways, her ideas about community, neighborhood, collaboration, compromise, all based on the interweavings of the prairie and pioneer life, came from nowhere more than from Cedarville, Illinois. The hometown girl, however, came from the leisure class, and we would be wrong to exclude class as a marker in her way of viewing the human condition. In her mind, the East Coast was the center of serious intellectual training, especially for women. Too, the East provided a safe harbor from the often chaotic democracy of the middle land. She had hoped to go to Smith College with its intensely intellectual education; during times of stress, she went to Cape Cod for rest; as she grew older, Addams vacationed in Bar Harbor, Maine, at Hull's Cove, in a cottage she owned with Mary Smith. Not surprisingly, we remember her, if at all, as Jane Addams of Hull-House, not Jane Addams of Hull's Cove; yet the truth is that she was both the public and the private woman.

Jane Addams is an appealing literary figure in that the books she wrote resist being merely decorative and all express a well-tuned moral imagination. Yet, or perhaps as a consequence, her books are seldom read today. Only her most obviously autobiographical work, *Twenty Years at Hull-House*, is always in print and is most often read only in anthologized snippets. In college classrooms, the essay most often read is "The Snare of Preparation," chapter four of her autobiography, an essay that can be discussed alongside Emerson's "The American Scholar," both suspicious of the academic enterprise. Nothing goes over as well in the American classroom as a good scolding of teachers. The book she herself liked best, *The Spirit of Youth and the City Streets*, has been reprinted from time to time and paints a fetching picture of adolescent exuberance that pushes beyond the shabby traps laid in its way by adults. In recent years, the University of Illinois Press has worked to bring all her books back into print.

I hope in this study of her writing to convince my readers to find Jane Addams's books in their libraries and bookstores and to curl up with them at home. At the turn into the twenty-first century there is every reason to reconsider the work of a Progressive Era writer like Addams. She wrote ten books of considerable literary quality and collaborated on three others.

The first chapter of this book, "Three Journeys," considers two seminal essays, "The Objective Value of a Social Settlement" and "The Subjective Necessity for Social Settlements" that first appeared in *Philanthropy and Social Progress* (1893), and a sociological study, *Hull-House Maps and Papers* (1895) that Addams co-edited with Florence Kelley. Chapter two, "Finding a Voice," discusses her three early books, full of the vitality of new ideas, *Democracy and Social Ethics*, *Newer Ideals of Peace*, and *The Spirit of Youth and the City Streets*. The third chapter, "Public and Private," looks at her autobiography, *Twenty Years at Hull-House*, together with her study of prostitution, *A New Conscience and an Ancient Evil*, and the propaganda she wrote for the Bull Moose Party. Chapter four, "Telling a War Story," views her pacifism through the collaborative history, *Women at the Hague* (1915), written by Addams, Emily Greene Balch, and Alice Hamilton. Her war stories include her most literary work, *The Long Road of Woman's Memory*, and the retrospective, *Peace and Bread in Time of War* (1922). The fifth chapter of this study, "Honest Reminiscence," examines the experimental nature of *The Second Twenty Years at Hull-House* (1930), together with *The Excellent Becomes the Permanent* (1932), a book of eulogies that includes her own. The concluding chapter, "Writing a Life," chronicles her work on the biography *My Friend, Julia Lathrop* (1935) at the same time that biographers, including James Weber Linn, eagerly sought material on her life, much as I do today.

Jane Addams's papers from dozens of collections—the University of Illinois at Chicago, Swarthmore College, Smith College, the Newberry Library, the Library of Congress, the British Library, the Chicago Historical Society, and the Cedarville Historical Society, among many others—are available to scholars in a microfilm edition, *The Jane Addams Papers, 1860–1960*, edited by Mary Lynn McCree Bryan, Nancy Slote, and Maree de Angury. This book relies on their long dedication to the project, collecting, sorting, arranging, identifying, and preserving thousands of documents associated with Jane Addams. Bryan, Barbara Bair, and de Angury are in the process of selecting material from the microfilm archive for book publication and have completed the first volume, *The Selected Papers of Jane Addams, Volume I, Preparing to Lead, 1860–81*. In this biography I am presenting all quotations as they exist in the original without emendation and ask the reader's indulgence for turn-of-the-last-century variants in spelling and usage.

I have come to know Jane Addams as a writer through her papers as well as her books and essays. Her literary inclinations can be seen as early as her college essays, where her didacticism collides with her desire to entertain, invent, embellish, or mythologize. "She wanted to write about something important," Davis says of these essays, "and she began to develop the habits of a writer while she was in college."[25] During her college years, she wrote for the *Rockford Seminary Magazine* and became its editor in her first literary job. And after college, as she worked her way through an eight-year depression, Addams's desire to write is evident in her letters and articles. Much of her ambivalence as a writer resolved itself during her first years at Hull-House. Influenced by the intensely political rhetoric of Florence Kelley, Addams helped to edit an early sociological study of her Halsted Street neighborhood. She emerged from that publishing failure as a more experimental writer, one willing to rethink the value and influence of her voice in a marketplace that would require more than careful arrangement of statistics and maps to attract the middle-class readers she would need in order to popularize her social ideas.

Her turn toward the literary and away from the social-scientific is perhaps the distinctive feature of her writing. In her first book, *Democracy and Social Ethics*, she sets her course as a writer, making the point that the story of American experience is to be found "by mixing on the thronged and common road where all men must turn out for one another" (6).[26] Explaining her method of argument by illustration, Addams points out that "ideas only operate upon the popular mind through will and character, and must be dramatized before they reach the mass of men." Or, as her favorite novelist, Charles Dickens, has Mr. Sleary, the impresario of the circus, put it to the industrialist, Mr. Gradgrind, in *Hard Times*, "Don't be croth with uth poor vagabondth. People mutht be amuthed. They can't be alwayth a learning, nor yet they can't be alwayth working, they an't made for it."[27]

Addams clearly sees the work of the imagination as the source of storytelling: "The popular books are the novels, dealing with life under all possible conditions, and they are widely read not only because they are entertaining, but also because they in a measure satisfy an unformulated belief that to see farther, to know all sorts of men, in an indefinite way, is a preparation for better social adjustment—for the remedying of social ills" (8). Addams's measure of literature—it allows us "to see farther, to know all sorts"—is precisely the way Grace Paley sees her craft today—the "illumination of what isn't known, the lighting up of what is under a rock, of what has been hidden."

Mikhail Bakhtin's theory of the dialogic urge of the novel, the orchestrating of diverse voices and the depiction of the novelist as ventriloquist, may help us understand how Addams's dramatic use of voices from the street, talking about the issues of the day—the conditions in the slums, the white slave trade in young girls, youthful behavior perceived as crime, immigrant culture, the warring instinct, urban culture and folklore—moved beyond the monologic or static voice of social tracts.[28] In developing her arguments, she dramatically juxtaposed the manners, customs, rituals, and values of the immigrant poor living on Halsted Street with those of the volunteer charity workers who come from communities situated a safe distance away. Her books, dialogic in nature, have much in common with novels in that she shed the garments of her gender and class in favor of a variety of costumes, a rhetorical cross-dressing, crossing the boundaries of gender, class, ethnicity, and race.

Jane Addams's creative impulse was to disregard convention in talking to her audience about two stories that she knew to be true: immigrants, as they poured into Chicago, were negotiating their way into an ethnically textured culture; and wealthy, educated women who had no intention of going back home were negotiating their way into male-defined professions. Her books brought voices from Halsted Street into conversation with the voices from Hull-House. Her literary goal was to establish her identity and the authenticity of her voice by writing an autobiography, in a sense, of the collective community. All her books may be read together as a single, long study of memory and consciousness. She began by mapping the terrain of Cedarville, Illinois, and then of the countries of Europe and Asia. As she moved to Chicago on the outskirts of academia, she worked to map the immigrant communities that made up the Halsted neighborhood. Much of the energy of her early books comes from her relaying of voices from the community as though the immigrants can only have force through her writing, as though she is a credible conduit. Her writing, at these times, has much in common with drama.

Later in life, as she questioned her ability to speak for the group, Addams shifted emphasis from the street to the terrain of her own mind, her memory, and her consciousness as they registered the events of the outside world. In 1930, mindful of her advancing age (claiming sixty-something but not the evident seventy she was that year), she introduced the story of *The Second Twenty Years at Hull-House* with a telling portrait of herself: "Even if we, the elderly, have nothing to report but sordid compromises, nothing to offer but a disconcerting acknowledgment that life has marked us with its slow stain, it is still better to define our position. With all our errors thick upon us, we may at least be entitled to the comfort of Plato's intimation that truth itself may be discovered by honest reminiscence" (6). With the marks of what would come to be called literary modernism everywhere present in this late book, Jane Addams insisted that "honest reminiscence" might gain validity through its typicality. She wrote what others of her generation had experienced. The reader could rely on her, she pledged, to record a collective consciousness in her reminiscence.

William James, her most insightful critic, wrote to tell her that he thought *Democracy and Social Ethics* was "one of the great books of our time."[29] After reading *Newer Ideals of Peace*, he wrote again, admiring the force of her voice: "Yours is a deeply original mind, and all so quiet and harmless! Yet revolutionary in the extreme."[30] Of *The Spirit of Youth and the City Streets*, James put it even more eloquently: "Hard not to cry at certain pages! The fact is, Madam, that you are not like the rest of us, who *seek* the truth and *try* to express it. *You inhabit* reality; and when you open your mouth truth can't help being uttered."[31]

She inhabited reality by blending other voices into her own, allowing her to speak through and for the people surrounding her at Hull-House. She kept James's letters and noted his critique in *The Long Road of Woman's Memory*: "[W]hen I really want to learn about life, I must depend upon my neighbors, for, as William James insists, the most instructive human documents lie along the beaten path" (xi). The stories she told about her own life interwoven with the lives around her make for good reading still. I am convinced that reading her books, articles, speeches, even her college essays, and surely her letters will allow us to see beyond the public woman to glimpse the writer at work.

Jane Addams's birthplace,
drawing of Cedarville, Illinois.
(University of Illinois at Chicago,
the University Library, Jane
Addams Memorial Collection,
JAMC neg. 924)

Jane Addams at age eight, 1868.
(University of Illinois at Chicago,
the University Library, Jane
Addams Memorial Collection,
JAMC neg. 2)

[Sarah] Alice Addams
(Haldeman), age nineteen,
1872. (Photograph by
G. W. Barnes, Rockford,
Illinois; Jane Addams
Collection, Swarthmore
College Peace Collection)

Jane Addams, about eighteen
years old, ca. 1878. (Photograph
by Samuel V. Allen, Freeport,
Illinois; Jane Addams Collection,
Swarthmore College Peace Collection)

Jane Addams in
Rockford Female
Seminary class picture,
ca. 1881. (Photograph
by Wallace Kirkland;
University of Illinois at
Chicago, the University
Library, Jane Addams
Memorial Collection,
JAMC neg. 1105)

Hull-House neighbor-
hood and people.
(University of Illinois at
Chicago, the University
Library, Jane Addams
Memorial Collection,
JAMC neg. 314)

Ellen Gates Starr.
(University of Illinois at
Chicago, the University
Library, Jane Addams
Memorial Collection,
JAMC neg. 920)

Jane Addams and Mary Rozet Smith, ca. 1896.
(Jane Addams Collection, Swarthmore College Peace Collection)

Jane Addams, age forty,
ca. 1900; "Faithfully yours."
(Jane Addams Collection,
Swarthmore College
Peace Collection)

Richard Ely, ca. 1910.
(University Archives,
the University of
Wisconsin, Madison)

Ida M. Tarbell, ca. 1907, by Misses Wilson and Kelly, as seen in *The American Magazine* (1911) advertising Ida Tarbell's series on the American woman. (The Ida M. Tarbell Collection, Special Collections, Pelletier Library, Allegheny College)

Jane Addams's and Mary Rozet Smith's summer home, Hull's Cove, Bar Harbor, Maine. (Jane Addams Collection, Swarthmore College Peace Collection)

International Congress of Women at The Hague, 1915. The women on the platform include Jane Addams (sixth from left) and Rosika Schwimmer (fourth from left). (Records of the Women's International League for Peace and Freedom, Swarthmore College Peace Collection)

Second International Congress, Zurich, 1919. The back row includes Mary Church Terrell (eighth from left), Alice Hamilton (twelfth from left); the front row, seated, includes Jeanette Rankin, Jane Addams (sixth from left), Lucia Ames Mead, and Emily Greene Balch. (Records of the Women's International League for Peace and Freedom, Swarthmore College Peace Collection)

Jane Addams and Mary Rozet Smith in the 1920s. (University of Illinois at Chicago, the University Library, Jane Addams Memorial Collection, JAMC neg. 592)

Jane Addams with Mary Rozet Smith and family of Stanley Linn, Hotel de Plaza, Carmel, California, 1928. (University of Illinois at Chicago, the University Library, Jane Addams Memorial Collection, JAMC neg. 1716)

James Weber Linn, ca. 1920.
(University of Illinois at Chica-
go, the University Library, Jane
Addams Memorial Collection,
JAMC neg. 500)

Paul Kellogg, in the
1930s. (Paul Kellogg
Papers, courtesy of
the Social Welfare
History Archives,
University of Minne-
sota Libraries)

Jane Addams laughing with unidentified woman at the
Democratic Convention, 1932. (Jane Addams Collection,
Swarthmore College Peace Collection)

Jane Addams, ca. 1926.
(Jane Addams Collection,
Swarthmore College
Peace Collection)

1 *Three Journeys*

Affronting Destiny, Europe, 1883

On board the *SS Servia* from August 22 through 29, 1883, during the warm evenings in the mid-Atlantic, a notable meeting in American literature nearly took place between courses at dinner. As the young Illinois traveler Jane Addams eyed the middle-aged New York writer Henry James, he seemed oblivious of her. They were, in a real sense, crossing paths: she eager to see Europe for the first time to learn the terrain of the Old World, and he anxious to leave the New World and return to the familiar expatriate landscape of Europe. They both sailed as orphans, the recent deaths of their fathers much on their minds, and they both thought of the journey as a sea change, literally and figuratively. James had spent the past few years in the imaginative company of Isabel Archer, the young American heroine of *The Portrait of a Lady,* and may well have been musing on similarities between the fictional and the real as he looked up from his plate. The young American woman before him had much in common with his fictional heroine. She dressed in somber clothes and pulled her dark hair back from her thin face with a severity that marked her seriousness. Addams sat visibly erect from the pressure of a thick back brace that, ever so slightly, inhibited the flexibility of her young body.

Many years later, in his preface to the New York edition, James would claim that his novel had grown from Isabel herself, "a certain young woman affronting her destiny," a character very like the young woman who sat staring at him with her head bent slightly forward, giving her dark deep-set eyes intensity. For James, Jane Addams was, no doubt, indistinguishable from the others of her type: "Millions of presumptuous girls, intelligent or not intelligent, daily affront their destiny, and what is it open to their destiny to *be,* at the most, that we should make an ado about it?"[1] His phrase for them all was "smaller female fry," and Jane Addams, on the voyage in late summer, may not have offered the artist's imagination anything new as he returned to his mutton.

Undaunted by the supposedly imposing figure of the forty-year-old gentleman writer and very much in the character of Isabel Archer, the twenty-three-year-old woman from Cedarville, who had the one distinction of having graduated first in her class from Rockford Female Seminary, took her own measure of the great man. Utterly unsentimental in the penetration of her gaze, she wrote to her sister Alice Addams Haldeman about the celebrities making the Atlantic crossing with her. "Celebrity, no. two, is Henry James the novelist, who I look at most of time between courses at table"; she noted in youthful defiance, "[H]e is very English in appearance but not especially keen or intellectual."[2] What, after all, could James have to offer her imagination?

Face to face with Henry James, Addams felt no need to defer to him. His letters and journal of the time record no conscious notice of the young Illinoisan. Ironically, the creator of Isabel Archer may have appeared neither keen nor intellectual to Jane Addams because, looking into the face of "the real thing," he may have failed to see her at all. What James had no way of knowing was that the young woman before him already thought of herself as a writer and would spend her life experimenting with language, much as he would.

Addams's earliest writings that have survived are letters to her sister Alice, then a student at Rockford Female Seminary. The first, in January 7, 1869, came from the child of eight who called herself Jennie. Just learning how to use written language, she shaped each letter of the alphabet deliberately in an ornate block, with the Ps and Ds often backwards. Her words were interspersed at times with detailed drawings—one of a beehive catches the eye. Language and pictures merged in her early greetings, a smudge signaling a kiss, as though the very mark touched the cheek. The little girl worked hard to get the genre right, to begin with a greeting and to ask about her sister first, to thank her for having written and, especially, to encourage her to write again. "As I take my pen in hand to let you know that I am wel at pressent," the first letter started.[3] She expressed her loneliness in her sister's absence: "Fleels very lomscone since you are gone." Are you lonesome? she asked Alice in each letter, spelling the word in different ways—"lomcsone," "lomsome," "loesome"—all in echo of her own feelings as the baby in a dwindling family. 1868 had marked a radical shift in what she thought of as her family, and every detail of these early letters, the very fact that she began to write letters at all, reveals her consciousness of the change and her vulnerability in the face of it.

Her mother, Sarah Weber Addams, had come to the Midwest from Pennsylvania in 1844 with her new husband, John Huy Addams, and had bore eight children in Cedarville before her death during another pregnancy when she was forty-five and Jennie was only two years old. The family story had it that she was midwiving at the time though pregnant herself, that she fell on her way home and died as a result. Sarah Addams's story has all the features of nineteenth-century female experience with fertility; the only detail that might raise an eyebrow is that she was as old as forty-five when the ninth pregnancy killed her. According to family accounts, she was an emotionally resilient woman who lost, including the one she was carrying, four babies. As she lay dying, she supposedly asked that the horrified toddler be allowed to see her.

The Papa of Jennie's early letters was perhaps the most distinguished man in Cedarville. John Huy Addams owned a sawmill and a gristmill on the Cedar River, served as Illinois state senator from 1854 until 1870, and founded the Second National Bank of Freeport. Addams served his community by urging the expansion of the Galena and Chicago Union Railroad to Freeport, and by creating the public school, sharing his gentleman's library, giving land for the town cemetery, and even sending a local regiment into the Civil War. Legend contends that his house was a station on the Underground Railroad, and he was a pal of Abraham Lincoln. As a political figure, he participated in one founding meeting of the Grand Old Party, this one in Ripon, Wisconsin, in 1855.

The family in Jennie's letters to Alice was not the household of Sarah and John and no longer the household of the Addams family only. Family legend includes a strange story of his courtship of his second wife, although nothing in it seems unnatural when we think of John Addams the man, rather than the father. Supposedly, on a day in 1867 as he made a usual trip to Freeport, he began to lust after another man's wife: "'What a good wife for me Mrs. William Haldeman would make!'"[4] She was attractive, stylish, accomplished, just the kind of wife for a successful, widowed entrepreneur if only she weren't already married. As luck would have it, he arrived in town to be told that William Haldeman had died in the night. Such a mark of divine providence, if not mere synchronicity, must have had meaning for the widower as well as the new widow. In a year, they were married, and it is her arrival in Cedarville that may well have stimulated Jennie's letter writing. The new stepmother, Anna

Hostetter Haldeman Addams, was the type of mother to encourage her new young daughter to take up the pen.

Too, the loneliness everywhere in these letters signals the shift in affection in the Addams household. The oldest sister Mary, who had performed the motherly tasks after Sarah's death, was sent to Rockford Female Seminary before her own marriage to John Linn, a Presbyterian minister (their son James Weber Linn would later write a biography of his aunt). Another sister, Martha, died in 1867 when she was only sixteen. The letters talk about the beloved nursemaid Polly, perhaps the most nurturing figure in the household. Years later, Jane remembered her deathbed visit to comfort Polly in a lonely farmhouse during a blinding storm: "I heard a feeble call of 'Sarah,' my mother's name, as the dying eyes were turned upon me, followed by a curious breathing, and in place of the face familiar from my earliest childhood and associated with homely household cares, there lay upon the pillow strange, august features, stern and withdrawn from all the small affairs of life. That sense of solitude, of being unsheltered in a wide world of relentless and elemental forces, seized me."[5] The letters to Alice have the same tone of a child who feels "unsheltered in a wide world of relentless and elemental forces," outside the protection of her sisters, Mary, Alice, and Martha. Apparently John Addams, relieved of his parental duties by his new wife and, too, of the burden of adult solitude, did not offer his youngest child the kind of shelter she sought.

Sad as she was in the early letters to Alice, Jennie returned to the exuberance of childhood. Anna Addams may well have warmed to the idea of mothering a daughter. The letters to Alice are punctuated with suggestions from the stepmother for the improvement of her new charge. Her brother Weber was away at school at the University of Michigan. And Alice, the beloved sister, was a student at Rockford Female Seminary. The stepbrother Harry Haldeman, who would later feature (oddly enough) as Alice's husband, was practicing medicine. The letters are full of news about Jennie's playful exploits with Georgie Haldeman, Anna's younger son, who was becoming a playful companion.

Although the many portraits of the young Jennie Addams stress her malformed spine, her frailty, her humorlessness, her difference from the other kids, these early letters reveal a vital spirit of youth. The fact that she would live longer than anyone in the household, nearly 75 years, belies the family myth of her frailty. In the cold, snowy Illinois winter of 1870, she wrote, "[W]e had lots of fun slideing downhill with Ida [Carey] . . . we had three sleds . . . and when we got tired we whent in the mill to warm."[6] Rough rural play continued throughout her teenage years.

In the spring of 1877, Addams exchanged letters with a young friend, Vallie Beck, each hoping the other would come for a visit. "March has been displaying his lionlike nature ever since he arrived, it snows and storms almost every day," Jennie boasted, "we are having better sleighing now, than we had at any time this winter."[7] At school as well as at home, her young life was full of activity; "Our school gave an evening entertainment last Friday, the hall was perfectly jammed and it was pronounced a perfect success."

As they moved into teenage society, both Jennie and Vallie wanted to be pretty or, at least, remarkable. The girl talk in the letters is fairly normal. When Vallie worried over adolescent gawkiness, Jane cautioned, "[I]f you begin I shall feel sort of duty bound to follow suit and could cover *pages* trying to vindicate my *nose* which is simply a piece of flesh, expressing no character whatever and contains eight freckles! horrible to relate (I counted them this morning)." Vallie enticed her to visit with promises of usual female entertainment, but in her responding letter of regret that she would not be able to come, Jennie noted the difference in their experiences as teenage girls. "I haven't the least doubt but that I should have the nicest kind of time and would not miss the 'gay,' for I cannot number dancing among my accomplishments, and my knowledge of 'cards' is very limited indeed."[8] She continued the letter three days later by noting that along with dancing and card playing, she had little experience with sewing. "You asked if I understood working on Turkish toweling, I think I do in theory, although I have never worked on it." Her mind was always lively, theory being nearly as satisfying as practice.

In these letters to Vallie, she painted a picture of playful rural life in Cedarville. Returning the invitation, Jennie noted with rustic humor, "I could safely promise you picnicing, boating, horse-back rides and so forth, but nothing very far out of that line, for you know 'we are six miles from a lemon.'" Although the older kids watched over her and she appeared to have sciatica and scoliosis, the letters portray the normal exuberance of childhood with its active life of the body.

Traces of an active mind, one nurturing itself on literature and politics, emerge from her early letters as well. As early as 1871, she told her sister about a literary society that she had helped to found: "We go to school and I will tell you about it . . . we have a Littery Society and we have a President and a Vice President to it and a secretary."[9] Then in some detail the woman who would one day run a settlement house and establish a pacifist league laid out the structure of the society, the shape of the thing more compelling than its mission. Book talk did not become a feature of her letters until she was a teenager and began to exchange views with Vallie Beck. Louisa May Alcott caught her imagination as she has that of many, many girls: "I have read and re-read *Little Women* and it never seems to grow old," she wrote in 1876.[10] And of Oliver Wendell Holmes, she admitted, "*Young Americans Abroad* is all I have to judge . . . it contains some events which are rather improbable." Romance would never have the appeal of literary realism to her imagination.

Later in her letters to Vallie, interspersed with worry over the shape of her nose, she reviewed *Jericho Road*, the book she had just finished reading: "I suppose we meet characters like those in that every day only we are too blind to see them rightly; excuse that moralizing but I feel in a very contemplative mood to day."[11] The terms "moralizing" and "contemplative" suggest the desire of the sixteen-year-old to be taken seriously as an intellectual and a moral thinker. At the end of the letter, she commented on the presidential election of 1876 (one that seems familiar to us in 2000), dubbed "the stolen election." Samuel Jones Tilden, the wealthy Democratic governor of New York, carried the popular vote (4,300,500) in his run against Rutherford B. Hayes (4,036,298) and thought he had 196 electoral votes, enough to win. As a result of political machinations over the fifty days between the elections and the inauguration, however, nearly 14,000 votes in Louisiana and Florida were voided and Hayes won the presidency by one vote in the Electoral College, causing humorists to brand him "Rutherfraud." Addams, young as she was, responded to the public drama. She wanted to talk politics with Vallie Beck: "How are you pleased with the ending of the Presidential campaign? I enjoy politics very much, and was especially interested last fall and winter. It seems rather tame now when the excitement has suddenly stopped." John Addams strongly supported the Republicans, and the party wrangling must have been aired in his household. Young as she was, his daughter's ear heard what were, no doubt, lively political discussions, and she delighted in the energy such events generated in small-town America.

A letter written on March 30 and April 2, 1877, tells us much about the bookish side of her nature: "I am enjoying a quiet afternoon sandwiching *Martin Chuzzlewit* and letters up in my room." The soul, as Emily Dickinson put it, selects her own society. "Pa and Ma are visiting Sister Mary at Winnebago, George has a young friend spending his vacation with him, and so I am 'left alone in my glory.'" She even interrupted the writing of the letter "to read awhile." Her father preferred that she read history books, but his daughter wanted to read what she called standard writers. If history writers were only "as interesting as Dickens I think I could really enjoy them, but possibly I have not been 'worked-up' to that fine and appreciative point," she joked. The letter ends in mild self-rebuke: "Please do not think I wish to appear learned, or any thing of that sort." And later that spring, she wrote as Vallie planned a visit to Cedarville: "I am reading Barnaby Rudge, also, and am about half way in it, I like it of course for Charles Dickens never wrote any thing stupid, I have a great love of the marvelous and consequently am much concerned about Mrs. Rudge."[12] Not unlike other young readers of her generation, Addams preferred fiction to nonfiction, realistic novels to the romance, and the colorful excesses of Dickens to the tedious scholarship of pedants.

Among her papers Jane Addams saved a diary she had written from perhaps 1874 or more probably 1875 until sometime in 1883. The first page begins with a flourish and records her handwriting over time—a decorative looping of lines and a stately "Jane Addams" on January 1, 1874, followed by "Jennie Addams" in 1875, and then a series of signatures moving from "Jane Addams" to, simply, "Jane."[13] Throughout the diary, we can hear her voice as it changes over the eight years, from public school and through college, until her trip along with Henry James on the *SS Servia.*

She recorded sliding, snowball fighting, playing ball and croquet, and horseback riding. In March 1875, she wrote that she and her friends "nearly killed" themselves playing hopscotch. With her stepbrother George, she studied natural history and played chess, usually winning the game. After a lecture by a phrenologist, she jeered, "I heard her hold forth quite a string of gab." We hear the midwestern twang in the voice of the young skeptic. After a sermon on the evils of theaters and card playing, she mused, "[H]e said that they might not be worng in them selves but it was going very near the precipice where the least influence would throw you over. In other words it was going as near hell as possible and go to heaven." Mark Twain depicted that same youthful weighing of odds by Huck Finn, a rural kid from nearby Missouri, who likewise resisted the efforts of adults to civilize him.

Jennie, every bit a fifteen-year-old, whined about the unfairness of the universe. "Everything has been going worng lately maybe it is because I complain so much. So I must quit it, I find it in every page of my diary," she chided herself. One big problem was the public school: "I am dreadful sick and tired of it and am glad it is near the end." And three days later, she wrote that she "crept like a snail unwillingly to school." Once there, of course, she was perfectly content to watch the discomfort of others: "We had a spelling match and William Ilgin who is a very poor speller went shifting from side to side no one wanting to claim him. It presented quite an amusing spectacle." The teacher, too, must have been hoping that school would end soon. Jennie joked about her move with Clara to the boys' side of the room: "[I]n the coner it is ever so much plesanter than it was over at the grave yard side." In the corner with the boys, however, she was distracted by a young fellow who was "ever lastingly picking his nose and that makes a body awful nervous and figity." In the privacy of her diary, the Cedarville teenager emerged with all her freckles, a regular kid after all.

At the end of high school, when Jennie Addams pleaded her case for a male-styled college education, her father supposedly allowed her to take the entrance exams at Smith College. Victorian Bissell Brown in *The Education of Jane Addams* (2003) argues that the family story had to be fictional because the young woman was not academically prepared to go to Smith. The story, whether fact or fiction, tells us much about the family drama. Addams always claimed that she passed the exams only to find her father's stubborn resistance. John Addams preferred Rockford Female Seminary because he was on the board of directors, his other daughters attended, and Jennie would remain close to home, not far from George, who would attend the all-male Beloit College. At Rockford she would, he must have thought, remain tethered to the Midwest and to her family. It may have been simply that John Addams favored this youngest child and wanted her close to him.

As it turned out, proximity to Cedarville gave the young woman much to rebel against in affronting her destiny. What was open to her destiny to *be*? That was the question most in her mind in the diary that continued into her years at Rockford; she apparently picked it up as the mood struck her. The seemingly random snippets of poetry and prose record the growth of a nascent writer. In September of her freshman year, she wrote a couplet: "What am I? Whence produced, and for what end? / Whence draw I being to what period tend?" Miss Adeline Potter, in a class on modern history, had sent her girls into the cool morning air with the somber example of Napoleon and a stern "little 'sermon' on human responsibilities." Addams wrote the couplet ruefully, knowing that a seminary education was going to bring with it many such mornings of admonitory lectures. The vignette from her diary made its way into a column, called "Home Items," that Addams wrote for the *Rockford Seminary Magazine*, a more public venue for her literary experiments.[14] She began to publish essays in the magazine in 1878 and took her first literary job as editor in 1879.

The diary also exposes the innocent underbelly of academic life, revealing Addams's whimsy in humorous anecdotes, jokes, and fictional experiments. The young women loved to read popular novels, ones that teachers and parents thought unsuitable to their impressionable and supposedly innocent minds. Addams warned first in her diary and later in the magazine that such novels were "certainly not the most inspiring theme for us to spend our leisure hours over." Recreating a classroom discussion of the novel *Guy Mannering,* she played with the contrast between what girls were supposed to do and what they actually did: "One student expressed it as her opinion that the descriptions [in the novel] were overdrawn. 'Why,' she says, 'it is just like those affected scenes that I've read dozens of in cheap novels.' A warning punch stops her—'Don't confess it,' whispers her neighbor, and the class generally look scared."[15]

Later in the diary, she returned to the subject of trashy novels that seemed to her, after all, not "absolutely vicious and degrading," but merely "enervating and foolish." She observed that they were everywhere in the dormitories: "We have seen in various rooms books poorly print-ed, poorly bound and on paper tinted blue or pink, in short of late we have seen a good deal of 'trash.'" The literary critic who prided herself on be-ing somehow superior to the lure of such fiction, we should note, was herself familiar with the plots: "A hero and heroine are madly in love—it is not very clear to the reader why they are, for both are destitute of qualities eminently lovable—they have a misunderstanding in which a dark rival figures, suffer untold trials and are reunited with a dash of marriage bells." She was right about the storyline and its endless varia-tions, revealing more than she intended to tell even herself about herself.

Addams's youthful arrogance often took the form of moral earnest-ness, though never piety. She wrote in her diary that undergraduates ought to be "gaining a reserve store of feeling and beautiful ideas, to be finding a sort of clue to the highest intellectual life which we can hold fast to, when we have no longer leisure and quiet at our command." The witty diatribe on trashy novels surfaced in the magazine as part of an editorial just before she graduated in 1881. There she refined her thinking by ex-pressing the thought metaphorically: "While we have a fire to ourselves and time to think, we had better be diligent to gain a clue to an intellec-tual life, which we can hold fast to when we no longer have a fire to our-selves and time to think, when it may require all our tact and principle to hold fast to our reserved store of beautiful ideas, and will not care a cent whether Imogene married Victor or Clarence."[16] What her published version lost in directness, it gained in humor as she rebuked her class-mates for thinking about the amorous adventures of an Imogene and, even more absurd, those of a Victor or Clarence.

Her letters during her years at Rockford explored the sexual urges that are as startling as they are irrepressible during adolescence. The young women, like their sisters at other women's colleges, giggled and flirted and fell in love with one another. In the fall of 1877, Jane composed a series of letters on the question of intimate female relationships, sending them to her long-time epistolary friends, who reported the seemingly ubiquitous ritual at their colleges. Vallie Beck responded by protesting her innocence: "I shall certainly never race around the halls hugging and kissing every girl good night and that seems to be the way to secure a host of most intimate friends."[17] Likewise Ida May Carey responded: "The girls here are afflicted with the same sentimental 'spooning' malady, which you say, infects Rockford! I heartily agree with you, Old Fellow, that it is both disgusting and horrible and demoralizing to us as women." The letter made the further point that "the girls carried the things so far as to actually *flirt with one another,* in a way similar to the different sexes." Apparently the situation brought on a reproving lecture from a Miss Bentley who worked to cool the air. Carey continued her letter by wooing Addams: "Now in your last you said you admired *cold* people." She urged her to be more intimate: "I think that in you, I have found my affinity." Addams found affinity in several young women.

For all her disappointment over not going to Smith, Jane Addams seemed to have recovered quickly and to have thrown herself into the society of Rockford with little self-pity. She was young, enthusiastic, witty, and popular. Corinne Williams, a classmate who later attended law school at the University of Michigan, remembered seeing Jane Addams for the first time one evening after they had suffered through the absurdly austere ritual of a Rockford dinner. Face to face, she recalled the "brown hair drawn plainly back, with a decided inclination, never encouraged, to fall apart on the side, the chin raised, the head slightly bent to one side, the face turned at an angle to me as she gave her attention to the speaker."[18] Williams reported that Addams's room was "always crowded when the sacred 'engaged' sign was not hung out," and she "just knew there was always something 'doing' where she was, and that however mopey it might be elsewhere there was intellectual ozone in her vicinity."

The room that was always crowded belonged to the girl who, although she resisted the hugging and kissing or maybe because she did, charmed classmates with her charisma. She, too, took special notice of Williams, emoting in her diary in November 1877: "Dedicated. Ever connected in my mind and surrounded by the same halo of glory are the names Md de Stael and 'Corinne' Williams—the one the champion of the liberties of France the other the champion of woman's best and noblest qualities. To the latter I dedicate this humble effort." The two young women had been pondering the question of female power in France, pitting George Sand against Madame de Stael, in a series of essays and pub-

lic debates. In the diary entry, Addams's juxtaposed the great French leader and the ordinary Illinois student with only the mildest irony. Rockford gave her true friends, girls she could love.

The seminary had been founded by Anna P. Sill in 1849, and the
teacher Adeline Potter had graduated as its first valedictorian in 1854. The
guiding principle of the seminary was to produce useful Christian wom-
en, and to that end the seventeen seniors in Addams's class, who called
themselves "Bread Givers," studied mental and moral philosophy, trig-
onometry, botany, astronomy, chemistry, geology, history, English literature, ancient languages, modern languages, music, drawing, and painting, a blend of female and male curricula of the mid-nineteenth century.
Her training in a female seminary was inherently contradictory in that
women were supposedly intellectually and physically frail and yet the
curriculum demanded intellectual rigor and physical stamina.

During an American literature course, the young Addams recorded
the books read along with the ideas given in lectures. Here we find Margaret Fuller, Louisa May Alcott, Miss Phelps, Mrs. Holmes, and Augusta Evans, all grouped as "domestic writers." Miss Sedgewick is ranked
"about the same" as James Fennimore Cooper, and Lydia Maria Childs,
Lydia Sigourney, and the poet Anna Lynch are singled out for praise.
Harriet Beecher Stowe is deemed "the most successful living American
novelist," according to Addams's notes. The male canon includes Edward
Everett, Wendell Phillips, John Pierpont, Richard Henry Dana, Horace
Greeley, and Bayard Taylor, an eclectic group of writers who have faired
no better over time than the women have. To add rigor to her education,
she joined a study group that read Shakespeare, Thomas Carlyle, Robert
Browning, John Ruskin, and two women (albeit with male pseudonyms),
George Eliot and George Sand.

Jane Addams was no passive student. She once corrected Miss Sill
on the pronunciation of Don Quixote, insisting on the Spanish rather than
the British version. A classmate, Eleanor Frothingham, later told the story
of the incident: "We backed her up with laughter at Miss Sill's 'Don Quix-
ott.' Miss Sill suspended the whole class for two days, then took us back
without comment."[19] The young purist, who would go on in life to battle ward bosses in Chicago, was honing her political skills. During chapel, she took her friend's hymnal and wrote:

> Life's a burden, bear it.
> Life's a duty, dare it.
> Life's a thorn-crown? Wear it
> And spurn to be a coward!

Mocking needlepoint doggerel, Addams hit two targets: the idea that Christian females ought to be docile and the idea that Rockford Seminary was supposed to be an intellectual institution.

Outside of class, Addams joined a literary society, a scientific association, a phrenology society, and attended lectures by speakers including Louisa May Alcott's father, Bronson Alcott, on transcendentalism and read Darwin's *Origin of Species* and *The Descent of Man*. She studied Latin, Greek, natural science, ancient history and literature, philosophy, French, and had private tutoring in English composition, and even lessons in taxidermy. She and classmate Catherine Waugh argued for a course in calculus so that they would be allowed to receive a valid bachelor's degree. Rockford, as a female seminary, had never awarded traditional degrees. Jane Addams would return to her alma mater a year after her graduation in order to be among the first to receive a Bachelor of Arts degree, the prize she had so desired from Smith College.

Reading Addams's college essays, we discover that spelling errors and disregard of grammar are perennial traits of young writers, even those who go on later in life, as Addams did, to make a living with the pen. Her teachers rarely seemed to notice her errors and, in fact, wrote very little commentary on the essays. The set of papers, as the work of a young mind over four years, is astonishing in its willingness to take on big ideas, to grapple with the meaning of personal experience, and to explore the possibilities of language by expressing what the mind thinks it has in its grasp.

Reading her diary and letters alongside the essays tells us much about Addams's routine of writing, habits she would have all her life. She jotted down ideas, talked about them with friends, gave speeches in class, wrote drafts of essays, and sometimes published polished versions in her college magazine. In designing an essay, she placed pieces of writing together, cutting and pinning sections. Her college writing comes loaded with nascent ideas that she would continue to refine over her lifetime. Woven into her essays are quotes from her classmates and teachers, as well as from philosophers, poets, and novelists, most incorporated into her own writing without citation. Her impulse to blend other voices into her own prose would become the dominant creative feature of her prose. Often she revised and reproduced sections of essays in several venues, tinkering with language, ever mindful of expanding her audience.

An early essay, "Bellerophon," began as an exercise in her diary and made its way into a class assignment.[20] She painted what she called a "fasle Chimera" and struggled to describe the meaning behind the myth. Brave men, as the early version goes, use philosophy, reason, and finally physical force to slay the monster, yet they fail. "It is only by the aid of poetry than that it may be subdued that the mind may be gradually turned away, and a pure ideal given to it." The later revision retained the image of battle and sharpened the language: "A false Chimera holds sway in a fair land, the people are weakened and broken by prejudice or driven and governed by a blind fanaticism." She exposed the metaphor in order to reveal her underlying argument: poetry holds the power of saving the fair land. The voice in this early essay is distinctively her own: "It is truly by the aid of poetry that delusion may be subdued; the ideal alone posesses power to conquer it and rises in the air above it. Producing a series of delusions, better and therefore stronger than the false one, it gradually draws the victim out of the monster's power, it is not by philosophy but it is something deeper and truer. This is the mission of poetry, its practical use in the world and beyond this it dare not go."[21] The young Jane Addams celebrated the practical use of the poetic imagination to subdue prejudice and fanaticism at the same time that she warned against the unbridled power of poetry itself.

The young writer revealed a moral seriousness about the nature of literature. In 1878, she wrote a series of drafts of an essay that responded to Corinne Williams in the debate "Resolved: That French Women Have Had More Influence Through Literature Than Politics. Representative Women: George Sand and Mde. De Stael."[22] Addams admired the power and influence of Madame de Stael, even as she delighted in the fiction of George Sand. Woman since the 1830s "discovered that she posesses an intellect as acute if not as powerful as that of man, by the use of which her influence may be as vigorous in power as her charms are persuasive in society." The Rockford student may well have had her own life in mind as she marked "a new confidence" in her generation of women. The literary voice of Aurore Dupin, who "at fourteen . . . was a philosopher and a sage," became "an electric shock" to readers in the late nineteenth century. As Dupin transformed herself into the novelist George Sand, she forged a model for young women. "For the first time in the history of the world woman spoke out for herself with a voice as powerful as that of man." Genders, we should note, blur in the essay: "George Sand's soul and brain were exuberantly and splendidly feminine and she threw the full force of his vigorous mind into her literature." The slip of using "his" suggests that, for Addams, the brain may be exuberantly feminine but the mind itself behaves in forcefully masculine ways. She may well have absorbed the conventional views of her day. The young writer, oblivious to the gender confusion, jokes about her own literary aspirations: "Written for *Harper's Magazine* but not yet published." Williams took the opposing position in the debate, the two of them generating considerable excitement about the topic and affection for each other.

The same year, Jane Addams disturbed her teacher Caroline Potter by writing "Teeth," a parody of Victorian essays on social progress. Turning the Biblical narrative inside out, she playfully reverses the story that God created man in his image: "Man alone seems to be an exception to the ordinary course of creation, his soul seems to have been created first entire and complete, it contained immortal life, the forces of nature trying their best could not evolve a body which would likewise be immortal; the soul then must have organized for itself a body of perishable flesh." The youthful writer points out the irony that in fashioning his mortal flesh, man imprisoned his immortal spirit rather than embodying it. To illustrate the problem, she uses a prosaic and visceral example: "Still his vexation and chagrin were not complete until he examined his teeth until he found what a failure they were." She depicts the battle to wrestle back from nature the potent forces that man has unwittingly ceded to her: "reeling onward, falling rising again, staggering forward, a wounded felon daring to escape from his prison." The wrestling match ends in bathos: "[W]e can still see in all his laws and inventions his efforts to give his soul a chance to expand in other words his progress in the manufacture of teeth." Creation is a muddle, she acknowledges, and the best we have to show for social progress against natural imperfection is false teeth.

As a midwestern pragmatist, she knew that teeth, disappointing as they are, might be aided by "progress in the manufacture of teeth," inexpert as such devices must have been in the nineteenth century. At the same time, she feared that humans may work "simply for the body" and not for the soul. The assignment called for serious exposition, yet the nascent writer felt the pull of imaginative expression, eliciting a "speak to me of this paper" response from Miss Potter, who must have been pleased to have such a spirited student although, perhaps, troubled by her unconventionality.

In 1878, Jane Addams published her first essay, "Plated Ware," in *Rockford Seminary Magazine.* She had written the first version of the essay as a class assignment, one that drew a cryptic response from her professor: "Pythagorean theory—sounds of heavens control movements of universe and seasons" (whatever that might have meant to either of them). In the published version, Addams worked to develop an analogy between electricity used to plate metals and intellectual energy that has the power to plate ideas onto minds. "Plated Ware" is clever and thoughtful without being as playful as the writing in her diary: "Just as easily and in a similar manner are minds and characters of every age, plated with a certain cast of thought; all the thought of the populace are gathered together as the little bits of metal, suddenly some great mind arises and applies the electric current, it acts like magic and every negative mind receives the impression, everyone is surprised to find his neighbor talking about the one sole subject that he has been thinking of ever so long and expressing the same ideas that he has carefully cherished in secret for months."[23] The essay, for all its stiffness, articulates her doubts about the use of power: "[T]he tidal wave of skepticism flowed over almost the entire world, every good and sincere purpose was tainted with it, there was no room for honest doubt it gave a sham effect to many solid thoughts and under this heavy plate it was hard to find the true substance of anything." "Plated Ware" has the markings of the earlier essay "Bellerophon," with its creation of the false Chimera—"the people are weakened and broken by prejudice or driven and governed by a blind fanaticism"— yet no poetry emerges in this essay as victor over the beast.

The literary spirit, the imaginative urge that creates poetry and fiction, continued to intrigue the young writer. By 1880 Addams herself was making the selections for *Rockford Seminary Magazine* and would keep the job until 1881. In her diary, she ordered herself to "get girls to write experances all on a certain thought, see how they agree, see the common subject of thought, through the school at high tide etc. general drift. Get them to write up a common experiance that comes to all girls ... Poems—'stories.'" Just as she worked to gather fiction and poetry from college students, she thought of ways to investigate the literary culture around her. "Write to different Colleges to the Literary editors, asking their opinions on Popular subjects. . . . Find out what Books are taken most from the societies libraries, deduce—criticize society work." The diary contains articles and editorials along with a practical consideration of her plans for the magazine.

In response to her insistent requests for submissions, she found her former classmates depressed after leaving school and homesick for Rockford. Catherine Dorr noted in 1881: "I have intended ever since you opened a contributions department to send some contribution, but I find home life not very conducive to literary persuits of that kind . . . but I supose it is with others as with myself."[24] Later that same year, Helen Harrington lamented, "I felt as though I was leaving the very best and happiest of my life."[25] And in a follow-up letter, "I never in my life before felt so utterly adrift." That same summer of 1881, Martha Thomas confessed, "I really am lonesome for girls' society" and am "disgusted by

Mr. D."[26] The Rockford women, after all, had not been trained to become writers; they were expected to teach or do missionary work or put up with Mr. D., whether they found him disgusting or not.

Addams herself had no intention of becoming a teacher, a missionary, or a wife. Her nephew James Linn claimed that Rollin Salisbury, the ablest fellow at Beloit College, proposed to Jane Addams as he was graduating, that she refused him, and that he remained a bachelor: "A romantic story, often whispered, probably true," Linn muses.[27] We do know that Salisbury wrote to Addams in the winter of 1881, inviting her to hear a lecture on evolution at Beloit, and that she declined. Writing to her father about an interstate oratory contest in Jacksonville that she attended without his prior knowledge, she described Salisbury to him: "I never saw anyone more despondent than he was after the contest."[28] He represented Beloit in the competition, and his team came in a disappointing fifth out of six teams—no way to win the lady's heart. In an awkward letter, Rollin wrote Jane to apologize for a band of Beloit revelers who performed what he considered to be "disrespectful lyrics."[29] The earnest young man, although valedictorian, did not have a chance with her. Her letters at the time talked about the news of her own graduation at the head of her class. "I am not puffed up," she wrote in letter after letter to her siblings and, especially, to her father. To her stepmother, she stressed her bargaining skills in ordering a graduation dress made of blue silk worth $76 that she bought for $50.

It was not marriage that she sought but, in vague ways, a profession, one that would allow her to use the education she had received at Rockford. The very idea at the heart of her later experiment at Hull-House appeared first as a diary entry of a letter she crafted to E. G. Smith, a county Bible agent in Cedarville who had been a close friend of John Addams. The early draft of the letter with many crossouts is dated December 5, 1880. What she managed to articulate is not as revealing as her struggle with language:

> I was embarassed and unnatural most of the time I talked with you the other day, prehaps it was because I had never before tried to define my purposes and ideals and [crossed out: did] saw how shallow [crossed out: useless] they were. Feelings that I was neither accurate or just in my representation of myself in trying to become [crossed out: struggling myself I fear] clearer my expressions and ideas were bungling. I am much obliged to you for what you said, I see that my idea of that so much as I embody[crossed out: -ing] Truth in myself that much I could attract from other people and bring out what was best in their lives a well as my own, can never be carried out unless I have the sacred flame to start with.

She crossed out "useless" and settled for "shallow" to describe her purposes and ideals in the knowledge that she was only beginning to define herself. And she decided against the phrase "struggling myself I fear," replacing it with the less melodramatic "trying to become clearer," to avoid exposing her anxiety to Mr. Smith, a man she did not know well. He pressed her to make a deeper commitment to Christianity, and she resisted, even as she promised to read her Greek testament and to add religion to her "culture." What the letter tells us is that very early in her life Addams had a core idea nearly within the grasp of her mind if not quite within the grasp of language: "as I embody Truth in myself that much I could attract from other people and bring out what was best in their lives as well as my own." She would continue to refine that idea over her years at Hull-House as she created the idea of social work and, too, as she struggled to find a literary voice, one that would blend others into her own.

In her letters from Rockford to her former classmate Ellen Gates Starr, Jane Addams felt free to sort out her religious beliefs. In January 1880, she admitted that she preferred a recitation to a prayer meeting with Miss Potter and that she felt "preverted." She confessed to Starr, "I do not know that I have grown very much in spiritual things."[30] Instead of the Bible, she recommended Joseph Cooke's *The New Birth* and claimed that the book helped her to see the idea of knowing God as "a scientific necessity but not as a aesthetic necessity so to speak." To her close friend she confided, "I need religion in a practical sense . . . to be in perfect harmony with nature and duty." Yet the letter declared her more exuberant love for Homer: "I would be willing to study Greek for ten years." Her schooling at Rockford had the perhaps unintended effect of awakening her imaginative mind. What the education did not provide, in any ways that satisfied Jane Addams, was a practical religious calling.

After her graduation, she began what would become years of travel, providing an education of a different sort. In August of 1881, John and Anna Addams took Jane and George to Lake Superior, a trip that was to blend her father's business and the pleasure of a family holiday. The fifty-nine-year-old patriarch collapsed on a climb to see a copper mine, the stress apparently bursting a weak appendix. The family frantically worked their way home as his conditioned worsened, making it only as far as Green Bay, Wisconsin, where he died of peritonitis a week and a half later.[31]

The very force at the center of Jane's young life disappeared, leaving her little to rebel against, no clear way to establish her independence from a strong father. Her letters at the time reveal sadness and enervation. She asked Ellen Gates Starr to join her in Cedarville: "I will not write of myself or how purposeless and without ambition I am, only prepare your-self so you won't be disappointed in me when you come. The greatest sorrow that can ever come to me has past and I hope it is only a question of time until I get my moral purposes straightened."[32] The letter shows signs that Addams experimented with medical remedies to deal with her sorrow. In a spirited lecture, she admonished Starr, who was under the weather, to take, "a bottle of *malt* every day and use for your chief food *desiccated* blood, the first called Hoff's Extract and the second manufac-tured in Detroit." At her father's death, Jane Addams inherited an income of $3,000 per year on her share of $50,000 from John Addams's estate, including 247 acres of farmland and 60 of timberland in Illinois. With his money and land, she became a modestly wealthy, single young woman, independent in her own right.

For all of her immediate loss of purpose in the summer of 1881, Jane Addams looked to her future education. She considered finishing her bachelor's degree at Smith College to give academic muscle to her stud-ies, but decided instead to go to medical school. Although she dreamed of studying at the University of Edinburgh, she settled for the Women's Medical College of Philadelphia. Her stepbrother and brother-in-law, Harry Haldeman, enrolled in graduate study at the University of Penn-sylvania, and Jane and her sister Alice began medical classes together at the female institution. The family moved to Philadelphia.

The study of science had always seemed to Jane rigorously intellec-tual, the sort of thing serious young men did. What she discovered about herself at the age of twenty-one was that she was wrong. She would have agreed with Henry James's brother William that medical school seemed fraudulent. "My first impressions are that there is much humbug there-in, and that, with the exception of surgery, in which something positive is sometimes accomplished, a doctor does more by the moral effect of his presence on the patient and family, than by anything else," William wrote about his experience at Harvard in 1864.[33] Medical school, especially in the first year, may have seemed to Jane "humbug" indeed, intellectually unimaginative and tediously detailed. Addams wrote in her diary, "I am growing more sullen and less sympathetic every day." She passed her exams but continued to slide into a depression, diagnosed as "hysteria," that she claimed consumed the next eight years of her life.

The most fashionable way of dealing with hysteria, the mysterious female malaise of the late nineteenth century, was to visit Silas Weir Mitchell, the creator of the famous "rest cure" that promised to take the stress of something like medical school off the body of a young woman and to caress her back into the indolence of wealth. Addams placed herself in Mitchell's care at his Hospital for Orthopedic and Nervous Diseases in Philadelphia. The young woman seemed to have responded well to the treatment that allowed her to abandon the dreary study of Gray's *Anatomy*. She was not at all unusual in her depression; Mitchell and his colleagues treated many prominent women, including Henry's sister, Alice James, and the wealthy novelist Edith Wharton. Charlotte Perkins Gilman, who would later flee Hull-House because she could not keep her windows open at night, rebelled against the stifling paradox of the imposed relaxation. Mitchell, himself a dapper literary man, would later read her gothic short story "The Yellow Wallpaper" and change his treatment as a result of her clear rebuke of his ideas.

Weir Mitchell's rest cure gave Addams, perhaps for the first time in her life, a "luxurious consciousness of leisure," exactly what her doctor intended, and permitted her the freedom to abandon medical school. "I remember opening the first volume of Carlyle's *Frederick the Great* with a lively sense of gratitude that it was not Gray's *Anatomy*," she acknowledges in *Twenty Years at Hull-House*, "having found, like many another, that general culture is a much easier undertaking than professional study" (65–66). Mitchell, so vilified by Gilman, seemed not to have troubled Addams, but rather, as Edith Wharton had done, she took books with her for her rest, and while not being cured, seemed at least not to have been harmed by the treatment. Mitchell, after all, thought of himself as a literary man by the time Addams fell into depression.

The rest cure gave Addams permission to sink into a life of comfort; however, as with Gilman, the cure left her mind more anxious than ever about what she would find to do next. In the spring of 1883, the Addams family returned to Cedarville with the prostrated Jane, whose back became the scapegoat of her maladies. Getting her "moral purposes straightened" took the strangely literal shape of surgery to correct the bend in her back. No one knows exactly what her stepbrother Harry Haldeman did that summer in Iowa to relieve the pressure on her spine, but he sent her into the world in a constricting back brace that, presumably, he expected her to wear for life. What better outward sign could she have of the constrictions she faced in affronting her destiny?

The journey to Europe that year, surrounded by family and friends, promised relaxation, the warm indulgence of sight and sound and movement, just what a leisure-class woman supposedly needed to deepen her sense of privilege and to mark her social status. She sailed with her stepmother, Anna Addams, two Rockford friends, Mary and Harriet "Puss" Ellwood, and their aunt, as well as a stepcousin, Sarah Hostetter. The women traveled for nearly two years in Ireland, Scotland, England, Holland, Germany, Austria, Italy, Switzerland, and France, followed by a second circuit through London, Berlin, and Paris. Her journal and letters home suggest a growing vitality, signaled by casting away the back brace that was designed to straighten her backbone and restrict her physical activity. As her letters chronicle, she moved easily across Europe, studying cathedrals and mounting stairs, following the routes of poets through mountain trails, touring museums filled with classical and modern art and paintings from Medieval and Renaissance Europe. No casual tourist in Europe, she studied the development of the Gothic cathedral, attended concerts and operas, took classes in German, Italian, and French, and pondered the positivism of August Comte and the aesthetics of John Ruskin. As a tourist might, however, she visited Thomas Carlyle's house and the graves of Matthew Arnold and William Wordsworth. As she traveled, she read. Ruskin and William Dean Howells both pointed out what she should be noting, and George Eliot brought fiction to bear on the historical landscape before her.

Throughout her travels, she kept a writer's notebook, recording the many details caught by her eye, and planned to use the material, as she had done in college, to craft essays after she returned. Her handwriting, in this most private of literary places, is nearly impossible to read (her handwriting was quickly becoming less and less legible, no doubt the mark of a tired hand). "She was deliberately setting down at this time almost the 'million words' which all of us have been enjoined to write in practice," Linn observed, "before we attempt publication."[34] It is clear from the literary exercise that Addams was beginning to see herself as a writer. A long essay came from her travel journey, a creation of memory and imagination, that she titled simply, "Five Sunday Mornings in England."[35] She wrote it with the dry humor of her college essays. Her observations seem scattered, as though she could not find a clear point of view. By the end of the five weeks in the countryside as she visited Winchester Cathedral, Addams was homesick for the midwestern landscape of Illinois. When she returned to London, she openly admitted her longings for Rockford and the class of 1881. Addams never published the essay in the college magazine although she clearly had that audience in mind.

Another European essay, "Three Days on the Mediterranean Subjectively Related," recounts the agonies of seasickness, and this one was published in *Rockford Seminary Magazine* in 1886. The tone mocks the earnest younger self who has traveled to Athens. Of self-consciousness, she jokes, "I thought I had choked the fiend in Rome, but here he is as self-assertive as ever."[36] The imaginative enchantments of consciousness overwhelm the experiences of travel. In one anecdote, she describes an attack of seasickness. As nausea clouds her perceptions, she suspects a Turkish cabin boy and the Jesuit priest and even the organ grinder of sinister intent: "These thoughts were part of a vast system, and they closed around me as the meshes of a fine net, or as the soft substance of a jelly fish smothers its victim." We might read this essay as a sign of her depression, especially the image of the jellyfish, had she not written it in such a lively spirit. As her seasickness lifts, she reports eating a hardy nine-course meal with a "reviving appetite" and, after docking in Naples, she laments, "Never again will we embark from a shore where Homer is still a household poet."

Henry James, had he noticed Jane Addams, would have known that the young woman from Illinois was headed to Europe to finish her education by reacquiring the sights and sounds of the Old World that had been traded away by her ancestors for the fresh possibilities in America. Art, architecture, opera, orchestral music, theatre, along with the more commercial delights and refinements of clothing and food and the subtler intangibles of culture, gesture, nuance, tone—all of these markers of social class supposedly awaited newly moneyed Americans as they traveled back to Europe as tourists. Addams may have found his company as stimulating as anything she had yet experienced. In her own middle years, she would meet his brother William and, later still, she would write an enthusiastic review of a biography of Charles Eliot Norton written by William's son, Henry James Jr. She could not yet know her link to his family. And they had no formal introduction, one that might have led them into conversation. The two were writers, after all, and might have said much to one another as they sailed from America to England.

Mapping the Terrain, Chicago, 1889

As Jane Addams dabbled in writing during her years of depression, she felt the pressure most women feel in their twenties: that their real job is to marry. "I am afraid I will never be the typical old maid," she cautioned her stepmother.[37] Being an old maid amused her; the idea of marrying did not. Her stepmother, oddly enough, hoped that Jane would follow her sister Alice's example and marry the other Haldeman son. The family moved east to Baltimore, where George studied at Johns Hopkins. The idea of marriage to George, the sibling companion of her youth who was already sinking into a depression much greater than her own, was repugnant to her. Surely in her mind this match had the taint of incest. Twisting free of conventional marriage seems to have lifted her depression, allowing her less conventional ways to affront destiny.

On her return to Europe in 1887 and 1888, she pondered a riddle that Leo Tolstoy called "the snare of preparation." Why is it that young people, so full of energy in the waning years of adolescence, are sent off to college and forced into a long period of intellectual and academic training that imposes inactivity, a curiously counterintuitive response to youthful vitality? And after college, why are young women of a certain social rank packed off to Europe to learn even more about leisurely inactivity? Why, Addams posed the question, train the mind of a woman if society offers her no meaningful labor after college? A woman's very inactivity, as Charlotte Perkins Gilman in *Women and Economics* and Thorstein Veblen in *The Theory of the Leisure Class* explained it in 1899, may mark her value to a husband. Women of the upper classes are simply more valuable if they do not work. But if not marriage and the domestic life, then what is a woman to do?

Tolstoy's unease over being an idle aristocrat was the very feeling that Jane Addams had after leaving college, and she turned to writing to express her anxiety. His phrase, "the snare of preparation," made its way into her writing in the 1890s as she composed essay after essay, refining the language each time she returned to the idea. The impulse to write and rewrite, to define and refine, to publish and republish her writing can be seen in all her essays, from first to last. No formulation of an idea could satisfy her as a writer, and certainly no payment for work changed her sense that she owned the material. Addams first explained the plight of the college "girl" in "The Subjective Necessity for Social Settlements" (1893): "In our attempt then to give a girl pleasure and freedom from care we succeed, for the most part, in making her pitifully miserable. She finds 'life' so different from what she expected it to be. She is besotted with innocent little ambitions, and does not understand this apparent waste of herself, this elaborate preparation, if no work is provided for her."[38] As she moved into womanhood, the problem continued to form the central place in her thinking about professional life. In "The Claim on the College Woman" (1895), she echoed Tolstoy: "The College woman is more or less a new development of the age. She has suddenly had knowledge given her and now the question is—What use shall she make of it?"[39] In "The College Woman and Christianity," an essay published in 1901, she again altered his language as she noted that the college woman "has fallen into 'the snare of self-preparation,' to borrow a phrase from Tolstoy."[40]

Much later in her autobiography, *Twenty Years at Hull-House*, she would put the words more directly into his mouth: "It was not until years afterward that I came upon Tolstoy's phrase 'the snare of preparation,' which he insists we spread before the feet of young people, hopelessly entangling them in a curious inactivity at the very period of life when they are longing to construct the world anew and to conform it to their own ideals" (88). Answering an American woman's version of Tolstoy's question—What to do?—took the eight long years from 1881 until 1889, the very years that Addams would later claim as years lost to depression, what she called "the snare." Her activity over that time belies the severity of the depression and suggests that her illness was as metaphoric as it was literal.

Addams and Sarah Anderson traveled back to Europe in 1887 over familiar terrain, this time in the company of Ellen Gates Starr. The small entourage moved from London to Paris to Stuttgart and Munich before returning to Paris in the spring and on to Rome and Florence and then Madrid before returning to England. The trip was decidedly briefer than the first tour and significantly more intense. The young women toured the poverty in East End London and studied the social experiment at Toynbee Hall, where young Oxford men lived and worked among the poor. Addams would later make claims about the journey that, as her biographers have all puzzled over, have the look of fiction. It should come as no surprise to us in the twenty-first century that autobiography is a close relative of fiction. She used fictional techniques to embellish plot, create characters, embroider details, set the stage, and heighten suspense—nothing usual for an autobiographer.

The most famous of her reconstructions is a bullfight in Spain, near the end of their travel. She wrote to her sister-in-law Laura Addams in the spring of 1888, "The great event of our stay in Madrid after all was the thing we are all rather ashamed of, and that was a bull fight or Festa del Toros, as we rather prefer to call it."[41] In colorful language, Addams described the bull: "He was a beautiful creature as lithe and active as a cat and as fleet and graceful as a deer with nothing of the awkwardness one associates with a bull." Ernest Hemingway might have been pleased to read the letter with its careful delineation of the acts involved in the drama of killing the beautiful creature. And she ended the letter with a line that surely her fellow midwesterner would have understood: "[W]e were rather ashamed and surprised to find that we were brutal enough to take a great interest in it." Writing to her stepcousin Sarah Hostetter, she recorded a similar ambivalence, "Shame for having yielded, admiration for its magnificence, and wonder at my own brutality in enduring it so well."[42] And later to Anna Addams, she reiterated her fascination, "The excitement and interest were so great as to throw the cruelty and brutality quite into the background. . . . so much does skill and parade do toward concealing a wrong thing."[43]

Anyone reading these letters would come to doubt that she was suffering from an enervating depression. She found herself captivated by the long death in the afternoon, as Hemingway called it. Nothing in the immediate letters links the bullfight to her calling in life although she does seem genuinely surprised that the brutal killing of the bull held her imagination. Only later in her autobiography, in the chapter entitled "The Snare of Preparation," would she claim that the bullfight not only transfixed her but also transformed her life.

In recreating the moment of conversion in *Twenty Years at Hull-House*, Addams would borrow again from Tolstoy. Her style of writing with its vivid blends of fact and fiction came to look much like the autobiographical writing that the great novelist was doing in his later years. Tolstoy's sense of drama was as keen as that of any writer in the nineteenth century, and his power of fictive presentation continued, not surprisingly, after he had supposedly abandoned fiction. On his first trip abroad in 1857, Tolstoy recorded in his diary a public execution: "What a senseless thing! A strong impression which did not pass in vain." Later in *My Confession* (1882), he recreated the execution scene to mark a blood-filled rite of passage away from fashionable notions of rationality and progress and toward radical pacifism: "When I saw the head divided from the body, and heard the sound with which they fell separately into the box, I understood, not with my reason, but with my whole being, that no theory of the wisdom of all established things, nor of progress, could justify such an act."[44] Addams had marked the passage in her copy of his book in seeming agreement with him that "the great mass of all the rest of mankind have an unreasoning consciousness of life which gives a meaning to it."[45] Tolstoy confessed that his conversion came as an epiphany as he watched with fascinated horror the decapitation of a fellow being.

Addams's imagination made similar use of a bloody spectacle to dramatize her own rite of passage from casual tourist to social activist. The bullfight in Madrid came as close as anything in her experience to a public execution. In *Twenty Years at Hull-House*, she refashioned the event, giving it full status as a blood-filled rite of passage: "Nothing less than the moral reaction following the experience at a bullfight had been able to reveal to me that so far from following in the wake of a chariot of philanthropic fire, I had been tied to the tail of the veriest ox-cart of self-seeking" (86). The epiphany supposedly ended her depression and transformed her from an indulged traveler into a professional woman, the founder along with Starr of the radical social settlement at Hull-House patterned after Toynbee Hall.

Jane Addams wrote of her move in 1889, along with Ellen Gates Starr, into a fine old house with pure Corinthian pillars, "Probably no young matron ever placed her own things in her own house with more pleasure than that with which we first furnished Hull-House."[46] Her letters home to Cedarville are full of requests that any young bride might make for family heirlooms and usable mahogany furniture, the accouterments of leisure-class housekeeping. She sent the lace curtains back to her sister, perhaps sensing the incongruity they signified.

As she looked through the stately windows of the Hull mansion, she saw the "Bloody Nineteenth" ward, an urban immigrant neighborhood. In her book *Newer Ideals of Peace* (1907), Addams would describe the urban landscape: "Insanitary housing, poisonous sewage, contaminated water, infant mortality, the spread of contagion, adulterated food, impure milk, smoke-laden air, ill-ventilated factories, dangerous occupations, juvenile crime, unwholesome crowding, prostitution, and drunkenness are the enemies which the modern city must face and overcome would it survive" (182). No literary naturalist could have said it better. If the individual is caught in an environment that is unsanitary, poisonous, contaminated, contagious, adulterated, impure, dangerous, unwholesome, how is the human organism to thrive? If such conditions are the result of hubris, avarice, greed, lust, sloth, anger and gluttony—the seven deadly sins after all—then the moral onus is on individuals, working in concert, to ameliorate the conditions and thereby free those trapped in the sinful city. "We must search in the dim borderland between compassion and morality," she admonishes her readers, "for the beginnings of . . . cosmopolitan affection" (11). The borderland of a twentieth-century American city like Chicago, where seventy-five percent of the people were immigrants and their offspring, allowed a commingling of vital forces in centers of radicalism.

Addams argues—and this is the heart of her radicalism—that "the idealism fitted to our industrial democracy will be evolved in crowded sewer ditches and in noisy factories" (94). Ditches and factories, situated on the outskirts of the urban landscape, become for her the central feature of the city, the cultural ooze of human evolution.

We find Progressive Era women like Addams writing about such morally vexed human activities as gambling, prostitution, and crime, as well as more mundane vulnerabilities that require accident insurance, old-age pensions, sick benefits, unemployment insurance, rent control, and health insurance. Their concerns continue to be our concerns in the twenty-first century, especially issues of world peace, a living wage, environmental pollution, and immigrant cultures in America. Addams's list of social, political, economic, and cultural remedies has been at the center of public discourse over the years that separate our lives from hers. What moral and ethical issues today seem more immediate than environmental racism and sustainability or ethnic and religious conflicts that threaten economic stability and, especially, the human impulse toward war rather than peace?

Addams's writing in the 1890s moved slowly toward big social questions as she worked out the personal dilemma of justifying her career. In a series of essays written over the years after college as she was reading Tolstoy's books and before she and Mary Smith went to Russia to talk with him, Addams reformulated the nascent idea embedded in her letter to the Bible salesman, E. G. Smith: "I could attract from other people and bring out what was best in their lives a well as my own." She professed that her life would be essentially active rather than contemplative and her writing persuasive rather than decorative.

"The Subjective Necessity for Social Settlements" and "The Objective Value of a Social Settlement" began as earnest formal lectures at a summer school in 1892 sponsored by the Ethical Culture Societies at the School of Applied Ethics in Plymouth, Massachusetts. The school's curriculum of study was interdisciplinary, bringing together comparative religion, ethics, and economics in the four-week summer course. She joined Robert Woods, J. O. S. Huntington, Franklin Giddings, and Bernard Bosanquet, whose lectures were folded into *Philanthropy and Social Progress* (1893), edited by University of Michigan professor Henry C. Adams. Later, she blended the lectures into the narrative of *Twenty Years at Hull-House*, telling the story of the two essays that served as the root of her thinking about her profession. "Some of us had numbered our years as far as thirty," she confides to her reader even as she shaves nearly two years off her age. And there is nothing modest about her claims, even in 1910: "I doubt if anywhere on the continent that summer could have been found a group of people more genuinely interested in social development or more sincerely convinced that they had found a clew by which the conditions in crowded cities might be understood" (114). It was not until her last book, *My Friend, Julia Lathrop,* that she looked back with a humorous eye, admitting that the collection of lectures in the summer of 1892 was "a fine Victorian example of rose water for the plague" (60–61).

"The Subjective Necessity for Social Settlements" opens with the image of Hull-House as a "mere foothold of a house, easily accessible, hospitable, and tolerant in spirit," a space to ensure domestic tranquility by bringing seemingly disparate people together within the city. In her poor neighborhood, both the African American and the European immigrant live in "practical social ostracism." And, ironically, on the wealthy end of town, educated young people "feel a fatal want of harmony between their theory and their lives." Addams captures the longing for cultural cohesion in a single sentence of the type that marks her writing style in its philosophical moments:

> These hopes may be loosely formulated thus: that if in a democratic country nothing can be permanently achieved save through the masses of the people, it will be impossible to establish a higher political life than the people themselves crave; that it is difficult to see how the notion of a higher civic life can be fostered save through common intercourse; that the blessings which we associate with a life of refinement and cultivation can be made universal and must be made universal if they are to be permanent; that the good we secure for ourselves is precarious and uncertain, is floating in mid-air, until it is secured for all of us and incorporated into our common life. (7)

The Platonic image of democracy "floating in mid-air" blends poetry with politics, and yet she yields to poets the power to articulate and inspire us toward what she calls "the race life": "[I]t is hazardous for any but a poet to attempt it." The poet she, no doubt, had in mind was William Wordsworth, especially his lines in "Intimations of Immortality": "To me the meanest flower that blows / Doth give thoughts that lie too deep for tears."

Addams herself plays with poetic language that ruffled later feminists as much as it soothed her contemporary readers. Urban professional women, as she put it, were doing "civic housekeeping," merely tidying the city as rural women have always tidied the farmhouse. And on a grander scale, Addams compared settlement work to a woman's urge to nurse a hungry baby. Her contemporary readers seemed never to have raised an eyebrow as she offered her maiden breast: "A more poetic prayer would be that the great mother breasts of our common humanity, with its labor and suffering and its homely comforts, may never be withheld from you" (11–12). The breast itself, homely and comfortable, nurtures and sustains culture and, by implication, without a mother's milk, a culture fails.

The companion essay, "The Objective Value of a Social Settlement," maps the Hull-House neighborhood at the intersection of Halsted and Polk Streets, the Fourteenth Precinct of the Nineteenth Ward, the latter made up of fifty thousand people from Italy, Poland, Russia, Bohemia, Canada, France, and Ireland. "The streets are inexpressibly dirty, the number of schools inadequate, factory legislation unenforced, the street-lighting bad, the paving miserable and altogether lacking in the alleys and smaller streets, and the stables defy all laws of sanitation," she tells her reader.[47] Civic housekeeping, as the Hull-House residents imagined, included a book club, a library reading room, college extension courses, a gallery of art, a day nursery, a kindergarten, a diet kitchen, a cooperative boarding club for working "girls," and even a coffeehouse. Along with traditionally female concerns, the women of Hull-House muscled their way into labor unions, the city Health Department, and the Bureau of Justice. The women established the Working People's Social Science Club, a group that met every Wednesday evening at eight o'clock to debate the issues of the day.

Her essay on the value of settlements led directly to her second book project, moving her toward objective investigation and away from subjective storytelling. Florence Kelley and Julia Lathrop worked alongside Addams to map the terrain of the Halsted neighborhood, collecting essays on sweatshops, child workers, labor unions, charity services, and the arts, along with studies of specific ethnic groups, including Jews, Bohemians, and Italians. Kelley, a determined radical who had translated the work of Frederick Engels, insisted that the study include intricate cloth maps of the neighborhood so that the book would carry weight in the academic community, especially the School of Social Thought developing at the University of Chicago. Richard T. Ely from the University of Wisconsin edited the book in his Economics and Politics Series under the title *Hull-House Maps and Papers: A Presentation of Nationalities and Wages in a Congested District of Chicago together with Comments and Essays on Problems Growing Out of the Social Conditions*, published in 1895. The title reflected the many interests of the writers, the editors, and the publisher. The maps, after a heated dispute about their viability in book form, appeared in reduced size, a sign of the compromises necessary in such an ambitious and experimental project.

The book is useful to scholars in the twenty-first century for its sociological data on the nature of cities, more useful perhaps than it was in the nineteenth century as a tool for social reform. Mary Jo Deegan, in her book *Jane Addams and the Men of the Chicago School*, claims that Addams, Lathrop, and Kelley developed the methodology that the Chicago School would make famous, although the men at the University of Chicago would never give women the credit for the seminal work.[48] Their scientific study of ethnic groups and income in the poor immigrant neighborhood surrounding the settlement house sold fewer than one thousand copies.[49] In an ironic twist, later critics would hit Addams hard for moving away from the sociological model of writing in her later books. In "Women Reformers and American Culture, 1870–1930," Jill Conway, angered by Addams's refusal to use the rational logic and statistical data of male-designed sociology, dismisses her work for its lack of scientific rigor: "[T]o base one's social criticism upon the idea that feminine intuition could both diagnose and direct social change was to tie one's identity as a social critic to acquiescence in the traditional stereotype of women."[50] Jane Addams's intuition would lead her toward imaginative writing rather than scholarly analysis.

Following the literal mapping of Chicago, Addams ended *Hull-House Maps and Papers* with an essay that indulges in storytelling. "The Settlement as a Factor in the Labor Movement" displays her talent for coherent argument although the prose is stiff. In the earnest essay, Addams experimented with language. Upton Sinclair and Frank Norris would surely have admired the line: "We must learn to trust our democracy, giant-like and threatening as it may appear in its uncouth strength and untried applications." Democracy as a threatening, uncouth, untried giant served as a dominant metaphor of the literary naturalism that Sinclair and Norris were writing. Leo Tolstoy and Henry James would have preferred the philosophical line: "But life teaches us nothing more inevitable than that right and wrong are most confusedly mixed; that the blackest wrong is by our side and within our own motives; that right does not dazzle our eyes with its radiant shining, but has to be found by exerting patience, discrimination, and impartiality" (198–99). As a writer, Addams would never be content with reporting data and drawing conclusions. Linguistic play and imaginative narrative intruded into any argument she worked to construct.

Talking with Tolstoy, Russia, 1896

With the confidence that came from publishing substantial parts of two books, *Philosophy and Social Progress* and *Hull-House Maps and Papers*, Jane Addams sailed across the Atlantic in April of 1896 on her way to talk with an unwitting literary mentor, Leo Tolstoy. She traveled this time with a wealthy Chicago debutante, Mary Rozet Smith, the two comfortable in each other's company and pleased to be away from Chicago. They were a remarkable couple. Jane pulled her hair back from her face, having the effect of making her eyes its distinguishing feature. The dress she wore was practical for travel, dark and relatively unadorned, yet the yards of silk in the sleeves signaled her wealth; she lived in the luxury of her social class, even though she resided much of the year in one of the poorest neighborhoods in Chicago. Mary was more relaxed with brown wisps of hair that resisted being pulled back from her open face.

When asked about their relationship, Jane referred to Mary as her niece; certainly they had begun to think of each other as family.

Mary may have had in her mind lines of poetry Jane had written about her in the fall of 1895 as Jane suffered through typhoid fever:

> One day I came into Hull House,
> (No spirit whispered who was there)
> And in the kindergarten room
> There sat upon a childish chair
> A girl, both tall and fair to see
> (To look at her gives one a thrill).

Mary Smith was tall, fair, youthful, and thrilling to Jane Addams, who had discovered, perhaps by surprise, that she was in love. The painfully conventional poem ends with an unconventional admission:

> Like mothers, who work long and late
> To rear their children fittingly
> Follow them only with their eyes,
> And love them almost pityingly.
> So I was blind and deaf those years
> To all save one absorbing care,
> And did not guess what now I know—
> Delivering love was sitting there.

The lines promise the thrill of passion yet mask it as motherly affection. Jane's poems to Mary—none of them showing any more talent for poetry than this one does—were very different in tone from her college letters that rejected sentimental female friendships with their strong hint of sexuality. The trip to Europe in 1896 was a vacation for the two women, a continuation of Jane's recuperation, and an opportunity for privacy.

Both women traveled to Russia after a thorough reading of Tolstoy's *What to Do?* and a considerable discussion of the strengths and weaknesses of his arguments. The residents at Hull-House lived much as they would if they lived in a wealthy neighborhood of Chicago. "I deprecate very much anything that makes the movement strained or unnatural," Addams acknowledged as early as 1891.[51] The notion that a Russian count would adopt peasant dress and spend his mornings working in the fields—time that he might use more judiciously as a writer and a social philosopher, if not as a novelist—seemed dramatic to her, even melodramatic. Letters in 1895, just before their journey, give us a clear sense of how the realist in Addams resisted Tolstoy's idealism. Mary Smith, after reading Tolstoy's book, winced under his attack on those with money. "I am sorry that Tolstoy gives you such a hard time with your principles," Addams wrote her friend. "I had an awful time the two years before I came to Hull House." After reading his books, she could never quite shed her sense of guilt. "I do not like it now when my farmer pays his rent, but do not believe that Tolstoy's position is tenable," she explained pragmatically. "[A] man cannot be a Xtian by himself."[52] Tolstoy's insistence on an unambiguous moral ideal irritated both women, each reassuring the other that he went too far.

In *Twenty Years at Hull-House*, Addams claimed that during the economic depression of 1893 and 1894, as the Colombian World Exposition took place on Chicago's South Side, she came close to agreeing with Tolstoy "that the Settlement, or Hull-House at least, was a mere presence and travesty of the simple impulse 'to live with the poor,' so long as the residents did not share the common lot of hard labor and scant fare" (260). She organized a Settlement Congress in Chicago during the Exposition to expose the dire poverty exacerbated by the economic depression.

For all of her later writing about her vulnerability, the truth is that by 1896 Addams felt enormously successful as a public figure and modestly successful as a writer. She and Smith arrived in London before going on to Russia and were feted by the Socialists at the home of Eleanor Aveling, the daughter of Karl Marx, during a reception for Karl Liebknecht, who was returning to Germany to serve a prison term for his criticism of the Reichstag. Addams later wrote that his gesture "gave us a glimpse of the old-fashioned orthodox Socialist who had not yet begun to yield to the biting ridicule of Bernard Shaw although he flamed in their midst that evening" (264). They mingled with Sidney and Beatrice Webb, Walter Besant, Octavia Hill, the novelist Mary [Mrs. Humphrey] Ward, and the head of Toynbee Hall, Samuel Barnett, and his wife Henrietta, all leaders in social reform eager to talk with the two women about Addams's successes in Chicago. Addams left the company of her British colleagues in high spirits and traveled on to Russia, anxious to meet the great writer.

On a hot afternoon in July 1896, Jane Addams and Mary Rozet Smith boarded a train in Moscow to travel 130 miles across the Russian countryside, chatting along the way with a young Britisher, Aylmer Maude, and his wife, who were also on their first journey to Yasnaya Polyana, the estate of Leo Tolstoy. They arrived to find that Tolstoy had gone to meet a train at the Toulá station in search of a letter that had been intercepted, as much of his correspondence was, by the Russian authorities. The sixty-seven-year-old man returned thwarted, tired, dusty from his trip, and yet greeted the young arrivals cordially, standing before them tall, gaunt, bearded, and clad in peasant garb. He was used to such folks arriving at his door, traveling as pilgrims on a sacred mission; his biographer George Noyes would refer to them as soft-headed cranks and freaks of all sorts.

William Dean Howells and George Bernard Shaw had preceded Jane Addams and, likewise, took his measure. Of the dinner ritual at Yasnaya, Howells later wrote in "Shaw's Criticism of Tolstoy": "[Tolstoy] sat in a ploughman's dress eating a ploughman's faire at one end of the table, and at the other end of the world, economic and aesthetic, [I] sat served with costly viands."[53] To friends, Howells humorously called himself an "old Tolstoyan manqué," adding wryly "Tolstoy himself is a Tolstoyan manqué."[54] Shaw captured the dramatic absurdity better than any visitor, saying of Tolstoy: "He put on the dress of a moujik exactly as Don Quixote put on a suit of armor. . . . And he was neither honest nor respectable in his follies. He connived at all sorts of evasions." As Jane Addams arrived that afternoon, follies began to unfold.

Her vulnerability in being both female and young (at thirty-five) made Count Tolstoy especially willful that afternoon as they all walked to a little river at some distance from the house where he liked to bathe. Maude, who would become a translator of Tolstoy's work, was to learn that the great man spoke English rather well, although he found using the language cumbersome. "I have to say not what I want to but what I can," he told them.[55] The language served him well enough as he observed the obvious wealth of the women and questioned them about what they did in Chicago and how they viewed their place in the world around them. Addams answered his questions unaware of the trap he was setting for her.

She had come to Russia to tell the great man that he was wrong, if we can imagine such effrontery. In her work at Hull-House, she believed she had discovered a way around the obstacles he had found in the path of philanthropy. Jane Addams had been spending the years since her sighting of Henry James affronting destiny by crafting the profession of social work. Two books that had much to do with the development of her thinking were Tolstoy's *My Religion* and *What to Do?* She discovered over the day that neither of them understood the culture of the other. In truth, Tolstoy had little interest in anything she had to say.

Addams admired Tolstoy's repudiation of his own fiction, the decorative art that he eschewed in his radical sixties, turning the power of his well-tuned moral imagination to intensely autobiographical musings, a literary genre much to her liking. In *What to Do?* he described living and working among the poor in Moscow during an especially brutal Russian winter in 1881, enlisting the help of the wealthy, visiting the homes of the poor, searching for those he might help with his money. Over his months in the city, however, Tolstoy grew cynical of himself as a rural patrician amongst the urban poor, who, as it turned out, held him in contempt. Jane Addams's experiment at Hull-House had been more nuanced than his experiment in Moscow. She and Ellen Gates Starr lived among the poor, raised money from the wealthy, but discovered that they themselves had much to learn from their poor and working-class immigrant neighbors. Their professional philanthropy had little to do with mere charity and more to do with cultural and social cohabitation. "The curious thing about this visit," Maude would later point out about the meeting, "was that Tolstoy had now an opportunity of comparing notes with one of much greater experience in these matters than himself, and whose experience pointed to quite a different conclusion" (527). An opportunity, perhaps, but no one recorded a "comparing of notes" that day.

Tolstoy had convinced himself that philanthropy was fraudulent and that the transformation of society depended on individual will alone. He took little note of the fact that the young woman before him had been living among the poor for seven years and had managed through mutual effort to effect significant change in her Halsted Street neighborhood. She wanted to say to him what she had already said many times to Mary Smith: Tolstoy was a hero to her because he had managed to lift his life to the level of his conscience, to translate his theories into action. He embodied her ideal of something she called "an incarnate idea." Addams wanted him to know that she had performed that transformation in Chicago, building a professional life based on living and working among the poor, struggling along with them toward progressive social and political reform.

From the familiar terrain of England, the two women traveled into the exotically foreign land of Russia. "The fair of Nijni-Novgorod seemed to take us to the very edge of a civilization so remote and eastern, that the merchants brought their curious goods upon the backs of camels or on strange craft riding at anchor on the broad Volga," she remembered in *Twenty Years at Hull-House* (266). A meeting with the Russian novelist Korolenko heightened their sense of cultural incongruity, "that strange mingling of remote past and a self-conscious present." They saw what looked like medieval pilgrims, their bleeding feet bound in rags, trudging to monasteries, tombs, and even the Holy Land, alongside fevered political rebels who would soon lead ancient Russia into a modern revolution. Tolstoy stood at the crossroad as both Russian count and harmless revolutionary.

Her travel diary in July 1896 simply, and characteristically for her in this period of her life, recorded the fact that she and Smith met Count Tolstoy. Her letters home suggested her preoccupation with Hull-House affairs, Chicago Commons, Canadian immigration, and the death of a friend, Mr. Colvin. After his death, she wrote to Gertrude Barnum that she was finding it "hard to go on being interested out here for seven or eight weeks longer, in the shadow of such a calamity, when one cares so much more to be at home. I have not had a letter from Hull House for ten days, and find myself getting a little fussy." The letter detailed her trip to visit Tolstoy, giving a version that she felt comfortable sending home: "We were entertained to supper taken at ten oclock outdoors under the porches, and were almost as much fascinated by his family as himself. One of the daughters had been working in the field all day. They took us over their village to make calls &c and were charming in every way. Tolstoi himself is one the gentlest and kindest of human creatures I ever saw. He was tired so that the actual conversation did not amount to so much as his presence and spirit." We have little reason from the initial letters to think that anything unusual happened that day at Yasnaya Polyana and note only the disappointment she registered about his fatigue.

We have Addams's various and varying accounts of her visit with Tolstoy and two versions written by Aylmer Maude, one in his *Life of Tolstoy* and the other in an article, "A Talk with Miss Addams and Leo Tolstoy," published in *The Humane Review*. "We all walked together towards the little river that flows at some distance from the house," Maude reported. Turning to the women, Tolstoy asked them where "they had come from, what work they did, and what their views were."[56] Jane Addams began to talk about her settlement house experience, about the groups of immigrants in Chicago, living in wretched conditions, and about collaborative accomplishments of the working poor and social workers.

As they reached the riverbank, Tolstoy turned his full gaze on his guest and acted out an old routine. Seemingly distracted by her clothes, Tolstoy turned his head and took hold of an edge and pulling out one sleeve to an interminable breadth, said quite simply, "There is enough stuff on one arm to make a frock for a little girl." The black silk dress indeed had a billowing sleeve, popular in Illinois, marking in its subdued color the seriousness of her mind and in its lavish fabric the degree of her wealth. As he held the loose, puffy silk fabric, he asked in amusement, 'And what is this for?'" The gesture completely disarmed her, as he knew it would. The last thing she had expected to do that afternoon was defend her clothing, and, had she not been rattled, she might have turned the question back on him. Why in the world would he adopt peasant garb of such fine fabric?

Addams found herself a player in his drama. Why had she not adopted peasant dress herself? "You should not like to be dressed differently from them," he admonished her. "I could not dress in all their national costumes!" she answered back. Warming to the argument, he continued, "All the more reason why you should choose some cheap and simple dress any of them could adopt, and not cut yourself off by your garments from those you wish to serve." The Countess Tolstoy, weary of her husband's rudeness, intervened with "a recital of her former attempts to clothe hypothetical little girls in yards of material cut from a train and other superfluous parts of her best gown." Take a firm stand against him, she advised. But his point had been made, reducing Addams to a leisure-class woman, a vain one at that, standing before him condemned by her clothes.

The old man knew how the drama would play out. Before she could recover her footing, he changed course. How did she, as a wealthy American, earn her living? Addams responded cautiously that she lived from money earned from her family property in Cedarville. "So you are an absentee landlord?" he responded, closing the trap.

Maude, who did his best to stay in the conversation, diplomatically claimed in later versions of the story that "there was not a shade of offence given or felt between these two." And yet Addams's accounts record a fiery exchange that afternoon. Tolstoy insisted on a rigid consistency, deliberately missing the point that to work among the poor in America required her to leave rural Cedarville for urban Chicago. And once in the city, she thought it false to pretend that she belonged in another social class. She took with her the wealth her father had created and the clothes her stepmother would have advised a young woman of her social rank to wear.

Marking the difference between men and women of whatever social rank, the party that warm afternoon divided at the river's edge, the women walking back to the house and the men remaining to swim. Grateful for male camaraderie, Maude bathed with the Russian Count from a wooden shed built on the edge of the stream. Tolstoy was muscular and vigorous in his old age. "He swam well, being expert at that, as at all kinds of physical exercise," Maude remembered. Unlike the ladies from America, he was invited to stay for several days as a houseguest, doing more swimming and even learning from Tolstoy how to ride a bicycle.

Later the group gathered in the garden where a leisurely dinner was served in the open air, the women from Chicago meeting the Tolstoy family and visitors from Germany and England. Countess Tolstoy turned her attention to Mary Smith, quizzing the lovely woman about her marriage plans. Smith good-naturedly listened to a lecture she had, no doubt, heard many times from family and friends about finding a husband while she was still young enough at twenty-seven years.

Addams's immediate reaction after the visit was to write a candid letter on July 30, 1896, to Maude about her anger, a letter he later quoted in his biography. Tolstoy's principle of nonresistance to evil, his insistence on pacifism, flew in the face of his treatment of her that day. For all his gentleness of tone, he condescended to her with the force of a moral bully. (He was, after all, a crank himself.) "A radical stand such as Tolstoy has been able to make throws all such effort as that of Settlements into the ugly light of compromise and inefficiency—at least so it seemed to me—and perhaps accounts for a certain defensive attitude I found in myself," Addams admitted to Maude. What irritated her most was Tolstoy's jeering at any solution that seemed to contradict or compromise his own. She noted the irony to Maude: "Beware of losing your own sweetness, in your anxiety to give other people light." Tolstoy could not resist the impulse "to push at a benighted man, and give him two black eyes for being blind." The patronizing tone the Russian patriarch used with any female may well have surprised Jane Addams, a woman who had come to think of herself as a social leader, comfortably acknowledged by the male world.

Caught between two forceful egos, Aylmer Maude, who was a young man affronting his own destiny, decided upon a middle course, one that would allow him to defer to both figures. His tactic was to calm her: "No doubt a fiery prophet (like Tolstoy)—& still more his 2nd & 3rd-rate followers (like myself) are apt to go too far."[57] Clearly the ritual of bathing with Tolstoy and being urged to stay on as a visitor erased the old man's fierceness from Maude's mind. As he chronicled the event in the biography that was published in 1910, however, he gave the argument to Addams, who had become by that time an impressive intellectual and social figure herself. "She had, I now feel sure, a much better perception of the next steps in progress than I or even Tolstoy, and as a result of this she succeeds in achieving considerable results" (II, 367). What we might note here is that Maude's "I or even Tolstoy" reveals his own good opinion of himself.

Tolstoy's charge that Addams was an absentee landlord hit a nerve. Her relationship to the family land was always vexed. Modest wealth had come from her inheritance; her leisurely travel in the 1880s had been provided by her tenant farmer's work, and even her move to Chicago and the establishment of Hull-House had come as a result of land ownership. As early as 1885 Addams, who was spending money in Paris, sold off some land, joking to Alice: "I never intend to invest in any more land—it does not pay to a 'European traveller.'"[58] She sold land again in September of 1885 to help her sister out: "I never counted on my property there at any rate, and would not miss it."[59] The following January, she offered to sell farmland at $60 per acre but failed to find a buyer: "I am sorry for many reasons that I was unable to sell my farm this fall,"[60] she wrote to Alice. As she shed her father's land, she purchased other properties, one at Lakeside, Michigan, in the summer of 1895, where she joined the country club. By 1904, she and Mary were traveling to the East Coast to escape the summer heat and the hard work in Chicago. It was not until November 1912 that Jane decided to sell the farm in Stephenson County for $125 per acre, receiving $20,531.25 in January 1913. Money from that sale may well have gone into the purchase of a cottage at Hull's Cove, the Bar Harbor home she bought with Mary. In New England, among the moneyed Easterners, Addams escaped the chores of settlement house work. The solitude and natural beauty of Hull's Cove, most importantly, gave her a place to write.

Apparent from all the versions of what happened on the hot afternoon in 1896 was that neither Addams nor Tolstoy quite understood the other. The boundaries of age, gender, class, language, and even politics and philosophy held them apart. Addams could see, as he could not, that translating his ideals into anything like an American urban setting would be absurd. She and the women working at Hull-House had no intention of joining the poor in the literal way he advocated. Gender was as barbed a barrier as social class and nationality. Addams knew that Tolstoy had ended *What to Do?* with a call to women: "Women, mothers of the wealthy classes, the salvation of men of our world from the evils from which it suffers is in your hands!"[61] And she agreed with him that women are more natural, instinctive, intuitive than men, especially men of wealth and education. He intended his call to be read literally—that women, as mothers, ought to direct in their traditional domestic and maternal roles. Addams, all along, intended her language to be metaphorical. Her talk about civic housekeeping and mother breasts was an imaginative way of cloaking radical ideas in familiar dress.

The figure of Tolstoy over that hot afternoon served as imaginative material for Addams, who would return to their meeting over and over again in her writing. The Russian figure became a literary character for her, one she shaped and reshaped in speeches, essays, and books over many years. In transforming Tolstoy into a character, she stressed those of his ideas that coincided with hers. In 1902, she lectured in Chautauqua on "Count Tolstoy" and his life as the "sermon of the deed."[62] In "Tolstoy's Theory of Life," she let him say the very things she would say. She alluded to her visit only to note that he displayed the "sweetest and humblest attitude possible" over the afternoon she spent with him at

Yásnaya Polyana, avoiding any trace of disagreement at their meeting. She summed up his positions as they reflected her own: "You must leave out art for a selfish end, for self-cultivation, or it will crumble in your hands." We might wonder at her last line: "But there is great affection in the family, and perfect tolerance and sweetness in their family life."

Nothing in her later book *Newer Ideals of Peace* suggested her actual experience with the man; instead, she used the symbolic figure to give force to her thesis. After arguing that newer ideals come from the jostling of immigrants in American cities like Chicago, she returned to Tolstoy's stress on the nobility of peasants: "He has nevertheless reached down into the moral life of the humble people and formulated for them as for us the secret of their long patience and unremitting labor" (233–34). The example of Russian peasants, who preferred to work in the fields rather than go to battle for the czar, recurred frequently in Addams's writing about peace, and she usually linked the Russian soldiers to Tolstoy as well as to the Doukhobors, the Utopian sect who lived by the ideal of passive nonresistance to evil he advocated.

Twenty Years at Hull-House chronicled a more detailed version of her visit. By 1910, she was a recognized sage and saint in her own right, and Tolstoy had died. She recreated the visit to Tolstoy because of its dramatic power in the same way that she embellished the bullfight in Spain, using each incident to punctuate changes in her narrative. In the autobiography, she folded together the trip to Russia and a subsequent visit to a Doukhobor colony, artfully using it to illustrate her grievances with him. The members of the pacifist sect display "the peace of mind that comes to him who insists upon the logic of life, whether it is reasonable or not—the fanatic's joy in seeing his own clear formula translated into action" (279). She used her pen to refute his ideas by slyly contrasting the successes of Hull-House with the failures of his followers, the Doukhobors.

Ironically, as she moved into late middle age, Addams developed a rigidity of her own. During the First World War she exercised her own penchant for insisting on the logic of life in her unbending pacifism. As a writer, she returned to Tolstoy to give credence to her increasingly unpopular stand against the fighting. In her essay "Tolstoy and the Russian Soldiers," she used the Bolshevik Revolution to illustrate the unwillingness of Russian soldiers to continue fighting the war. Tolstoy appeared in the essay to argue that peasants are naturally opposed to war, making the point that militarism should not and indeed could not be forced on the masses who instinctively seek fraternity, not fratricide. As a character in her essay, he supported her belief that the war instinct can be overcome by the urge to build community, an instinct especially prevalent in the ethnically and racially diverse urban culture of Chicago.

Not until 1931 was her pacifism vindicated and then only in part. The Nobel Committee awarded her the Peace Prize in tandem with Nicholas Murray Butler, the president of Columbia, who had advocated America's entry into the First World War. It was at this time, late in her own life as she visited with Alexandra Tolstoy, who was touring the United States, and just before she won the Peace Prize, that Addams wrote an introduction to Aylmer Maude's translation of the book he titled *What Is to Be Done?*—the book that, perhaps more than any other, influenced her thinking and her writing. She traced the world of 1880 Russia for her twentieth-century audience, who by the 1930s had little interest in the nineteenth century.

Toward the end of the essay, she echoed the skepticism of her earliest college essays. "Social and moral questioning, stimulated by some of the greatest leaders of English thought had driven deep furrows in the smooth surface of nineteenth century satisfaction with the belief that progress was inevitable."[63] During this period many of her generation had turned to Tolstoy as a moral force. "Realizing also as we grow older that life can never be logical and consistent, it still remains the fact that Tolstoy makes complacency as impossible now as when *What Then Must We Do?* first appeared." The scene was the final literary meeting between the writers, the two sages oddly crossing paths—she in her seventies passing literary judgment on the writing he had done in his fifties.

2 *Finding a Voice*

Cassandra in Cross-dress

In 1881 Jane Addams dressed herself, rhetorically speaking, as Cassandra to dramatize the fate of the first generation of American women to graduate from college. In her senior essay to her classmates at Rockford Female Seminary, she cast the new woman as the mythic Greek heroine: "The frail girl stood conscious of Truth but she had no logic to convince the impatient defeated warriors, and no facts to gain their confidence, she could only assert and proclaim until at last in sooth she becomes mad."[1] The heirs of Seneca Falls grew up during and after the Civil War in a culture defined by military conflict, economic competition, and social division by race and class, as well as by gender. Over half of female college graduates—and Addams was no exception—would never marry, and of those who would try to move into professional life, many would indeed become "mad" in long stretches of hysteria.

She sought a way for Cassandra to overpower Apollo, who had granted her the gift of prophecy but cursed her with the inability to be understood. We can hear the feminism of the late nineteenth century in Addams's prodding of the Rockford women to resist Cassandra's fate through education: "I would call this a feminine trait of mind, an accurate perception of Truth and Justice which rests contented in itself, and will make no effort to conform itself, or to organize through existing knowledge." How might this transformation be accomplished? Addams, at twenty-one, thought she had the solution: If women would study at least one branch of physical science, they might avoid Cassandra's madness by expressing what they knew through the language and logic of masculine discourse. Women might wield revolutionary power by transcending gender through the synthesis of intuition (inherently female) and reason (traditionally but not inherently or exclusively male). "All that subtle force among women which is now dream fancy, might be changed into creative genius," Addams asserted, if women can gain *auethoritas* through the power of a public voice. Jane Addams's Cassandra might be trained to talk like a man.

Training Cassandra would take the next twenty-five years. We can hear the maturing of her literary voice in her writing, especially in *Democracy and Social Ethics, Newer Ideals of Peace,* and *The Spirit of Youth and the City Streets.* It was in *Democracy and Social Ethics,* published in 1902, that she found a dramatic mode of presentation and established the authority of her public voice. The book, containing an introduction and six essays she had already delivered as speeches or published as articles, sold 4,500 copies in the first eighteen months and continued to sell well over the next ten years, with a total of about 10,000 copies. Its success stood in sharp contrast to the sales of *Hull-House Maps and Papers,* and it vindicated Addams's turn away from a purely academic genre. Most books on social ethics fail because they are bookish and remote from the actual, she explained to her readers, promising to talk with them more intimately.

Culling characters from her experience and imagination, Jane Addams dresses, re-dresses, and even cross-dresses the Cassandra figure. As she put it in *Democracy and Social Ethics,* "[I]deas only operate upon the popular mind through will and character, and must be dramatized before they reach the mass of men" (227). Blending narrative and analysis, she juxtaposes the manners, customs, rituals, and values of the working class with those of the volunteer charity workers from leisure-class communities situated at a safe distance from poverty. In the background of her argument lies metaphorical Halsted Street, the "common road where all must turn out for one another, and at least see the size of one another's burdens" (6). The mingling of the poor with the wealthy acts as the catalyst of the new social ethics she advocates: "Thus the identification with the common lot which is the essential idea of Democracy becomes the source and expression of social ethics" (11). Through a series of dramatic disguises, Jane Addams found a literary voice that, at least until the First World War, managed to thwart Apollo.

Rockford Female Seminary reinforced gender differences embedded in Victorian ideology. Woman, like the mythical Cassandra, supposedly knew about the world from intuition, an irrational, subconscious, even mystical source of knowledge, and expressed herself in associative logic. Less educable, more primitive than man, the female was seen as naïve, naturally pure, and morally good. A female's body, like her mind, was considered frail, and at least that was true for a leisure-class woman, whose father or husband provided the money that made her work outside the home unnecessary. Woman's sense of justice came from her innate tendency to nurture, empathize, cooperate, and to create order in the domestic world. As John Ruskin counseled young women in "Of Queens' Gardens": "The woman's power is for rule, not for battle,—and her intellect is not for invention or creation, but for sweet ordering, arrangement, and decision."[2] Her activities, however, were restricted to the home, "the shelter, not only from all injury, but from all terror, doubt, and division." The message was clear: a woman might reign only as long as she was an angel and even then only within her house. Jean Bethke Elshtain's biography *Jane Addams and the Dream of American Democracy* places Addams's social work in this tradition, even ending the story of her life with the line: "Come in, she said. There is shelter from the storm."[3]

In the conventional dichotomy, a male, specifically the moneyed, educated man, supposedly possessed a rigorous intellect that expressed abstractions in linear patterns. He thought and spoke in the rational logic of the Enlightenment, basing his conclusions on scientific experimentation and scholarly research. The male presented to the public world his physical as well as intellectual power. His innate strength caused him to favor aggression, competition, even combat, so that his sense of justice had its basis in conflict. Male discourse, like his muscular presence, overwhelmed the female, at least in public life. His voice carried authority in the social, political, business world beyond the domestic space where women spoke. Apollo had the power, after all, to curse Cassandra. The female seminary education shaped the way young women were to view their place in the world by stressing both the strength of the manly presence and the moral goodness of the feminine sensibility.

The tension created by this juxtaposition clearly confused Addams and her generation, eager to fulfill their duty and use their energy and, at the same time, aware of the restrictions on the female enterprise. If they did not marry and raise children, what were they to do, how were they to free themselves from "the snare of preparation"?

At the turn into the twentieth century, a time of social change expressed by Henry Adams and his generation of aging men as the breakdown of Western civilization, young women of Jane Addams's generation welcomed change. Moving away from small-town life, eager to transform notions of domesticity, Addams and her female colleagues resisted small-town restrictions and embraced city life. Mary Wilson Gibson argues in *The American Woman in Transition: The Urban Influence, 1870–1920* that upper-middle-class women found the urban world a freer place to live. They discovered ways to expand their dominion beyond the home; women's charity groups and social clubs moved into the public and political life of the city. Addams and her colleagues created professions out of what was thought of as volunteer work. Beth Fowkes Tobin in her study of early nineteenth-century England, *Superintending the Poor: Charitable Ladies and Paternal Landlords in British Fiction, 1770–1860*, documents the takeover of aristocratic charity work by the middle class, a newly educated group of Englishmen who successfully transformed noblesse oblige into professional work, gaining new areas of management and dislodging the rich from political control of the country. Addams and colleagues in the social settlement movement attempted a similar coup in America by transforming philanthropy into a profession. The new female professionals in social settlements, education, nursing, and industrial relations fought hard to gain political credibility that might come to include suffrage and public office.

Addams's first book, *Democracy and Social Ethics*, synthesizes masculine and feminine modes of thought and speech, blending rational and intuitive knowledge, intellectual and visceral experience, objective and subjective points of view into patterns of rational and associative logic. In order to discredit what her younger contemporary Mikhail Bakhtin would call "authoritative discourse"—the inflexible monologic rhetoric of businessmen and pseudoscientists—Addams sets on her stage a polyphony of voices from the Chicago streets, those of charity workers, immigrants, laborers, and tenement dwellers.[4] Her writing, as a result, often has the look and sound of fiction. The experiences of working-class women, children, and men pour forth from street scenes in narratives that tell the story of urban poverty from the inside out. She celebrates the dialogic world of independent and equally valid voices. Addams's strategy is to garner the support of sundry people who together have the power to gain public attention and credibility. She crosses the boundaries between classes and genders, casting herself as first one character and then another, transforming the female voice from a private into a public one.

The book argues that "the cure for the ills of Democracy is more Democracy" (11–12) and illustrates its thesis through the behavior of three female characters: a youthful volunteer, a professional settlement worker, and the writer herself. She tells the story of the writer's experiences, first as a daughter resisting her father's dominance at home and then as a commentator speaking on a range of social issues. Beneath the surface movement of the book lies a static set of ideas, all embedded in what Addams believed are innately female ways of knowing and behaving. Social ethics grow naturally from the melding of cultures, the rich with the poor, the native-born with the immigrant, the old with the young, and especially the male with the female. "To attain individual morality in an age demanding social morality, to pride oneself on the results of personal effort when the time demands social adjustment, is utterly to fail to appreciate the situation," she cautions. Morally healthy society grows from associated, not individual, effort and from cooperation, not competition.

In *Democracy and Social Ethics* Addams dresses herself as a novice charity volunteer, then as a seasoned settlement professional, and finally as "the writer," the ultimate authority who observes, intercedes, and most importantly records the activities on Halsted Street. All three characters may be read as evolutionary stages of female sensibility and, finally, as aging versions of Addams herself. The novice charity worker looks like Cassandra with a Rockford education: "The daintily clad charitable visitor who steps into the little house made untidy by the vigorous efforts of her hostess, the washerwoman, is no longer sure of her superiority to the latter; she recognizes that her hostess after all represents social value and industrial use, as over against her own parasitic cleanliness and social standing attained only through status" (16). Borrowing from Charlotte Perkins Gilman's *Women and Economics*, Addams portrays the modern, leisure-class woman as an economic and social parasite.

She presents male ideas in cross-dress. The "dainty" apparel is deceiving in that when the charity worker speaks, she sounds like a bourgeois businessman, full of the rhetoric of Ralph Waldo Emerson and the social Darwinists. Dressed like a woman, she talks like a man. The dainty charity worker chides the poor for not practicing cleanliness, hard work, thrift, temperance, and self-denial, the modes of conduct traditionally assumed to bring men material success: "She insists that they must work and be self-supporting, that the most dangerous of all situations is idleness, that seeking one's own pleasure, while ignoring claims and responsibilities, is the most ignoble of actions" (17). In a review for *Charities* magazine, Edward T. Devine, misreading the text, criticized Addams for creating a straw man that served only to weaken her logic.[5] Her goal, however, was not to use the rhetoric of argument but rather the narrative of drama to pull the reader along with her from one perspective to another. The daintiness of charity work gives way to the subtler intelligence of "the sensitive visitor," a professional social worker who adds experience to the fledgling intuition of the younger woman. The visitor understands that she cannot play the role of social leader in a working-class neighborhood. The charity worker (whose own grandmother would have understood real labor) begins to see the absurdity of her position. She learns that the ethics of the poor grow out of their relationship with each other and their shared economic vulnerability.

In the background of the drama lies the "common road," a polyphonic chorus of poor women, children, and men who have developed their ethics through firsthand experience. The writer listens to the stories and narrates them, sometimes using dialogue. The genuine charity of neighbors contrasts sharply with the artificial charity of the volunteer. In a passage modeled after Tolstoy's *What to Do?*, Addams records the protest of the poor against the efforts of the volunteer: "'What do you want, anyway?'" they jeer. "'If you have nothing to give us, why not let us alone and stop your questionings and investigations?'" (23–24). In the multilayered narrative, the charity worker begins to shed the rhetoric of the businessman, along with her dainty clothes, and to see the world through the eyes of the poor.

Yet it is the writer who finally sees it all—creates the characters, records the scenes, and moves her readers toward solutions to class differences. Cassandra, dressed daintily as a charity worker, is no match for the writer, who has shed dainty apparel to become a professional woman. In another passage that echoes Tolstoy's *What to Do?*, Addams writes: "She discovers how incorrigibly bourgeois her standards have been, and it takes but a little time to reach the conclusion that she cannot insist so strenuously upon the conventions of her own class, which fail to fit the bigger, more emotional, and freer lives of working people" (38). Big, emotional, and free are all more democratic traits than small, rational, and constricted. The volunteer charity worker personifies the "pseudoscientific and stilted state" in an evolutionary process. At one end is the primitive community, represented by the immigrants in Chicago who behave instinctively through intuitive knowledge, and at the other end is the social settlement, conceived by the writer who has blended her intuition with experience in the world. On the common road, the charity worker has "stumbled and fallen" because she has mistakenly believed that she could "push forward the mass" (69). Until she learns "to walk for many dreary miles beside the lowliest of His creatures," she will have it wrong (70). The common road metaphorically marks the progress of Addams's ideas throughout the book.

Addams attacks paternal behavior of all sorts. In "Filial Relations" she tells the story of the social worker and her struggle to pull herself away from the rule of her father, the claims of family, and the power of social class. Although she does not mention S. Weir Mitchell by name in *Democracy and Social Ethics,* Addams criticizes his treatment of the wealthy young woman who falls prey to depression: "Her life is full of contradictions. She looks out into the world, longing that some demand be made upon her powers, for they are too untrained to furnish an initiative. When her health gives way under this strain, as it often does, her physician invariably advises a rest. But to be put to bed and fed on milk is not what she requires. What she needs is simple, health-giving activity, which, involving the use of all her faculties, shall be a response to all the claims which she so keenly feels" (87). By the time he treated Jane Addams in the 1880s, Mitchell was already nurturing his own literary life, publishing several novels from 1882 until 1913, including *Circumstance* (1901). A reviewer in the *Post* linked Addams and Mitchell as writers who had the same theme in mind.[6]

Female hysteria, as Addams sees it, results from the tension between a woman's desire to own herself and her family's notion that she is their possession, that "her delicacy and polish are but outward symbols of her father's protection and prosperity" (83). The daughter is, in truth, her father's chattel. John Addams had been dead for twenty years when the book was published, yet his daughter continued to resist him. She illustrates her point about female freedom by dressing her father as King Lear and herself as Cordelia to retell the story from the daughter's point of view. Pity for Lear blinds us to his flaws. "Cordelia made the awkward attempt of an untrained soul to be honest and scrupulously to express her inmost feelings" (95), but Lear's mind could not accept the idea that his daughter might have a life beyond her attachment to him: "It was impossible for him to calmly watch his child developing beyond the stretch of his own mind and sympathy" (97). Cordelia was right in her desire to stretch beyond her father, Addams argues, and Lear was wrong.

We might expect Addams to argue that same course of action for the working-class daughter. But not so. In "Household Adjustment," the maid, as a member of the working class, is advised to live among her own people, not in her employer's house. There are strong ironies in Addams's depiction of the working-class home as a haven for daughters. The very writer who rails against the family claim on the wealthy daughter argues that home is where the working girl belongs so that her parents can protect her until she can find a proper husband: "It is well to remember that women, as a rule, are devoted to their families; that they want to live with their parents, their brothers and sisters, and kinsfolk, and will sacrifice much to accomplish this" (123). Poor girls will always work, in the home and outside, in factories, offices, stores, or in other homes.

Addams's profession, as the reviewer from the *International Socialist Review* understood, was based on a stratified class system. Poverty and social vulnerability, we are to believe, make her jobs as social worker and writer necessary.

Just as domestic workers should live among their own families, industrial workers should live in their own communities. "Industrial Amelioration" makes that point by attacking George Pullman and his construction of worker communities in Chicago: "He socialized not only the factory, but the form in which his workmen were living" (143). Addams argues that paternalistic philanthropy, like paternalistic family life, is doomed. George Pullman and his Palace Car Company constructed a model community for workers south of Chicago. Although the town provided such bourgeois amenities as churches, stores, parks, even a library, the fact that workers had no freedom to live elsewhere coupled with a reduction of wages in 1893 caused unrest. Eugene Debs organized workers into the American Railway Union and called for a strike that erupted across the country (Addams served on an investigative committee and delivered speeches on the topic to the Chicago Woman's Club and the Twentieth Century Club).[7] The story of Pullman parallels the drama of the dainty charity worker: the wealthy cannot foist manners, customs, and morality on the working class and expect loyalty in return. Paternalism operates from a wrong set of ideas: "He honestly believed that he knew better than they what was their good" (144). Trade unionists, Addams points out, know more than Pullman can know about how to manage the working-class community. What poor people need are shorter work hours, regulated wages, and a minimum age for child laborers.

The patriarchal figures in the book begin to merge: the charity worker schooled on male ideas, the wealthy father claiming rights over his daughter's life, the bourgeois family enslaving the working girl, King Lear insisting on Cordelia's sacrifice, George Pullman hoping to buy worker loyalty. Paternally conceived relationships suffer from a lack of democratic ethics.

Why wasn't *Democracy and Social Ethics* written by a working-class immigrant? Addams addresses the question indirectly by condemning education in America for its tie to business. Like Lear and Pullman, the businessman wants loyalty and obedience from students because he is interested, finally, in financial gain: "'Teach the children to write legibly and to figure accurately and quickly; to acquire habits of punctuality and order; to be prompt to obey; and you will fit them to make their way in the world as I have made mine'" (191). The young man on Halsted Street finds such an education stultifying: "Partly because so little is done for him educationally, and partly because he must live narrowly and dress meanly, the life of the average laborer tends to become flat and monotonous, with nothing in his work to feed his mind or hold his interest" (194–95). Addams advocates a more intellectually rigorous education to compensate the worker who cannot rise socially and economically: "He, more than other men, needs the conception of historic continuity in order to reveal to him the purpose and utility of his work" (206). Unlike the businessman—and we hear the condescension—the worker supposedly has little sense of his own effort. Her view of workingmen seems to come from the outside in, not from the inside out as her portraits of women so remarkably do.

Denying the authority of the male voice—that of businessmen, social thinkers, as well as workingmen—has the effect of granting credibility to the female voice. Addams moves her reader toward a willingness to hear what a woman has to say. Her final chapter, "Political Reform," narrates the story of her struggle against Alderman John Powers, the head of the Democratic machine in her Nineteenth Ward. Working to oust him from power, she begins to see his function from the point of view of her Halsted Street neighbors. Powers gains support through another type of social work that Addams describes as the "stalking survival of village kindness." The alderman pays the mortgage when a family is in trouble, bails a wayward son out of jail, gives turkeys to women at Christmastime, attends and pays for funerals, gives uniforms to the Salvation Army, and protects men who want to gamble and drink after hours. The corrupt alderman thus becomes the hero of the poor immigrant community and sets its moral tone.

The roles of hero and moral guide are, of course, the ones Jane Addams is creating for herself. In a surprising reversal, she claims that his ethical system may be more democratic than that of paternal reformers (kin of paternal fathers and businessmen) who fail to live and work among the poor. "Would it be dangerous to conclude that the corrupt politician himself, because he is democratic in method, is on a more ethical line of social development than the reformer, who believes that the people must be made over by 'good citizens' and governed by 'experts'?" (270). The social reformer, like her dainty charity volunteer, must learn to live among the lower classes if she is to have a profession, taking lessons from the corrupt alderman, boodler though he may be.

The last scene displays the social reformer in her most exotic disguise. We see her cross-dressed, marching shoulder to shoulder with the workingmen of Halsted Street: "This necessity of reducing the experiment to action throws out of the undertaking all timid and irresolute persons, more than that, all those who shrink before the need of striving forward shoulder to shoulder with the cruder men, whose sole virtue may be social effort, and even that not untainted by self-seeking, who are indeed pushing forward social morality, but who are doing it irrationally and emotionally, and often at the expense of the well-settled standards of morality" (274). Timid charity workers are pushed aside, along with anyone without the muscle to thrust forward with the crude men of the street. The jostling of descriptive clauses in the sentence has the effect of coupling the social worker and the workingman in an image of brute physical strength. The cruder men, under their costumes, look like Cassandras—female figures in the garments of the workingmen—who speak, as women supposedly always have, from intuitive, irrational, emotional knowledge.

How successful was Jane Addams in convincing readers that the female voice carried masculine authority, that Cassandra might "convince the impatient defeated warriors"? A workingman who supported Powers in the political battle wrote her a blunt letter about the place of a woman in the Nineteenth Ward. "God created woman as a companion for man. To be loved, cherished, and honored, by man. But no man can love a woman who takes her place among men as you do," the letter reads, each cursive line tilting slightly backward in a hand that looks suspiciously young. In language that must have raised eyebrows at Hull-House, the voter accuses her of wanting to be a man and warns: "Did it ever occur to you while on a tour of inspection, through alley ways old barns and such places where low depraved men with criminal records may be found (such a place a virtuous woman would be afraid to go.) You might for a small sum induce one of such men to sell you his pecker and balls. It would not be much loss to him, and will be your only chance to prove yourself a man."[8] To prove herself a man was, of course, the challenge. In her book, she boldly links arms with workingmen like this one from her ward. It was not genitalia but the manly costume that she desired.

She was impressive in cross-dress. Edwin Seligman wrote to her in April, praising the book: "It is long since I have read so sane and so inspiring a book." The image of the female social worker dressed as a workingman apparently convinced him of her authority as a writer: "[N]o other book by a woman shows such vitality—such masculinity of mental grasp & surefootedness."[9] Oliver Wendell Holmes got the point, too, writing to Richard Ely that Addams is "a big woman who knows at least the facts and gives me more insights into the point of view of the workingmen and the poor than I had before." And gazing upon her there in the street, he notes, "How excellent her discrimination between doing good *to* them and doing *with* them."[10] Harriet Monroe referred to Addams's "mountaineer venturesomeness."

The image of a big woman with a masculinity of grasp and the venturesomeness and surefootedness of a mountaineer attests to the virility of the writer. Over the course of the book, the masculine voice, daintily clad, loses ground to the feminine voice, crudely arrayed. Dressed like a man she was free to talk like a woman.

The Marketplace

For a writer two moments hold, perhaps, the greatest risk: one when the idea comes into consciousness and the other when the book finds its way into the reader's hands. As Jane Addams was completing the manuscript of *Democracy and Social Ethics* and finding her voice as a writer, she thought hard about her next book, *Newer Ideals of Peace.* If she were to become a writer, after all, her first book must be followed by a second and a third. Her first book lay in the hands of readers, even as the second lay precariously in her mind. The gestation time for the second book, as it turned out, would be six long years.

In January 1901, she lectured in Burlington, Iowa, as she sought her footing on the new book project. "I made my attempt to outline the chapters of the book and hand it to you at the date you requested," she wrote to Richard Ely, "but the outline was so unsatisfactory and meagre that I gave it up."[11] She was reading Stanton Coit's *Ethical Democracy* and collecting her own thoughts in lectures she was crafting. Talking and writing always developed in tandem for her, and she used one activity to beg off from the other. Ely responded, as good editors do, that he was "confident, however, that your book is going to be helpful." And he urged her to "steal the time from other things."[12] Write simply a dozen lines, he coaxed her, that indicate the direction the book might take: "P.S. Can you not, without going into details and mentioning chapters give me ten or a dozen lines indicative of the general character of your book." Getting just that dozen lines would take considerably more time than he imagined or than we might think and, even then, her words would be nearly indecipherable.

The year she ought to have been writing, she procrastinated by taking on a series of tasks—arranging for the visit of the anarchist Prince Peter Kropotkin in April, traveling to New Orleans and St. Louis, planning a summer school course at Rockford, visiting the Pan-American Exposition in Buffalo in August, selling her sister Mary's property in Lake Forest, and attending a family wedding. Even as she busied herself with reading, lecturing, and administering, she could feel Ely at her heels, demanding not only the final draft of *Democracy and Social Ethics* but also some clear sign of her next book. "I will certainly get at the material this summer," she promised. "I have been swamped with work for the past three months."[13] What swamped her, of course, was the running of a social settlement, especially in its early days. "I am ashamed of my delay but often Hull-House is of more importance than my feeble utterances." Writing a single book does not make one a writer—she knew that much.

In August 1901, Addams embarked on her usual summer holiday, going first to Mackinac Island, Michigan, to spend a week with Alice Hamilton, and then to Buffalo, New York, for the Pan-American Exposition (Theodore Roosevelt had opened the event in the spring) and to see Niagara Falls. Days after her return to Chicago, on September 5, President McKinley arrived in Buffalo and also visited the Falls only to be met the next day at the Exposition by his assassin Leon Czolgosz, an immigrant anarchist. The murder put Roosevelt into the White House. Across the country police arrested anarchists, including Emma Goldman, in confusion and paranoia over a possible plot to kill the president. In Chicago, Abraham Isaaks, a Russian immigrant who edited *Free Society* and often attended meetings at Hull-House, was arrested, pulling Jane Addams into the struggle to free the radicals being detained. She found herself at the center of the political storm without thinking of herself as a radical, much less a revolutionary. Clarence Darrow wrote her about the fiasco, "Of course, I would gladly avoid this if I could," full of sadness and ambivalence over the moral and ethical responsibilities of public intellectuals at peril in a national crisis.[14] Reading the flack in the London newspapers, William Stead wrote, "There is always an immense danger in times of popular passion and fury that perfectly innocent philosophers may be confounded with bloody handed assassins."[15]

Her letters that summer, surprisingly, seem as concerned with the events in her own family and her planned trip with Mary Smith to Saratoga as with the national trauma. Addams confided to Florence Kelley (who was helping her market an essay at the *North American Review*): "Prof. Ely has been here for three weeks and talked to me daily about the book."[16] He urged her to publish with him first and not to release material to magazines beforehand, and she suggested to Kelley that they drop the project with the magazine. Ever the negotiator, she urged Macmillan, that summer, to read her nephew James Weber Linn's manuscript, "The Second Generation," and they accepted the book, publishing it in March 1902.

Her work with editors, most of them men, would vex her all her life. She hated being bossed by anyone and, it should come as no surprise, thought of her writing as her own property. As early as November 1901 she had begun to dig in her heels with Ely, who wanted revisions on the manuscript of *Democracy and Social Ethics:* "I am the more ashamed of my delay because it has amounted to nothing and I am sending the manuscript at last in practically the same condition that it was a month ago."[17] By inclination a hairsplitter, Ely lectured her on writing style: "As I already mentioned, good writers do use split infinitives and it is better sometimes to use one than to avoid one in an awkward manner. I think, however, that with sufficient pains the split infinitives can almost always be avoided without any awkwardness in style."[18] Addams thought about the art of writing in ways that Ely never imagined.

Her literary instincts were sound, even as she struggled to rely on them. As she had explained to William Vaughn Moody: "I am enough of a Tolstoyan to care for 'art'—as it enables me to express 'that which one feels but finds inexpressible.'"[19] How might she, as a writer, find a voice to express the inexpressible? The question clearly perplexed her. She did keep in mind another of Ely's cautions: "Of course, books are uncertain, and no one can tell in advance what a book is going to do."

After *Democracy and Social Ethics* appeared in 1902, Addams traveled to the East on a lecture tour, including talks at Vassar and Bryn Mawr and a meeting of the Consumers' League in New York City. By the end of March, Macmillan sent her $50 on the sale of the first 1,000 copies of her book, and by April she reported to Mary Smith that she had cleared $500 in lecture fees. The schedule was grueling and, even as she collected the money, she complained about having to speak every day for more than two weeks.

All that year, letters and reviews piled up, most of them appreciative of her work as a writer, having the counterintuitive effective of making her less confident. J. David Thompson from the Library of Congress wrote praising her work: "I spent the whole evening with you for as I read your new book I could hear distinctly the very tones of your voice."[20] He urged her to publish more of her lectures. As she read his letter, she wrote Anita McCormick Blaine, a friend and generous Hull-House donor, "I have had some terrible qualms since it has been issued but perhaps that is inevitable."[21] Edwin Seligman assured her that the book had moral authority, yet she confided to Mary, "I feel a little better about it, but it is all I can do not to tear out the leaves."[22]

Aylmer Maude, reviewing the book for *The Whim*, waxed and waned in his enthusiasm for her as a writer. He credited the value of the book as its relation to Addams's experience in social work but criticized her work as a writer. Apparently, he found the book too hard to read: "One criticism may, I think, fairly be made. Miss Addams—whose greatest work is Hull House, Chicago—is not primarily an author, and she has not spent the time, or taken the trouble, that would have been necessary to make her book quite easy reading . . . and even one who has thought about the questions she treats of, may find some passages the meaning of which remains somewhat doubtful, even after a second perusal."[23] The passage suggests Maude's own trouble with language and, curiously, his limitations as a thinker.

Addams sent copies of the book to various writers, scholars, and friends, among them William Dean Howells, who wrote to thank her for the book, "I shall read with instruction and pleasure."[24] Much of Howells's letter, however, discusses her reading of his work. She had written him to explain a newspaper account of what she was quoted as having said about one of his plays, probably "The Mother and the Father." He good-naturedly responds, "As I have not yet seen what you said of my poor little fables, or the newspaper perversion of your words, I am . . . in no present pain." The two writers had first exchanged letters in October 1899 after a "Howells night" at the Twentieth Century Club in Chicago and a subsequent trip to Lake Forest. Addams called him her "charming comrade" and he enthused over theater at Hull-House: "As I told you, I hope somehow, sometime, to do something worthy of the Hull-House stage, which seems to me a real Théâtre Libre, and forms an opportunity for a conscientious drama which is quite unequalled in America, so far as I know." Howells imagined Hull-House attracting "future Tolstoys, Ibsens, and Maeterlincks."[25] Shannon Jackson in her study of performance at Hull-House, *Lines of Activity: Performance, Historiography, Hull-House Domesticity*, links the theater to other modes of representation, exploring the subtle power of language in its dramatic guise.

We know from her letters that Jane Addams often luxuriated in the comfort of her social class. A writer, after all, cannot be always at her task. At the end of her lecture tour, she vacationed with Mary Smith's parents at the posh Hotel Chelsea in Atlantic City. Writing to Mary, who was traveling in Europe, Addams basked in her surroundings: "Here we are, most comfortable and happy in a fine hotel, with excellent things to eat and every inducement to loaf."[26] She liked staying in the sumptuous hotel and indulged herself with food and books. "Perhaps when we are old and retired into a rear flat on Irving St.," she joked, "we will be able to read together but not write—we won't do that any more!"[27] Even on vacation, or perhaps especially on vacation, Addams brooded about the book that she was supposed to be writing. "I have here time to think about you a great deal and you have been a great solace in the midst of terrible throes about the awful book—if I could only do it now and then dedicate it—á la Prof. James!" She clearly associated her second book with the work that William James was doing. The idea of dedicating her next work to him and placing herself in his literary company, however, unnerved her.

In May 1902, Jane Addams traveled to Los Angeles with Florence Kelley and Julia Lathrop to participate in a meeting of the Federation of Women's Clubs. Along with her loneliness, she recorded in her letters to Mary candid criticism of the meetings: "Oh! So infected with woman folk." She lamented having to deal with her southern hostess: "I find the atmosphere a little difficult."[28] Henry Ward, a thirty-eight-year-old American carpenter, shrewdly observed in a letter to Addams, "I don't doubt that you have noticed that some of the speaking is a very common hash."[29] And Addams wrote to Smith about the hash, "[I]t all seems terribly remote and save for the color question without any real issue."[30] By the end of her month, she was homesick: "[A]nd you must know, dear, how I long for you all the time—and especially during the last three weeks. There is reason in the habit of married folk keeping together."[31] The sustained company of women only put her more in mind of the one woman she desired.

Correspondents and reviewers continued to urge her to write. A friend she called a "consistent democrat," William Kent, admonished her: "The time has come when you should do a great deal more writing."[32] Vida Scutter praised *Democracy and Social Ethics*, especially its "profoundly moving effect," and yet hesitated over the book's structure: "I am afraid that a good many people may miss in some cases the structural unity that really exists, and see only a series of independent tho stimulating reflections."[33] Scutter was right that Addams moved her argument through a series of "stimulating reflections," a technique that she would develop over many years.

She struggled to make changes in *Democracy and Social Ethics* for its second printing. William S. Booth, irritated by her desire to reshape the book, warned about expenses: "I have been carefully through all the corrections which you have made in your book, and as far as I can see they will demand the entire resetting of the book, as they are so numerous and so lengthy that every page will have to be overrun to the end of each chapter in which the corrections occur."[34] Booth lectured the novice writer on the art of bookmaking and the craft of making plates. George Brett, the publisher at Macmillan, wrote to soothe her: "We have, of course, supposed that you would follow up the success of this book with another one and we should be very happy indeed if you were willing to let us know as to when in all probability your new book will be ready and the subject thereof, in order that we may make an offer for its publication." Richard Ely advised her on the merits of publishing with a single press, stressing the royalties that would be advanced by Macmillan on her new work.[35] The double assault from Brett and Ely had the effect of moving her toward her second book.

We imagine her dragging her chair to the desk as she worked to deliver the dozen lines that Ely had been urging her to write. "I have thought of putting some lectures into a book form altho I am afraid the book would be rather small," she told him.[36] She offered three preliminary titles: "The Newer Ideals of Peace," "Dynamic Peace," and "War & Labor." Attached, somewhat mysteriously and certainly awkwardly, to the letter is a page of notes, apparently the dozen lines he wanted to see. Her writing signifies the tentative nature of her creative process so early in her writing career. Scrawled at an angle, moving downward across the page, the lines go something like this:

> women dwelling—tending within
> the house—conventional—
> 1st
> [women] entering into the commercial
> life & worker industrial conditions
> with its element of warfare, of
> competition, of 'owning' your work
> withdraw the combative—in
> a certain sense
> Spinning, weaving, dying blankets for
> keeping the family warm
> or working in an emporium in order
> to buy blankets—to keep
> family warm—

I say "something like this" because the writing is nearly inscrutable, especially after the word "withdraw." She may have selected the words conventional, competition, and combative as she imagined a way for women to redirect human behavior. From the looks of it, Addams had in mind using warfare as a metaphor. The question for women, both working women and the professional women at Hull-House, was how useful their work might be in an industrial, capitalist economy. If they were to give up blanket-making in order to work in a store, what might they gain? With such irony in mind, she could not think beyond the dozen lines.

The writing of the book moved haltingly even after she signed the contract in January 1903 with a $200 advance and the promise of 13 percent for a book to be part of Macmillan's Citizen Library series, as her first book had been. She warned George Brett even as she signed the contract that she was doing so only with the "assurance that it was possible to allow three years between such signing and the appearance of the book."[37] We can hear all her hesitations in her negotiation: "I find little time for writing and my ideas are as yet by no means clear." Although she had, by this time, fixed the title, "The Newer Ideals of Peace," she had written only one chapter and some notes. She requested that no announcement be made of the promised book until she had more of it down on paper. Having put some distance between herself and her putative book, she relaxed by continuing to lecture and to work on other writing projects.

Addams continued to mull her ideas about peace. Richard Watson Gilder, the editor of the *Century* magazine, sent her some of his poetry in the spring. Reading the poems stimulated her thinking. She responded that it "gives one new courage in the quest for the 'moral substitute for war' to know such writing."[38] The idea of finding a moral substitute or equivalent for war linked her to William James and kept her mind on the book that she thought she would dedicate to him.

Ely kept after her, asking again in April when she would have the book done and advising her to write it before the presidential campaign, which would take public attention away from any book, however well written. Her letter back to him reveals the process she was going through as she worried that Hobson may have said it all in his book *Imperialism*, a work that she hoped to use in building her own argument. Another letter in June to her sister Alice arrived with a copy of W. E. B. Du Bois's *The Souls of Black Folk*, a book that she and Mary Smith had just read together during a trip to Atlanta. The structure of that book, with its folding together of seemingly scattered vignettes and observations, appealed to her, offering as it did a narrative based on associative thought rather than chronology or argument.

Her writer's block was—what else could it have been?—the product of her imagination. She wrote to Raymond Robbins about his sister's appreciation of *Democracy and Social Ethics*, "I certainly wasn't annoyed when you told me of her reading of my book—but embarrassed. Any reference to that unhappy volume seems to throw me into a state approaching a childish panic."[39] Her anxiety about the book, however, did not keep her from other writing projects. She worked on the topic of child labor and pauperism during the fall of 1903, giving lectures and publishing versions of her essay as part of the campaign for passage of the Illinois Child Labor Law. In September she published a pamphlet, "Newsboy Conditions in Chicago," an exposé that included photographs of boys living in wretched conditions that resembled the work Jacob Riis was doing in New York City. After her friend and colleague Henry Demarest Lloyd died in October, Addams wrote a tribute to the Chicago journalist and public activist. Ely continued through the year to encourage her writing, even arranging for her to receive her first honorary degree, LL.D., from the University of Wisconsin.

In the late summer of 1904, she and Mary vacationed in Bar Harbor, Woods Hole, and Gloucester, Maine, relaxing into their "marriage." As Jane traveled alone to Chautauqua, she wrote back to Mary: "I feel as if we had come into a healing domesticity which we have never had before and as if it were the best affection offered me, and you?"[40]

Addams lectured on "Newer Ideals of Peace" with her new book in mind. She met with William James that fall at the Thirteenth Universal Peace Conference in Boston and published her essay "Women's Peace Meeting" in the *Woman's Journal.* Ely continued to encourage her to write the next book: "It seems to me that for years there has not been so favorable a time for its appearance. . . . There is a disposition to consider peace measures such as there has not been for many years."[41] Addams could finally tell him, "The book is moving on slowly but after all is in motion. I think it would be safe to announce it for the Spring, if that means that I not have the manuscript ready before February."[42] It would be hard to say who was more relieved by the news.

Addams was the first female convocation speaker at the University of Chicago that year, and she proudly sent a copy of her speech to Ely, admitting playfully that she was sending it in "accordance with my absurd custom of considering you my *'sociological godfather.'*"[43] Clearly delighted by the metaphor, he responded: "It seems to me to have wonderful insight and to say just the things that need to be said. I indeed feel gratified and encouraged greatly by your thought of me as your 'sociological godfather.'" He thought of himself as her literary mentor, and she listened to his advice indulgently, as mentees often do, without always heeding what he had to say.

Her article "The Immigrants and American Charities," which appeared in the *Proceedings* of the Illinois Conference of Charities in 1905, drew strong praise from William Hard, editor of the *Chicago Tribune,* who admired her combination of intellectual grasp and tenderness of touch. "You have told me that you found it hard to write. I cannot believe it. Your paragraph on humanizing the new scholarship has exquisite expression along with it profound discernment."[44] She might have responded, as we all might, that expression and discernment come from long, often difficult labor.

George Brett told Addams in February that he would speed publication of her new book, pledging to produce it in four weeks for a May date; and, perhaps because he knew his woman, he warned that if the book was not ready by spring, then a September date would have to do. In the midst of what might have been a writing season, Addams traveled to Oberlin College and to New York, returning to find a letter from Du Bois, inviting her to attend the Tenth Annual Conference to Study the Negro Problems, along with Edgar Gardner Murphy and Professor Walter F. Wilcox, and to give a twenty-minute talk. Under pressure from Ely to get the book done, she declined Du Bois's offer even as she pointed out that she would rather attend his conference than meet other commitments. "[Make] it a habit of staying with us whenever you come to Chicago," she told him.[45]

As Addams traveled east for rest in the summer of 1905, the writing project most in her mind was the editing of Lloyd's last book, a combination of two pamphlets, one that had never been published and another that first appeared in *North American Review*. The title that she had in mind was "A Coming Religion of Love and Labor: Suggestions of Social Hope," although she decided on the more secular *Man, the Social Creator*.[46] She wrote to Walter Hines Page about possible publication as Ely suggested a September deadline for "The Newer Ideals." In responding to Ely, she used her promise to Mrs. Lloyd and the burden of the obligation as an excuse and asked for an extension to October 1. Yet even with the extension, she turned her mind to duties in Chicago, taking on the chairmanship of the School Management Committee, a tricky political task that would take much of her energy and savvy over the next year.

Walter Page, who had heard that Addams was in the process of writing her reminiscences for a series to be published by *Ladies' Home Journal*, assured her that should she want to publish her next book with him, he would "make it as profitable an undertaking for you as possible."[47] Even as she hesitated with Ely and Brett, we note that she was writing and negotiating to publish her work. Exasperated by her procrastination, Ely invited her to give a dozen lectures at the University of Wisconsin in the summer of 1906 with an honorarium of $250 (she negotiated for 10 lectures at her usual fee of $50 each). The idea in the back of his head, and in the back of hers as well, was that the lectures would spur the thinking and finally produce "The Newer Ideals." She concurred, "It will be the only way to get my book written if indeed it is ever done."[48]

One wonders, reading through her letters, why she did not simply abandon "The Newer Ideals of Peace," especially because the ideals, whatever she may have had in mind originally, were still hazy five years later. It may be that she kept at the book because readers of all sorts responded enthusiastically to her writing. *Ladies' Home Journal* published "Fifteen Years at Hull-House" in a three-month series in 1906 that featured her early social work in Chicago. The articles elicited responses from ordinary readers. Mrs. M. from Syracuse confided, "I hope you will not think me a crank for writing but I saw your picture in a magazine and took a great liking to you your face is so pleasant."[49] The letter is typical in its appeal for help. "Believe me Miss Addams I am not in the habit of asking assistance but having read of your kindness to the poor and being in great need myself, how I wish you could find it possible to help me a little." She explained that she was exhausted and both she and her husband were out of work and, therefore, without money to buy medicine. "I hope you will not let my letter or name be published." Asking for charity of any sort was a sign of moral failure, and the letter survives without a full name. Angelique Kilmer of Paw Paw, Michigan, wrote that although she was an educated woman and had managed over the years to establish an eighty-acre fruit and grain farm, conditions had changed over the past year. "My eldest daughter had appendicitis in November, one of the worst forms, and I have had an enormous expense for a surgeon from here and other necessities to save the child's life," she explained. As a result, she could not pay her mortgage and would lose the farm.[50] She, too, did not ask for charity. "I am not afraid of work, having always lived an energetic life. I can execute rapidly work I understand." Her plan was to leave her four children with a maiden sister in order to come to Chicago to work. Many rural and small-town women yearned to make such a move, hoping to earn financial independence through labor in the city. Jessie Goldner from Ontario, Canada, boldly wrote, "I feel impelled to write you—and tell you something of myself, and what I would like to do with my life."[51] She explained to Addams that the people around her thought she was "much too outspoken (naturally!)." Addams's story of moral improvement also resonated with college students who identified with her literary persona.

Sensing possible profits, publishers and editors vied for her writing. Robert Adger Brown urged her to consider D. Appleton and Company: "I am writing to ask whether you have disposed of the book rights of this article, and if not whether you would be willing to entertain a proposition from us as to its publication in book form."[52] Samuel S. McClure complimented her on the series and invited her to publish the book with him. Edward Bok, the editor of *Ladies' Home Journal,* suggested that he could find a publisher for a book: "I am glad and proud of the fact that the material has reached the public through our magazine. . . .[D]o you wish to elaborate these articles into a book, say during the coming summer?"[53] Walter Hines Page wrote in April offering her a contract for sixty thousand words or more. In her response, she mentioned her commitment to Ely to complete "The Newer Ideals" manuscript. A negotiator at heart, she slipped in the news of other offers from McClure and Appleton, ending the letter innocently enough: "You are all very kind to believe in the success of an unwritten document, if anything will make it possible it will be letters such as yours."[54]

Among her friends, she joked about the pressure of writing and the irony of fame. "The Ladies' Home Journal has been hounding me for 'copy' at such a rate that I have hated the very notion of writing," she confided to Julia Lathrop as she finished work on the series that included "The First Five Years at Hull-House" in April, and "How the Work at Hull-House Has Grown" in May.[55] She always felt comfortable with Lathrop. "For two days I have the honor of 'keeping' all the presses waiting, and Mary Smith was moved to say that if I could keep them permanently in a state of suspended animation that she would be reconciled to my writing!" Her sense of humor saved her from irritation. She was in charge of her literary career, after all, as much as she was in charge of Hull-House.

Addams was full of work in 1906. She battled on the Chicago School Board, lobbied in Washington for women and immigrants, and worked on the National Child Labor Committee and for the Federation of Women's Clubs. As H. G. Wells visited Chicago, she hosted him at Hull-House. The biggest scandal of the year was the charge that the National Juvenile Improvement project accepted $5,000,000 from the notorious Standard Oil man, John D. Rockefeller. She found herself refuting that story as she raised "honest" money for Hull-House projects. After lecturing in Madison that summer, she retreated to Fisher Cottage on Mackinac Island to write. She sent Ely notice, "My book, such as it is, is about in shape for a final type."[56] Ely's blend of encouragement and irritation finally drove her to finish the volume in September, even as she complained, "I am sorry it isn't better, but I do not believe that I will improve it by working on it any longer."[57] As it turned out, Ely himself was on holiday by the time the manuscript arrived in Madison, and Brett explained to Addams that the press would wait, this time, for Ely to do his work.

As he read the manuscript, Ely grumbled, as she must have known he would, that her writing style was undisciplined: "Some of the sentences are rather long and involved, and I would have you bear in mind in looking through the proof the importance of simplicity and lucidity in style." He "corrected" her writing by adding punctuation, especially semicolons and dashes.[58] And Addams continued to revise the drafts, in part to please him but, more so, to please herself. He wanted an academic book and she wanted a more imaginative one. A letter of corrections from Ely prompted several responses from her, as she battled with him over literary license. He insisted that she use footnotes: "This is generally regarded as more scholarly."[59] Her attempts to appeal to general readers irritated the venerable Wisconsin professor, whose name would be associated with her experiment. She included the words of scholars to give power to her own voice, but she never meant to write an academic book with footnotes that might divert the attention of her readers. To his mind, she was free to quote her working-class neighbors without citing them, but she crossed the line when she expropriated the language of scholars. He chided, "I would not say that it is necessary to mention every book or article from which you have quoted; but where the quotations are of some length or of special significance, the reference is worth while." And she bristled: "I can, of course, give the authors of the quotations in footnotes, although I did not do that in *Democracy and Social Ethics,* and assumed that the book was to be kept popular and colloquial in style rather than exact and scholarly."[60]

Addams fired off agitated letters to George Brett, complaining about the time Ely was taking with the manuscript and quibbling over her payment for the book after it finally arrived at Macmillan. She reminded Brett of the promised $50 advance for delivery of the manuscript. Brett responded diplomatically that the sum was actually $200 to be paid on the day of publication, and, after looking again at the contract, she conceded that he was right. In the end, Addams urged Brett to rush the publication, not because she needed the money, but because she hoped the book would help with her lobbying in Washington, D.C.: "Affairs here are very critical in regard to the Immigration bill, and I am very anxious to have some of the spiritual results of immigration put before certain people."[61] She asked him to send copies to President Roosevelt, Senator R. M. La Follette, and James R. Garfield at the Department of Commerce and Labor: "This request is not that of the 'vain author' but a desire to put a certain aspect of the immigration question before men who are seriously debating the question and who really want to get this point of view." Brett complied and worked to soothe the writer: "[T]rust that you have already received our telegram and that your anxiety in regard to the matter was thereby relieved."[62]

At the end of the long labor, perhaps especially at the end, Addams worried about what her readers would think, book in hand. Writing to Julia Lathrop on February 12, 1907, she sounded a strong note of regret:

"I am sending you a copy of the book which I regard with mixed emotions—one is gratitude that it is out at last and the other regret that I didn't fuss with it longer."[63] We can hear Ely sigh.

A Harmless Revolutionary

William James settled into his armchair in Cambridge in the winter of 1907 after a hectic trip to New York City and found himself transported into the Chicago of Jane Addams. "I soothed myself by the perusal of your book," he wrote to her. "I find it hard to express the good it has done me in offering new points of view and annihilating old ones."[64] *Newer Ideals of Peace* coincided with ideas he had been mulling since he had met her in Chicago. "Yours is a deeply original mind and all so quiet and harmless! yet revolutionary in the extreme," he assured her, "and I should suspect that this very book would act as a ferment thru long years to come." Her book, in odd ways, never suited her fellow sociologists, but James was the exception. "I don't care about this detail or that," he told her, certainly not worried, as her editor Richard Ely had been, about irregularities in style or the eclectic nature of her imagination. As for genre, James admitted that he had read "precious little sociological literature" of late and so could not say whether what she had written sounded academic. And as Jane Addams relaxed into her chair with his letter in hand, she must have been pleased to have the words of her most admiring reader: "I am willing to *bet* on you."

Addams met James in 1898, two years after her encounter with Tolstoy, as they attended the Tolstoy evening at the Twentieth Century Club and the Peace Jubilee in Chicago. James spoke against imperialism but questioned the ideal of passive nonresistance to evil. In a letter to Mary Smith, Addams mentioned the Jubilee but only amid news that their friend Aylmer Maude planned to visit Chicago on November 28: "P.S. I am so glad that you are coming home for Bro. Maude. I hardly dared hope you would!" Almost as an afterthought, amid a discussion of the handles she would prefer for her chest of drawers, Addams added: "I sat in Mrs. Potter Palmer's box at the Peace Jubilee and otherwise exposed myself to its fascinations, but can do nothing but feel a lump in my throat over the whole thing. I have been really quite blue, not play blue but real depths and will have to be more of a Tolstoyan or less of one right off."[65] As she listened to James and thought back to her talks with Tolstoy, Addams mused on the warring instinct. "The same strenuous endeavor, the same heroic self-sacrifice, the same fine courage and readiness to meet death may be displayed without the accompaniment of killing our fellowmen," she declared in "Democracy or Militarism," a talk she gave a year later at the Chicago Liberty Meeting of the Central Anti-Imperialist League.[66] In responding to the Spanish-American War and its brutal influence on the relatively peaceful community of Halsted Street ("seven murders within a radius of ten blocks"), she sought what she called "a moral substitute" for the warring instinct, an idea akin to James's "moral equivalent."[67] James sought a rite of passage that would curb male aggression in young college men, the sort of students he had at Harvard. Addams had in her mind the young immigrant workers living on Halsted Street, the types she talked with at the Social Science Club on Wednesday evenings at Hull-House. The differences between such young men— ethnicity, experience, social class, labor—were stark. For James, the men of Harvard might lead the way to peace.

Addams turned that idea on its head, claiming workingmen as her heroes in *Democracy and Social Ethics:* "It is possible that we shall be saved from warfare by the 'fighting rabble' itself, turned into kind citizens of the world through the pressure of a cosmopolitan neighborhood." As an example, she cited the creation of the International Association of Workingmen by workers in London in 1864. "They recognized that a supreme interest raised all workingmen above the prejudice of race, and united them by wider and deeper principles than those by which they were separated into nations." The modern city brings together so many differing types of people that the only way to survive is through mutual effort.

In Chautauqua in July 1902, Addams lectured on "The Newer Ideals of Peace," interweaving her notion of a moral substitute for war with stories of her visit to Tolstoy. Certainly proximity to the Russian count gave credibility to her voice. Cobbling together material for a talk at the Ethical Culture Society of Chicago in January 1904, she formulated ideas under the title "A Moral Substitute for War." The *Friends Intelligencer* in January 1904 reported that Addams used two examples in her talk, the German emperor and the Russian czar, to illustrate the distance between those who mandate military action and those who actually do the fighting. If the German emperor were to live among the poor for ten years "He would see that his nation rests on labor and commerce, and not on his army and navy." And in Russia, she ominously predicted: "Who can tell at what hour that great multitude of peasants will decide that the time has come for them to put into operation Christ's principles even as Tolstoi has decided?"[68] Responding unambiguously to Tolstoy's ideal, she proclaimed: "I do not believe in non-resistance. Do not let things alone, but take hold with a firm hand, guided by a higher, finer morality than the code of war requires."

She and James lectured together in Boston at the Thirteenth Universal Peace Conference, she giving three addresses and he one, and both talking about what he called "the rooted bellicosity of human nature." Her letters to Mary chronicled the events: "The Sunday evening of the Peace Congress was one of the most magnificent services I ever attended. Mary McDowell wept by my side while I gave vent to my emotions in ways such as I seldom do." Although she displayed emotion, Addams eyed the event with detachment: "[T]he meetings are pretty continuous and some of them filled with 'platitudes' but on the whole it is a fine group of people trying to do a real thing and I get up from time to time."[69] From "time to time" included a banquet address on Friday evening, October 7, and talks on the interest of labor in international peace and on the responsibilities of women. Albion Small collected the papers at the Congress and published hers in the *Official Report.* In a real sense, both James and Addams worked together to ward off the kind of conflagration that would erupt into the First World War and would continue, as we know, to bedevil pacifists to this day. (James wouldn't live to see the First World War, and Addams would die before the Second.)

William James worked out his theory in a series of lectures over the early years of the twentieth century and finally in written form in "The Moral Equivalent of War," an essay published through the Association for International Conciliation in *McClure's Magazine* (1910) and *Popular Science Monthly.*[70] Marshaling his argument, James brought into his essay an array of writers: Virgil, Thucydides, Matthew Arnold, and, in considering the "innermost soul of army-writing," General Homer Lea (in *The Valor of Ignorance*), and S. R. Steinmetz (*Philosophie des Krieges*), and, in pacifist thought, Leo Tolstoy, Lowes Dickinson, and, finally, H. G. Wells, of whom James claimed, "I believe as he does" (670). He sought to redirect male instinct: "The fatalistic view of the war-function is to me nonsense, for I know that war-making is due to definite motives and subject to prudential checks and reasonable criticisms, just like any other form of enterprise" (667). Although American culture in the nineteenth century found itself in the grip of the war-function, James saw every reason to believe that the behavior might be satiated in a more peaceful way. "If now—and this is my idea—there were, instead of military conscription a conscription of the whole youthful population to form a certain number of years a part of the army enlisted against *Nature*," James argued, then men might through a rite of passage that required order, discipline, service, devotion, physical fitness, exertion, and responsibility find an equivalent that would curb the human appetite for aggression and thereby change cultural modes of thinking (669).

In fashioning his pacifism, James left out Jane Addams, the very woman he had been talking with in conversations, speeches, lectures, and letters. Could it be that on the topic of war and in a discussion of manly activity a female voice would strike a wrong note?

Daniel Levine in *Jane Addams and the Liberal Tradition* (1971) establishes a common theme among scholars who have considered her relationship to the male thinkers of her day, especially to William James: "Miss Addams, in adopting both the recapitulation theory and James's view on instincts, was thus simply absorbing currents of thought around her, not originating anything."[71] That line with its emphasis on absorbing suggests that Addams never really learned the intellectual game and, consequently, never became a major player. Levine argues that she used the ideas of James and his student G. Stanley Hall, along with other powerful members of the Chicago School, especially Albion W. Small and John Dewey. Allen Davis follows the same line of thinking, albeit with more subtlety and precision, when he argues: "In citing the 'predatory spirit,' the primitive instincts that lay close to the surface, especially in young people, she was borrowing from the thinking of psychologists G. Stanley Hall and William James."[72] It is only recently that scholars have begun to consider Addams as an original thinker. Louis Menand, in *The Metaphysical Club: A Story of Ideas in America* (2001), narrates the story of an argument between John Dewey and Jane Addams over Hegel's dialectic. Addams argued that antagonism in an argument actually got in the way of reason rather than, as Dewey believed, advancing it. In a letter to his wife Alice, Dewey conceded: "'She converted me internally, but not really, I fear. . . . [W]hen you think that Miss Addams does not think this as a philosophy, but believes it in all her senses & muscles—Great God.'"[73] It may well be that men absorbed her ideas without thinking of her as a philosopher or a sociologist.

Newer Ideals of Peace was original, revolutionary in its own soothing way. And William James was not the only reader to puzzle over how to categorize it. One reviewer linked her to Shakespeare: "Miss Jane Addams of Chicago in her latest book, 'The Newer Ideals of Peace,' cites [Shakespeare] as illustrating perfectly that liberalizing, expanding effect which transfer from rural to urban scenes often has on men." Another reviewer called it "The Epic of Nations," sensing its literary texture: "[I]t treats principally of the elemental feelings of individualized life in neighborhoods made up of many different races."[74] Her writing resembles drama and epic, the imaginative work of Shakespeare and Homer.

Florence Kelley thought the book should have been titled "The Newer Manifestations of Government." In her review, she snapped, "The title of Miss Addams's volume is not altogether a happy one."[75] In summarizing the book, she significantly revised the book's underlying idea: "For a new history of government begins with an attempt to make life possible and human in huge cities, in those crowded quarters which exhibit such undeniable tendency to barbarism and degeneracy when the better human qualities are not nourished." Kelley saw the poor as barbaric and degenerate rabble—a conventional view. Francis Hackett in her review came closer than Kelley to understanding Addams's presentation of the "rabble": "Speaking as association has entitled her to speak, she emphasizes the human kindness of the motley throng in the cosmopolitan wards, bristling though they are expected to be with every antagonism that militarism has invented."[76] Curiously, Hackett denied the book literary merit: "Miss Addams is not primarily a writer of books." And then she puzzled over the nature of the book itself: "As the book stands it is more than a contemporary essay, much more. It is more, on the other hand, than a cool, professorial analysis of the moral issues of to-day." What kind of a book was *Newer Ideals of Peace*?

Readers contemned the book for too little sociology or, ironically, for too much. As one reviewer complained: "Sociology is a new science which has yet to find itself and know its proper scope and purpose." For that reason, "Miss Addams' book is valuable when she gives facts, for her opportunities of observation among the toilers have been large, but her argument is befogged by 'sociology' so that her deductions are worthless."[77] The *New York Tribune* reviewer upbraided Addams for not following convention: "It is a pity that the subject matter could not have been more logically organized about the central theme. It is disappointing to pick up a self-professed monograph and to discover that it is only a collection of somewhat miscellaneous essays."[78] The reviewer in the *Nation* chided her, as well, for not plowing "a little deeper" into the issues. Her close friend George Herbert Mead, husband of Lucia Ames Mead, wrote in the *American Journal of Sociology* a long admiring essay on the issues in the book, though he ended with a mild rebuke: "One does not feel, in reading Miss Addams, the advance of an argument with measured tread."[79] The question, of course, is what tread to measure. Years later, Allen Davis apologized for the book by arguing that she wanted the flawed book out of the way so that she could work on her real masterpiece, and her own favorite book, *The Spirit of Youth and the City Streets* (1909).

The key to reading the book may be her dedication. Amid the letters that flew between Chicago and Madison in October 1906, Addams appends a postscript: "May I send the enclosed dedication for the first page of the book. It is an effort to show that I am presenting the immigrants from an American's point of view."[80] Far from emerging as she had intended in her letter to Mary Smith "á la Prof. James," the dedication reads "to Hull-House and its Neighbors." The voice that finally surfaces in the book is not that of William James, Harvard professor; rather, we hear in the long middle passage of *Newer Ideals of Peace* a chorus of voices from the street. The book argues that the nurturing instinct trumps the warring instinct and tells the story of immigrants relying on cooperation rather than combat to survive.

What experience had she, after all, with the terrain of war itself, especially on the battlefields where literal combat takes place? William James, of course, had no idea either, although they both had in mind the American militancy of their day, and they had listened to family stories about the American Civil War. R. W. B. Lewis argues that James came to an understanding of the battlefield experience in an analogous way when he found himself in the earthquake in San Francisco in 1906, but surely his ideas about warlike behavior had been gestating for years by that time.[81] Addams used James as a colleague and supporter when necessary to give credibility to her arguments, but the truth is that neither figure spoke with any firsthand knowledge of war. Their writing comes, rather, from the moral imagination and its creation of a fiction of peace.

The landscape of Chicago emerges in *Newer Ideals of Peace* as the scene of an epic battle: "It is a long dreary road, and the immigrant is successfully exploited at each turn." Addams places herself—and this is what gives artistic energy to the book—in the literary company of Walt Whitman. "'As I stand aloof and look, there is to me something profoundly affecting in large masses of men following the lead of those who do not believe in men.'" The passage situates the moral imagination in the modern American city. A sensitive and alert onlooker, she searches in the "dim borderland between compassion and morality for the beginnings of cosmopolitan affection."[82] In the poorer quarters of Chicago, she discovers the "mass of the unsuccessful" (13) with what she calls their "nascent morality," stimulated by a "commingling" (16) of vital energies. Chicago is a cultural ooze, a commingling of nascent and radical possibility. From the fetid yet fecund mass might come, she imagines, a new creation. The image of Eden blends with another Christian symbol, the Catholic cathedral, a massive structure requiring generations to build.

Addams brings William James to her aid, creating him as a character in her urban drama, footnoting his distinction as a Harvard professor. He appears in her book to tell her reader, in a sense, "She's all right; she's with me." Addams cloaks herself in scholarly robes, quoting rather freely from a variety of works by her contemporaries, putting such academics as Delos Wilcox in *The American City: A Problem in Democracy* (1904) in conversation with Adna Ferrin Weber in *The Growth of Cities in the Nineteenth Century: A Study in Statistics* (1899). Her passage from L. T. Hobhouse's *Democracy and Reaction* (1904) seems to have come from memory: "[T]o our grandchildren the world will present itself, not as a white oligarchy, ruling and exploiting millions of yellow, brown, and black, but as a system of self-governing peoples linked by mutual respect and international agreement rather than by bonds of authority and subordination."[83] The page number is wrong and the language imprecise, or rather the language is more nearly her own. She quotes Josiah Royce in *The Spirit of Modern Philosophy* (1901) that the Declaration of Independence has been "rendered meaningless by the modern doctrine of evolution."[84] Here, too, she truncates his language, if not his meaning (32). John Morley's *On Compromise* (1886) argues that progressivism "can only work its way through the inevitable obstructions around it, by means of persons who are possessed by the special progressive idea."[85] She quotes him only in part, leaving out his next line that may have seemed to her too self-serving: "Or he is one of those rare intelligences, active, alert, inventive, which by constitution or training find their chief happiness in thinking in a disciplined and serious manner how things can be better done." And she agrees wholeheartedly with Karl Groos in *The Play of Man* (1901) that two human impulses work to build society: one is the desire for aggression and the other the desire for communication. Only after parading the academic speakers through the early section of the book does Addams strike out on her own. It may be that reform will come from the city itself and not from academia: "Although the spiritual struggle is associated with the solitary garret of the impassioned dreamer, it may be that the idealism fitted to our industrial democracy will be evolved in crowded sewer ditches and in noisy factories" (95). Evolution comes from the crowded sewers and noisy factories, the very toxicity of the city. "The sickening stench and the scum on the branch of the river known as Bubbly Creek at times made that section of the city unendurable," Addams reports from the scene. "The smoke ordinances were openly ignored, nor did the meat inspector ever seriously interfere with business, being quite willing to have meat sold in Chicago which had not passed the inspection for foreign markets," (105) she continues by laying the blame at the door of the manufacturers who are more eager to make money than to consider consequences for the working class, who, by necessity of cheap rents, live amidst the stench, scum, and smoke in what we would call today the conditions of environmental racism.

The poorer the community, the newer the immigrants, and the darker the skin, the nearer people are to the literal poisons of the city. The working poor, Addams reminds her reader, are left to find their own sustenance: "One of the most touching scenes during the strike was the groups of Macedonians who would sit together in the twilight playing on primitive pipes singularly like the one which is associated with the great god Pan. The slender song would carry amazingly in the smoke-bedimmed air, affecting the spectator with a curious sense of incongruity" (109). Music lightens the brutality of life and places the immigrant within a mythic past. And it is at the very center of the contagion, among the lowliest characters in her story, that Addams reverses the Fall from Eden, seeing in urban contagion a vision of creation.

The environmental wasteland of Chicago's South and West Sides presented then, as it does today, a deadly serious urban problem. "The sanitary condition of all the factories and workshops, for instance, in which the industrial processes are at present carried on in great cities, intimately affect the health and lives of thousands of workingwomen. . . . surrounded by conditions over which they have no control" (188). The world of polluted Chicago is especially brutal to the young and female. Her battlefield is urban, environmental, cultural, as well as economic and political. And the newer ideals of peace come from communal effort toward bringing the city back from despoliation, pollution, and contamination and into natural harmony.[86] The immigrants, the poor, and women of all classes form the vanguard of the pacifist movement she has in mind as she tells her reader, "[W]e should find in the commingling of many peoples a certain balance and concord of opposing and contending forces."

What may seem odd to us is that Addams gave very little ground to William James in her book, just as he ceded nothing to her in his essay. Perhaps James settled so easily into the book because he found his own ideas placed fairly early in the text: "An American philosopher has lately reminded us of the need to 'discover in the social realm the moral equivalent for war—something heroic that will speak to men as universally as war has done, and yet will be as compatible with their spiritual natures as war has proved itself to be incompatible'"(24). For Addams "something heroic" comes from the epic landscape of the modern city.

Her illustrations bring together the people of Halsted Street, the very people she will dedicate the book to, and, as they take the stage, we feel the creative energy of her writing. The dreary, pedantic, academic prose of the opening passage is dislodged by the throng from the street. We have crossed from a scholarly realm into a creative, even fictive one. She marches her characters down Halsted Street, the very folks that academics fear. My friends, she declares, are a gambler, a prostitute, and a murderer! Her reader comes to attention. It is in this band of criminals that Addams proclaims she discovers "the very energy of existence, the craving for enjoyment, the pushing of vital forces" (60). The narrator delivers a crushing blow to the would-be reformer: "For one short moment I saw the situation from the point of view of humbler people, who sin often through weakness and passion, but seldom through hardness of heart, and I felt that in a democratic community such sweeping condemnations and conclusions as the speaker was pouring forth could never be accounted for righteousness" (59). The community, she argues, is divided between the repressed and the repressive. Her goal is to find a path between scholarly research and imaginative art. The scholar, she suggests, might learn more from the streets than from books. What she is seeking to portray in her writing is not the accumulation of academic knowledge but rather the power of firsthand experience, what she calls a "study of origins, of survivals, of paths of least resistance—refining an industrial age through the people and experiences which really belong to it and do not need to be brought in from the outside" (65).

The inside story for Addams, and this is what irritated Ely and Kelley and pleased James, comes from her street tales. She is not doing anthropological ethnography as Franz Boaz thought of it.[87] She is retelling, embellishing, even fictively creating street scenes that give her reader a view of "the very energy of existence, the craving for enjoyment, the pushing of vital forces" (60).

"I have taken a Chicago street-car," she begins a section of the book that explodes into a series of street tales: "The boys and girls have a peculiar hue—a color so distinctive that one meeting them on the street, even on Sunday when they are in their best clothes and mingled with other children who go to school and play out of doors, can distinguish them in an instant, and there is on their faces a premature anxiety and sense of responsibility, which we should declare pathetic if we were not used to it" (156). The street children speak in the book much more freely than the scholars do. One young worker who had after sixteen years of hard labor become a tramp describes his situation in blunt language. "At last I was sick in bed for two or three weeks with a fever, and when I crawled out, I made up my mind that I would rather go to hell than to go back to that mill," he tells us, sounding very like Huck Finn (158). Addams tells of another boy who had worked so hard for his family that at the age of sixteen he contracted typhoid fever and, never really recovering, he too became a tramp. The development of imagination in children, she notes, is the source of art and may provide "enough individuality of character to avoid becoming a mere cog in the vast industrial machine" (170).

The penultimate chapter brings the argument, loosely woven as it is by this time in the book, to the question of women. We can see the first dozen lines she struggled to write under pressure from Ely—"Women dwelling—tending within the house—conventional—1st/women entering into the commercial life & worker industrial conditions with its element of warfare." These ideas function as a climax to her story of urban experience. "The men of the city have been carelessly indifferent to much of this civic housekeeping," she notes wryly in a rare moment of good-natured humor, "as they have always been" (183). She imagines the urban woman on an epic journey: "Sometimes when I see dozens of young girls going into the factories of a certain biscuit company on the West Side of Chicago, they appear for the moment as a mere cross-section in the long procession of women who have furnished the breadstuffs from time immemorial, from the savage woman who ground the meal and baked the flat cake, through innumerable cottage hearths, kitchens, and bake ovens, to this huge concern in which they are still carrying on their traditional business" (188–89). She uses female scholars, notably Florence Kelley and Beatrice Webb, to argue that civic work is a "mere continuation of woman's traditional work," blending the duties of women across time.

In the last scene of the book, Jane Addams returns to the platform she had shared with William James at the International Peace Conference in Boston in 1904. The book ends by calling men of authority to the stage for a reprise that puts the prose back into the scholarly voice—this time with a dramatic twist. Tolstoy appears, alongside August Comte, Hobson, Lecky, St. Paul, Perris, Bandereff, and Ruskin. The narrator, dressed in biblical garb as the prophet Isaiah, puts the final imprimatur on the book: "Swords would finally be beaten into plowshares and pruning-hooks, not because men resolved to be peaceful, but because all the metal of the earth would be turned to its proper use when the poor and their children should be abundantly fed" (238). William James, the man seated at her side, muses on her harmless revolution, and, as a character in her drama, says nothing at all.

Hot Property

After *Newer Ideals of Peace* appeared in 1907, Jane Addams became, in the mind of her readers and would-be publishers, and in her own mind, a literary figure of considerable reputation. As Macmillan sent off copies to college professors in order to stimulate sales, Addams began to receive a steady flow of letters from them as well as from what Virginia Woolf would call "common readers." Florence Kelley assured her, "It is noble and wise and parts of it are very beautiful," in spite of the fact that Addams deliberately veered away from scholarly writing.[88] And Ely conceded, "I am proud to have my name associated with the book."[89] Margaret Dreier Robins spoke for many readers: "I am so very glad that you manage to find time for writing."[90]

Kate Kimball from the Chautauqua Press, who was issuing a cheap edition of the book, requested a softening of tone on the issue of race in the South. In place of the line: "In the southern states, where a contemptuous attitude toward a weaker people has had the most marked effect upon public feeling (page 153)," she suggested: "In the southern states where the peculiar importance of the race problem has had the most marked effect upon the public."[91] Addams knew from her travels in the South that "a contemptuous attitude toward a weaker people" was bland enough phrasing. She wouldn't budge, and the line remained unsoftened. Her essay "Chicago Settlements and Social Unrest" resonated with African American readers. H. J. Pinkett wrote to her after reading the essay in *Charities:*

> Your interpretation of the state of mind of the residents of your settlement toward American 'excitement' when some offense has been committed somewhere by one of them, and your lofty rebuke to narrowness and hate and prejudice, constitute a complete defense of the cause of my race in this country. What the Jews of Chicago have recently experienced my race has been experiencing for forty years, and I am most grateful to you for having given the point of view of the oppressed elements which, like those of my race, seldom have anyone to speak for them who will be heard.[92]

She must have been pleased, his letter in hand, to know that her literary voice was convincing. Pinkett heard not only the voices of Jewish people but of African Americans as well.

Addams sought ways to cross what W. E. B. Du Bois called "the color line." She wrote to him as she traveled to Atlantic University in the spring of 1908 to lecture. He was anxious to have a transcript of her speech: "This is to circumvent the Associated Press which will ignore or misquote us."[93] The two exchanged itineraries for the day, he worrying over usual indignities in the South: "May I not urge that you come and stay at the University at least from Tuesday morning until you leave? Our experience is when our guests stay with friends in the city the most extraordinary series of accidents are sure to occur which nearly always mar or spoil our exercises." Although Addams visited the university, she never met with Du Bois. Ida Wells-Barnett explained in a letter to Du Bois that Addams had tried and failed to see him during the day, and he wrote Addams about the subtleties of the "color line": "I should have called on you elsewhere but so many of our friends from the North are—well not anxious to see us here, that I have grown perhaps over-sensitive & usually await for rather positive signs of welcome before I venture to visit."[94] She responded by welcoming him and his wife to Hull-House, the beginning of a cordial and collegial friendship.

A curious apology arrived in March 1907 that reflected the squabbles in Chicago as Addams battled the political machine of Alderman Powers. James Keeley, the managing editor of the *Chicago Tribune*, diplomatically worked to set the record straight about comments he had supposedly made: "A copy of the Examiner has just come into my hands, and on page four I find an affidavit by a member of the grand jury before whom Mayor Dunne took his case against The Tribune, in which he alleges that I stated that you were a freak and a monomaniac."[95] The report had surely fallen under her gaze. "I trust that I hardly need say that the statement is an unqualifiedly false one, and inside of twenty four hours I think I will be able to submit to you statements from State's Attorney Healy, Assistant State Attorney Judge Going, and other members of the jury which will substantiate my word." The terms "freak" and "monomaniac" hit a nerve with Addams. She had become a central figure in Chicago and, therefore, a target of criticism. The language itself and the swiftness of response suggest the power of the woman.

"[Y]ou can never strike a time when anything from you will fail to be welcomed eagerly,"[96] Norman Hapgood telegraphed from *Collier's* in the winter of 1908, urgently requesting 1,500 to 2,000 words on Chicago politics. Edward Bok asked her for an article on parents and children for *Ladies' Home Journal,* as though she were the foremost authority, and paid her $500 for "Why Girls Go Wrong," a provocative essay that triggered many letters to her throughout the year. James MacArthur wanted her to review Professor Thomas's *Sex and Society* for *North American Review,* clearly seeing her as the female authority. Ray Stannard Baker sent her the April 1907 issue of *The American Magazine* with its emphasis on the "negro question," believing her to be an expert on race in America. Joseph Esenwein offered her two cents per word for signed editorials to be published in *Lippincott's Monthly Magazine.* Horatio Krans tried to arrange a meeting between her and George Putnam as Addams visited New York City in April. Edward Marsh wrote to remind her that Macmillan would welcome another book: "May I suggest that we are greatly interested in the possibility that you may have a new book ready for publication before long?"[97] In a more tentative tone, Robert Adger Brown, from D. Appleton and Company, asked: "You did not leave us altogether hopeless that you might at a later time [publish with us]. . . . Is the time any riper now?"[98]

Addams traveled to Boulder, Colorado, with Smith in the summer of 1908 and then to the coast of Maine for their usual holiday; as she confided to Alice, "[I] am eager to get to the coast of Maine, I cannot stand constant public speaking as well as I used to and do not mean to take more summer engagements."[99]

As soon as she relaxed into her vacation, she began to think about *The Spirit of Youth and the City Streets*, the graceful book she wrote over the next year. Edward Marsh worked to secure its publication, suggesting the didactic title, "Juvenile Delinquency and Public Morality," but she jotted down at the bottom of his letter more imaginative possibilities, "The Spirit of Youth" or "The Modern City."[100] He urged her to sign the contract for 13 percent on the first 1,500 copies and 15 percent after that, but she resisted, at first, because his title sounded "a little more 'sociological'" than she wanted it to be, wary of getting into another academic project just as she had freed herself from Ely's editorial control.[101]

"The Spirit of Youth and the City Streets has occurred to me, or some title which would be distinctly literary," she explained to Marsh. "'Juvenile Delinquency' implies facts and figures and investigations into Juvenile Court records etc. for which I am not prepared, although of course many of the illustrations are taken from the Chicago Juvenile Court cases." Her plan was to gather a series of lectures and essays into the book, and she sent Marsh an outline that was legible and confident:

Public Recreation & Social Morality (1)
N.Y. Playgrounds speech (2)
Religious Ed. Speech (3)
Averbuch Article (4)
Why Girls Go Wrong (5)
Industrial Ed. N.Y. (6)
Sage Foundation Article (7)

Working as her own agent, she complained that he had not offered enough money. "I have just looked over your account rendered April 30th, 1908, and find that I received 16 per cent upon 1112 copies of 'Newer Ideals of Peace', and 16 percent upon 497 of 'Democracy and Social Ethics.'" Why, she asked, was he cutting her pay? He diplomatically schooled her in reading accounts: "The maximum royalty we have paid you on the two earlier books is 13%, or 16¼ cents on each copy sold at $1.25."[102] He meant to give her a raise by offering to pay 15 percent for copies over 1,500, and she signed the contract even as they continued to negotiate the title of the book that she called "rather small and rather light" with a title he called "a little vague and abstract."

She got her way on the title and worked to his schedule, publishing the book by the end of the year, even as she bargained with *Ladies' Home Journal* to publish "The Bad Boy of the Streets" and "When Youth Seeks a Mate," material from the book, in the fall of 1909, and "Why Women Should Vote" in the winter of 1910. *Ladies' Home Journal* had named her the foremost living woman in America in March 1908, and they clearly wanted to publish more of her material. Edward Bok, who did not believe that women ought to vote, congratulated her for "so completely pleasing an editor who does not believe in what you say!"[103]

Experimental Moralist

Jane Addams was especially pleased with *The Spirit of Youth and the City Streets* (1909), perhaps because she spent so much time in it telling stories. What do the stories tell us about her as a writer? The answer may lie in the French novelist Emile Zola's portrait of the naturalist writer as an "experimental moralist." In a discussion of his influence on American fiction, Lars Ahnebrink noted, "Zola, especially, had a reformer's zeal. He believed that society was responsible for all the misfortunes that befell the French people."[104] In his famous essay, "The Experimental Novel" (1880), he set out a theory of literary naturalism, urging his generation of writers to replace novels of pure imagination with novels of observation and experiment, a literature that might embody the spirit of an age of scientific investigation. In naturalist novels, writers record the links between heredity and environment in stories about the reciprocal influences of society on the individual and the individual on society.

The moral task of the writer, in Zola's paradigm, is to expose the conditions that cause human misery.[105] He urged writers at the end of the nineteenth century to examine the human condition in order to gain control, as a social scientist might, over the mechanism that controls fate: "We disengage the determinism of human and social phenomena so that we may one day control and direct these phenomena."[106] The novelist might overwhelm nature, or at least lead the way in the task, and thus become an experimental moralist, one who takes up the burden of curing social ills through progressive social reform.

Jane Addams's method of writing, in a sense, turned Emile Zola's theory inside out. He and the American naturalists who followed him, writers like Theodore Dreiser, Frank Norris, Upton Sinclair, and later, Richard Wright, believed that literature ought to become more like science. They sought to objectify imaginative fiction by imbuing it with science. Addams turned the theory inside out by making social science more like imaginative fiction.[107] She hoped to attract middle-class and leisure-class readers who were armchair moralists and reformers, people who would support settlement efforts even without visiting Halsted Street. *Democracy and Social Ethics* and *Newer Ideals of Peace* moved considerably away from the scientific discourse of *Hull-House Maps and Papers* and toward a literary style based on synthetic and impressionistic depiction rather than strictly rational argument. Sales went up strikingly.

Addams, however, remained suspicious of art as a purely imaginative medium because of its power to transport the reader beyond the quotidian world. For the social reformer, transport poses a real problem in that readers may ignore the social problems surrounding them. Addams had in mind Karl Groos's *The Play of Man*, a book she had read as she worked on *Newer Ideals of Peace*, especially his assertion that play is instinctive. Groos had borrowed from William James's *The Principles of Psychology:* "There is another sort of human play, into which higher aesthetic feelings enter. The lowest savages have their dances, more or less formally conducted. . . . We have our operas and parties and masquerades."[108] Groos warns, in a somber academic voice, "When a child becomes absorbed in solitary musing (see the youthful reminiscences of George Sand), he should be aroused by application to useful occupation or by social stimuli which bring him in every possible way into contact with the external world." And here is the problem that artistic transport poses: "Even the noble gift of imagination may from overindulgence degenerate into a deadly poison." Imagination and creativity are suspect, even poisonous. Addams kept her mind on that problem.

As she talks about cinema in *The Spirit of Youth and the City Streets*, she questions its seductive power: "From a tangle of 'make believe' [people] gravely scrutinize the real world which they are so reluctant to reenter, reminding one of the absorbed gaze of a child who is groping his way back from fairyland whither the story has completely transported him." As she explained in a letter to the filmmaker Carl Laemmle, one that he used in his advertising, film is too often "associated in the public mind with the lurid and unworthy." Yet she valued its power of transport for what she believed were socially constructive purposes as entertainment in schools and churches.[109] She applauded the showing of fairy stories, foreign scenes of Italy and Greece, and adaptations of *Uncle Tom's Cabin* and *The Bishop's Candlesticks*, all images and narratives that she believed may reveal, as art often does, "an inner beauty, not suspected before."

Her suspicion of make-believe or mere transport as a costly diversion extends to other forms of art, including writing. Later, in *Twenty Years at Hull-House,* she would use an anecdote about Thomas De Quincey, who tells the story of a time when he was trying to recall a line from the *Iliad* as he saw an accident about to happen right in front of him, to illustrate her contention that art may stand in the way of action. De Quincy struggles to disentangle his mind from the line of poetry in order to save the hapless couple. "This is what we were all doing," she warns, "lumbering our minds with literature that only served to cloud the really vital situation spread before our eyes" (70). Addams desired a limited transport, a brief journey that would double back and leave the reader with a heightened sense of moral responsibility to reform the flaws of the world.

The Spirit of Youth and the City Streets is, in significant ways, a book about the power and the limitations of art. It opens with a tribute to poets and artists who through art "reveal to others the perpetual springs of life's self-renewal" and laments that literature is unavailable to those who remain illiterate, the working-class poor in the Halsted neighborhood (3). The common folk of Chicago, she suggests, experience the "perpetual springs" through the vitality of youth itself.

The book's opening chapter comes from a speech Addams had given at a banquet in New York City to honor Mary [Mrs. Humphrey] Ward, a decorous British novelist, who had been lecturing in the United States. The novelist Edith Wharton, who had become Mary Ward's friend in 1905 and might have attended the banquet had she not been in Paris, turned a cool eye on the coupling of literature and social action. She wrote to her longtime friend Sara Norton: "Mrs. Humphrey Ward's progress through the 'States' is very amusing. She seems to like all the things that would most appall me—I mean the publicity, reportering &c. But I fancy she'll have more than enough before she bids goodbye to Liberty enlightening the world."[110] Jane Addams, in many ways the midwestern antithesis of eastern literary and intellectual reserve, was herself among those "enlightening the world" and worked to make Ward's visit successful.

She began the banquet speech much as she would begin her book: "Nothing more is certain than that each generation longs for a reassurance as to the value and charm of life, and is secretly afraid lest it lose its sense of the youth of the earth. This is doubtless the reason it so passionately cherishes its poets and artists—as we eagerly testify tonight, in honoring our artist guest who has for many of us thrown upon life 'the fugitive and gracious light' which alone reveals and explores its inner meaning."[111] In the book version, Addams simplifies the language: "This is doubtless one reason why it so passionately cherishes its poets and artists who have been able to explore for themselves and to reveal to others the perpetual springs of life's self-renewal" (3). Addams depicts a world made comprehensible and joyous by art. The poetry of Wordsworth, the essays of Emerson, the plays of Shakespeare and Ibsen (note that the minor female novelist Mary Ward disappears entirely as the speech makes its way into her book) record and preserve "the perpetual springs" for the upper classes who have been trained to read and appreciate literature. She argues that the literal spring of nature is a source of expression and delight. Her readers have the leisure and the money to travel beyond the despoiled city of Chicago to restore themselves in the pristine landscapes of northern Illinois, southwest Michigan, or southern Wisconsin. Looking around at the immigrant laborers in Chicago, Addams questions how that spirit might find its equivalent among the lower classes.

An urban landscape, Addams laments, offers only debased forms of art and nature to its laboring youth. Popular romances, movie theaters, vaudeville shows, gin mills, soda shops, and bawdy songs all signify for her the efforts of commerce to defraud the young. Popular culture clearly frightens Addams in its seductive power: "The newly awakened senses are appealed to by all that is gaudy and sensual, by the flippant street music, the highly colored theater posters, the trashy love stories, the feathered hats, the cheap heroics of the revolvers displayed in the pawnshop" (27). The ultimate in vulgarity for her is a song with the refrain "snatching a kiss from her ruby lips"—clearly, every word offends. One might argue that the very vitality of the city, then and now, resides in the gaudy, the sensual, the saucy.

Certainly, the portrait of a twentieth-century Sodom captured the imagination of the middle-class reader, an armchair tourist who traveled into the slums without the risk of an actual encounter with the dangerous classes. Addams knew as much as Upton Sinclair or Frank Norris or Theodore Dreiser or Zola knew about the power of such descriptions to sell books. One of her readers wrote to her in 1906 afraid for her life after reading Upton Sinclair's *The Jungle,* begging Addams to say that "it isn't true—I mean, that Mr. Sinclair has used the prerogative of the novelist to produce emotional effects."[112] The plight of the Lithuanians was trouble enough, but the idea that the food supply could be contaminated and that the filth of the stockyards might permeate her kitchen appalled her. Jane Addams understood that if the story of the stockyards were considered merely fiction, readers might relax back into their armchairs, gnawing contentedly on a bone after dinner, without having to trouble with messy social and economic realities.

Jane Addams read novels by Upton Sinclair, Theodore Dreiser, Frank

Norris, Henry Blake Fuller, and John Dos Passos, all followers of Zola's theory of literary naturalism. Her correspondence includes several letters she exchanged with Sinclair and Dreiser over the years that reveal her relationship to writers in the movement. In 1905, Upton Sinclair wrote to apologize for his treatment of her during his visit to Chicago as he researched his novel: "I have always had a feeling that I owed you an apology for having been in an argumentative mood when I met you."[113] He explained his bad behavior in a curious way. "Chicago & the things I saw there had got on my nerves," he whined, as though Jane Addams hadn't any nerves of her own. In 1922, he invited her to verify gossip he had heard as he collected material for *Goose-Step, A Study of American Education:* "I am going out for the colleges." He had heard that she was "denied use of the university hall by the board of regents" at the University of Michigan in 1912. "Will you tell me if this statement is true?"[114] A month later, he wrote again asking her to verify a "story of the long fight with the Association of Commerce over occupational schools." Exasperated with his tactics, she finally responded to both letters as she vacationed at Hull's Cove. She reminded him that she had been a guest of the University of Michigan on many occasions and had never been mistreated. The topic in 1912 had been women's suffrage, an issue that was at the time "before the voters for a referendum vote." University officials wanted to avoid political controversy and, therefore, arranged for her to speak in Ann Arbor. She clearly did not want her story exposed in his attack. Her letter turned the table on him: "It does not seem to me . . . germane to your thesis."[115] Even during the very last days of her life, Sinclair pressed her for details about John De Kay, whose daughter had been a resident at Hull-House. In this request, however, he promised that the information would be confidential. She wrote frankly and graciously that De Kay was an elusive but kindly man who lived in Switzerland, and that his daughter committed suicide while at Hull-House. Addams never cared much for Sinclair's manners although her stories of poverty in Chicago would resemble the stories he created.

Her relationship with Theodore Dreiser was more distant and professional. They corresponded through James E. West, who invited her to write an article for *The Delineator* on "The Widow and Her Children." He enclosed a letter that Dreiser had sent to him about the prospects of securing such an essay: "She understands the problem so well, though, that you had better not suggest an outline unless she questions the method of treatment. I will pay her price."[116] His novel *Jennie Gerhardt* caught her attention and her peace work caught his over the years. After she won the Nobel Peace Prize in 1931, Dreiser wrote asking for money to support the legal defense of the Scottsboro defendants, a case of "lynching sublimated by legality." He enlisted her support, along with that of Lincoln Steffens, Burton Rascoe, John Dos Passos, Suzanna La Follette, and others, to combat the "epidemic of racial, industrial, and political persecutions in our country."[117] They both knew from reading Ida B. Wells-Barnett's *The Red Record* that lynching was indeed an epidemic in the United States.

Out from under the eye of Richard Ely, Jane Addams relaxes into storytelling in *The Spirit of Youth*, narrating events in her own life as a settlement worker and interspersing her observations with vignettes of immigrant life. The pleasure in reading *The Spirit of Youth* comes from the exuberance of the street tales themselves, tales that at times subvert the sociological argument. Her book looks much like the muckraking fiction of her day, especially Upton Sinclair's *The Jungle* and Frank Norris's *The Pit*, a novel that creates a mythic image of Chicago:

> There in the centre of the Nation, midmost of that continent that lay between the oceans of the New World and the Old, in the heart's heart of the affairs of men, roared and rumbled the Pit. It was as if the Wheat, Nourisher of the Nations, as it rolled gigantic and majestic in a vast flood from West to East, here, like a Niagara, finding its flow impeded, burst suddenly into the appalling fury of the Maelstrom, into the chaotic spasm of a world-force, a primeval energy, blood-brother of the earthquake and the glacier, raging and wrathful that its power should be braved by some pinch of human spawn that dared raise barriers across its course.[118]

Addams, at times, echoes Norris's vision of the city as a "world-force."[119] Yet, as an experimental moralist, she denies its absolute power over the landscape and, more especially, over humankind.

The Spirit of Youth continues to be popular with readers in the twenty-first century because we hear in the book the voices of common folk. The college-educated professional woman walks along Halsted Street observing and sketching lower-class life, popular movie plots, and scenes from literature. The tales she tells sound like naturalist fiction with its lurid scenes of compulsive and destructive sexuality, addiction, and brutality. Her story of "Poor little Ophelia," for example, might have come from a Zola novel. The lovely young woman is trapped in an abusive relationship with her menacing lover Pierre, who is addicted to whiskey and opium. As Addams tells the story: "I can see her now running for protection up the broad steps of the columned piazza then surrounding Hull-House. Her slender figure was trembling with fright, her tear-covered face swollen and bloodstained from the blows he had dealt her" (40–42). Like Gervaise, the heroine of Zola's *L'Assommoir*, Ophelia acquiesces, powerless to control her own cravings or his. "'He is apt to abuse me when he is drunk,'" she tells the social worker, who discovers that they are not married, have no children, and that Pierre has twice tried to kill her.

Addams puzzles over the irony that although the settlement workers have tried to convince the young woman to leave the brute, virtue is no match for vice. "A poor little Ophelia, I met her one night wondering in the hall half dressed in the tawdry pink gown 'that Pierre likes best of all' and groping on the blank wall to find the door which might permit her to escape to her lover." The Hull-House workers, horrified and fascinated by the power of sexuality, put the young woman in the hospital, yet after her release she returns to her lover who presses her into prostitution to earn money for drugs. Addams acknowledges what many parents know: "[W]e were obliged to admit that there is no civic authority which can control the acts of a girl of eighteen." The spirit of youth itself is the culprit.

The narrative unabashedly employs titillating details—the columned piazza, the slender, trembling, and scantily clad figure, the flowing tears, even the blood. Shakespeare's Ophelia comes dressed in a tawdry pink gown and tainted desire. Addams's fictionalizing of the account borrows heavily from sentimental literature, the tales of seduction and betrayal popular in the nineteenth century and secretly read at Rockford Female Seminary. Her hybrid constructions juxtapose sentimental plots with social issues to illustrate her naturalist philosophy. Like Zola and Sinclair and Dreiser and Wright, Addams thought that fate is determined by such things as hormones, poverty, and addiction. Ophelia becomes a "white slave," forced into prostitution by her addicted lover. The fictional episodes in *The Spirit of Youth* are so colorful that one wonders whether the middle-class reader is convinced to take up Ophelia's cause or whether the lurid details place the fallen heroine apart from the community Addams had hoped to establish. In the narrative, Ophelia leaves the Halsted Street neighborhood when she follows Pierre, letting the reader off the moral hook. Addams offers no further hope for her, no social reform that might curb her biological urge, and no cure for Pierre's addiction to drugs. These are, we know, perennial questions, none of them answered to this day.

Addams offers readers another tale of female behavior. Angelina (not exactly the opposite of Ophelia although the message is clear from their names) inhibits her sex instinct and waits patiently and hopefully for her father to arrange a proper marriage (45). Presumably, the father will be able to detect biological and social imperfections in other males and will not have such imperfections himself. Oddly, arranged marriage emerges as the safest solution to female sexuality in the book. With sex as with art, Addams fears the power of transport. She will return to the issue of "white slavery" in her fifth book, *A New Conscience and an Ancient Evil*, with many new portraits of sexual manipulation and without many more answers to the problem of female sexual desire.

A significant feature of Addams's naturalism is that although females are safest in their prelapsarian state, males cannot resist the fall. The book is full of stories about male juvenile delinquents from eleven to fifteen years old, accounts that she has gathered from court cases and newspaper articles about exploits along the railroad tracks. The male instinct for adventure seems natural to Addams and, if redirected by society, a healthy and vital resource for the community. The section of the book on boys is full of exuberance: "It is as though we were deaf to the appeal of these young creatures, claiming their share of the joy of life, flinging out into the dingy city their desires and aspirations after unknown realities, their unutterable longings for companionship and pleasure" (70–71). Her heroes commit petty crimes—they shoot craps, smoke cigarettes, keep bad company, experiment with drugs, hobo around the country—because of their urge to express "the unrecognized and primitive spirit of adventure, corresponding to the old activity of the hunt, of warfare, and of discovery" (53). The expectation is that in his lapsed state the boy will become "the steady young man of nineteen who brings home all his wages" (58). Maturity coming at nineteen suggests how quickly Addams would like to quell even male sexual energy. And how does the hero avoid the fate of the sadistic Pierre, whose instinct turned to perversion? Addams puts forward a set of social reforms, aimed at redirecting male instinct, such as athletic programs and industrial education to train the primitive urges into healthy and useful behaviors.

Jane Addams remained doubtful about the power of the experimental moralist to change the human condition. To give voice to these hesitations, she brings the body of a Russian "girl" to the stage as she makes her last appeal to the reader. The young woman can no longer speak for herself because she has committed suicide; but a surviving friend who likewise attempted suicide confides in the social worker. We can hear Addams's voice from beneath the shroud: "One of these latter, who afterwards talked freely of the motives which led her to this act, said that there were no great issues at stake in this country; that America was wholly commercial in its interests and absorbed in money making; that Americans were not held together by any historic bonds nor great mutual hopes, and were totally ignorant of the stirring social and philosophical movements of Europe" (147). The problem with democracy is materialism, the desire for property and wealth, at the expense of communalism, the desire for historic and philosophic bonds. The double voice is poignant, even to our ears.

In turning Zola's theory inside out, Addams employs fiction to aid scientific discourse, creating a hybrid literary genre that proved popular with middle-class readers and helped to transform thinking about parks, recreation, athletics, and education in America. Her third book was so successful that Macmillan reprinted it five times in the first six months and by 1911 included it in the Standard Library series of "cheap books." As an "experimental moralist," Addams worked through Hull-House to shorten working hours, provide kindergartens, form athletic teams, organize trips to natural environments, support community theater, and display immigrant crafts. We are all aware in the twenty-first century that the solutions she set into practice at Hull-House have not cured our social ills, and yet we read her books with a clear sense of her literary voice.

3 Public and Private

Literary Godmother

Jane Addams wrote her fourth book, *Twenty Years at Hull-House,* all at once in the late summer and early fall of 1909, surrounded by the calm and beauty of Bar Harbor, Maine. Her third book, *The Spirit of Youth and the City Streets,* was making its way into the hands of readers even as she created the story of her early experiences in Cedarville and Rockford and Europe. Out from under the scrutiny of her sociological godfather Richard Ely, she turned to a new literary mentor, Ida Tarbell. "I have written the first seven chapters—open of course to an enormous amount of change and elaboration—and think that I would better go through to the end," Addams confided to her in August.[1] "I am sure that I ought to do the book pretty well *en bloc* if it is to have real unity—it is quite different from the other things which I have done." The book she was writing, the one about her own life, is truly a work of the literary imagination, a sustained effort to please herself. "May I write you later," she asked Tarbell, "as the child grows and thank you then as now for being such a kind god mother!" Mary Smith arrived in Bar Harbor at the end of September, and the two women stayed through October, Addams telling her sister Alice, "[I]t is a perfectly heavenly place in which to write."[2]

The book's godmother, the midwestern journalist Ida Tarbell, was born in Hatch Hollow, Pennsylvania, in 1857 into an oil-producing family that would suffer from the machinations of John D. Rockefeller in his empire-building scheme at Standard Oil. She was the only female in her class at Allegheny College and later studied women's history at the Sorbonne, taking up the life of Madame Roland and the role of women during the French Revolution only to discover that Roland, no enlightened Cassandra, turned out to have been as callous as her male comrades. After graduation she was hired by *McClure's* magazine and doubled its circulation as she serialized a study of Abraham Lincoln. Turning her childhood experiences and journalistic research into an exposé of Rockefeller, she wrote a nineteen-part series on the history of Standard Oil, a project so convincing that Congress established the Department of Commerce and the Bureau of Corporations as a result. Teddy Roosevelt dubbed her and others of the Progressive generation "muckrakers," a term she never liked but one that was apt. Along with Zola, Sinclair, Norris, Dreiser, and Addams, she was an experimental moralist. In *The History of the Standard Oil Company*, published by Macmillan in 1904, Tarbell concludes: "As for the ethical side, there is no cure but in an increasing scorn of unfair play—an increasing sense that a thing won by breaking the rules of the game is not worth the winning."[3]

"I was deeply stirred on Tuesday night," Tarbell wrote to Addams after hearing her speak at the New York banquet for Mrs. Humphrey Ward in 1908. "I have been talking your address over with Mr. Phillips, and he is very anxious to have a reading of it, with a view to publishing it in *The American Magazine*," Tarbell wrote by way of introduction. "I hardly see how you could improve it. In understanding, in reasoning, and in form it was admirable." We can hear her falling under the spell of Addams's charisma. "Candidly, you quite took my breath away, and I am proud, proud, proud of you!"[4]

As editor and mentor, Ida Tarbell differed significantly from Richard Ely. Her desire was to see Addams again that very month, although she didn't actually visit Hull-House until July. The long letter of thanks that followed, belatedly, three months later, is full of personal detail about her family, suggesting how close the two women had become in such a short time. "I hope if you are in New York or are coming you'll let me know. It would give me such pleasure to take care of you while there. Of course that means leaving you perfectly free."[5] Taking care, for Tarbell, meant granting freedom, the very combination that made her a good editor for Jane Addams. Tarbell could joke with her about the New York leisure class: "I think we're going to have a lively *woman's* winter. Society in New York has determined to intellectualize itself! Of course the women must do it." Addams responded warmly, "Please don't feel disturbed over a delayed letter, nothing you can do will ever shake your standing at H.H. where you have made an abiding place for yourself."[6]

Tarbell wrote again in May to explain somewhat awkwardly why her boss, John S. Phillips, had rejected the essay, even as he wanted Addams to write something much longer for the magazine. Phillips wooed Addams through Tarbell. "Mr. Phillips seemed to feel that I could say what he wanted to say better than he could write it," Ida Tarbell explained, attaching sections of a letter that Phillips had written. "'But then Miss Addams comes down to the particular at once, properly, rightly, with great intelligence, in mind of the points she is after and the people she is speaking to, realizing their knowledge and their interest in the particular subject.'"[7] He rejected the speech because it was written for a specific occasion. What he wanted was the story of her life: "[S]he will, I am confident, prove to be one the most remarkable writers of our time." An autobiography of Jane Addams would "stand with the best of such books in our time." Phillips confides to Tarbell, "Really, she ought to do it." And Tarbell, as godmother to the project, relayed the message.

Readers wanted her to talk about Hull-House and about her own life. A reader from Kentucky wrote a letter to the editor of the *New York Evening Post,* calling on Addams to write more about her experiences at Hull-House: "After twenty years of service, when the period of experiment is long since gone, the public is interested in knowing what the settlement stands for, from one so well qualified to speak."[8] Walter Hines Page urged her to tell her private story: "You will recall, I hope, that several years ago I took the liberty to propose to you that you should write out your experience and your philosophy, your creed, or whatever you call it, in the form more or less of an autobiographical narrative."[9] He cajoled her with a warning that a Mrs. Breck, who was looking for something to do before she married, had been thinking about writing a biography of Addams. "But no marriage nor any other event, except the last final one that comes to us all, will ever get the conviction out of my mind that such a book ought to be written—that it ought to be written now, and that you, yourself, ought to write it." The genre is a noble one, he reminded her: "[S]ome of the greatest books are autobiographical." He told her that if need be he would come to Chicago to give her the "forty and one good reasons" why she ought to turn her hand to the project. "I can't think of a book that is likely to stimulate more minds nor, if you will permit me to say so, is there a method that I think of whereby the larger significance of your great labor will be made plain to the big public."[10] His metaphor moves from marriage to labor and, wistfully, to the birth of the book, one that Doubleday Page might expect to publish.

Addams began negotiations on the autobiography that Page implored her to write, but she did not, however, take him up on his offer to publish the book, remaining loyal to Macmillan. George Brett wrote in May 1909 acknowledging her discussions with Marsh: "We on our part are ready and indeed anxious to bring it out for you at such time as seems to you best suited to the publication of the book."[11] They completed the deal for the two books, the first in the autumn of 1909 and the second in 1910, and Addams continued to negotiate with Marsh at Macmillan and Bok at *Ladies' Home Journal* in order to allow time to publish in both venues.

Throughout the summer of 1909, Addams kept at the task of writing even as she traveled to the National Conference of Charities in New York City, where she presided. "I have fussed over the book all of the time between meetings," she reported to Mary. This time she dictated the whole manuscript to a stenographer, an expense that she hoped would save her "the remorse inspired by New Id of P."[12] She soothed her companion: "Keep up courage Darling—I am expecting to have a restored Lady by the time we move into the little brown house which I think of with much affection—Always yrs." The two women planned to share a cottage in Highland Park for two months as Mary recuperated and Jane wrote. "I am afraid that life in the little brown cottage will be too lively for book writing," she complained, considering "the heat and burden of the day luncheon and dinner parties every meal and philanthropic talk expected '*all* the time.'"[13] Talking all the time, of course, dissipates the urge to write. And the literary woman wanted, more than anything, to write.

In New York, she met with Ida Tarbell to work out details of the publication in *The American Magazine*. A representative at Macmillan agreed that she could copublish anything from the book in the magazine. "I am not in the least sure that there will be anything worth publishing after the end of my efforts altho I mean to do what I can this summer," she wrote, and we can hear her reticence. Phillips offered her $500 for each installment but reserved the right to choose material and to call for revisions. Although she accepted the deal, she would never be comfortable with the way things would work out.

By the end of October, Phillips was reading a full manuscript of *Twenty Years at Hull-House*. "You have written a very beautiful and remarkable book," he assured her. Walter Hines Page responded to the news: "I cannot conceal from you my regret that you did not see fit to allow us to publish this in 'The World's Work', of which we should have been very proud, and also in a book which we should have given our best attention."[14] Publishers everywhere were eager to publish whatever she had to say. Charles Nutter wrote from Appleton that they were sorry to have missed the chance of publishing her autobiography, and Julia Tutwiler wrote from Henry Holt, requesting the opportunity to publish the book, apparently not having heard the news that Macmillan had already won the competition. The editorial board at *Harper's Bazaar* invited her, along with William Dean Howells, Henry James, Mark Twain, Margaret Deland, and Mary Wilkins Freeman, to participate in a series of three-thousand-word essays on "The Turning Point of My Life." Elizabeth Jordan wrote to Addams, noting that Howells was to write about why he became a novelist and not a poet and James about why he became a novelist and not a lawyer.[15] Addams, caught up in the writing projects at hand, declined the offer, although it must have pleased her to be in such company.

In the fall of 1909, after a short and successful gestation, the first version of her autobiography arrived at *The American Magazine*. It was Tarbell, her very godmother, who had the guts to call the manuscript into question. "Mr. Phillips, Mr. Baker and I have just had a confab over your manuscript," she wrote in November.[16] "The only regret is that you did not feel like going on in the vein of the first four or five chapters, and making a story which could run for a year." They wanted a full autobiography of the woman. Tarbell explained to Addams that Phillips was "much disappointed that you do not see your way to do this, but I have told him that I did not think you would be willing to reconsider." Then she added, "If we could persuade you to do it, of course, we should be most happy." The fact that Tarbell asked the question and that Addams ignored it tells us much about how to read the autobiography.

Ventriloquist and Dummy

The literary costume that best fitted Jane Addams was her imaginative construction of herself in *Twenty Years at Hull-House* in which she could speak as both character and writer. Her autobiography is her one book that is still read today and often taught in university classes, where she sits comfortably alongside Benjamin Franklin, Henry David Thoreau, Frederick Douglass, and Henry Adams, all men who cast their own stories as revelatory of American experience. Addams sits less comfortably alongside Margaret Fuller, Harriet Jacobs, and Edith Wharton, because they all, as women, diverted readers from the details of their private lives. In melding these two autobiographical traditions, one male and the other female, Jane Addams preserved the sacred myth at the heart of American culture: the upward mobility of the individual. In the process of reinvigorating the myth, she told, in essence, two stories—one about herself and the other about her Halsted Street neighbors. For the little girl who was rich to begin with, mobility had nothing to do with money; rather, she moves upward in moral growth. Much like the Transcendentalists

Thoreau and Fuller, Addams casts herself as a character who yearns to find the mystery beyond the quotidian world.

The daughter of a moneyed family takes the train from Cedarville to Chicago, leaving the bucolic landscape behind in search of meaning in a city slum. Much to the reader's amazement, she refines her moral sensibility among immigrants crowded into blighted tenements. To transcend the material world of the nineteenth century, a woman must live at the very center of the city and not, as the Transcendentalists would have us believe, in nature. She walks out of the natural world onto what she calls the common road, shoulder to shoulder with workers who battle rapacious capitalists like Pullman and corrupt politicians like Powers. The essence of the story is not the climb from rags to riches, but rather the journey from riches to rags. And it is there, in the ragtag neighborhood of Halsted Street, that she slips away from the narrative. *Twenty Years at Hull-House* satisfied readers, then and now, because the upward struggle is cast as a communal one, the triumph of concerted human effort.

Addams couldn't have written a more popular tale. The account of her twenty years at Hull-House first appeared in *The American Magazine* in 1910. Readers followed the story in serial form, anxious for new installments—her awkward childhood in Illinois, her relationship with her politically savvy father, her female education at Rockford Female Seminary, and her neurasthenic discomfort with leisure-class travel.

The early sections of *Twenty Years at Hull-House* could be titled "Twenty-Nine Years before Hull-House." About a third of way into the book, however, the heroine disappears, leaving Hull-House itself as the hero of the tale. She confesses in the Preface, "[N]o effort is made in the recital to separate my own history from that of Hull-House during the years when I was 'launched deep into the stormy intercourse of human life' for, so far as a mind is pliant under the pressure of events and experiences, it becomes hard to detach it" (viii). The reader is left to wonder about the distance between Addams and her persona. "No effort" has been made by whom? And where does the "launched deep" quote come from? What are we to make of the more suggestive phrase "the stormy intercourse of human life"? Who exactly is speaking to us? The transition from personal to public story, from Jane Addams to Hull-House, is subtle and artful.

In blending autobiography with the story of Hull-House, she expropriated language from the early essay "The Subjective Necessity for Social Settlements," published in *Philanthropy and Social Progress* in 1893. She had a good deal of trouble trying to get back the rights to her essay.

Thomas Crowell, who had published the book of essays as well as *Hull-House Maps and Papers*, did not want her to recycle his copyrighted material. She had written to him in March 1906 asking for permission to republish her essay. He responded in irritation: "[W]hile the sale of this book is not large, we think that what sale there is is due largely to your contributions to the book, and it seems to us that to use the material in the way you suggest might interfere with our sale."[17] Crowell refused the request: "We hope, therefore, that you can see your way clear to make some other arrangements for the present." She went back to him again in January 1907, hoping to use the essay in her autobiography, and Crowell responded officially, refusing even to sign his name, that she had his permission to use the material only if she agreed to mention him.[18]

Referring to Crowell in her autobiography, however, she chided him for not doing more to promote *Hull-House Maps and Papers*: "The first edition became exhausted in two years, and apparently the Boston publisher did not consider the book worthy of a second edition" (153). Richard Ely, siding with Crowell, took Addams to task for the comment, lecturing her in his old way: "I do not believe you understand the facts, and I think I ought to make some comments upon this passage. It seems to convey a certain reproach to Mr. Crowell."[19] We can hear the condescension in Ely's voice: "I do not think he deserves any reproach in this matter, and that seems to be conveyed by implication. With Mr. Crowell it was not a question of the worthiness of the book, but a question of profit and loss. While I do not know, if I were going to make a guess I should say that Mr. Crowell probably lost as much as $500.00 on the book. The maps were extremely expensive." In the business of publishing, the men stood together. His rebuke may be a sign of how free Jane Addams had become as a writer.

Circumventing Crowell's legal request, Addams used the original text of the lecture she had given in 1892 to the Ethical Culture Societies. Using the oral version of the paper allowed her to manipulate the text, introducing it with a scene of pure fiction: "I remember one golden summer afternoon during the sessions of the summer school that several of us met on the shores of a pond in a pine wood a few miles from Plymouth, to discuss our new movement" (113). We note that she places herself in the imaginative company of Thoreau and in the literary venue of Walden Pond. The essay, she urges her readers to believe, "should have a chance to speak for itself" (a cheeky response to Crowell and Ely) (115). The passage appears in smaller font, presenting itself as the very voice of Jane Addams, the younger. Yet what she gives us is not really a quotation at all, but rather an edited version (we imagine Ely peering over her shoulder, red pen in hand). She combines short sentences, adds punctuation, omits sentences, skips sections, and removes references to Tolstoy, Mary Ward, and Frederick Harrison.

Jane Addams appears before us in a double guise. As she deftly moves her hand into the puppet, she becomes both ventriloquist and dummy. The writer of fifty speaks as the young woman of thirty-two, the two voices sounding together. The passage marks the transition in the story from Jane Addams to Hull-House. Just as her readers settle comfortably into the story of her private life, she slips away, leaving us, book in hand, with very little trace of the writer.

We might argue that she never wanted to tell the story of her private life. She claimed that she hoped by writing her autobiography to halt two biographies in the making: "The unworthy motive was a desire to start a 'backfire,' as it were, to extinguish two biographies of myself, one of which had been submitted to me in outline, that made life in a Settlement all too smooth and charming" (vii). Her early years in Cedarville, Rockford, and Philadelphia, and in London and Madrid, provide literary terrain for a popular tale of individual accomplishment, the rebellion of an upper-class daughter against the family claim on her energies and imagination. Her question, as a writer, is what to do with herself once she matures? The continuation of her private story would require details of her life with Ellen Gates Starr and, later, with Mary Rozet Smith. It would take us to Lakeside, Michigan, by motorcar and to Mackinac Island by boat. We would be packed along on trips to Bar Harbor and would take our place at the table on the long warm summer evenings on the Atlantic shore. The writer, however, never intended to tell the story of female intimacy and camaraderie.

Even the story of her early years comes to us as fable. She told Elizabeth Jordan, editor of *Harper's Bazaar*, that one fairy tale stood out in her childhood: "If by fairy tales you mean imaginative stories which pleased one as a child, one of the first I remember with vividness is Andersen's 'Ugly Duckling.'"[20] A version of that fairy tale appears early in the autobiography as she describes herself: "the ugly, pigeon-toed little girl, whose crooked back obliged her to walk with her head held very much upon one side" (7). On the traditional Sunday walk, she claims to have avoided her father's hand so that his "fine head" might not be associated with hers, bent as it was. "In order to lessen the possibility of a connection being made, on these particular Sundays I did not walk beside my father, although this walk was the great event of the week, but attached myself firmly to the side of my Uncle James Addams, in the hope that I should not remain so conspicuously unattached that troublesome questions might identify an Ugly Duckling with her imposing parent." The use of the fairy tale is clever because her readers all know that the ugly duckling turns into a lovely swan, just as she tells the tale of a later meeting with her father in the public square when he tips his hat to her.

The Andersen fairytale is followed by a biblical variation, Joseph's coat of many colors. Addams, as a girl of eight on her way to Sunday School, wears "a very pretty cloak—in fact so much prettier than any cloak the other little girls in the Sunday School had." (13) Her father lectures her on conspicuous consumption: "[H]e would advise me to wear my old cloak, which would keep me quite as warm, with the added advantage of not making the other little girls feel badly." In a third variation on the story of female dress, she includes her trip to Yasnaya Polyana and Tolstoy's pulling on the sleeve of her dress as he admonishes her to dress in the mode of the peasant.

In another early scene, waiflike she presses her thumb against the miller's stone to force her body into the shape of her father's, whose thumb has been worn flat by hard labor early in his life. "Even when playing in our house or yard, I could always tell when the millstones were being dressed, because the rumbling of the mill then stopped, and there were few pleasures I would not instantly forego, rushing at once to the mill, that I might spread out my hands near the millstones in the hope that the little hard flints flying from the miller's chisel would light upon their backs and make the longed-for marks" (5). Such a suggestive crossing of genders, coupled with an even more suggestive image of masochistic pleasure, appealed to her readers without raising eyebrows as such scenes might a century later.

Her heroine is spiritual, fervent, intense, moral, self-effacing, and worthy of attention, even emulation. The scenes of her tour of the slums of London, as she traveled in leisurely splendor, and her epiphany in Madrid as she delighted in the bullfight have been favorites of readers. W. A. Bradley, writing in *Bookman*, recounted the bloody conversion scene in Madrid and its ramifications: "For other times and other men, this book, with its explicit statements of spiritual fervours and tense moral crises leading on to a career of singularly self-effacing effort to lead the life dictated by the impulses and convictions of a profound personal religion, will constitute a document of extraordinary interest and value as a clue to the recrudescence of mediaeval idealism in modern life."[21] His reading of the narrative as chivalric, even quasi-religious, with its roots in medieval idealism, no doubt, pleased Addams. Francis Hackett wrote in the "Book of the Week" column for *The Chicago Evening Post*: "Most books on the social question are agreeable, inert, dead books, capable of dissection on doctrinaire lines. But Miss Addams' is a book with all the richness, all the complexity, and all the self-justification of a living being. To estimate it is like trying to perform a vivisection, out of curiosity."[22] If her persona embodied mythic meaning, she also seemed vital, tangible, and likeable to readers. The reviewer at *The Sociological Review* praised the book's structure: "The narrative of schemes begun and developed, or attempted and abandoned, is interwoven with passages of personal reminiscence and confession, with stories of tragedy and heroism, drawn from a marvellously full store."[23]

The full title of the book is *Twenty Years at Hull-House with Autobiographical Notes,* and the qualification is significant. Jane Addams promises only notes about her personal story, and not a full accounting of her fifty years. The story she tells begins with the noble young woman from Cedarville, but she abandons her to tell a story about a settlement house in Chicago. The most revealing sentence in her preface is the line: "No effort is made in the recital to separate my own history from that of Hull-House." She leaves herself free as the ventriloquist to move from a private to a public voice.

Magazine Heroine

Jane Addams's autobiography appeared first in *The American Magazine.* As she read the magazine over the year she was writing her book, she found much to agree with in its socialist politics and philosophical naturalism. And, more to the point, the character she was constructing, the Cedarville girl who would become the social and spiritual center of the settlement house movement, fitted comfortably between the pages of the magazine. In the issues leading up to Addams's autobiography, Ray Stannard Baker wrote a series linking religion and reform. William Allen White summed up the new morality of the Progressive reformers: "And so with all our reforming conditions about us, by the millions and millions we are first of all reforming ourselves. We are promoting democracy by forgetting ourselves in the thought of others." The magazine's credo was hinted at by White: "This self-abnegation is the greatest movement in our National life."[24] Surely, the magazine reinforced Addams's own thinking about the nature of autobiography—she may forget herself in the telling of the story, secure in the belief that self-abnegation is a virtue. The magazine also included fiction that may well have caught her eye. In 1909, Susan Glaspell, Jack London, and Zona Gale contributed stories, all written in the mode and mood of literary naturalism. Exploring our animal nature, William James published an article, "The

Confidences of a 'Psychical Researcher,'" that attempts to locate the spiritual world and our study of it.

Ida Tarbell gave a long introduction to Jane Addams by way of a series of articles over the months leading up to the April 1909 issue. "The American Woman" traces the story of female achievement from 1776 through the years of the Civil War and makes the case for female involvement in the public sphere, including the natural right to education and political power. In the November issue, Tarbell covers the Revolutionary War, a time when women preserved the machinery of society by managing the shop, farm, school, and church while men were battling for independence from British rule. In the issue that begins with the story of Jane Addams, Tarbell talks about the ways that women responded to the Civil War by taking up tasks usually assigned to men, much as they had done in 1776; she featured the work of Elizabeth Blackwell, Harriet Beecher Stowe, Clara Barton, Dorothea Lynde Dix, Anna Ella Carroll (a woman who freed all her slaves at the outbreak of the War), and Julia Ward Howe. The logical next woman in the series was Jane Addams.

The readers of *The American Magazine* opened the pages in April to find two photographs, one an image of Addams as a writer at fifty and the other of her as a child of four. The writer appears at a desk, pen in hand, her dark lace sleeves pushed above the elbow, ready to compose the story of her life. The wisps of her hair are dark, not gray, and the part in her hair looks (as Corinne Williams noted) as though it is about to fall out. The facial expression is calm, assured, comfortable with the pen she holds gracefully in her hand. Looking more closely, however, we see that the single sheet of paper on the desk is empty; there are no books in sight, and her eyes are cast upward, perhaps at the suggestion of the photographer, Eva Waltson Schutze. The photo is framed with an elaborately trimmed card beneath it, shaped as a lady's calling card with scrolls on either end. "Jane Addams," the card reads, "AT A TIME WHEN WOMEN ARE TAKING A GREATER PART IN PUBLIC AFFAIRS THAN EVEN BEFORE, MISS ADDAMS MAY WELL BE CALLED THE FOREMOST AMERICAN WOMAN."[25] On the opposite page, the reader sees the young Jane, standing beside a chair that highlights her size. At four, her shoulders come to the top of the chair; she is dressed in a dark plaid dress with capped sleeves that have been slipped just over her shoulders, and in her left hand she holds a fur muff. Her hair is severely parted in the middle, drawn back behind her ears—no chance for the part to fail—and her eyes gaze to the right of the camera, probably at the suggestion of the photographer. She is elegant and graceful, even at four—clearly, a child of privilege.

The frame of the photo has a scalloped roof, supported on each side by angels who hold the image in place. The art nouveau design makes the obvious point that even as a professional woman, Jane Addams is angelic. Another card, ornately bordered, announces, "AUTOBIOGRAPHICAL NOTES UPON TWENTY YEARS AT HULL-HOUSE BY JANE ADDAMS ILLUSTRATED WITH PHOTOGRAPHS." The publisher introduces her as the culmination of female destiny:

> Hull-House of Chicago, which has just finished its twentieth year's work, is to-day the most extensive and important social settlement in the United States. No other one institution, perhaps, has had more influence in shaping and inspiring the present movement toward social reconstruction in this country. Behind every vital institution stands a great and vital personality. Without the inspiration of a prophetic vision and abounding faith in carrying it out, without noble qualities of courage and sympathy, with a high order of administrative, social and even political capacity, no such original institution could rise to a place of power and influence.

Addams is portrayed as vital, prophetic, abounding in faith, courageous, sympathetic, and able. The photographs, language, and design denote social rank and breeding.

As readers turned the pages, they saw lush half-page photographs of her birthplace, a graciously balconied house surrounded by leafy trees, and across the page a side view of arched windows and delicate brackets. The text declares: "It is a great human story of a great woman: of her beautiful early home life, of her education, of her struggle with ill health, of the influences, both of men and of books, which led her finally to the settlement in the slums of Chicago." A single picture could not capture the stately charm of her home, the one that marks her social status through the accomplishments of her father, a man shown on the next page across from another picture of Jane at seven. The whole seventh page consists of a drawing of the Addams homestead in Cedarville, with accompanying labels—village, barn, house, mill—to show the relationship of the family to the town and to stress their ownership of land. Two pages later, a photograph of Pine Hill appears. "The Pine Grove on top of this hill was planted by John H. Addams in 1844," the caption emphasizes, together with a picture of the mill that he built as his first business. Clearly readers were meant to understand Jane Addams's place among the landed gentry in the Middle West.

Addams continued to work on the book manuscript at the same time that *The Spirit of Youth and the City Streets* attracted an admiring audience. William James wrote in the *Journal of Sociology*, "Certain pages of it seem to me quite immortal statements of the fact that the essential and perennial function of the youth-period is to reaffirm authentically the value and the charm of life."[26] Vida Scudder enthused, "There is a rare and lovely tenderness suffusing it, that goes to the heart. Your attitude reminds me of that of the Pater Shakespeare."[27] She basked in the glow of her reputation and, at the same time, worked to sell the remaining sections of *Twenty Years at Hull-House* to other magazines. *Ladies' Home Journal* considered publishing her chapter on Tolstoy; even as Florence Converse wrote from the *Atlantic Monthly:* "How very good of you to give us an opportunity to consider your article on Tolstoy!"[28] The article finally went to *McClure's.*

Addams reported to Mary, "All the articles have gone to the American and the Tolstoy to McClure's, so when the Book is off, nothing remains in way of literary labor, but the St. Louis speech!"[29] By April Jane and Mary traveled to Hot Springs, Virginia, enjoying motor rides as Jane recovered from a surgery to repair her botched appendectomy. The two women visited Lakeside, Michigan, in June and then went to New Haven. In 1920, Yale University honored Jane Addams's social work and her writing by conferring on her their first honorary degree ever awarded to a woman. Still recovering from illness and fatigue, Addams spent the late summer months in Maine with Mary.

Princess Alice, consort of Alexander, the Prince of Teck, wrote in July, seeking Addams's help for young women in Europe. "Their youth and inexperience, linked with their slender resources and lack of knowledge of the language, expose them to unforeseen and grave dangers in a strange land, where many watch them for evil and few have any regard for their good."[30] The theme of Addams's next book, *A New Conscience and an Ancient Evil,* could not have been articulated any better than this, and we imagine Jane Addams storing the long sentence away in her mind.

In the late summer and fall of 1910, she worked to revise her autobiography for its final publication in book form. From her letters, we learn much about her habit of writing. "I have been digging away on The Twenty Years," she wrote Clara Landsberg from Maine.[31] "It is really coming out much better and I am awfully sorry that it must go to Macmillan before you have a chance to see the improvement in the ungainly child." In a letter to Graham Taylor, Addams described her day: "I work on the book for four to six hours a day, altho I write so slowly—that it is hard to realize there are so many hours of work on it."[32] In the end, she lamented releasing edited sections of the book to *The American Magazine:* "It is certainly better than the American articles altho that is not my highest praise—they are so cut and mangled."[33]

Addams continued the long labor, writing this time very much in control of her schedule and sure of her talent. She joked to Florence Kelley, "I have simply been swimming in proofs for the past two weeks," and repeated the metaphor in a letter to Clara Landsberg, "I am swimming in proofs—it is an awfully big book 115,000 words!"[34] She savored the long days of late summer on the Maine coast that allowed her the leisure to indulge in imaginative play with language.

George Brett wrote in October about the next book, making the argument that Edward Marsh would "probably be very glad" to publish whatever she had in mind. She resisted: "I am quite sure that I can do nothing in regard to the other book during the winter beyond collecting material, and I am afraid we must regard its publication as problematical."[35] Edward Marsh, knowing Addams well, responded: "[T]here is a crying need for a book on the problem of the girls in large cities."[36] *Collier's*, too, had asked her to write a two-thousand-word article, one they hoped would be titled "The Problem of the Growing Girl."

After her return to Chicago, she succumbed to the doubt every writer feels as a book is about come out. Her "child" would appear on November 16, and she confessed to Mary Smith (who had stayed behind in Maine): "I find I rather dread it."[37] They were separated from time to time as Mary suffered a string of illnesses—asthma, lumbago, rheumatism, bronchitis, pneumonia, and nervous exhaustion, all akin to the illnesses that marked Addams's youth. Jane wrote to reassure Mary: "Do write to me Dear One and know that if I am too rushed to write that I am never too rushed to be conscious of you and our affection."

Addams was sick both in body and mind. She had a distressing abscess on her face from a bad tooth; both tooth and abscess were removed, causing her days of pain and months of anxiety over the gap between her teeth. More significantly, however, she suffered from her brother Weber's continuing mental illness. His episodes of "aural delusions" worsen as he visited the family in Cedarville. Although he tried to keep control of his senses in front of the family, what he wanted was to return to the hospital. The depression that his sister experienced in her youth was never as severe as his.

The publication of *Twenty Years at Hull-House* in 1910, as Hull-House entered its twenty-first year and Addams celebrated her fiftieth birthday on September 6, might well have signaled a triumphant end to a long career. Her friend Robert Woods wrote what she considered the best letter she received about her autobiography. "I see that you have laid down the classic of settlement literature, existing and to come," he assured her and then made the suggestion that she "let others carry many of the less significant burdens you have so long borne, and save your strength of vision and creation for the further chapters in the story."[38] She might have retired, more or less, from Hull-House and devoted herself more exclusively to her writing. Mary Smith returned for the holidays and Addams planned a trip to New York City in January, one that would not include speaking engagements.

The person she most wanted to see over lunch was Ida Tarbell, the editor who had served as her literary godmother. The narrative they both labored over in *The American Magazine* series and the subsequent book proved to be popular with critics and readers. Edward Marsh sent word of the review in *The Nation:* "Such whole-hearted approval is rare with The Nation, and you can hardly be more gratified over this review than I am."[39] They all took credit for the achievement.

Her letters home to Mary, however, revealed ambivalence: "N.Y. is very gay and I am quite invigorated by all I see and hear—almost a stirring of the old ambitions—but not quite—of confidence to 'do & dare.'"[40] Addams saw the end of *Twenty Years at Hull-House* as a pause in her long life. With Mary Smith she could be candid: "Darling, Here we are still in N.Y. but incognito as it were so that it is as restful as Lakewood and I have begun seriously on my paper which however is not going very well—but I am sure would not anywhere else owing to interior reasons."[41] Her age and health, fatigue from her work over the summer and fall, waning energy for crowds, and the leafy retreat of Bar Harbor were all in her mind. "I am afraid that my speaking days are over perhaps it is well that I have my operation to fall back on. . . . I am distressed about your rheumatism, Dearest—I do wish we knew what to do!" Respite, maybe, but not retirement, lay ahead as Addams turned back toward Chicago.

Slum Angels

Her autobiography made its way into her readers' hands in 1910, and editors and publishers begged for her next book, a study of "white slavery," the most sensational, even lurid, topic in America before the outbreak of war in Europe. They hoped she would write a book about the sexual life of young women in the city. George Brett assured her in October 1910 that Marsh "would probably be very glad to publish it."[42] Jane Addams held him off for a year, fearing that he would announce the publication that would require her to write more quickly than she thought possible or wise.[43] Edward Marsh himself urged her to focus her new book "on the problem of the girls in large cities," flattering her by adding that she would give the topic "a serious and unsensational treatment."[44] A month later, Brett wrote again to ask for "another book which I think is much needed, on the position of young girls and women when they first come to the city to take up work in the great manufacturing and mercantile establishments."[45] She reported in January, "[W]e are getting together a great deal of interesting material in connection with the Juvenile Protective Association," even as she warned him not to make any announcement of the book because she saw "a danger of over-statement" on the topic of girls alone in the city.[46]

The publishing business in the United States had mushroomed after 1891 when international copyrights were established, ending the cheap reprint of books by European writers and, as a result, making American authors a good buy. According to historian John Tebbel, the gentlemanly editors of the late nineteenth century—George Palmer Putnam, Charles Scribner, Henry Houghton, and James T. Fields—were followed by a new breed of more competitive men like Frank Doubleday, Walter Hines Page, who had encouraged Addams to write her autobiography, and George P. Brett, who sought out Jane Addams and then struggled to keep hold of her.[47] He offered her advances and assiduously reminded her of new projects, explaining from the start of their relationship that she would do best by keeping their publishing marriage together. Literary agents were popular after 1900 as best-selling writers commanded the attention of publishers. What distinguished Jane Addams from other successful authors was her insistence on making deals for herself. Her letters are full of artful negotiations with Brett and editors of popular magazines as she marketed her writing in more than one place, enhancing her readership and garnering income.

Addams turned her attention to many projects after publishing *Twenty Years at Hull-House* that took her away from writing. She arranged for a Chicago showing of the Child Welfare Exhibit at the Coliseum, managing to get funding from Mrs. Cyrus McCormick Jr. She joined the Committee of One Hundred, which endorsed the creation of a National Department or Bureau of Health. With the financial help of Anita McCormick Blaine, she helped to organize the Chicago chapter of the National Association for the Advancement of Colored People, telling her sponsor: "You know, of course, how vexed the entire problem is and how necessary that some one should do some clear thinking and plan some decisive action in regard to it."[48] She supported the Committee on Crime and Immigration, especially in the effort to oppose a literacy test for immigrants. The same month, Theodore Roosevelt made his first trip to Hull-House, setting into motion a political relationship that would lead them both to the podium at the Bull Moose Convention in 1912. Addams traveled from Chicago to Springfield to lobby state lawmakers on child actors and newsboys, and to Birmingham, Alabama, to speak at a child labor conference. She returned to Hull-House to help stage John Galworthy's play "Justice" at the Hull-House Theater.

Little wonder that she found herself exhausted during the winter of 1911 and that she planned an especially long summer away from Hull-House. By April, George Brett had heard the news. "Someone told us the other day that you were expecting to take a long summer holiday this year," he began his spring letter, pointing out that the vacation would allow her "opportunity for the getting together of the material for the book."[49] And she responded, "I hope to do some work this summer upon the book concerning girls in the city, but as I wrote before I am quite unwilling to have it announced because I am not sure that the material which I have will be of any value."[50] The book would be her most controversial one—Jane Addams could hardly take up the subject of female sexual vulnerability without drawing attention.

Even as she stalled Brett, she encouraged McClure, who had read the Vice Commission report and recommended that she read an article by Professor Ford in the January *Scribner's*. Likewise, James Tower from *Good Housekeeping* had read Graham Taylor's report in *Survey* on Chicago's Vice Commission and wrote Addams to say: "I know no one else in the United States whose views on the servant problem seem to me as sound and helpful as yours."[51] He wanted, as they all did, to publish anything she might write, and he was willing to pay her any amount of money.

As she thought about the confining nature of the city, she grew fonder of the unconfined nature of the Maine coast. Her letters that spring are the first to dwell on Bar Harbor. Addams invited Lillian Wald "to see me in my house at Bar Harbor," and signed her letters from June to September from Hull's Cove, Maine.[52] She described what she called "this beautiful spot." Hull's Cove offered seclusion from public life and privacy to write. It is a strange irony that as she moved into the leisurely community of Bar Harbor, she began to write about the dangers of living in Chicago. "McClure is hurrying me for the first 'reading' of my stuff," she wrote Grace Abbott. Her new book about young women and sex stimulated her imagination. "I have quite enjoyed writing it altho the subject is grisly—I have tried to hide it, under the title 'A New Conscience and an Ancient Evil.'" Perhaps she enjoyed writing the book because the subject was grisly.

Through the late summer, she continued to bargain with George Brett and Samuel McClure to secure publications, first in the magazine and then in a book. She always relished making the literary deal. Her Macmillan royalty statement in the spring of 1911 totaled $3,922.10, including the sale of 407 copies of *Democracy and Social Ethics*, 409 copies of *Newer Ideals of Peace*, and 2,756 of *The Spirit of Youth and the City Streets*. The Chautauqua "cheap edition" of *Twenty Years at Hull-House* had a surprisingly high first-year sale of 16,877 copies. As a result of her success, publishers competed even more for the next piece of writing.

Her article on the social evil, promised to McClure, had grown into a book of seven chapters. "As I begun it with the magazine article in mind," she explained to Edward Marsh, "I have tried to keep the phraseology and tone, so that it might be read by the general public without embarrassment."[53] She offered the chapters for his perusal, and Brett responded that he wanted the book, even without having read the chapters, "sure of a wide reading" for anything she had written.[54] She hoped to publish the book in March 1912, leaving her time to use the same material in magazine articles during the fall of 1911 in order to avoid problems with copyright law. Addams still had the argument with Crowell in mind and wanted to control her literary property for as long as possible.

The two men wrangled over the proper venue for a book that, whatever the tone she used in whatever veiled language, promised to be a surprisingly sexy book for Jane Addams to write. Hoping to keep the material for himself, Brett advised her that it was not suitable material for a magazine. At the same time, McClure urged her to publish in the magazine, where a readership of five hundred thousand families would surely boost book sales. McClure's letters display a playful courting of her, even as he shrewdly made his case. "I am setting up nights for the manuscript," he told her.[55] When she finally sent the manuscript, he responded: "I feel that it is just the sort of material that I want for my magazine."[56] Unlike Brett and Marsh, he read the manuscript, offering to use all of it over five months, from December 1911 through April 1912, well past the March 1912 publication that Brett hoped to secure. McClure's offered her $1,000 for the series, praising the writing for its "singular nobility of tone." Two days later, Marsh's next letter arrived, cautioning her about serialization in the magazine: "I doubt whether they are the kind of readers you want." Realizing the implication, he added: "Of course, your handling of the subject is at the farthest remove from the sensational."[57] He hoped to dissuade her from selling the material before Macmillan could sell the book. And her goal was to collect as much money and as many readers as possible.

Addams responded coolly to McClure's offer of $1,000, writing hastily in pencil that he should consider the effect on a writer who is "unduly compensated" for her work and suggesting that he return the manuscript. "*The American* paid me more for my articles than you offer and I shall have to say 1500.00 for the series of five."[58] Of course, the deal was struck with both men who were eager not to offend her. She arranged for the book to be published by Macmillan in March and for two articles to be published in November and December in *McClure's*. McClure even extended the deadline to September 11. He implored her in his playful way, "[P]lease do not fail me."[59] Brett humored her by promising to use a union binding shop, something he neglected to do for the last book. Prior to publication, Addams read from the articles in a talk to the Chicago Ethical Society, prompting McClure to coach her on how to avoid having the press quote her verbatim before publication.

As she bargained with publishers, Addams was utterly at home in Bar Harbor and comfortable with her writing schedule. She invited Florence Kelley to have a look at the "little book" she was writing. But, perhaps more so, she was eager for her friends to see her place. She wrote to Lillian Wald that she was "so anxious to have you see this beautiful island."[60] Alice Hamilton, who had read the manuscript, wrote enthusiastically from Mackinac Island: "The stories are awfully good and illuminating, especially Olga's."[61] After a long separation from Mary Smith, who had been recuperating in Hot Springs from a variety of ailments, Addams gently reassured her: "Dearest—I do wish you could really believe that I would rather be with you than anyone else."[62]

Jane Addams was reading Theodore Dreiser's second novel, *Jennie Gerhardt* (1911), during the winter of 1912 as she finished writing *A New Conscience and an Ancient Evil*, the two books becoming linked in her mind. She had traveled from Chicago south to Augusta, Georgia, in February with Louise DeKoven Bowen to stay at the Hampton Hotel. The working holiday provided escape from the winter in Chicago and the business of Hull-House, but, more so, it gave her solitude. She wrote her sister Alice that the Hampton was a comfortable, even gorgeous hotel: "I am working on the new book at the rate of about ten hours a day."[63] What she wanted was time to write, and her trip allowed her to finish the book manuscript due at Macmillan by the first of March. After the long hours of work, she relaxed in the evenings.

"The Lady works like a galley slave, and I shall be glad to get it off for all kinds of reasons and get my mind freed of the subject," she confided to Mary about her writing project. As for the reading she was doing in the evening, she was selective: "I have very little time for reading novels just now." The one novel that held her interest was Dreiser's second novel, especially the ending: "Jennie Gerhardt seems to me a clever story but the Bed of Roses is too much."[64] She was composing a book about young women in the city and looking for a way to end her story that would be credible, and Dreiser's story of his sister's experience stimulated her thinking.

Both writers were eager to impress the public. Dreiser made his career as a novelist on tales of Emma, Mame, and Sylvia, his alluring, fecund, and flashy sisters who were bored with small-town, working-class life in Terre Haute, Indiana. As Emma later mused, "I don't know whether it was because we were poor or because Father was so insistent on the Catholic faith, but I was wild for anything that represented the opposite of what I had."[65] Her beleaguered and confused father lamented, "I done the best I could. The girls they won't ever agree, it seems." Jane Addams spotted such girls, immigrants or daughters of immigrants, disenchanted with the life their parents provided. "As these overworked girls stream along the street, the rest of us see only the self-conscious walk, the giggling speech, the preposterous clothing," she observed in *The Spirit of Youth and the City Streets*. "And yet through the huge hat, with its wilderness of bedraggled feathers, the girl announces to the world that she is here" (8). Perhaps no figure intrigued the American middle-class reading public more than the small figure under the bedraggled feathers. They wanted to hear about her experience in the city, and, at the same time, they wanted reassurance about her innocence. Any writer who wanted to appeal to this audience would need a plot that titillated readers and, at the same time, left the heroine an angel, albeit of the slums.

Florence Mabel Dedrick, a missionary at the Moody Church in Chicago, insisted, "There comes a time in nearly every girl's life when her cry is to go to the city."[66] As Herman Melville's Ishmael headed for the sea in the nineteenth century, midwestern girls headed for Chicago. Dedrick's essay appeared in a sensational exposé, *Fighting the Traffic in Young Girls or War on the White Slave Trade* (1910), that pandered to an excited public. The book's cover features a white slave behind bars, a pale but shapely young victim with a slim waist, bare shoulders, and long wavy hair, whose eyes stare hopefully upward to heaven as a ghostly male figure grabs for her body. The book features a series of essays on the sex trade in Chicago, written by associates of Jane Addams, including Edwin W. Sims, a U. S. district attorney, and Clifford G. Roe, a state's attorney. Although she mentioned Sims and Roe in her book, Addams worked to distance herself from the sentimental presentation of women and the hysterical prose of *Fighting the Traffic in Young Girls*.

Getting beyond the sensationalism of white slavery to tell stories about female experience in the city was nearly impossible for a writer of any sort. Addams's study of prostitution and Dreiser's second novel struggle to portray the poor woman in Chicago as mobile, intelligent, experi-

mental, pugnacious, and imaginative, but they fail because the manuscripts could not get beyond the public hysteria over white slavery. They
wrote for an audience obsessed with the vulnerability of the untended
"girl" from Europe or rural America imperiled by the seductions of urban life. In the popular imagination, young women adrift in the city were
unsuspecting victims of sexual predators. The public preferred that story to a more realistic depiction of young women forging neighborhood
communities, organizing labor unions, claiming their place in the city
and even shaping the manners and mores of middle-class America. Ostensibly investigations of the sex trade served as a warning to young
women in order to save them from crime but in reality they limited her
movement into the city and curbed her freedom, professional and educational as well as sexual, once she got there.

Sexual slavery functioned as an urban myth, used to scare the adventurous woman whose "cry is to go to the city." Florence Dedrick, of
course, understood the cry because she herself yearned for city life, as did
Jane Addams from small-town Illinois and the Dreiser sisters from Indiana. "It may be necessary through force of circumstances, or to develop
herself along the line of her cherished ambition, or a thirst for knowledge," Dedrick argued, certain that she had come to Chicago because of
her missionary calling, professional ambition, and desire for knowledge.
The women at Hull-House journeyed into Chicago for those reasons, too.
Dedrick carefully separated herself from the mass of working-class and
poor women who enter the city supposedly for tawdry reasons: "If it is
to satisfy the desire for mere personal happiness and enjoyment and craving for excitement, I say, 'Beware!' for here it is many slip and are lost."[67]
Any woman desiring happiness, enjoyment, and excitement is under
suspicion, and any woman succumbing to sexual cravings is beyond social respectability and, her message implied, beyond religious salvation.
It is difficult in the twenty-first century to imagine the distance created
in the early twentieth century between licit and illicit sex, the very borderland that Addams and Dreiser sought to depict.

Sexuality, then as now, is tied to gender but perhaps more so to social class and race, and certainly that was true in Chicago. From 1880 to
1900, the city's population tripled, bringing in poor women—European
immigrants, rural Americans, and southern African Americans. Close
quarters in tenement houses encouraged people to meet on the streets
and in public places, such as dance halls, ice cream parlors, amusement
parks, and nickelodeon theatres, where women and men intermingled
with a familiarity unapproved of in middle-class society. Crime commis-
sioners and social reformers labeled a wide variety of activities "prosti-

tution." Kathy Peiss, in *Cheap Amusements: Working Women and Leisure in Turn-of-the-Century New York* (1986), discovered in the actual records of the time that many young women flirted and engaged in sex for "treats," things they could not afford to buy with the money they earned from factory work, domestic service, or even sales and clerical jobs.[68] George Kneeland argued from his research that often such women, known as "charity girls," refused direct payment for sexual favors, preferring instead presents, attention, and pleasure from their encounters with men, the very vices that Dedrick noted. Historians have uncovered a central irony in the vice commissions at the turn of the last century: the moral panic over prostitution and sexual slavery in the United States came at a time when prostitution may have been waning because the availability of birth control devices allowed freer sexual behavior in dating. Perception of freer sexuality among middle-class women may explain the exaggerated attention to the white slave.

Sexual slavery, as an issue, had grown out of the movement against regulation of prostitution in England, led by the crusader Josephine Butler and Jane Addams's friend, the muckraking journalist William Stead. As a zealot to the cause, he had arranged to "buy" thirteen-year-old Eliza Armstrong from her parents for five pounds to prove that sexual slavery was indeed a national trade and, after the purchase was completed, used his success to launch a series of sensational articles in the *Pall Mall Gazette* entitled "The Maiden Tribute of Modern Babylon" (1885).[69] International conferences on sexual slavery—Geneva in 1877, Genoa in 1880, and Paris in 1902—led to the International Agreement for the Suppression of the White Slave Traffic, ratified by twelve nations in 1904. The United States responded with the Mann Act in 1910, prohibiting movement of women into the country and across state lines for purposes of sexual activity (over one thousand people were prosecuted under the Mann Act from 1910 to 1918). Judith Walkowitz, in *City of Dreadful Delight: Narratives of Sexual Danger in Late-Victorian England* (1992), notes that public outrage over white slavery had the unintended effect of dislodging feminists from power in England, handing the problem of prostitution over to male professionals, conservative churchmen, and advocates of social purity. The social purity movement advocated the burning and condemning of literature, especially novels by Balzac, Zola, and Rabelais in Europe. Sister movements in the United States had their eye on Dreiser after he published *Sister Carrie* in 1900.

Although contemporaries and scholars have found evidence of schemes to sexually enslave girls, the moral panic appears to have been a gross exaggeration. A report from the police department of the city of

Boston, issued in 1907, concluded: "Sober-minded persons employ [the term "white slavery"] as a convenience, often with an apology; but because of its sharp appeal to popular imagination it has become a plaything for persons of a different type, who use it to stimulate as well as to express a certain form of hysteria."[70] The police found no grounds for suspicion that young women were being forced into prostitution in the city. Teresa Billington-Grieg, likewise, called into question the sensational accounts of the period in an essay, "The Truth about Sexual Slavery" (1913); the truth being that she could find no official proof that "organized trapping" was occurring.[71] The following year in Massachusetts, a crime commission reported that stories of white slavery appeared to be based on hearsay and on fiction itself: "Several of the stories were easily recognized versions of incidents in certain books or plays."[72]

That is not to say that women were not coerced into sex for money. Coercion, however, most often took the form of economic necessity, as Emma Goldman metaphorically identified the beast in "The Traffic in Women" (1910): "Exploitation, of course; the merciless Moloch of capitalism that fattens on underpaid labor, thus driving thousands of women and girls into prostitution." Goldman voiced the radical view that the difference between marriage and prostitution was "merely a question of degree whether [a woman] sells herself to one man, in or out of marriage, or to many men."[73] Economic conditions for single women prohibited living on their own because factory workers or salesgirls earned $8 to $10 per week in 1910, hardly enough money to pay for room and board, certainly not enough to pay for clothing or amusements. A bargirl might earn $25 per week, a prostitute even more. Jane Addams, in *A New Conscience and an Ancient Evil*, warned that working-class women were especially vulnerable: "Their unspoiled human nature, not yet immune to the poisons of city life, when thrust into the midst of that unrelieved drudgery which lies at the foundation of all complex luxury, often results in the most fatal reactions" (161).

The Vice Commission of Chicago, in its report *The Social Evil in Chicago* (1911), typifies the official portrait of female sexual vulnerability: "Huddled away among coarse and vulgar male companions, lonely, underfed and hungry—hungry not only for food, but for a decent shelter, for a home, for friends, for a sympathetic touch or word; tired from a hard day's toil even to the point of recklessness—starving for honest pleasures and amusements—and with what does she meet?"[74] Huddled, hungry, filthy, outside the shelter of a sympathetic sisterhood, tainted by the indecencies of male companionship, poor women were seen as easy prey for white slavery, an international conspiracy to traffic in young women and girls. Although "white" explicitly distinguished the trade from black slavery, it tacitly supported the racism of American culture by focusing attention on the sexual enslavement of European American women even though traffic in women of color, especially Asian women sold in California, was more verifiable.[75]

Narratives of white slavery, like those in the Juvenile Protective Association report that Jane Addams used for her examples, follow a fairly regular pattern. The poor woman, always young and beautiful and usually white, leaves the country for the city (or Europe for America), finds herself tricked by wily slave traders, dark, suspicious types, often Jews or Italians, who lie in wait at train stations, hotels, dance halls, ice cream parlors, or movie houses, or linger outside sweatshops or in department stores. The swarthy men promise marriage or offer help with lodging, or they sometimes drug the heroine with chloroform or spiked drinks and haul her off to a brothel, where they force her to surrender her street clothes for filmy, lacy, flashy garments and lock her up. Her debasement and isolation heighten a plot meant to arouse the reader, who gets to peek at the life of sexual excess and vicariously experience the rape of innocence, from a comfortable middle-class armchair.

The white slave narrative offered a reductive and stylized version of female sexual experience in response to what Jeffrey Weeks terms a "moral panic" over the relocation of poor women to the city.[76] As Peter Stallybrass and Allon White theorize in *The Politics and Poetics of Transgression* (1986), the culturally high may seek to eliminate the low as a measure of prestige and status and yet ironically embrace the low as a "primary eroticized constituent of its own fantasy life." The dynamic results in a seeming paradox: "[W]hat is *socially* peripheral is so frequently *symbolically* central."[77] The socially marginal poor woman alone in the city, often an immigrant or a daughter of immigrants, came to symbolize the central issues surrounding women and social change in America. The movement of women out of the domestic sphere, female sexuality, divorce, birth control, venereal disease, female education, and even suffrage coalesced around her. Add to those issues nervousness over the rapid influx of immigrants to American cities, suspicion of differing racial and ethnic groups, fear of miscegenation and the taint of foreign blood, lamentation over the loss of rural agrarian culture, and anxiety over the strength of urban industrial capitalism.[78] The poor woman, pressed by economic necessity, reared outside genteel culture, often rebelling against immigrant customs, threatened middle-class society, who feared she might ignore their social codes, manners, and mores.

The pressure on young women workers, Addams concludes in *A New*

Conscience and an Ancient Evil, might cause social and economic rebellion. "The long hours, the lack of comforts, the low pay, the absence of recreation, the sense of 'good times' all about her which she cannot share, the conviction that she is rapidly losing health and charm," Addams warns her middle-class readers, "rouse the molten forces within her" (77). The molten forces suggest a power that might lead to labor unions, political demonstrations, and insistence on radical change in family life, domesticity, sexuality, and labor, as well as in the merging and blending of ethnic and racial groups in the city. Addams gets to the brink of a revolutionary course of action for poor urban women: "The girls, realizing [the] inability on the part of their mothers, elated by that sense of independence which the first taste of self-support always brings, sheltered from observation during certain hours, are *almost as free from social control as is the traditional young man* who comes up from the country to take care of himself in a great city" (29; emphasis added). The depiction of young women "almost as free" as young men would seem to embody the radical social change that Addams's economic analysis would seem to advocate—higher wages, better jobs, more leisure time for athletics, and more discretion in choosing amusements. She gets all the way to this image of the unfettered working-class female and then recoils.

Why, we have to ask, did Addams back away from the logical conclusions of her own argument? The problem for Jane Addams in writing a book about fallen women, even prostitutes, is that she could not write a convincing story about her encounters with them. As Allen Davis observes, she never actually talked with young women who had gone "wrong."[79] Without firsthand knowledge, and with an apparent distaste for personal or professional contact across the sexual borders of middle-class respectability, how could she tell any story with credibility? That limitation made her wary of writing the book in the first place. What rings false about *A New Conscience and an Ancient Evil* is that Addams does not adopt the dress or the voice of a prostitute. Unlike portraits in her earlier books, her stories come third- or fourth-hand from vice commission reports that themselves come from court cases based supposedly on the testimony of prostitutes and investigators. As a result, Addams's stories take the form of the conventional narrative. The effect of the process is to remove the dialogic texture and to flatten the prose. What she promises her reader is the voice of a mature onlooker: the book "endeavors to present the contributory causes, as they have become registered in my consciousness through a long residence in a crowded city quarter" (10). She delivers a series of plots that might come from fiction as much as from fact. The young women are all angels of the slum akin to the heroines of white slave narratives—gullible, unskilled, uneducated, confused, powerless, inarticulate, and very much in need of a mother. The mature narrative voice, belonging to the professional settlement worker, makes the argument through a series of "grisly" stories.

Often no more than children, the slum angels enter Chicago as innocents and fall under the weight of forces they never understand. Marie, "a French girl, the daughter of a Breton stone mason, so old and poor that he was obliged to take her from her convent school at the age of twelve years" (18), is accosted on her way to buy milk by a procurer who plies her with sweets and pictures of show girls in America. Once she has been lured to Chicago, she is pressed into prostitution, earning $250 per week for the "pander," or pimp, nothing for herself. Olga, whose mother returns to Sweden, is left in Chicago to fend for herself, but "a friendless girl of such striking beauty could not escape the machinations of those who profit by the sale of girls" (30). Driven mad by her pursuers, Olga is arrested, and at the point of being sent to prison she is rescued by the Juvenile Protective Association. Her story reinforces Addams's point that "no one can safely live without companionship and affection" (33), that is to say, without the support and direction of other women, especially the social workers in the city. Likewise, a young factory girl from a Bohemian family living in Milwaukee is fooled by the promise of marriage (38).

In every configuration, the girl appears in Addams's evolutionary model as an urban primitive: "Because she is of the first generation of girls which has stood alone in the midst of trade, she is clinging and timid" (66). The young woman may wish to assert her independence: "We all know that the American girl has grown up in the belief that the world is hers from which to choose, that there is ordinarily no limit to her ambition or to her definition of success" (67). But such exaggerated self-confidence is dangerous, Addams warns in example after example, because everywhere hovers the pimp or "cadet." She concludes that society must keep girls in school for an additional six and a half years, not a bad idea if education were the goal, but it is not.

Addams assumes—here the eroticized transgressor loses her power as a symbol of social change—that poor women eventually want to become wives and mothers: "[T]he great business of youth is securing a mate, as the young instinctively understand" (167). Young women are to be protected by the strong moral arms of the new professional class of women who come from colleges and universities, the type of professionals Jane Addams gathered at Hull-House. Her answer to patriarchal sexual exploitation, as it turns out, is matriarchal protection arising from the "primitive maternal instinct" to nurture and defend (192): "The chastity of the modern woman of self-directed activity and of a varied circle of interests, which gives her an acquaintance with many men as well as women, has therefore a new value and importance in the establishment of social standards" (211). Social workers have come to the city for adventure but have earned respectability by not indulging in cheap amusements. Margit Stange has it right when she describes the New Woman in her study *Personal Property: Wives, White Slaves, and the Market in Women* (1998): "Remaining erect at her public post, she must endure public exposure without falling into commodification, repeatedly fulfilling her civic obligations while still guarding her chastity."[80] Addams makes the same point that Florence Dedrick makes: "As woman, however, fulfills her civic obligations while still guarding her chastity, she will be in position as never before to uphold the 'single standard,' demanding that men shall add the personal virtues to their performance of public duties" (211). The urban woman must avoid even a hint of sexuality and thus serve as a model even to urban males.

Walter Lippmann, in *A Preface to Politics* (1914), puzzles over the tone of *A New Conscience and an Ancient Evil*, calling it "an hysterical book, just because the real philosophical basis of Miss Addams' thinking was not deliberate enough to withstand the shock of a poignant horror."[81] Allen Davis pronounces it "an hysterical book, also sentimental and naïve."[82] He complains that Addams took up the issue of sexual slavery because it was a popular topic that served to heighten her public image as "Saint Jane"; moreover, he charges that she bullied *McClure's Magazine* and Macmillan into paying her twice for the same material.

If we were to strip the book of its "poignant horror"—by which term Lippmann meant the stories of sexual slavery—and follow the logic of Addams's argument about poor women and work, we would find an economic analysis closely paralleling Charlotte Perkins Gilman's in *Women and Economics* (1899). The two women first met in California in 1894 at the annual meeting of the Federation of Woman's Clubs, Gilman claiming Addams as a friend and advocate. Addams found the meetings themselves uninspiring, and yet she stayed in contact with her new friend, inviting her to stay at Hull-House after Gilman was gracelessly evicted from California for "debt and failure." Gilman traveled from California to Chicago in 1896, spending three months at Hull-House with Jane Addams. Their discussions resulted in a curious cross-pollination, each woman borrowing from the other without either woman, as it turns out, finding the trade quite comfortable.

Gilman, gratified by the intellectual audience at Hull-House, had found visceral contact with the poor repulsive. Well before the obligatory six months residency was over, Addams arranged for her to run a settlement house on the North Side in a neighborhood known as Little Hell. Gilman eyes the grim prospect in her autobiography: "The loathly river flowed sluggishly near by, thick and ill-smelling; Goose Island lay black in the slow stream." The social ideal of living among the poor placed her in a toxic environment, much as it would today. "Everywhere a heavy dinginess," she writes, "low, dark brick factories and gloomy wooden dwellings often below the level of the street; foul plank sidewalks, rotten and full of holes; black mud underfoot, damp soot drifting steadily down over everything."[83] She turned the work of running the settlement over to Helen Campbell—"my interest was in all humanity, not merely the under side of it, in sociology, not social pathology"—and spent the next years traveling and giving lectures.

Gilman was already thinking about her sociological treatise, *Women and Economics*, and was pleased to have Addams's support for the project: "She is really impressed with the big new idea. To have her see it is a great help," she wrote in her diary.[84] Her study compares prostitution to marriage, both providing the payment of money for the comfort of sex. "Because of the economic dependence of the human female on her mate," Gilman theorizes, "she is modified to sex to an excessive degree."[85] Addams's study of the sexual behavior of poor and working-class women owes much to Gilman's analysis. Sex becomes a commodity in the public square as surely as it does in the private sphere, yet for Addams the vulnerable young woman must seek the moral sanctity of marriage. Her reading public would have found any other ending deeply offensive. An educated, upper-middle-class woman might avoid marriage altogether by finding a professional equivalent or substitute for marriage, one that would provide a comfortable living, but beyond that putatively asexual existence, no writer—Gilman, Addams, or Dreiser—would dare venture.[86]

Dreiser had asked Jane Addams for an essay on the topic of the widow and her child in the summer of 1910 because it was the very topic that perplexed him as he finished writing *Jennie Gerhardt*. Although he began writing the novel in 1901, immediately after the publication of *Sister Carrie*, Dreiser fretted over the story, abandoning it for years. When he finally finished it in 1911, he kept his eye on the Boston Watch and Ward Society and the New York Society for the Suppression of Vice (sister societies to the Chicago Vice Commission and the Illinois Vigilance Association that Addams relied on for her book), knowing that the threat of censorship would force deep editing of his manuscript and fearing that without successful publication of his second novel, his career as novel-

ist—he was thirty-nine and author, at the time, of one morally questionable novel—might well be over.

He had tried but failed to interest George Brett in his book and finally published a version of his early manuscript, one bowdlerized by Rip-
ley Hitchcock at Harpers. The editors removed Dreiser's depictions of the
coarseness of city life, his descriptions of drinking, the dialogue he had
written in slang, and all profanity. Hitchcock pandered to the social purity crowd by excising discussions of birth control, descriptions of the
hero's "feral" sex drive, and any trace of the heroine's sexual desire or
power.[87] The published edition that Jane Addams read in the winter of
1912 denied its heroine adventure, desire, and especially pleasure.

Dreiser's question was one that Addams had not been able to answer
herself. What community would be likely to accept a fallen woman?
Dreiser finally places Jennie Gerhardt in Sandwood, a neighborhood of
lake-short cottages north of Chicago, her erotic energy exhausted. Her
lover has died as well as their daughter; she, as a widow of sorts, adopts
two children and embodies the sanitized safety of the suburbs, where
second-generation Americans were being absorbed into bland patterns of
economic and political conformity. As Elizabeth Ewen explains in *Immigrant Women in the Land of Dollars* (1985), "Successful adoption of
the suburban consumer ideal meant hiding all traces of one's roots. All
telltale signs of the old way were smothered."[88] The smothering of even
his own immigrant culture may have soothed Dreiser as he made his way
into American literary society.

Addams also sought suburban retreat from the city. With money from
the estate of Joseph Tilton Bowen, Louise DeKoven Bowen's husband, and
a $50,000 gift from Julius Rosenwald, the Chicago settlement bought a
version of Sandwood, establishing the Joseph Tilton Bowen Country Club
in June 1912, a natural landscape that seemed untouched by human design. The motto of the country club was: "Secure from the slow stain of
the world's contagion." The sexual energy of the city left her in as much
doubt as it did Dreiser about the effect of the "slow stain." Addams didn't
buy the "bed of roses" ending at Sandwood, perhaps because she thought
the ease in which Jennie joins middle-class society was unconvincing.
And yet, Addams hadn't found any better way to end the tale. The slum
angel in her analysis could find shelter only in the hands of the nurturing professional women of the settlement house, and, ultimately, in legitimate marriage. Dreiser's novel and Addams's narrative may have
calmed readers eager to deny the social changes that poor, rural, and
immigrant women brought with them to Chicago.

Macmillan advertised *A New Conscience and an Ancient Evil* in language that fell just short of the rhetoric of lurid exposés. "A work to be seriously pondered by every serious man and woman," the copy read. "Actual experiences of those who have investigated the 'white-slave' traffic, and often the stories of girls who have been drawn into the net— are the things of which Miss Addams's book is made," the publisher promises. "Absolutely frank in its treatment of the social evil, startling in its revelations, judicious in its suggestions and sympathetic in its viewpoint." The advertisement itself teeters between startling and judicious. The audience for the book differed, as Brett had predicted, from the readers of the series in *McClure's* magazine, but both publishing venues attracted the curious, many of whom sent letters to the author.

Young female readers felt camaraderie with Addams, prompting many to write intimately. Charlotte Howett Lansey, for example, wrote a mash note, of sorts: "It is impossible for one woman to make a declaration of adoration for another, and yet this is exactly what I am doing."[89] Phoebe Willets saw the sensationalism of the white-slave narrative as literary sightseeing. "Your book is another example of this method of money getting; is it not?" she queried.[90] Willets placed Addams's own sexual experience under scrutiny, noting that she had never "been married to a good man and attained a normal view of certain relations." Another letter from Willets arrived the next week, this one even more admonitory. "'Miss Addams is beginning to see the *world* through Hull House *windows*' and I feel you should be asked to consider if this is not *true?*"[91] As Addams gained celebrity, the letter charged, she lost her ability to judge her own writing. "You are *too certain* of general acclamation," she continued. "You do not see your limitations, perhaps because of flattery." Willets showed her hand at the end of letter as she condemned Addams's efforts in the suffrage movement as evil and hysterical.

A typical complaint among magazine readers was her use of "cadet" as a term for a pimp. She received a flood of protests from military men, who thought of themselves as cadets. Charles N. Sawyer, for example, wrote: "It is with a sense of pain that I have of late seen it used in anything but a manly sense."[92] The letter serves as a signal of how quickly Addams will fall from grace as she opposes the First World War. "And with more pain," Sawyer warned her, "have I found it in the articles of a noble woman whose life has been devoted to the service of others." As many readers perceived her to be openly political, they became critical of her as a writer.

Her book hit a nerve with readers who questioned her view of gender difference. H. H. Herbst, from the Huron Valley Building and Savings Association, read the magazine version and took Addams to task on the issue of frankness. "So far as I can learn, there is but slight difference in the sexual passions of boys and girls from 16 years up," he observed, adding that it would "appall the ordinary reader" to learn how many boys and girls between the ages of 15 and 22, "school mates, companions and ordinary acquaintances," indulge in unlawful sexual intercourse. He pointed out that, in his experience, males are no more likely than females to be sexual aggressors: "They enter into such relations thoughtlessly, spurred on by passion, at times favorable to the act."[93] The sexually inquisitive and aggressive Dreiser sisters, languishing in Terre Haute and yearning to try their luck in Chicago, may have been more typical than anyone wanted to say.

B. A. Behrend of the Institute of Electrical Engineers was considerably agitated about the very idea that illicit sex might leave a woman relatively unscarred.[94] He wanted Addams to know about a twenty-seven-year-old woman, who was president of her church society, vice-president of her college fraternity, a teacher at a women's college, and a seemingly respectable member of her community. Behrend knew, however, that for five years she had had an affair with a young Harvard lawyer and that they had engaged in acts, "which included every indecent practice known to degenerates like those practiced by Stanford White." More astonishing to Behrend was the medical report: "A physical examination showed that owing to the unnatural nature of the practices, no physical injury had been done to her." Moreover, the young woman, seven years later, appeared mentally and intellectually normal, not to say professionally successful. He confided to Addams that he had read the letters written during the affair, although "the offending man had used such gross immoral expressions and such utterly vile degenerate language that even the hardened detectives blushed with shame and declined to act, stating that no woman could be so innocent and ignorant as not to know the moral wrong of such matters." He concluded that the "fallen" woman is a Jekyll and Hyde and admitted he had continued to introduce her into polite society. Perhaps hoping for expiation, he sent Jane Addams a check for $50: "Please accept it as a sacrifice on the altar of human suffering." The letter suggests the strong desire for sexual knowledge that readers of the white-slave narratives must have felt, coupled with their perplexity about what to do with the new knowledge when they got it.

Bull Moose Woman

It is not too much to say that from 1912 to 1915, Jane Addams became the best-known public woman in the world and that her writing became more political than literary, more practical than philosophical. The man who wooed her into politics was Theodore Roosevelt. He began courting Jane Addams in a 1911 Halloween letter marked *"Private."* The letter ostensibly delivered a review of *A New Conscience and an Ancient Evil,* lecturing her on sexuality and proper behavior. Considering the Vice Commission in Chicago and its effort to extinguish the social evil, he concurred that boys and girls ought to be treated in the same fashion, and he endorsed, as Addams did, chastity for both genders. Yet Roosevelt questioned equal suffrage as the way to promote fairer treatment of women in society. "I am a woman suffragist," he announced, only to take it back, "but I have never regarded the cause of woman suffrage as being of really capital moment."[95] Sounding thoroughly conventional, he reminded her that a woman's primary duties are wifehood and motherhood. How could he have missed the irony that Addams had never married or had children? As a good politician, however, he ended the letter with a hook, urging her to let him know when she planned to be in New York City.

By July, Roosevelt was back in touch with Addams through their mutual friend Ben Lindsey. She and Roosevelt were at loggerheads about how the Progressive Party, newly organized and scheduled for a convention at the Coliseum in Chicago in August, should respond to the issue of female suffrage. She wanted an equal suffrage plank in the party platform. Lindsey relayed the message to her that Roosevelt was having a "change of heart," coming to agree with her that the convention might be energized by championing the cause of women. Certainly, he knew that the women in the United States had strong networks of clubs, associations, and committees that might coalesce around his campaign, giving his candidacy the vitality it would need to win male votes.

When the Bull Moose came to town in August 1912, Addams participated with remarkable vigor in the rough exchanges of ideas on the convention floor. As she focused her attention on arguments for women's suffrage, she was blindsided by the issue of race. Teddy Roosevelt had seated white delegates, whether from the North or the South, but drew a line (the old line, actually) between northern blacks and southern blacks, some of whom he opposed seating. Addams stood before the platform committee to oppose Roosevelt's decision, urging that black delegates be seated, all of them, alongside whites. Letters of support came swiftly from around the country. The Colored Woman's Civic Club cheered her effort: "We extend heartiest thanks for the courageous stand taken in defense of the Negro."[96] J. F. Ransom offered the "thanks of my race for your brave stand before the platform committee of the National Progressive Convention."[97]

Other observers viewed the event with skepticism. W. M. Trotter responded from Boston that she must not sell out to Roosevelt and betray the cause by seconding his nomination. Trotter pointed out the irony: "Women suffrage will be stained with Negro blood."[98] In the fullest response to the political machinations going on in Chicago, a minister from New York, P. C. Allen, wrote: "To the national Progressive association I wish to state that on spite of the edict or stand of Colonel T. R. he have made the greatest mistake of his life. I had taken stand for him in this so call bull moose Party despite his stand againts the Black Race. I am a minister of the gospel I did think he was taking the rite stand but seeing the stuff he is maid of we shall do all we can to defeat him. Remember we are men and flesh and blood as any other man and if this is free country we want to be free not part free & part slaves."[99] Caught between two inequities, Addams chose the one closer to her experience and stood before the convention to second the nomination of Roosevelt.

Hamlin Garland called her performance at the convention a "thunder-bolt" speech.[100] Wallace Thayer, a delegate, described the nomination scene as a revival meeting to bring Union and Confederate soldiers together for the first time since the Civil War. Roosevelt's compromise had the effect of blurring differences between the North and South. "Indeed," Thayer remembered, "the keynote of this convention was not struck till the afternoon of the third and last day, when the first and most beloved woman in the land—the first woman ever called to the platform of a national political convention—seconded the nomination."[101] Her speech moved the group into female territory. The Progressive Party was worth the effort, she argued, because of its pledge to protect children, the aged, and the laboring poor: "Committed to these humane undertakings, it is inevitable that such a party should appeal to women, should seek to draw upon the great reservoir of their normal energy so long undesired and unutilized in practical politics."[102]

The plank that won her support read: "The Progressive Party, believing that no people can justly claim to be a true democracy which denies political rights on account of sex, pledges itself to the task of securing equal suffrage to men and women alike." On August 8, Roosevelt's thank-you arrived by telegraph—impersonal, detached, very much in the tone of a thundering statesman: "I PRIZE YOUR ACTION NOT ONLY BECAUSE OF WHAT YOU ARE AND STAND FOR, BUT BECAUSE OF WHAT IT SYMBOLIZES FOR THE NEW MOVEMENT. IN THIS GREAT NATIONAL CONVENTION STARTING THE NEW PARTY WOMEN HAVE THEREBY BEEN SHOWN TO HAVE THEIR PLACE TO FILL PRECISELY AS MEN HAVE, AND ON AN ABSOLUTE EQUALITY."[103] Not mollified by his slippery use of the passive verb, "have thereby been shown to have," Addams and her cohorts demanded clarification. His critics tried to warn Addams that Roosevelt was, at heart, a "blooming hypocrite." A second telegram arrived the next day in a more playfully pragmatic voice: "DID I PUT INTO TELEGRAM THE FLAT FOOTED STATEMENT WITHOUT QUALIFICATION OR EQUIVOCATION THAT I AM FOR WOMAN SUFFRAGE THAT THE PROGRESSIVE PARTY IS FOR WOMEN SUFFRAGE AND THAT I BELIEVE WITHIN HALF A DOZEN YEARS WE SHALL HAVE NO ONE IN THE U.S. AGAINST IT IF NOT PLEASE WIRE ME IF THERE IS ANYTHING FURTHER OF ANY KIND YOU WISH ME TO PUT IN."[104]

The political heat she took for her seconding speech can be felt even today in reading the letters that followed. The Anti-Imperialist League attacked Roosevelt for opposing Philippine independence and supporting tariffs and the appropriation of the Panama Canal. Her Socialist friends saw Roosevelt as a double-dealer. Her pacifist friends wondered how she could overlook Roosevelt's bellicosity. The Prohibition Party noted dryly that they had always included a platform plank in favor of suffrage, although Addams had never supported their candidates. Some members of the Progressive Party itself announced that they were leaving because of the compromise on race.

The *New York Times* telegraphed a request for her to write an article, and she scribbled at the bottom, "Sorry impossible to take on any more writing."[105] After the fireworks, Addams slipped out of town, seeking the solitude of Bar Harbor. From her retreat, the newly politicized Jane Addams began her campaign to bring other women along with her into the Progressive Party. She enlisted Lillian Wald in a letter that reveals the state of her mind following the Bull Moose Convention: "In spite of much criticism and difference of opinion, I have never doubted for a moment that my 'place' was inside when there was a chance to help or back a program as this one."[106] And then she turned to the personal: "How are you, dear Lady! I came yesterday, and am enjoying it mightily here in spite of the fact that I torn away from my new political duties very abruptly." A woman over fifty could make such an escape. Louise Bowen hosted her at Bar Harbor, and she planned to see Mary Smith in Bethel, Maine, later in the week.

Addams exchanged 135 letters—counting only the ones that have survived—in August, receiving and writing sometimes five or six a day. Although she was on holiday in Bar Harbor, her friends, colleagues, and new political cronies found her. Mary McDowell wrote as a supportive friend and admiring colleague: "How great you were to carry off a political party at the strategic moment."[107] She had read the story unfolding in the newspapers. Addams managed "to seize that moment when a new party was born," she declared. "[Y]ou and no one else was ready by experience and personality to do the deed and you did it perfectly, I think." Anna Howard Shaw, president of the National American Woman Suffrage Association, praised Addams's speech as "so different from those wearisome and fulsome addresses," including Roosevelt's own.[108] "I wish I could believe in him," Shaw confessed, echoing what many women were feeling.

Mabel T. Boardman, President of the woman's advisory committee of the Republican Party, wrote a letter to the *New York Times* that drew a strong response from Bar Harbor. In a neat reversal of the female sphere, she accused Addams of using Hull-House, a public and professional institution, for personal and political ends. The Boardman letter reminds us how unironic public life in the United States can be. In her letter of response, Addams coolly pointed out that association with Hull-House did not disqualify anyone from citizenship, nor did it cancel out the constitutional guarantee of free speech. "I have followed my best judgment and conscience," Addams found herself confessing, "and cannot agree with Miss Boardman that I have violated any obligations to Hull House or any other associations with which I may be connected."[109] In a Lincolnesque line, she concluded: "It is a question whether any society or institution has a right to stultify its officers. On the contrary an institution reveals its own weakness when it cares more for its position and influence than for the very cause itself." Roosevelt hoped to harness her charisma for his campaign, asking her the very next day about the possibility of turning her attention to the Progressive Party and its causes. "I wish very much you would write one or two pieces on the new movement and what we Progressives are striving for in the way of social justice."[110] He knew that no other female writer in the country had more admiring readers.

Edward Bok was suspicious of her overtly political writing and returned articles she sent him about the Progressive Party, making the excuse that they arrived too late for publication before the election. He pledged to vote for Roosevelt, no doubt, to placate her. What he really wanted was a series of regular columns to appear after the election in *Ladies' Home Journal.* He suggested topics such as labor issues, social welfare, and ethical questions, knowing that these were the issues that most appealed to her. "I would rather have you than any other woman in the land," he flattered. "What it calls for is an easy, popular explanatory style."[111] He suggested twenty-five hundred words per topic, not too much for his female readers, intellectually delicate as he believed them to be, and he offered to pay $250 per piece.

Addams took on both tasks in the fall of 1912, writing the baldly political articles that Teddy Roosevelt needed and sending them to Edward Bok for the "easy, popular explanatory" column he desired. The columns were, however, too political for Bok, who complained, "[T]hey are newspapery in style." He wanted her to add characteristic tales from the street, the literary dressing and cross-dressing her readers enjoyed. "I see no reason why if you elaborate these articles by stories &c, and omit any Progressive Party references, much the same material, worked over, could be used."[112] He sent detailed outlines for each article and hoped to toss out the one she wanted on women's suffrage. "[Equal suffrage] is the only 'plank' in the Progressive platform that I can't 'see.' Dense, am I not?" He ordered six columns: experience in politics, problems of the working girl, vital needs of children, high cost of living, supporting a family from prison, and amelioration of labor wrongs.

At the same time that she made the deal with Bok, Addams found an agent, Virgil V. McNitt, from the Central Press Association, to market her six Progressive Party Platform statements to newspapers around the country. She put herself to the task in August and September, writing six short position papers from eleven hundred to fourteen hundred words in length: "The Progressive Party and the Needs of the Children," "The Progressive Party and the Protection of the Immigrant," "The Progressive Party and the Claims of the Disinherited," "The Progressive Party and Safeguards for Working Girls," "The Progressive Party and Organized Labor," and "The Progressive Party and Woman's Suffrage."

Selling political propaganda, as we might imagine, was not easy. McNitt tried to explain his failure to find buyers: "In the first place, I owe you an apology for my poor guessing as to the financial results which might be counted upon."[113] Any other series by Addams would be expected to sell well, but newspapers that did not support Teddy Roosevelt certainly did not want to pay her to campaign for him. McNitt managed to collect $925 with $616.66 going to Addams. Papers in the Scripps McRae League paid $175, the *New York Evening Mail* $200, and the *Kansas City Star* $125, but other papers, including the *Chicago Tribune*, were reluctant to pay much for a series that would be available for free as her speeches were reported. The articles showed up in the *Chicago Tribune* and other places across the Midwest—the *Indianapolis Star, Detroit News, Kansas City Times*—and in the Eastern papers—*Boston Traveler and Evening Herald, New York Evening Mail,* and *Philadelphia North American*—and as far west as the *Los Angeles Daily Tribune.* Not every paper picked up every piece but her voice was a clear and strong one in the drive to elect Teddy Roosevelt. After selling the political statements to newspapers, Addams recycled them into editorials for the *Ladies' Home Journal* series, beginning in January 1913 with "Philanthropy and Politics," followed each month by "The Children of the Nation," "Current Legislation for Working Women," "Prison Labor and Prisoners' Families," "The Protection of Immigrants," "Public Dance Halls: The Need of Supervision," "The Need of Woman's Vote in the Modern State," and "Recreation—A Function of City Government." Bok got much of what he wanted along with the editorial on woman's suffrage that he did not.

It was at the Bull Moose Convention that Jane Addams began to redesign herself as a professional woman. Her writing at Bar Harbor during the fall of 1912 did much to establish her identity as a public figure. In the essay "Philanthropy and Politics," she argued for women on the public stage, urging them to enter national politics on a journey that would lead women in general and her in particular into international public life.[114] Increasingly, Addams saw the necessity to move settlement work into public policy (the effort would have, although she could not know it, the unintended consequence of diminishing the power of women in public life). Another political position paper, "The Progressive Party and Organized Labor," warned that eight-hour workdays and six-day weeks ought to be legislated to protect the working class from industry and to protect the middle class from the trauma of social upheaval.[115] In the paper that Bok discouraged, "The Progressive Party and Woman Suffrage," she took issue with the notion that only when women remain outside the political arena can they comment on the turmoil of men with a disinterested wisdom reserved for nonparticipants. The world outside politics resides in "chilly places remote from real life," and women who remain outside the public sphere "also keep out of the real life."[116] Addams used herself as a character in "The Steps by which I Became a Progressive."[117] Her long experiments and struggles led her to the Progressive Party, the collective hero of her tale, a hero who is "intelligent and conscientious," committed to social justice. She sent the longer essay, "Philanthropy and Politics," to Bok on September 18, 1912.

On the same day, Addams sent another essay to McClure, entitled "The Progressive Party and Social Legislation," telling the story of how various constituencies—the American Economic Association, the National Conference of Charities and Corrections, the Civil Service Reform League, and others—hammered out a party platform that met "the fundamental obligation of adapting the legal order to the changed conditions of national life."[118] One compromise that troubled her was the Progressive Party plank that called for the building of two battleships. In a moment of candor, Addams reviewed her own early book on peace: "[F]or many years I had . . . followed one line, pursuing the subject through a long dull book entitled the 'Newer Ideals of Peace,' I had contended that peace is no longer an abstract dogma but that marked manifestations of 'a newer dynamic peace' are found in that new internationalism promoted by the men of all nations who are determined upon the abolition of degrading poverty, disease, and intellectual weakness with their resulting inefficiency and tragedy." The Bull Moose Convention forced her to forego the purity of pacifism for the pragmatism of industrial amelioration. Another compromise that haunted her in the essay concerned the seating of delegates from the South during the Bull Moose Convention.

Her long-time friend Jenkin Lloyd Jones, the liberal Unitarian minister and editor of *Unity*, read the essay in October and cautioned her about the price of party affiliation: "I think it is partly because of a feeling that you are 'too big a man' to be identified with any party agitation or as a leader of party enthusiasm, which under the best of circumstances destroys the perspective and does violence to the proportions."[119] Jones had it right that the only man who fitted the Bull Moose platform may have been Roosevelt himself. Clearly those carrying the water for him felt the weight.

Norman Hapgood forced a considerable compromise from Addams in another version of the essay, this one entitled "Pragmatism in Politics," published in *Survey*. "Mr. Paul Kellogg gave me the pleasure of reading this article because he wanted to know what I thought of the political effect of the negro part," his letter to her cautiously began. Kellogg, the editor of *Survey*, employed Hapgood to deliver the message about the political advantages and risks in publishing the longer essay: "Of course, if it squared with your conscience the best thing politically would be to use the rest of the article with the negro part left out."[120] Jane Addams "squared" things with her conscience and agreed to literary segregation: *Survey* published the white version of the essay without the "negro part," and *Crisis* published the black section of the essay as "The Progressive Party and the Negro" with a frank admission: "Possibly this is all we can do at the present moment."[121]

With fatigue in her voice, Addams wrote to Sophonisba Breckinridge in September, "I have finished six articles for the Central Press, hoping they may help the Progressive Party."[122] In the midst of such practical toil, she was grinding away on a longer piece for McClure. "I have to remind myself quite often," she joked, "of the $500.00 fee and the good of the cause."

We are reminded that while she was a political figure of some note in 1912, she was also a woman over fifty supposedly on vacation in Bar Harbor. On September 6, Jane Addams turned fifty-two, celebrating her birthday with Louise Bowen and Mary Smith, whose gift was a trip to

Egypt, one they planned to take in the next year. As Mary watched the changes in Jane, she yearned to spend more time together. The Maine Coast that late summer was especially lovely and the three women found time, even in the face of the political battle and the pressure of authorship, to relax in the privacy of their retreat. After visiting them, Bok noted, "I was delighted to see you look so well and rested the other day."[123]

The essays she crafted in the fall made their way into newspapers across the country, bringing the recognition of her name and face—one that functioned as an icon especially after the success of her autobiography—to the cause of the Progressive Party. The final essay was "The Progressive's Dilemma: The New Party," an article that appeared in *The American Magazine* just before the election. Under a banner that caricatured candidates and mascots—an elephant, a donkey, a goat, and a moose—Addams testified to her twenty-three years of social work as the basis of her political credo. "I have become identified with the Progressive Party," she began, and followed that statement with a string of sentences, all beginning with "I": "I have seen," "I have known," "I have witnessed," "I have lived," "I am happy," "I believe," and "I am further convinced."[124] Reading the short essay is like watching the grand finale at a fireworks display on the Fourth of July.

Addams left Bar Harbor after six weeks of rest and writing and began a month-long campaign trek across the Northeast and Midwest by train, speaking along the route for woman's suffrage and for Teddy Roosevelt. She traveled first to Barraboo, Wisconsin, on October 3, for a political rally organized by Zona Gale. On October 10, she arrived in Detroit and then moved on to New York City, Boston, Indianapolis, Gary, and back to Saginaw, Michigan. After only a day of rest, she arrived in Oklahoma City on October 21; from there she traveled to Kansas, Nebraska, Iowa, Minnesota, North and South Dakota, Colorado, and Missouri, all before November 4. Along the campaign trail, the Jane Addams Chorus rallied the troops with "The Song of the Child-Slave" sung to the tune of "Old Black Joe." Olive Dorsey Gray, also know as "Daisy Deane," had penned the lyrics from the Hotel del Rey in California:

> See the child-slaves, such a tired toiling band
> Prisoned in factories in our fair freedom's land
> Toiling in mines, underground and dark as night:
> With weary little eyes that never see daylight:
> Oh, the children, little children:
> With weary forms bent low:
> Toiling in the mine and factory
> For—Pluto.

The Progressive Party, all the songs promise, would battle against wage slavery. The campaigns of the early twentieth century, carried on at local rallies on routes along the railroad tracks, looked a good deal like campaigns today staged for a mass television audience.

Surrounded by cheering crowds and unembarrassed by the music, she delivered speech after speech, declaring in a letter to Alice, "I am quite enjoying my campaigning."[125] Voters wanted to hear her voice, publishers wanted to print her words, and she emerged from the throng invigorated by the visceral experience.

The day after the election as the Progressives won over four million popular votes and eighty-eight votes in the Electoral College—not enough to win but enough to split the Republican tally with William H. Taft and hand the victory to the Democrat Woodrow Wilson. Teddy Roosevelt moaned, "WE HAVE GONE DOWN TO DISASTER."[126] Addams wrote ostensibly to console him in his loss: "Perhaps I may have an opportunity to tell you then the tremendous impulse the campaign has given to social reform. I had never dared hope that within my life-time thousands of people would so eagerly participate in their discussion."[127] More in triumph than defeat, she traveled to Philadelphia for the National Suffrage Convention on November 24. Returning to Chicago, she spoke at the City Club on November 27, telling her audience how pleased she was with the Progressive Party and its power to move local issues onto a national stage.

George Brett had watched Addams through the weeks leading up to the election. He called Roosevelt's bid "problematic" and suggested that the effort may well reach fruition during the 1916 election, an idea that most Progressives wanted to believe. "It seems to me that you might," Brett enticed her, "if you choose, aid very much in this success if you felt able, and willing, to write a little book which should give in short chapters, i.e., one devoted to each subject, an account of the chief ills of our present civilization."[128] The project he had in mind would allow her to collect the political pieces she was smoothing out for Bok at *Ladies' Home Journal* into a book. Two days after the election, Addams suggested that the six articles she was finishing for Bok might grow to twelve. "If I find that any of the material would be available for a book, I shall be very glad to communicate with you later," she wrote, and then to slow him down, she added, "although I rather doubt it."[129] And thus he had his answer—yes and no. "I may, I hope, confidently count upon the material being sufficient for the making of a book," he responded, trusting that the seed would take root.

Addams wrote to Robert Underwood Johnson, the editor of *Century*

Magazine, that she would send him fourteen hundred words in an open letter: "I am afraid I cannot promise to have them there in time for the January number as I find an accumulation of work upon my return here."[130] Johnson had worked in Chicago early in his career and was sympathetic to the social work that Addams was doing. Along with John Muir, he worked to establish Yosemite National Park and shared with Addams, the Pinchots, and other Progressives a desire to conserve natural resources. A month later, Addams retracted her offer: "I have already promised so much writing that I find it utterly impossible to write one word for the open letter."[131] Her play with language in the letter sounds like Teddy Roosevelt's rhetoric: "I am sorry to have marched up the hill so vigorously and then apparently to march down again, but I am unusually busy this fall and have less time than usual for any writing." On November 26, Addams met with Progressive Party leaders, including Teddy Roosevelt, at the home of the Pinchots. Gifford, an environmental advocate and organizer of the Progressive effort in 1912, and Cornelia, an advocate for women's rights, had become friends and political allies of hers over the course of the campaign.

Ida Tarbell, who had been invited to the meeting, wanted to see her friend but wanted nothing to do with the others. She explained in a note: "[I]f you are get-at-able anywhere this evening I should like to run in and see you."[132] Explaining her reticence to join the group, Tarbell confessed, "I have always felt that the journalist should be free of all political affiliations." Addams was herself struggling with the obligations of party loyalty. She freed herself, at least temporarily, from the pressure of public life by retreating with Mary Smith on their planned trip to Egypt in February 1913.

Although Addams attended an organizing meeting of the Progressive Party in Chicago, she did not go to the executive board meeting in New York City. The board lamented her absence and asked her to take charge of the Bureau of Social and Industrial Justice. Gifford Pinchot enlisted her help in the effort of the National Conservation Association to prevent Congress from disbursing public lands into private hands. "The movement to turn the National Forests and all they contain over to the States is stronger in Congress this year than I have ever known it," he told her.[133] Environmentalists feared that the administration in power—at that time, the Democratic Party—would trade away natural resources to placate business interests and those who advocated states' rights. "In producing such an understanding few things would be so effective as a letter from you which I might make public at the proper time." A sign of Addams's political and literary stature in 1913 is Pinchot's appeal. He joked to friends that Roosevelt had grown suspicious of the social worker crowd except for Jane Addams, and he was afraid of her.

Edward Bok felt the shortness of time in December as he urged her to complete the articles she had promised him. He made the considerable mistake of urging Addams to model her own writing on Louise Bowen's little books, "The Department Slave Girl," "The Girl in Hotels and Restaurants," and "A Study of Public Dance Halls." The hint of plagiarism made little difference to him as he suggested that using Bowen's language to "make your work easier, and enable you to prepare enough articles for us."[134] His letter drew an angry response from Addams. "Of course, your page must absolutely remain your own and appear over your name," he mollified her. "My thought of the material by Mrs. Bowen was that you would sort of digest it and then give your version of the material, of course giving Mrs. Bowen and the Juvenile Protective Association credit."[135] As she packed, he gave deadlines for promised articles, cautioning that continuity is a virtue. As she sent him "The Family and the State," he responded sheepishly, "[I]t *is* delicious, and very, very clever!"[136]

The long trip to Egypt had the intended effect of freeing Addams from the bonds of the Progressive Party. The Atlantic crossing in March turned out to be a rough one. Mary Smith reported: "There is a new baby in steerage and three of the poor Italian passengers have died since we sailed."[137] Addams was wretched from "bowel trouble" while at sea; and, once they arrived, she found Egypt too hot. She admitted to Helen Culver that she felt like a "deserter" as she retreated to the luxury of the Grand Hotel in Jerusalem.[138] Once in the cool luxury of the hotel, however, she relaxed, telling friends that she had not "felt so stimulated and refreshed for years." She was pleased to discover that Egypt revived her imagination: "The ancient history was much more vivid than I had imagined it," she told Culver. Later she would write an insightful and elegant essay about the trip. Clara Landsberg and Louise Bowen joined them in Naples in May, and the women traveled together to Sicily and Rome. Smith and Landsberg sailed back to the United States on June 4, and Bowen and Addams motored through Umbria and Tuscany before attending a world conference of women in Budapest, where they linked forces with Rosika Schwimmer, a relationship that would build over the next year as Europe found itself at war. They returned to New York on July 2 and took the train to Chicago on the Fourth of July, staying at the Bowen Country Club before going to Maine with Mary. Addams spent her time writing an introduction to Graham Taylor's book *Religion in America* and a preface to Louise DeKoven Bowen's *Safeguards for City Youth at Work and at Play*. She was pleased with her annual royalty statement in 1912, totaling $2,329.90 from Macmillan. All five of her books were in print and *The Spirit of Youth* and *Twenty Years at Hull-House* were selling remarkably well. The newest book, *A New Conscience and an Ancient Evil*, sold 9,083 copies in its first year.

The political climate had not improved over the summer, however. May Childs Nerney reported that Hull-House could not afford to pay its staff in Chicago, apparently because Anita McCormick Blaine had not yet sent a promised $1,000. "Can you think of any tactful way of reminding her?" Nerney pleaded. Addams sent Nerney's letter to Blaine with a playful though pointed appeal: "Is this a 'tactful' way of reminding you! It is at least direct and certainly embarrassing."[139] The budget was in the red for 1913, with income of $57,677.12 and expenses of $61,040.58. Addams worked to raise additional money that summer to avoid carrying the deficit into the next year's budget.

The situation in Washington, D.C., was especially difficult for African Americans. Oswald Garrison Villard sent a letter to friends of the NAACP detailing the effect of Jim Crow in the nation's capital: "[S]oon we may expect to have 'nigger' sections in all the Washington departments." The Civil Rights Act had been annulled and Villard called on Addams and others to help him fight back. An NAACP letter to Woodrow Wilson, on August 26, 1913, signed by Addams and many others, protested the segregation in civil service. Two months later, Blanche Wright, a woman who had played the wife in Hull-House's enactment of Charles Chestnut's "Wife of his Youth," sent Addams a sad letter. Chestnut's graceful play tells the story of an upwardly mobile man, who, after suffering slavery, embraces the comforts of a genteel life until his former wife, a battered and poor woman, arrives on the scene. In acknowledging his bond to the former slave, he nobly accepts his humble past even at the cost of his newly earned status. The irony was stark: as a civil worker in the nation's capital, Wright had no civil rights. Restaurants and even toilets were segregated. "Now I absolutely refuse to put my foot in any separate convenience for color people exclusively," she confided to Addams. "I have eaten nothing for two weeks, and some nights I lie awake all night."[140] Little had changed in America fifty years after the Emancipation Proclamation: national discussion, then as now, avoided serious questions about race relations.

Edward Bok wanted Addams to end her series in *Ladies' Home Journal* with a column on peace, not a controversial topic before the war in Europe. Tempted, even at the end of their work together, to dictate the tone, he cautioned, "[A]ny treatment of it must be other than in the sentimental note."[141] George Brett had found Addams in Maine to remind her that he was looking forward to her next book, one on "anything which you may have to give us."[142] Norman Hapgood suggested an article for *Harper's Weekly*, sending her a copy of "Jane Addams Favors Fashion's Scant Garb," a provocative report on the Social Workers' Conference in Pittsburgh. The quote that caught Hapgood's eye came from Addams: "I do not believe that women are being degraded by the fashions. The less clothes we can wear with modesty the better it is. It is better for the health and allows more freedom of movement."[143] The warm summer weather continued into the fall that year and Addams may have been responding as much to visceral experience as to moral implications.

Reading Addams's letters over the year before the outbreak of war in Europe provides a portrait of the dutiful political woman she had become. In December, for example, she traveled to Washington, D.C., with Louise Bowen to speak at a Suffrage Convention; from there, the two women took a train to New York City, where Addams spoke the next day in Brooklyn to a group that Ida Tarbell defined as women of leisure and professional women. Addams served on the board of the Chicago Commons Association, a group headed by her friend Graham Taylor, and she remained on the board of *Survey* as a favor to her friend Paul Kellogg. In Washington, she worked on the Committee on Industrial Relations and the Committee on Organization for an International Congress on Social Insurance. By the end of 1913, however, it seems clear that Jane Addams had backed away from Progressive Party politics, preferring to work as a nonpartisan, especially in municipal affairs. Albert Beveridge sent her an editorial from the *Indianapolis News* that proclaimed her defection from the Progressive Party, as Teddy Roosevelt beckoned in December, seeking her commitment to attend the Lincoln Birthday dinner on February 12, 1914. Addams wrote to Beveridge that she planned to attend the Lincoln celebration: "I hope that will silence any talk of deflection."[144] Slipping an "l" into defection would have caught Freud's eye; Addams certainly wanted to deflect any criticism of her defection from Roosevelt's cause.

A Woman over Fifty

In the middle of her fifty-third year, Jane Addams opened a letter from Edward Bok at *Ladies' Home Journal*. "I am very anxious," he confided, "to stir up the woman whom I constantly hear say, when she reaches fifty, that she is too old to do any social service or civic work."[145] He detailed how he would rouse "old" women by speaking through Addams's voice. "Of course, such an article should show that a woman reaches her prime at that age and that with her background of experience and her riper judgment she can do the most effective work of her life." Bok wanted to play ventriloquist to her dummy. In twenty-five hundred words, she was to make his argument that when a woman reaches fifty, she is "prime," even "ripe," and she ought to use her financial prosperity in public service. He worried that his female readers were withdrawing from public activity, preferring the comforts of the private world.

Jane Addams, as she held his letter in her hand, may have been thinking about the comforts of the private life as she and Mary shopped for a house in Bar Harbor. She certainly understood what worried Bok—wealthy women, even those who had been active in urban life, might turn inward in their fifties, exchanging the commotion and contagion of the city for the solitude and shelter of a hermitage, shaded by leafy greenery and cooled by watery breezes. A professional woman, especially one of her generation, who had worked all her life to move from the private to the public sphere, might reverse course.

An editor sure of his goal can be a bully. What Bok wanted—and here he went too far—was a precise accounting of the hours in her day: "Then I should like it very much, for the personal guidance of these women, if you would tell in such an article the management of your personal life, so as not only to interject the personal note, which, you know, is so valuable in an article of this kind, but by your example and method of living to show these women how they can live along sensible lines and plan their days so as to make them effective." His female readers (we note that Bok opposed women's suffrage) ought to be sensible and useful under his guiding hand.

When her editorial arrived on his desk two months later, he discovered that a woman over fifty might speak for herself. "The article on the woman over fifty is excellent, so far as it goes," he responded.[146] He was surprised and irritated by her refusal to give him what he asked for: "But you have omitted all reference to yourself,—the very basis on which I hoped the article might rest." He fretted over her reluctance, guessed at her motivation, and ordered her to do more work. "All I want is a statement of how you regulate your life & work: how you plan your days: husband your strength." The verb "husband" must have amused Jane Addams, who had no intention of telling anyone, much less Edward Bok and his readers, the details of her daily life. She was, to be sure, a woman with a clear sense of the privacy that comes with age and wealth.

"Need a Woman over Fifty Feel Old?" Addams asks in the editorial, published in the October 1914 issue of *Ladies' Home Journal.* In the past, she reminds her readers, women became mothers and then mothers-in-law, losing the authority of their voice within the home, even as their husbands gained business and professional authority. Middle-class and wealthy women drifted into placid irrelevance, or they struggled to fill their leisure with vapid occupations: "[W]e certainly deplore those women of seventy years occasionally seen rushing from one social function to another, attired in modish gowns, with picture hats surmounting their elaborately coifed heads."[147] She cannot resist a playful gibe worthy of a writer like Edith Wharton. Ornamental women, she continues, who in their youth knew "no exercise more violent than playing croquet, no dietary more rigid than preserves and sponge cake," might spend their still considerable energies and their late husbands' considerable fortunes on civic and artistic projects. Hull-House, of course, depended on such patronesses. In all these examples, Addams gave Bok what he wanted.

But in place of the daily schedule of her personal life—we imagine he wanted to know that she rose at seven o'clock, wrote through breakfast until, say, eleven, and worked on legislation or attended meetings all afternoon, and saved her evenings for public lectures—Jane Addams talks about the activities of other professional women. She mentions the social and political work of Ella Flagg Young and Anna Howard Shaw, and the literary careers of Edith Wharton and Margaret Deland. Other professional women who are close friends to her—Florence Kelley, Lillian Wald, Julia Lathrop, and Louise DeKoven Bowen—remain nameless; Addams lists public accomplishments but refuses Bok any closer view. Jane Addams had no intention of bringing her readers into the private spaces at Hull-House, much less at Hull's Cove. The coast of Maine sheltered Addams from social work, public speaking, and the pressures of being a public woman.

A woman in her prime at fifty, as ripe as she would ever be, was an image that applied to Addams perhaps more than to any other woman of her generation. As a writer, she had become the colleague of Theodore Dreiser, W. E. B. DuBois, Hamlin Garland, Zona Gale, Charlotte Perkins Gilman, William Dean Howells, William James, and Ida Tarbell in the United States and of Leo Tolstoy, Mrs. Humphrey (Mary) Ward, and Emile Zola abroad. In the essay she wrote, she placed herself alongside Margaret Deland and Edith Wharton.

Looking at Jane Addams that summer, we might think that she had little more to offer the public. Hilda Satt Polacheck, a woman who had grown up in the Halsted neighborhood, recorded in her memoir *I Came a Stranger: The Story of a Hull-House Girl* the changing nature of Addams's involvement at Hull-House: "As more and more people found their way to this haven of love and understanding, [Addams] began to relegate the work to other people and to seek rest at the home of friends."[148] Her personal life absorbed more and more time, and in the mood, perhaps, of semiretirement, Addams announced to Lillian Wald that she and Mary Smith planned to "move into our little house next Monday."[149] The two women finally lived in a home of their own at Hull's Cove, the antipode of Hull-House. Had the summer proceeded as usual, Jane and Mary may have moved into the house and begun even more to recede from public life, having earned, as women over fifty, a right to privacy and leisure.

4   *Telling a War Story*

A Moral Adventure

In the summer of 1915, Zona Gale wrote to Jane Addams from Portage, Wisconsin, a small midwestern town seemingly well away from the war in Europe, and yet the fighting was foremost in Gale's mind and in her fiction as she worked on a didactic novel, *Heart's Kindred*. She was struggling to depict a brutish hero who wants to become a soldier. "'Women are lame lucks in the war game,'" he proclaims, adding "'I want to be in on it.'"[1] Traveling to a peace rally in Washington, D.C., however, he falls under the spell of Jane Addams, who becomes a character in the novel: "The silence became a hush, contagious, electric, and he saw that a woman on the platform had risen" (194). Gale presents the scene of Addams's emergence as a pacifist heroine: "She stood hatless, her hair brushed smoothly back, and her hands behind her." The hero admires her saintly and maternal composure as she commands the crowd: "There was no applause, but to his amazement the whole audience rose, and stood for a moment, in absolute silence. This woman spoke simply, and as if she were talking to each one there." In epiphany, he sees the female figure—the Cassandra of Addams's college essay—as the voice of reason: "It astonished the man."

As she worked on the manuscript that summer, Gale searched for a literary mentor, a godmother of sorts, and wrote Addams asking for advice, approval, and more material about various pacifist speeches given by several women, including Rosika Schwimmer, who also functions as a character. "I should be delighted to see the proof," Addams exclaimed, adding the curious line: "It always gives me great pleasure to *write* what you *read* " [emphasis added].[2] Literary mentoring can be peculiar, one writer looking on as another writer works. Addams, perhaps laughing at the slip, corrected the line, "It always gives me great pleasure to *read* what you *write*. " The tangle of verbs suggests the energy passing between the two women. "I am in no way writing this from a feeling of duty but with a sense of great pleasure in store for me," Addams reassured Gale. "It does seem most important that women should be able to formulate a sense of kindred, which certainly is sadly needed at this time." As a sign of the kindred spirit between the two women, Addams invited Gale to stay at Bar Harbor in August.

After reading the manuscript, she wrote to Gale, "I like the chapter very much as I do all the rest of the books, or at least all you sent."[3] Her letter began in praise and ended in caveat. "I have absolutely no fault to find with the woman's meeting but something might be added perhaps— a little of the sense of difficulty which women of the warring nations feel when they are obliged to protest." She made the appeal for "women of the warring nations" although her own protests were very much in her mind that long summer. She sent Gale her speech from the April meeting of women at The Hague, along with another invitation to come to Bar Harbor during the last two weeks of August. "[I]t would give Miss Smith and myself a great deal of pleasure," she told Gale.

Addams's escape that summer from public life was poignant. The long first year of the war in Europe, from the summer of 1914 through the spring of 1915, changed her public life, lifting her onto an international stage in performances that altered her image as a leader even as they damaged her as an icon in the American imagination.

Public events in Europe contrasted vividly with private life in Bar Harbor in the summer of 1914. Franz Ferdinand, heir of the Hapsburg dynasty, made his way into Bosnia in late June to observe the maneuvers of the Austrian troops and found himself in the gunsight of Gavrilo Princip. News of the assassination spread slowly in a confusion of responses. During that same week, Jane Addams journeyed to Hull's Cove. She and Mary Smith had purchased a spacious white cottage with black shutters, a dormered roof, and a porch bordered by a low balustrade. Surrounded by a green lawn and shaded by leafy trees, the house offered sanctuary, a place for reflection and writing. On July 3rd, Addams wrote to Lillian Wald that she and Mary planned to move into their new home on Monday, July 6. Nothing in the letters from Bar Harbor in July and early August hint at the events in Europe, events that would shatter the calm at Hull's Cove as well as Hull-House, much as the distant events of a Tuesday morning in September eighty-seven years later would shatter my placid view of a clear sky filled with late-summer sunlight. Distant catyclysmic events always intrude on the private world in ways we cannot know.

In response to the assassination, Austria looked to Germany for support before retaliating against Serbia, a hesitation that brought other countries into the conflict. It was July and many of those who might have acted more quickly were on holiday; no one seemed eager to get involved, and the crisis festered for a long month. Britain proposed a conference to mediate the disagreement but not in time to prevent Austria from declaring war on Serbia and attacking Belgrade on July 29, setting the pieces into play, pitting Britain, France, and Russia against Germany, allied with Austria, who declared war on Russia on August 5. During that first week of August, as the war took shape, the women of Hull's Cove faced a more personal emergency. Louise Bowen was taken to the hospital with an intestinal obstruction, and her friends, truly frightened, stayed with her for two days as she recovered from surgery. Her condition was grim and she would undergo a second surgery. Bowen's health, the prosaic reality before the women, was the central concern in Bar Harbor, and not, as we might imagine, the even grimmer events unfolding in Europe.

News of the fighting came to Hull's Cove in the middle of August in a letter from Rosika Schwimmer, the irascible political activist whom Addams and Bowen had met at the Seventh Congress of the International Woman Suffrage Alliance in Budapest in the spring of 1913. "I leave this hell called Europe on the 25th Aug.," she wrote in characteristic haste, "when I sail from Liverpool on the 'Arabic' White Star line."[4] She sought Addams in Chicago and found her finally in Bar Harbor, where Addams planned to stay until the middle of September. Schwimmer arrived in America expecting to talk directly with Woodrow Wilson and William Jennings Bryan about American involvement in a mediation to bring an early end to the war.

Jane Addams, who would eventually win the Nobel Peace Prize, was anything but sure of her own ideas during the long late-summer of 1914. She wrote candidly to Paul Kellogg, the editor of *Survey*, that the pacifists in Boston could not decide on even the wording of a manifesto. She gave Kellogg the names of Julia Lathrop, Graham Taylor, William Dean Howells, and Edwin Mead, fellow pacifists who might see ways "to bring the older peace efforts in line with this new one, if that is desirable."[5] Rosika Schwimmer prompted Addams's caution. "I am sending a copy of Miss Schwimmer's plan which you may have seen," she told Kellogg. "I have signed it reluctantly as a member of the National Suffrage Board, simply because I don't like to damp any plan which is so widespread, but it doesn't seem very feasible." Addams was fretting over her own statement on pacifism: "I am having my usual ill luck with the war editorial—or rather the subject is too much for me."

The subject was too much for anyone that summer. American intellectuals moved slowly into discussion of the war in Europe, a war that seemed far away in the fall of 1914. What Wilson wanted and most social and political thinkers in the country hoped for was a hand, not in the fighting, but in the peacemaking. How could the United States secure a credible and powerful place at the negotiating table? That was the question in Jane Addams's mind as she looked for ways to bring people together.

She handpicked a group of colleagues, inviting them to the Henry Street Settlement in New York City for a roundtable luncheon at half-past one on Tuesday, September 29, a meeting that was to last through an evening dinner. Lillian Wald wrote the invitation that blended social and political rhetoric. "We suppose that never before has Society been self-conscious enough carefully to note the subtle reactions of war, inevitably disastrous to the humane instincts which had been asserting themselves in the social order." "Society" is capitalized, a subtle reminder that the twenty-six guests had been chosen with care and discernment. The invitation included Felix Adler, Louis Brandeis, Thomas Edison, William Dean Howells, Samuel Lindsay, and other public intellectuals, together with Emily Balch, Florence Kelley, Paul Kellogg, Julia Lathrop, and Graham Taylor from the settlement movement. Settlements thought of themselves as centers of social work, handmaidens to industrial workplaces, crafting legislation to protect manual workers, shorten the work week, increase wages, limit female and child labor, and weave a social safety net. "We feel that, whatever the outcome of the conflict, we are concerned that certain things in the civilization of Europe and in each of the warring countries shall not perish."[6] The letter makes clear that the United States was not a combatant but that, as an onlooker, it had a responsibility to express its ideals of democracy and pacifism.

The goal was to preserve the civilized order that produced such an invitation. The earnest tone resonates for us reading it nearly a century later after viewing the wars of the twentieth and, indeed, the twenty-first centuries. The metaphorical language reveals the female hand: "This round table is suggested as a means by which, in humbleness and quiet, some of us who deal with the social fabric may come together to clarify our minds, and, if it seems wise, to act in concert." The carefully crafted words make clear that the luncheon is exclusive and that people have been selected because they are wise, judicious, and agreeable. We imagine them seated around the table at half-past one, lifting teacups, wiping moisture delicately from the corners of their mouths, listening thoughtfully, and speaking in calm, measured tones about what would become one of the most destructive, least civilized events in human history. Over the long afternoon, in the back of their minds was the unsettling suspicion that no matter how well they behaved during lunch and dinner in New York City, the effort could have no meaningful effect on the behavior of those not invited.

Little came from the luncheon. Addams turned back into her personal life, even as she returned to Hull-House. Alice Addams Haldeman arrived ill in October. In caring for her sister and meeting the demands on her in Chicago, Addams felt the strain. "I am sorry to play the 'public woman,'" she confided to Sarah Hostetter, "and it is very hard in the midst of distress and illness."[7] She continued to care for her sister at Hull-House and, later, at Mary Smith's house on Walton Place. Alice resented being there because the house was, after all, Mary's and not her sister's. With the duties owed an ailing older sister, Jane cared for her as she could and yet went ahead with her public speaking schedule through the midterm elections in the fall. The Progressive Party hoped to establish itself as more than the personality of Teddy Roosevelt, and women's suffrage had yet to be won. With the vote for women as her goal, Addams traveled to the West for two weeks in October, speaking in towns along the route.

Her personal life was ever more in her mind, especially her devotion to Mary Smith. "I had a wave of real homesickness for you in *Dead Wood*," she joked as she completed her political tour.[8] And then more tenderly, she wrote, "Dearest—I didn't know but I wanted you very much." Her sister's illness reminded her that she had lost her parents early in her life and that she had a strong fear of death itself. The tug between public and private life brought on the homesickness, and home reminded her of no one more than Mary.

As she lectured on women's suffrage, Addams grew increasingly wary of being defined by gender and confined by association with women only. She declined the honorary vice presidency of the National American Woman Suffrage Association. "You will have to defend me to Miss Shaw the next time you are in New York," she wrote Madeline Breckenridge at the end of November. "She evidently feels that I should not have withdrawn my name."[9] She did not like the idea of being the only candidate and wanted none of the pressures of office. "It put me again in a position of responsibility which I was not willing to assume," she bluntly admitted. The same letter committed her to the peace movement, although her attitude was characteristically cautious. Rosika Schwimmer and Emmeline Pethick Lawrence had been guests at Hull-House for ten days, having spent the fall forming committees in New York, Boston, and Washington to promote peace in Europe. They urged Addams to call for a peace meeting of women only, in a "War against War" effort. Although Addams admired the energy behind the movement, she demurred: "Personally, I should rather have a meeting of 'social workers' and others representing the new point of view, the saving of life by all sorts of social devices, and have men as well as women invited." Crossing the gender line made sense to her because a meeting at that border promised, as it always does, the infusion of male power and influence.

The war, after all, was a male enterprise. Carrie Chapman Catt, hearing of the effort to put together a national conference, wrote to Jane Addams in December, suggesting that the chief and largest women's organizations across the country might serve as a conduit for the effort. "Even a small group, say 25, if properly representative, would be influential enough to ask and secure hearing before the Congressional Committees which without doubt will consider at once the *necessity* (!) of increasing our own armament."[10] Her immediate concern was the national frenzy to arm for war in case of attack. "I feel that we should strike our blow at that movement at once." Addams accepted membership on a Peace Committee, chaired by David Starr Jordan, and suggested the meeting in Washington on January 10, 1915, as a response to grassroots efforts throughout the country. "There is great eagerness for some sort of expression," she told him, "and while I do not wish it to lead to a foolish demonstration it does seem a pity not to give definite form to so much zeal!"[11] And in another letter to Rosika Schwimmer, who was on the road, Addams warned, "I have received a number of letters from all over the country urging such a meeting, but the basis of constituency is very difficult."[12]

She feared that a mob of unruly women might well be viewed as irrational, even hysterical by the press. "There is naturally much emotional reaction against the war, and people are eager to meet and talk about it, but I must say that I dread a large and ill assorted assemblage and doubt if we could do anything with it." Negotiations with Catt continued throughout the month. "I quite dread gathering together women from all over the country merely because they are eager for Peace," Addams confided. "We would certainly confront a good deal of emotionalism and I doubt the value of such a conference."[13] The rational pacifists she had in mind—"such a group as lately had a very significant meeting in New York"—were the women and men that she and Lillian Wald had invited to tea.

In the letters, we can still hear the rub of ego against ego. Catt responded two days later that Anna Garlin Spencer had warned her that "the present management of the peace movement in this country is over-masculinized."[14] For that reason, Catt demanded a meeting of women only. A national meeting in Washington, reinforced by simultaneous rallies in Chicago, Philadelphia, New York, and other cities, would have dramatic impact. She gossiped about Lucia Ames Mead, a pacifist and the wife of Edwin Mead. "Mrs. Spencer was a little chagrined, I think, when Mrs. Mead took over the idea as her own, and has, I believe, already written the manifesto which she proposes such demonstrations should adopt." Mead chaired the Peace Department of the Council of Women, and Catt chaired the Votes for Women on the Empire State Campaign Committee. "Mrs. Mead is without question exceedingly well informed upon the peace question and a woman of very rare ability," Catt began. "On the other hand, for reasons which I have never been able to analyze, she is an extremely unpopular woman." She certainly was not popular with Catt, who had a strong visceral response: "I confess that while I cannot name a single sensible reason for my feeling, I always want to run when I see her coming." A good politician, Catt encouraged Addams as a foil to Mead: "I therefore write in confidence to you and express my opinion that you are the one woman in the nation who ought to call such demonstrations if they are to be held." What she offered Addams was permission to use her name in organizing the rally. A politician herself, Addams saw the wisdom of compromise: "I quite agree with you as to the masculine management of the existing Peace Societies. I have been identified with them for years, and while I believe that men and women work best together on these public measures, there is no doubt that at this crisis the women are most eager for action."[15] Even as she acquiesced, however, Addams voiced doubt: "I am undertaking all this with a certain sinking of the heart, knowing how easy it is to get a large body of women together and how difficult it is to take any wise action among many people who do not know each other well."

Sensing the makings of another book, Richard Ely wrote in December: "I need scarcely say how much I should like to have another volume by you in the Citizen's Library."[16] Any book in his series, he assured her, could later be published independently by Macmillan, allowing two editions of the same material. "If you have anything which you could submit to me first, I am confident that arrangements could be made to give you the same terms which you would receive for independent publication." Addams, a woman now well over fifty, was in the process of creating a new public self as the leading female pacifist in the long, failed effort to mediate an end to the fighting in Europe.

Jane Addams sought ways of bringing women together as a counter-force to male aggression and, ironically, found herself in the middle of an internecine feud among the women themselves. Rosika Schwimmer, exhausted and depressed from her speaking tour of the United States and furious with the press for misrepresenting her mission, complained to Addams: "I try now to harden myself against the terrible things that happen every minute. I feel absolutely helpless because I see that the world has *not* learned anything from this terrible disaster."[17] Reports continued to come to Jane Addams during the war about Schwimmer's abrasive personality and its effect on women in the United States and in Europe. Antoinette Funk wrote after spending an evening with Schwimmer in Indianapolis at a meeting of the National American Woman Suffrage Association: "I had listened to Mme. Schwimmer deliver her instructive and inspiring address in the afternoon, the same, I think, that she has been giving over the country."[18] Funk moved steadily toward her point: "I take it that she was exceedingly tired and nervous after a long and strenuous journey to the West, but in any event she seemed to me to lose control of herself entirely when evening came." Not only did Schwimmer criticize Wilson and Bryan for their reluctance to mediate a truce, but also she displayed "a degree of bitterness toward the American people that surprised me very greatly." To Funk and other midwestern women, Schwimmer was "nervous and hysterical" as she attacked them for being spineless in the movement to end the fighting in Europe and in their reluctance to question the leadership of Wilson and Bryan. No one wanted to hear what she had to say.

The Washington meeting in January 1915, that Zona Gale depicted in *Heart's Kindred* very nearly did not come off at all. Schwimmer told Addams that because of press coverage, she refused to take part in the Washington meeting scheduled for January 10.[19] Aletta Jacobs sent word through Carrie Chapman Catt that English women were headed toward supporting war rather than peace. German women appealed to their sisters in the United States to resist the export of ammunition to England and France, bullets and bombs that were to be used against them.

The letters between Addams and Catt, two strong-voiced women, record a long series of connections and misconnections, full of vitality and wit. Admitting that she had neglected to read her mail, letting it stack up on her table, Catt nevertheless attacked Addams for not letting her know sooner how prominently her name and reputation were being used by the pacifists in organizing the Washington meeting. She was especially angered by Emmeline Pethick Lawrence's controversial phrase, "Woman's War Against War." Catt kept her eye on the international stage and her role as leader of universal suffrage. "Especially is it important to keep my skirts clear at this particular moment, for a vote is on its round to determine whether or not we shall hold an international peace conference in Holland in April."[20] Lifting her skirts and moving aside in Washington would allow her a place on the international stage.

Bringing the disparate women together by the tenth of January called for diplomatic dexterity. Addams went first to New York City, meeting with women there and traveling with them to Washington. She flattered Rosika Schwimmer by insisting, "I cannot possibly let you off from the meeting!" and offering her a leading role.[21] Smoothing feathers, she explained to Catt and Schwimmer that metaphors are, after all, only metaphors; Pethick Lawrence was not advocating militarism when she used the phrase a "war against war." Moving her entourage from the Hotel Belmont in New York to the New Willard Hotel in Washington, Addams convinced Catt to join the meeting at 8:30 on the evening of the ninth. And thus the rally came off on the tenth, as scheduled. Schwimmer's postmortem characteristically focused attention on herself, whining that she had not been useful in Washington: "The World has come to such a point of indescribable misery that race suicide, an earthquake carrying us away at once, seems to me the most desirable thing."[22] We can hear her moan and Addams's responding sigh.

In the clashes among pacifists, Jane Addams found herself at the center of quarrels and quibbles. Antisuffragettes complained that they had been declined membership in the Women's Peace Party because of politics. Samuel Gompers refused to send representatives from the American Federation of Labor. Bella Caldwell Culbertson, president of the Women's Interdenominational Missionary Union, expressed dismay over the fact that the rally avoided prayer. News arrived from Chicago that the Peace Association had been torn asunder by the resignation of the treasurer, a man who left to join—of all things—the Navy League. In Boston, Lucia Ames Mead recommended a Mr. Welsh to organize the Women's Peace Party but admitted that it would look bad to have a man in charge and suggested that Addams appoint some prominent woman as titular leader, allowing Welsh to be "a sort of power behind the throne."[23]

The International Women's Congress at The Hague in April 1915 required Addams's skill as negotiator because, predictably, women in the Allied nations were growing increasingly bellicose. "They have now come to the conclusion," Catt quipped, "that they want the war to continue until the Germans are wiped off the face of the earth."[24] The militancy of former pacifists was palpable. "Between these German letters and the French letters my conviction has been emphasized that the world has literally gone mad, and I don't think we could get any International meeting with these warring people in attendance." Catt wrote in a knowing way and Addams appreciated her sardonic humor: "It would be too much like trying to organize a peace society in an insane asylum." The letter ended in a pragmatic appeal: "It is only under your leadership, however, that it could have an auspicious beginning." Rosika Schwimmer fumed through a letter in February, complaining about battles among various factions of the movement and admonishing Addams, "*[D]on't hesitate to throw me over.*"[25] "Haven't we hate and suspicion enough?" she asked wearily. And then she, too, indulged in gallows humor. Bernard Shaw might say about the battles among the pacifist women: "[H]ave they all become childish, or unreasonable, or villainous or cowardly or romantic or impossible like the other sex?"

In truth, Addams was more ombudsman than heroine as she managed, against considerable odds, to establish the Women's Peace Party. In justifying their pacifism, the women used an essentialist argument: "As women, we are especially the custodians of the life of the ages."[26] The very body of a woman abhors violence: "As women, we are particularly charged with the future of childhood and with the care of the helpless and the unfortunate." Women, likewise, have as their responsibility the protection of the home and hearth: "As women, we have builded by the patient drudgery of the past the basic foundation of the home and of peaceful industry." Beyond instinct, the group appealed to reason and called for justice. The "mother half of humanity" (a forgivable pun, perhaps) protested the war and demanded the vote. The Woman's Peace Party adopted a resolution denouncing preparations in the United States for entering the war. "We desire to make a solemn appeal to the higher attributes of our common humanity to help us unmask this menace to our civilization." The language sounds like Addams's own.

To separate her pacifism from her social work, Addams established an office of the Chicago Branch of the American Peace Society at 116 South Michigan Avenue. "Peace has never been so well housed in Chicago before!" she proclaimed in a letter to Lyra Trueblood.[27] The group sought money from the Carnegie Endowment for International Peace. Its acting director of the Division of Intercourse and Education was Nicholas Murray Butler, the man who would share the Nobel Peace Prize with Addams in 1931. Carnegie funded two projects, a production of Euripides' *Trojan Women* and a lecture series. A $5,000 grant went to the theatre project with the stipulation that funds would not be used directly for the Woman's Peace Party. Art promised to move the masses more than political rallies, and no other play seemed to Addams more apropos. The

Chicago Little Theater toured the United States, staging performances in Illinois, Indiana, Michigan, Ohio, Pennsylvania, and Maryland, as well as in Kentucky, Kansas, Nebraska, Colorado, Utah, and California. The ten-week tour cost $7,350. "I personally think," Addams advised her feminist supporters, "the Woman's Peace Party ought to have more attention to propaganda through plays and festivals."[28] She knew, as Dickens did, that people must be amused. The production ran into hard times, however, in labor disputes. Ironically, the legislation she had been working on at Hull-House threatened the peace project. As it turned out, the budget had not allowed for payment of union workers; to be consistent with her call for fair wages, the production required another $50 to $80 per week. Worse yet, the play called for the use of a child actor, forcing Addams to question the restrictions on child labor she advocated. In the end, the play flopped.

Addams gave the Carnegie series of lectures in 1915, beginning in Pittsburgh on March 5 and then in New York City with stops at Yale, Philadelphia, and Smith College. The trip was frenetic, and in the rush she forgot her drugs and her lorgnettes. "I am quite lost without the latter as I am blinder than ever," she joked to Mary. "Will you please send them to the Belmont for me—'p.d.q.'"[29] The pressure of time and the stimulation of audience exhilarated her. "I am really writing a good speech," she boasted. At the same time, she worked on a peace issue of *Survey* magazine, one that Paul Kellogg and other pacifists hoped might sway the country. "Toward the Peace That Shall Last" was published on April 2, 1915, with fifty thousand copies printed. Edward Bok wanted more writing from her, a follow-up to her essay about women over fifty. He suggested "The Unmarried Woman" and "The Idleness of the Suburban Woman" or a piece on "how the suburban woman can remedy her own condition."[30] His *Ladies' Home Journal* continued to tell the American woman how she ought to behave—shun pleasure, idleness, and self-indulgence and work for family and country—although she should never expect the right to vote and to conduct her life as a man does.

The plans for a peace meeting in Europe came at the same time that Jane's sister Alice Addams Haldeman was dying of cancer. She had discovered a malignant growth five years before and had undergone surgery; the tumor reappeared in July 1914, and she struggled with it until March 1915. Her daughter, Marcet, who assumed her mother's role in her Aunt Jane's life, was not told that her mother was failing. It is significant that Mary Smith wrote the letter of apology to Marcet explaining how the worsening of the illness surprised them and how it was that they had not written sooner. Alice had been a successful banker in Gerard, Kansas, taking up her husband's profession after his death, and her daughter had taken her mother's place at the bank.

In her grief, Marcet made Aunt Jane the sole beneficiary in her new will. It is a strange arrangement, one that marks Marcet's emotional need. Her letters to her Aunt Jane are full of detail about her own life and about the writing she was doing. Marcet wrote journalistic pieces and short stories, placing some in the *Atlantic Monthly.* It is fair to say that Marcet had her aunt's talent for storytelling without her gift for writing.

The official invitation to the International Women's Congress at The Hague, on April 28–30, 1915, was written by the Queen of Holland, although Schwimmer and Aletta Jacobs organized the Congress in Europe and Catt in the United States. By the end of March, Addams knew that she would be named president of the Congress. She prepared to leave at noon on Thursday, April 13, on the *Noordam.* Lillian Wald received an invitation from the executive council of the Woman's Peace Party, urging Wald to travel to Holland as a delegate to the Congress. Any invitation from the Woman's Peace Party came as an invitation from Addams herself, whose will was hard to ignore, much less defy. "All my inclinations lead me to accompany you," she wrote to Addams, "and to add one more protest against war."[31] Yet she declined the offer: "I will see you off on the thirteenth of April, and with deep regret that I am not in the goodly company." The very next day, writing from Hull-House, Addams admitted, "I am awfully sorry that you have decided not to go to The Hague."[32] She then confided, "The undertaking, of course, offers many possibilities of failure; indeed, it may even do much harm." The idea of traveling to Europe during time of war, especially for a woman who decried the male project of war, was exhilarating. "The whole enterprise has about it a certain aspect of moral adventure but it seems to me to be genuine." We can still feel the rush of adrenaline in her letter. "I think, too, that women who are willing to fail may be able to break thorugh that curious hypnotic spell which makes it impossible for any of the nations to consider Peace." She pleaded with Wald: "It would be a great thing for us if you would go with us!"

The letters she wrote that day echo the term "moral adventure." To Ray Stannard Baker, she mused: "The Conference at The Hague is uncertain and has about it, of course, a certain aspect of moral adventure."[33] She enlisted his help in talking Ida Tarbell into coming. Another letter to Emily Balch urged her to come as a representative of Wellesley College: "Of course, the whole undertaking has about it something of the spirit of moral adventure and may easily fail—even do harm."[34] She lured Balch by telling her that Grace Abbott and Sophinisba Breckinridge, from the University of Chicago, had already accepted the call. "Don't you think that there is a certain obligation on the women who have had the advantages of study and training, to take this possible chance to help out?" And then she released the pressure: "I don't want to be too insistent."

Mary Rozet Smith sat down to write a letter to Wald urging her to reconsider and yet, on the very same page, offering her good reasons not to go. "J. A. feels that you would be a *very valuable* member of the American delegation, but she says she could not urge your going, first because there is an element of danger on the high seas and secondly because it is all so uncertain a venture."[35] Mary explained that she was merely scribbling what she believed were Jane's thoughts: "She feels that it may be of some use but also contemplates the possibility of a flat failure. She seems awfully wishful of your going but firm in her conviction that she has no right to urge it, that it might prove a waste of good time and strength." How could the invitation be more forceful than in Mary's conciliatory voice? Wald declined the offer and, for several days, Addams did not respond to her telegram. It was Mary Smith who insisted that she write to Wald. "I had a telegram from Emily Balch this morning insuring her going, and it pleases me very much."[36] As further sign of coolness, she added: "[T]he New York Branch of the Woman's Peace Party is giving us a farewell dinner on the night of the 12th—where, I don't know, but I shall surely see you in New York."

The women traveled to The Hague on the *Noordam*, paying $95 each for double rooms and $120 for singles. The "moral adventure" provided a floating set of seminars meant to bring the group up to speed on the events and issues in Europe. "A class everyday at 11 o'clock, almost everyday at 3 o'clock, and every evening at 8 o'clock," Addams explained to Mary Smith. "[W]e have finally fused into a fine program."[37] The gatherings calmed the delegates, who were, after all, on the high seas in time of war. Addams, who always missed Mary's companionship, wrote in memory of their travels, "I have been quite homesick for you and the Adriatic through this long and peaceful voyage." Forty-two women traveled from the United States, including Emily Balch, a professor at Wellesley College; Alice Hamilton, a physician who would later join the faculty at Harvard; Sophinisba Breckinridge, dean of the Chicago School; Lucy Biddle Lewis, a trustee of Swarthmore College; Grace Abbott, member of the Immigrant's Protective League; Leonara O'Reilly, member of the Wage Earners' Social League; Annie E. Molloy, a union president; Alice Thatcher Post, the wife of the current Labor Secretary; and Madeleine Doty, a lawyer. Four men traveled with them: Demarest Lloyd, William Bross Lloyd, Louis Lockner, and H. J. Smith, all pacifists themselves.

Alice Hamilton described the voyage in long letters to Mary Smith: "I find the discussions ever so interesting and get quite absorbed in them, and then all of a sudden the whole thing looks absurdly futile."[38] She was a keen-eyed realist, and her letters give us a clear sense of what was happening. "Miss Addams is really having a good time. She has made every woman on board feel that she is a intimate friend and they all adore her. And she has the pleasant conviction that she has done a good job with not very promising material." All the women on board wanted to be her intimate friend, and all hoped to be invited to England after the conference, where simply being in Addams's company would give them entrée into the intellectual world of British salons. When she finally announces the trip to England, Hamilton noted wryly, "[S]he will have annexed a lot of them and I shall be lost in the shuffle."

The trip proved to be a moral adventure for them all. They passed a westbound ship marked "Belgian Relief," high in the water, apparently on the way to America for supplies. And crews on mundane fishing boats roared at the women in anger because the *Noordam* disturbed their nets. Hamilton found it eerie that the captain did not talk with any of the women as they crossed the ocean. She could be flatly funny: "It seems a little provoking that forty elderly female Peace delegates cannot be trusted to keep from fighting over war reports."[39] Their ship was halted in the English Channel for four days on the charge that they harbored two German stowaways, and two weary people were led away by British authorities. The American delegation arrived in the Netherlands only two hours before the opening session. Worse yet, as they landed, they became the target of jeering reporters who called the women "Pro-Hun Peacettes" and their Congress "The Palace of Doves." Only three British women managed to slip free of their government's blockade because they had begun their travel early. No woman from France would attend and, likewise, none arrived from Russia, Serbia, or Japan. Germany had twenty-eight delegates, who sat uncomfortably alongside five women from Belgium. The neutral nations of Norway, Sweden, and Denmark sent several women, as did the Netherlands.

Cassandra's Stumble

Telling a war story as big as this one would take Jane Addams years, and she would tell the story over and over again from various perspectives, never quite sure that her literary portrait was accurate or that the action she took was useful, always aware that any action drew sharply critical responses. In her first book on peace, *Newer Ideals of Peace*, she had imagined life on "a long dreary road" in urban America where the masses of the unsuccessful commingled. From the tightness of quarters and harshness of labor, the masses produced a culture on the "dim borderland between compassion and morality" (11). Democracy and even pacifism, she had argued, might evolve in "crowded sewer ditches and in noisy factories" (95). After the gunshots in Sarajevo, Addams faced young men in her neighborhood who planned to travel back to their mother countries to join their former countrymen in battle. Her early book seemed a misfire.

The historic gathering of women at The Hague in 1915 seems to be the type of story Jane Addams would be eager to tell. The characters are colorful and their deeds brave and the narrative of their struggle—woman against man, civilization against chaos, peace against war—epic in scope. Instead of writing it by herself, however, she collaborated with Emily Balch and Alice Hamilton on *Women at The Hague: The International Congress of Women and Its Results* (1915), cobbling together essays they had already published in *Survey*. The collaboration was a sign of ambivalence, much as her first book on settlement work, *Hull-House Maps and Papers*, had been. Addams wrote the introduction and three chapters; Balch added three more chapters; and Hamilton wrote one remarkably personal chapter, a meditation on the journey through Europe after the Congress as the women met with leaders in the Netherlands, Switzerland, Britain, France, and Belgium as well as in Germany, Austria, and Italy, to spur continuous mediation. The book was tentative, earnest, even vigilant, as the writers gazed upon the brutality of Europe. In the introduction, Addams apologized for the fact that much of the material was already in print and passed judgment on the book, calling it "obviously journalistic" and "slight material" at best. It is fair to say that the essays never quite merged into a book at all.

A single speech led to the hesitant tone of *Women at The Hague.* Jane Addams sailed early on her return home from Europe, leaving from Liverpool on June 26 aboard the *Old St. Louis.* Uppermost in her mind were Mary and Louise, who were waiting for her at Hull's Cove and, too, Ellen Gates Starr, whose father had died that month. She arrived in New York City on June 5 to a gathering of supporters and stayed on to talk with President Wilson, who was himself on vacation, before she traveled to Bar Harbor. As she waited for an audience with the president, she delivered her first speech about the moral adventure, telling the story of the war in Europe as she had witnessed it.

Cassandra in female dress—the very figure of Jane Addams herself—she stood in front of a full house at Carnegie Hall. She urged her audience to consider what she would say in the context of the highly emotional atmosphere in Europe. "It is difficult to formulate your experience when brought face to face with so much genuine emotion and high patriotism as Europe exhibits at the present moment," she cautioned her countrymen, perhaps not appreciating how emotional they themselves were.[40] "The situation is so confused, so many wild and weird things are said about it that you are afraid to add *one word that is not founded upon absolutely first-hand impressions* and careful experience; because for the world, you would not add a bit to this already overwhelming confusion" [emphasis added]. We see, from the perspective of time, that she unwittingly set the trap herself. How might a woman—outside of military activity and well away from the front lines—credibly offer firsthand impressions of the battle itself?

Her misstep, the most costly of her career as a public speaker, came in the context of the very stagecraft she constructed. She completed her speech, as she was so comfortable doing, by speaking for the soldiers: "Generally speaking, we heard everywhere that this was an old man's war; that the young men who were dying, the young men who were doing the fighting, were not the men who wanted the war, and were not somewhere in the high places of society, the elderly people, the middle-aged people, had established themselves and had convinced themselves that this was a righteous war, that this war must be fought out, and the young men must do the fighting." A Swiss soldier claimed that in all the months of fighting he had never "shot his gun in a way that could possibly hit another man." Germans, likewise, fear going into battle because "they might be put into a position where they would have to kill someone else." Her soldiers, all young men, are heroic in Addams's stories because they are pacifists at heart. In military uniform, they talk like "peacettes."

Had she stopped at this moment, she would have been denounced by the American public and, especially, by the press but probably not vilified. Warmed by the pacifist crowd before her, she told them about soldiers who abhor the bloody conflict, particularly the necessity of finishing off the enemy with a bayonet: "It is quite as foolish to think that if militarism is an idea and an ideal, it can be changed and crushed by counter-militarism or by a bayonet charge." She attempted a nuanced reading of the battlefield and struggled to make the point that trench warfare is actually an assault on the heroism of a soldier. Searching for the best way to illustrate her point, she adopted the male voice. A young soldier had supposedly told her that he rejected the use of the bayonet, and she quoted him directly, "'That is what we cannot think of.'" Cassandra-like, Addams continued, "We heard in all countries similar statements in regard to the necessity for the use of stimulant before men could engage in bayonet charges—that they have a regular formula in Germany, that they give them rum in England and absinthe in France; that they have to give them the 'dope' before the bayonet charge is possible."

Once she had made the charge that men must be doped in order to fight, the crowd saw her as an old woman who knew nothing about the trenches and had never even held a bayonet. Ironically, she had prepared them to question her authority by insisting that firsthand impressions were the only valid ones; worse yet, she had cautioned the group to resist emotionalism and sensationalism. The assaults on her came quickly and cruelly. Stanislas d'Halewyn, Vice Consul for France, read about the speech in newspapers that used her gaffe to sell copy. "Troops Drink-Crazed, Says Miss Addams," headlines reported. Speaking for French soldiers, d'Halewyn wrote to Addams that he would stake his life on the falseness of her charge: "If you knew better the men of France, you would understand, that the thought of avenging their womenfolk acts as a much more powerful inspiration than would absinthe, which, by the way, is not drunk anymore in France, a law having forbidden it."[41] As a woman she could not possibly know what motivated men to kill each other, and as a lady she faced the charge of being ungrateful for male chivalry. Echoing the indignation that men in general felt at her charges, Richard Harding Davis, a novelist and son of the novelist Rebecca Harding Davis, responded in a letter to the *New York Times*, "I have seen more of this war and other wars than Miss Addams, and I know all war to be wicked, wasteful and unintelligent, and where Miss Addams can furnish one argument in favor of peace I will furnish a hundred." He might give her, as a woman, the stage. "But against this insult, flung by a complacent and self-satisfied woman at men who gave their lives for men, I protest." His charge stuck, especially that she was womanish and had no right to speak for men.

Her supporters urged her to respond to the charges. "At present I am finding, as you no doubt are finding, that it is being absolutely interpreted even by many who conceive themselves in close sympathy with you and who certainly are in sympathy with the Peace movement," Elizabeth Evans, from the Massachusetts Branch of the Woman's Peace Party, cautiously warned her. "I hope, therefore, that you will answer misunderstandings and give interviews and perhaps arrange for syndicate articles in any way that you can."[42] Addams might have used a letter she received from Mary Page in the spring of 1915 that included a translation of a letter from the front, written by P. Fossé, the oboe player in the Boston Symphony Orchestra, who was fighting in the Compagnie de Vitrailleuses,

235th Infantry: "The last fifteen days has been terrible here. The boches have tried to mine my trench and attacked us furiously."[43] He detailed "a funnel-shaped hole" forty meters in diameter and eighteen meters deep that the Germans made beside the trenches as they prepared for the bayonet attack. "They sent men to attack us right after this drunk with ether," he wrote, providing her a firsthand account. Reluctant to give any story to the newspapers, however, Addams shied away from any defense that might lead to further distortions.

To her long-time friend Paul Kellogg, Addams made her case. "I am sorry that I was so dull when I got back. I was so filled with many contradictory impressions that I didn't seem to be quite clear beyond one or two points, and I was also held in the grip of the conviction that it is so easy to still further confuse the situation."[44] She promised to write a "more permanent" version of the story when time allowed, the volume that would become *Women at The Hague*. She warned him against naming her to a provisional peace commission, a nongovernmental international group sanctioned by Wilson, or sending any female names forward, for that matter. "I am afraid the President is not 'for women' and I am also afraid that the European countries would construe it as a very strange performance." Enervated by the Carnegie Hall speech and the drubbing she was taking in the press, she had little stomach for public battle.

After meeting with pacifists in Chicago and New York City, Addams retreated to Hull's Cove with Mary Smith. In the comfort of her own marriage, Jane wrote Marcet to say, "I do wish that you had a 'companion.'"[45] It is hard to imagine Jane as a doting aunt, but the letters between the two reveal their growing affection. Once in the middle of a ferociously busy schedule, for example, she received a night letter from Marcet imploring her to drop everything and find drapery fabric for her redecorating project. And Jane (who may look very familiar to those of us with children) dropped everything to make sure that Marcet got the "happy" fabric she wanted.

In August Addams fell ill with bronchitis that lapsed into pleurisy and pneumonia, conditions brought on by stress and conditions, too, that provided shelter from the many women—Emily Balch, Rosika Schwimmer, Aletta Jacobs, and others—who wanted to talk with her. Mary kept would-be visitors away as Jane rested and read. She offered Zona Gale advice on *Heart's Kindred*. True to her literary inclinations, she spent much of her time in Maine on her writing task, cobbling together the *Survey* articles on The Hague along with her address to the Congress and finishing the manuscript of *Women at The Hague* on October 10. "The book has gone off to Macmillan's today," she wrote in satisfaction to

Marcet, "and I am off to Chicago tomorrow so much better that I can quite easily pretend that I am well."[46] After the book appeared in stores, she proclaimed: "I have written out my impressions in the book which promises to have a good sale, and we are of course constantly receiving new evidence."[47] With much of her war story yet to write, the book in hand, not altogether hers although she claimed it as her own, succored the author, even as she braced for more attacks.

Interpretative Memory

Katharine Coman, an economics professor at Wellesley College, had written to Jane Addams in 1913 with news that life had changed significantly for her. Coman had undergone surgery late in 1911 and discovered breast cancer (a disease that would take her life in 1915). "Under the advice of my physician, I am resigning my professorship at Wellesley," she told Addams as she put herself in the service of the Progressive Party.[48] Coman wanted to work without pay and, as she traveled to Europe for recuperation, hoped to do some useful research, blending work with leisure. The reason she could afford to step out of academia and into private life was that she had become a wealthy woman through her partner, Katharine Lee Bates, the chairman of the Wellesley Department of English. Bates had visited the Columbian Exposition in Chicago in 1893 and journeyed from there to Colorado, climbing Pike's Peak on a particularly clear Fourth of July and composing "America the Beautiful" while the sight was potently in her mind:

> O beautiful for spacious skies
> For amber waves of grain
> For purple mountain's majesties
> Above the fruited plain!

The poem earned her and Coman a fortune. Lawrence Buell argues in *Writing for an Endangered World* that the song, arranged by Irving Berlin, has become "the single most iconic work of environmental literature in the U.S."[49]

Their letters, written over many years, reveal Addams and Coman as intellectual and literary confidantes. After reading *Twenty Years at Hull-House*, Coman had thanked Addams for its literary "vindication of American womanhood!" She understood the intent of the autobiography: "Indeed, it is not your own life, but the life of your neighborhood interpreted by you . . . it becomes a life philosophy."[50] Of *A New Conscience and an Ancient Evil*, Coman had claimed it was "fearless while restrained," assuring her that "no one will accuse you of muck-raking."[51] Knowing that Addams and Smith planned to visit Egypt in February 1913, Coman sent a copy of her new book for them to read along the way. *Economic Beginnings of the Far West: How We Won the Land beyond the Mississippi* is a two-volume work than Coman believed "contains the best there is in me."[52]

The scope of Coman's study stretches over time and distance, perhaps solacing its author as she faced her own mortality. She narrates a smoothly shaped, predictable story about the struggle for the West, the "richest portion of North America." Written as a tale of seduction and betrayal, the story ends, as women's novels often do, in rescue. The young American republic, female in gender, turns her attention and energy toward the West after defeating the British Empire in the East and purchasing Louisiana from the French. She demands Florida, Texas, New Mexico, and California, as well as the watershed of the Columbia River and Puget Sound, thereby completing manifest destiny. We can hear Bates in the background of the tale:

> America, America!
> God shed his grace on thee,
> And crown thy good with brotherhood
> From sea to shining sea!

Victory came, as Coman's story goes, from "the bread and butter struggle that must ever result in the survival of the fittest,—the ablest to utilize the resources of a virgin territory."[53] It is the sort of story that has to end at the Civil War if the ending is to be a happy one. The Republican Party under Abraham Lincoln committed the young country to free land and free labor and instituted the Homestead Bill on May 20, 1862. "The long struggle between forced and free labor, between land monopoly and the self-employed landowner, had ended in the triumph of the ideal American type—the homestead farmer" (II, 365). The homesteader serves as the hero of her story by rescuing the American West for family farms. It is the sort of book that could be written unselfconsciously in the United States before the First World War. Coman openly supports social Darwinist belief in "the survival of the fittest," sees the country as "virgin territory," and celebrates American triumphalism—all without ambivalence or embarrassment and, certainly, without a trace of irony.

In responding to the gift, Addams acknowledged a connection between Coman's scholarly work and her own imaginative writing. "I have always been enormously interested in those early beginnings, things which always seem curiously near my childhood experiences."[54] Coman's story of the West provided an historical palimpsest that Addams peeled back to reveal Cedarville, Illinois. The image of the homestead farmer folded John Addams into its many layers, and it was that link between past and present that caught her attention. She wondered, too, about race memory and whether a collective unconscious might contain a reservoir of imaginative material for writers and storytellers. Coman's narrative was in Addams's mind as she sailed across the Atlantic Ocean aboard the *Adriatic* on the cold morning of February 18, 1913, and it would influence the shape of her next book.

The Long Road of Women's Memory was Addams's second, and perhaps her most successful, war story. Certainly, it was her most literary project, one that traced myth back to its roots in the human and especially the female psyche. Content to ask questions and to leave answers open, Addams wove together neighborhood tales, dressing comfortably in the garments of working women and telling long stories through their voices. She actually wrote the last chapter of the book first as a long meditation on history and consciousness with autobiographical fragments that reveal much about her own psyche. She placed images of Cedarville over those of ancient Egypt in an experimental literary pattern she called "interpretative memory."

After she and Mary Smith arrived in Egypt in March 1913, Addams wrote to Coman, "I will confess to have fallen very much under the spell of this amazing country."[55] The trip made its way into an early essay, one that Addams sent to Ellery Sedgwick at the *Atlantic Monthly* after her return in July.[56] After reading the essay, Sedgwick assured her: "Your paper from Egypt will stir many readers to new questionings in a discussion which is never closed." He added, "I have read your essay with deep interest and shall be only too glad to print it in The Atlantic." Her musings on the nature of memory were difficult to classify, and Sedgwick read them as discourse on religion: "I think that our constituency was never more ready than now to listen to these ideas of yours."

The readers of the *Atlantic Monthly* found as they opened the issue in February 1914 a curious kind of travelogue, one that loops backward and forward geographically and chronologically. As she travels through Egypt, she thinks about Illinois, an imaginative juxtaposition that forms the basis of her essay. Looking at the temples and tombs of ancient Egypt reminds Addams of nowhere more than her own country. Seeing antiquity through American philosophy, she uses Emerson's advice "'to establish a relation between the days of our life and the centuries of the world.'"[57] Human history embodies personal experience. With that relationship in mind, Addams constructs a traveler's palimpsest that sketches a map of her own beginnings in Illinois over the terrain of modern and ancient Egypt. She sees her own childhood through the scene before her: "Nevertheless, what I, at least, was totally unprepared to encounter was the constant revival of primitive and overpowering emotions which I had experienced so long ago that they had become absolutely detached from myself and seemed to belong to someone else—to a small person who no longer concerned me and who was certainly not in the least responsible for my present convictions and reflections." As modern-day Egypt had buried ancient tombs under layers of earth, so Addams's conscious mind had concealed subconscious and semiconscious memories. The act of traveling unveils her early life, long dormant in her mind. The reader journeys toward Cedarville as Addams makes her way toward Cairo. The conquests of Ramses, the theology of Akhenaton, and the feminism of Hatshepsut express in hieroglyph a fear of death akin to the fear she had experienced as a child.

Travel has the counterintuitive effect of turning the tourist's eye inward. "[M]y adult intelligence would be unexpectedly submerged by the emotional message which was written underneath it all." What she calls "primitive emotion" sweeps away her conscious adult self along with the history being portrayed in the temples and museums, unearthing the bedrock of memory from her own "earliest childhood," memory that is "instinctive and universal" and therefore awakened by the juxtaposition of Jane Addams, the adult traveler, and Egypt, the historic monument.

Central to the shape of the book she would write from the essay is the idea that literature comes from memory and imagination. "Again there came a faint memory of the child's first apprehension that there may be poetry out-of-doors." She moves her readers toward her final point: "the discovery that myths have a foundation in natural phenomena." And she subtly links her prose to the poetry of Wordsworth and his "intimations of immortality." The essay ends in epiphany: "Such ghosts of reminiscences coming to the traveler as he visits one after another of the marvelous human documents upon the banks of the Nile may be merely manifestations of that new humanism which is perhaps the most precious possession of this generation, the belief that no altar at which living men have once devoutly worshipped, no oracle to whom a nation long ago appealed in its moments of dire confusion, no gentle myth in which past generations have found solace, can lose all significance for us, the survivors." The new humanism as she interprets it comes from a secular, and not a religious, pattern of belief. Altars, oracles, and myths from the past continue to hold meaning for twentieth-century readers.

The term "survivors" is prophetic, especially because the first draft of the essay was apparently written before the events of August and September 1914 that that would lead to the Great War. A woman over fifty might think of herself as a survivor, of course, especially with Coman's illness in her mind as she traveled in Egypt and began to think about how to describe her experiences.

The essay contains the nascent ideas of the book that Addams cobbled together over the next two years. Her vision of America is nearly an inversion of Katharine Coman's vision in *Economic Beginnings of the Far West*. Instead of telling the story of the triumph of the homestead farmer who secures the virgin land for the young country, Addams tells the story of failure and misery among immigrant women who worked to build America's cities. Katharine Bates had written another poem after visiting the Columbian Exposition in 1893, a year of economic depression in Chicago and throughout the world. "The Year of the Vision" includes the lines:

> Beyond the circle of her glistening domes
> A bitter wind swept by to waste and wither,
> A cry went up from hunger-smitten homes,
> But came not hither.

It is that cry that Jane Addams records in much of her writing, but never more poignantly than in the book completed in the midst of an upheaval that threatened any sense of social order.

Ghostly Fingers

The Long Road of Woman's Memory is Addams's most experimental book in its associative structure and its theorizing about the relationship between memory and art. She invokes Memory as the Mother of the Muses, placing her efforts alongside those of Euripides, who sought to transmute tales of sorrow and wrongdoing into song. The book places her back on Halsted Street in the company of her neighbors—the long road that ends her first book, *Democracy and Social Ethics*. She affirms: "[W]hile I may receive valuable suggestion from classic literature, when I really want to learn from life, I must depend upon my neighbors, for, as William James insists, the most instructive human documents lie along the beaten pathway" (xi). In the company of her old friend, Addams dresses herself in a series of costumes, all of them female this time, to tell the story of American experience. The literary journey begins with a rumor that the Devil's own child is living at Hull-House and moves forward and backward over time, ending with images of Jane Addams as a child in Cedarville.

The book is remarkable for its design, one that anticipates the literary experiments with fiction that will follow the Great War. Her willingness to expose the structure beneath her art, the very timbers that support her design, places her among modernist writers who explore states of consciousness. Moving from Euripides to William James to William Butler Yeats, Addams works to define the art she is creating. "I once tried to collect some folk-lore for Mr. Yeats," she explains, "to prove that an Irish peasant does not lose his faith in the little people nor his knowledge of Gaelic phrases simply because he is living in a city" (18). Is there such a thing as collective memory, even race memory or ethnic memory? Does a subconscious or semiconscious reservoir of memory operate on the individual or public imagination? If so, what is the relationship between group consciousness and individual experience? Addams struggles with such questions in her search for a connection between memory and art.

She comes to believe that the female mind may be especially receptive to memory and places herself beside Diotema, "the wisest woman of antiquity, who asserted that the life which above all we should live, must be discovered by faithful and strenuous search for ever-widening kinds of beauty" (82). *The Long Road of Woman's Memory* takes the reader on a narrative journey outward from the writer's experience into a discussion of art itself and then, surprisingly, uses the knowledge gleaned to penetrate the writer's innermost thoughts.

In the winter of 1916, Addams was diagnosed with tuberculosis of the kidney, a painful condition that led her doctor to demand rest away from the cold Chicago weather. As soon as she left Chicago to travel to California by way of Colorado, she turned her mind to writing "The Devil Baby at Hull-House," a blend of neighborhood stories and musings about their meaning. In February, Ellery Sedgwick found the manuscript waiting for him at the *Atlantic Monthly* office after his return from a holiday in the West. He beamed approval: "This is the Miss Addams in whom we all believe—militarists, pacifists, progressives, and the rest of us—and I shall take the very greatest pleasure in publishing the paper."[58] He chided her, however, for writing too much, reminding her that his readers resisted essays longer than ten pages. He was thrilled to find her back at her craft. A writer without politics sells magazines; certainly that was true in 1916 as the United States moved inevitably toward battle. The story of a six-week-long rumor that the women of Hull-House were sheltering the Devil's baby was published in *Atlantic Monthly* as well as the *American Journal of Sociology.*

"[I]t was the Muses again at their old tricks,—the very mother of them this time,—thrusting their ghostly fingers into the delicate fabric

of human experience to the extreme end of life," Addams begins the essay (x). The "ghostly fingers" of memory, like a hand in a puppet, shape
the stories the women tell. The essay offers a sociological and psychological study of urban myth, giving variations on the tale and suggesting
how versions of the story transmuted immigrant experience. The phe-
nomenon illustrates the power of memory to soften the harshness of reality for women who have little control over the forces that rule their
existence. She concedes that the opening and closing sections of the book,
the Devil Baby myth and the journey to Egypt, seem to move in opposing directions, the Muse of Memory being protean after all. At Hull-House
urban myth has the effect of bringing groups together to ward off the
dangers of the outside world, and in Egypt myth has the opposite effect
of separating Addams from the group in order to understand the dangers
in her own life.

As she works to define the transmutation of fear into myth, what she
does not tell us is that the book itself may be read as her own attempt to
deflect public criticism of her pacifism. As she grew less sure of her public and political voice, Addams wrote in private and imaginative prose.
The occasion for the book was the summer of 1915, as the war in Europe
exposed "the black depths of primitive human nature." Addams believed
that women in wartime are especially vulnerable: "Desolated women,
stripped by war of all their warm domestic interests and of children long
cherished in affectionate solicitude, sat shelterless in the devastating glare
of Memory." The women used myth to build a community in Chicago
and to forestall destruction.

The story of the Devil Baby came in several versions, depending largely on the ethnicity of the storyteller. The Italian version had a hundred
variations of a tale about a pious and pregnant young woman married to
an atheist, who tears a holy picture from the wall of their home with the
curse that he would rather have the devil in his house, only to discover
that the devil appears in the body of his child. "As soon as the Devil Baby
was born, he ran about the table shaking his finger in deep reproach at
his father" (3). The young man grabs the baby and takes him to Hull-
House and from there to church for baptism. The baby flees the holy
water, "running lightly over the backs of the pews." In the Jewish version, the father of six daughters swears that he would rather have the devil
himself than another female child. The Devil Baby suddenly appears.
"Save for a red automobile which occasionally figured in the story and a
stray cigar, the tale might have been fashioned a thousand years ago" (4).
Addams traces the story, analyzing the "contagion of emotion" along with
the "aesthetic sociability" of what becomes an urban myth. She suggests

that the tale—as was true of the white slave narrative, although she does not make the connection—serves as a warning passed to younger women by their mothers: "[D]omestic instruction is best given through tales and metaphors." The teller of the tale, too, gains respect in her knowledge of the story and her ability to retell it in vivid language. "These old women enjoyed a moment of triumph, as if they had made good at last and had come into a region of sanctions and punishments which they understood" (9).

The circle of old women in the Halsted neighborhood act as shamen in the community, transmuting their sorrows into an oral literature that makes sense of fragmentary experience: "[A]t least for half an hour the past seemed endowed also for me with a profounder and more ardent life." The Devil Baby suggests the mission that Jane Addams herself had in mind to transform the reality of the war into "long-accumulated folk-lore with its magic power to transfigure and eclipse the sordid and unsatisfactory surroundings in which life is actually spent" (18). She reveals her mode of storytelling when she admits that "tragic experiences gradually come dressed in such trappings" (21).

A good storyteller knows how to use the "ghostly fingers" of memory to shape events, however random, to create convincing and entertaining narratives. A well-told story has the power to give beauty and significance to rough reality and to transform resentment, unhappiness, and horror into art. An urban myth like the Devil Baby story acts as a taboo giving women the power to warn men about the results of infidelity. She theorizes that it is through words and not through brawn that women may have the means of subduing men by creating "a literature of their own" (29). That is certainly Addams's hope for her writing project, although she never says it openly.

The literary theory she struggles to define and illustrate is what she calls "interpretive art" (34). In one example, she quotes a long anonymous letter from a semiliterate neighbor who writes in what a modernist would call stream-of-consciousness: "[S]he say what youse talk with old drunk man for we shall come to their dance when it will be they will tell us and we should know all about where to see them that girl she say oh if you will go with them you will get devils baby like some other girls did who we knows" (33). Addams first gives the easy moral reading that the Devil Baby myth provides the community with an unambiguous case of sin and retribution: "if you will go with them you will get devils baby like some other girls." She, however, seeks a deeper interpretation, one that links her to other modernist writers. "I think, on the whole, such an explanation was a mistake; it is more probable that the avidity of the women demonstrated that the story itself, like all interpretative art, was one of those free, unconscious attempts to satisfy, outside of life, those cravings which life itself leaves unsatisfied" (34–35).

Our desire to tell a seamless narrative is illusory. The stories about the Devil Baby reveal the human desire to free the unconscious: "At moments, however, baffled desires, sharp cries of pain, echoes of justices unfulfilled, the original material from which such tales are fashioned, would defy Memory's appeasing power and break through the rigid restraints imposed by all Art, even that unconscious of itself" (35). Virginia Woolf sought such expression, as did William Faulkner. Experimental fiction in the early years of the twentieth century often focused on bafflement, cries, echoes, the residue of material left after the tale has supposedly been told.

Addams retells the Devil stories told her by the women of Halsted Street, smoothing out the narratives in her own cool voice. She turns seemingly random stories into art. "In the midst of the most tragic reminiscences, there remained that something in the memories of these mothers which has been called the great revelation of tragedy, or sometimes the great illusion of tragedy; that which has power in its own right to make life palatable and at rare moments even beautiful" (52). The tragedy she seems to want to tell is the story behind the surface of her study, a tale too close to her experience and too significant to human history for her to know yet how to tell it more directly.

In the voice of an old woman whose son has committed suicide to avoid telling his mother that his girlfriend is pregnant, Addams tells the reader, "'If you are kind enough to listen, I want to tell you my experience in all its grim sorrow'" (55). The voice is only thinly veiled, and we can hear Addams merging with the female voices around her, speaking with them and for them. Using an analogy, she explains, "[O]ur social state is like a countryside—of a complex geological structure, with outcrops of strata of very diverse ages" (65). Her literary effort is to make sense of the outcrops that reveal to us the exposed features of the mysterious structure at the core. A woman might be especially good at transforming random stories into art: "If she develops her craving for continuity into a willingness to subordinate a part to the whole and into a sustained and self-forgetful search for congruity and harmony with a life which is greater than hers, she may lift the entire selective process into the realm of Art; at least so far as Art is dependent upon proportion and so far as beauty hangs upon an ineffable balance between restraint and inclusion."

Addams has moved, at this point in her loosely woven argument, away from Euripides and toward Diotema, whom she calls the wisest woman in the ancient world in her search for "ever-widening kinds of beauty." A woman, as a new chivalric figure, stands as the lone creator of life through the visceral experience of birth and as an artist through the fusion of maternal memory and concern for the future of her children.

The penultimate chapter, "Women's Memories—Challenging War," finally gets to the topic that is closest to Addams. The elaborate structure of the book, with its many layers of narrative and argument, leads readers to the war in Europe. Many of them would not have read the book had she started there. Her pacifist vision of the world, surprisingly, comes in her most openly creative chapter. At this point in the narrative, Addams admits in a footnote that the story she is about to tell about the war is fictionalized in that the voices she will use are a "composite made from several talks held with each of two women"(115). The female voice summarizes the last letter she received from her son before his death in battle: "'He wrote that whenever he heard the firing of a huge field-piece he knew that the explosion consumed years of the taxes which had been slowly accumulated by some hard-working farmer or shopkeeper, and that he unconsciously calculated how fast industrial research would have gone forward, had his department been given once a decade the costs of a single day of warfare, with the government's command to turn back into alleviation of industrial conditions the taxes which the people had paid'" (119). The letter, unlike authentic battlefield prose, sounds like a treatise on government.

It certainly does sound like Jane Addams, who watched as the social programs she had worked to put into place suffered from the sharp turn of attention toward preparation for war. The son, before his death, had been working on poisonous gases, a project that forced him, ironically, to reverse his own early research to prevent hazardous gases from harming factory workers. The mother's voice pleads Addams's case: "'I know how hard it must have been for him to put knowledge acquired in his long efforts to protect normal living to the brutal use of killing men.'" And Addams pushes the point: "It was literally a forced act of prostitution" (121). The voice, at this point, is very thinly veiled: "The international mind, which really does exist in spite of the fact that it is not yet equipped with adequate organs for international government, has become firmly established, at least among scientists" (121). The double-dressing is clever—a character through the voice of her martyred son tells Addams, the writer, what Addams most wants to tell her readers.

The last chapter strangely puts the reader at the beginning of the book's actual composition, the travel essay on Egypt and Addams's memory of Illinois. What she does to reconcile use of the essay is to claim in her introduction that as the war escalated during the summer of 1915, she thought more and more about her previous journey into antiquity. The longer view represented by the Pyramids and the human desire to see a way past personal death and cultural extinction allows Addams to seem to end the book outside the immediate tragedy unfolding before her.

She sent a copy of the book to Vachel Lindsay, who warmed to her as a writer and sought her as a friend. "I can hardly wait a decent interval to answer your letter," he began his letter of thanks. "You do not know how eager I am for your friendship."[59] His literary friends in Chicago included Carl Sandburg, Edgar Lee Masters, and Harriet Monroe. In December he planned performances of his poetry, and, after the performances, he hoped to use Hull-House as a writer's retreat. "I have consecrated December and most of January absolutely to the business of writing, and I am wondering if I could be man enough to refuse most social invitations and write there a month and take in Hull House in the evenings through the skin as it were?" The association of Hull-House with literary art was a natural one for him as he finished reading *The Long Road of Woman's Memory*. "I sat down and read it all morning and half the afternoon the minute it arrived. It is a lovely book—the work of a Greek, a woman more Greek than Christian—as was 'The Spirit of Youth and the City Streets.'" Probably no compliment could have charmed her more. His letter is long, dense, full of the energy of ideas and language. He told her about his experimental book on photoplay and how he feared it might not get the audience he desired.

Lindsay talked frankly about the vulnerability of books: "Back of it all is the hope that my book shall be a live thing, a piece of ink-dynamite, not just a book pleasantly discussed by people who read my verses." Addams read the letter knowing that her own work, especially in time of war, was exposed to the same vagaries of the marketplace. He spoke for them both: "With so many books dying before my eyes, I cannot bear to write a dead one."

The Long Road of Woman's Memory, written amidst her political effort to turn the United States away from the fighting in Europe, reveals its message subtly. The very idea that the immigrant experiment in North America might end with a reprise of European hatreds was indeed horrific to her. She makes the point simply and personally that the little girl who had grown up without her mother in Cedarville, Illinois, remains frightened. The book closes with three paragraphs that work hard to take it all back, drawing a picture of modern-day Egypt that is meant to calm nerves. Yet after her assurance that she sees the flow of a life common to all centuries, she leaves the reader with a darker image: "These records also afford us glimpses into a past so vast that the present generation seems to float upon its surface as thin as a sheet of light which momentarily covers the ocean and moves in response to the black waters underneath it" (168). We feel the chill.

A Voice from the Silence

Zona Gale, who won the Pulitzer Prize for drama in 1921, began to read a book with keen interest in 1922. She might have been reading Eliot's *The Waste Land* with its suggestive images and fragmented lines or Joyce's *Ulysses* with its bold play of language and focus on individual consciousness. Gale's taste, however, was fairly parochial, as she explained in her essay, "The United States and the Artist": "Our breathless North American industrial towns, plump suburbs, motionless farms, preoccupied mountains; our desert, either as pure color today or as seed of the cities of tomorrow; and our little towns, faintly figuring the velvet of their vast fields, white or green—these are not mere material for art; these are stuff of the life of art." With Katharine Bates's "America, the Beautiful" in her ear, she declared: "[A]rt is the imaginative interpretation of the life of the people, *whatever that life may be.*"[60] Literary experiment, for her, had more to do with culture than with language.

The book in her hand was *Peace and Bread in Time of War*, a book written by her midwestern literary mentor. In a long, appreciative review of the book, Gale mused on the timing of the war story: "She is so honest and so logical that it is impossible for the open-minded to do other than to feel profound respect for her analysis, while for those who share her convictions she is a voice from the silence."[61] The silencing of a public voice as strong as Addams's was a story worth retelling in 1922. Certainly by the age of sixty-two, she unabashedly yielded to her inclination to tell a story without footnotes, without having to account for her sources or verify her dates. What she created is not scholarly history or imaginative fiction—it lies somewhere between the two. As a voice from the silence, Addams revealed modernist skepticism about the limits of objective truth. "During the writing of it, however, I found myself so increasingly reluctant to interpret the motives of other people that at length I confined all analysis of motives to my own" (vii). Addams had spent much of her own literary life in the dress of others, narrating their accounts and recording their motives in books that are dialogic in texture. This time, she pledged to write from her own conscious memory, giving a firsthand "autobiographical portrayal" of the war.

In creating her persona, she quotes from an article in *The Arena* magazine: "'We do not possess our ideas, they possess us, and force us into the arena to fight for them'" (vii). Jane Addams appears in an allegorical pageant of sorts. She shifts slyly back and forth from "I" to "we" throughout the narrative, moving us into her own mind and then away from herself into the collective mind of the Women's International League for Peace and Freedom, the organization that developed from the Women's International Congress at The Hague in 1915. The voice she offers pledges to revise the distortions imposed on pacifists in newspapers and magazines. "Our portion was the odium accorded those who, because they are not allowed to state their own cause, suffer constantly from inimical misrepresentations" (3). She feels free at last to tell her war story as a peace story and offers her credo as collective belief. "We believed that the endeavor to nurture human life even in its most humble and least promising forms had crossed national boundaries."

The war story unfolds anew. The meeting at the Henry Street Settlement in October 1914, so elegantly conducted over lunch and dinner, held the promise of "unfettered kindliness" amid alarm that society might devolve into chaos, where "all social efforts would be cast into an earlier and coarser mold" (4). Efforts over tea that afternoon, "somewhat exaggerated in tone," were in vain. The group feared that the war in Europe might represent "the reversal in the whole theory and practice of their daily living" (6). All their studied rationalism shed very little light on the problem or, especially, its solution. It was on that afternoon, however, that pacifists began to resist the flow of events in Europe.

Addams retells the story of the Women's International Congress at The Hague to register her disdain for the press, who willfully misinterpreted her efforts at the Congress and later of the delegation that traveled from country to country in Europe to offer mediation. "As I recall those hurried journeys which Alice Hamilton and I made with Dr. Alletta Jacobs and her friend Madame Palthe to one warring country after another, it still seems marvelous to me that the people we met were so outspoken against war, with a freedom of expression which was not allowed later in any of the belligerent nations" (18). She rebukes reporters and newspaper owners for distorting events and silencing opposition: "It seemed to us in our naïveté, although it may be that we were not without a homely wisdom, that if the Press could be freed and an adequate offer of negotiations made, the war might be concluded before another winter of the terrible trench warfare" (19).

As if the bayonet story wasn't enough to suffer, Addams struggled, even as late as 1922, to distance herself from Henry Ford's Peace Ship, the *Oscar II*, the venture across the ocean to organize a conference of neutrals and bring warring nations to the negotiating table. She notes wryly that "no fewer than sixty-four newspaper men finally sailed on the *Oscar II* " with a group of pacifists that did not include her. Prefacing her criticism of that moral adventure, she reminds her reader, "I was fifty-five years old in 1915; I had already 'learned from life,' to use Dante's great phrase, that moral results are often obtained through the most unexpected agencies" (37). However true that may have been, she certainly knew the Ford mission was a ship of eccentrics, if not fools. "Admitting the plan had fallen into the hands of Mr. Ford who had long taken an inexplicable position in regard to peace propaganda, and that with many notable exceptions, a group of very eccentric people had attached themselves to the enterprise, so that there was every chance for a fiasco, I still felt committed to it" (39).

The story behind the launching of the Peace Ship is not one Addams tells in her book. Among Addams's letters marked *"For Confidential Records"* is one from Elizabeth P. Dowling, at the Bureau of Credits in Detroit, that recorded early negotiations between Addams and Ford.[62] Dowling had talked with Frank L. Klingensmith, secretary of the Ford Motor Company, and he in turn had consulted with Henry Ford himself. The solicitation of funds was a sticky matter, and Dowling spent much of the letter outlining how Ford fended off direct appeals for money. "Miss Addams, you and the committee will bear me out in it, I am sure—*that neither directly nor indirectly* shall Mr. Ford be solicited for funds; nor shall he be required to divulge his own plans in the peace work." Although Ford admired Jane Addams, there was every reason for discretion. "There is a great deal of publicity afloat since Mr. Ford's declaration for peace, some of it is sense and some of it is very foolish." She then commented on the fate of public figures, all the while having Addams's bayonet speech in mind. "That falls to the lot of every person in the public eye. But such of it as can be controlled must be, from Mr. Ford's standpoint." Dowling put it fairly bluntly to Addams: "Can you imagine the fusillade outside the Ford plant if it were to become known that Miss Addams had come here for a conference with Henry Ford!" The two public figures met in private.

Rosika Schwimmer met with Ford, as well, to solicit funds. Her visit prompted a nervous telegram from Edwin Pipp to Jane Addams: "MADAM SCHWIMMER HAD AN INTERVIEW WITH HENRY FORD YESTERDAY. MR. FORD'S ATTORNEY WAS PRESENT, WAS HOSTILE, SKEPTICAL AND EVEN SEEMED DOUBTFUL OF MADAM SCHWIMMER. WOULD YOU KINDLY WIRE ME AT OUR EXPENSE FOR PUBLIC OR PRIVATE USE A STATEMENT AS TO HER WORK AT THE HAGUE CONFERENCE AS YOU OBSERVED IT."[63] Addams vouched for her but the lawyer heard the tone. Anna Garlin Spencer wrote to Addams, warning her about the collision between Ford's money and Schwimmer's personality: "I am dismayed after a visit to the Biltmore headquarters. Mme. Schwimmer is evidently secured in leadership. Mr. Lochner seems fanatically certain that Mr. Ford's preposterous slogan 'Out of the Trenches by Christmas' can actually be realized! The whole atmosphere there is surcharged with excitement and seems to me quite removed from that sober and humble attitude of mind which can alone enable one to be of real service in the awful time."[64] Spencer saw Schwimmer as the source of the problem, with her claim that the Peace Ship might actually stop the war, and worried that such a visible ship might be a target for the Germans. "I cannot be the guest of a man who is hopelessly under Mme. Schwimmer's control," she declared, adding privately to Addams that a man might control Ford but a woman would have no chance of controlling Schwimmer.

The *Oscar II* sailed on December 8, 1915, at two o'clock in the afternoon from New York without Jane Addams. As the day drew near for departure, Alice Hamilton telegraphed Schwimmer and Lockner: "DOCTORS SAY MISS ADDAMS CANNOT POSSIBLY PLAN TO TRAVEL BY DEC. 8TH."[65] Perhaps as a response to the stress, Jane Addams began to show signs of the kidney problem that would be diagnosed as tuberculosis. Her pacifist colleagues in Europe hoped she would come to the Mediterranean as she convalesced, but Mary Smith urged her toward the West Coast of the United States, well away from the Ford Peace Ship and the fighting in Europe. And she, too, was inclined to stay away from the unruly adventure. As Addams explained in *Peace and Bread:* "It became clearer every day that whoever became associated with the ship would be in for much ridicule and social opprobrium" (40).

The ship sailed and Ford pronounced it a success in an attempt to save as much face as possible. Louis Lochner loyally reported on the fiasco. "I cannot tell you how my heart sank when I read your cablegram here in Stockholm telling me that you have to go to California for two months," he wrote her at the end of January 1916.[66] He warned her, however, not to join the group later. "From what I have seen of Dr. Jacobs recently, I fear that she is not in complete possession of her faculties. Her attitude toward us has been most peculiar," Lochner explained. "After Mr. Ford broke down in health, and left with us enough money only to carry on the expenses of the Expedition, but said nothing further about the $200,000 gift to the women's work, you can see that Madame Schwimmer was put in an embarassing position." The letters back and forth narrate the rift between the European women. Rosika Schwimmer wrote Addams with her version of the story: "I think I owe it to you and to myself to tell you that Dr. Jacobs not only reached the limit, but overstepped every boundary of decency." She reported to Addams that Jacobs was "misusing your name and my name in connection with Ford."[67] Several members of the Women's Committee had apparently complained that the Ford Expedition would fail unless Jacobs resigned. Moreover, others had informed her that Addams had forbidden members of the International Committee to cooperate with the Ford people. Schwimmer confided, "They considered your sickness a 'diplomatic disease,' invented to protect you from open admission that you did not want to be connected with the affair." Addams began to refer to the group as a "Counsel of Imperfection" and watched from a distance, one that grew over the next months.

The story of her journey westward in the winter of 1916, likewise, did not appear in *Peace and Bread.* She escaped from Hull-House and the Peace Ship controversy, traveling with Mary Smith to Colorado and then to California, and both women relaxed into their companionship. Marcet began a letter in February, "Dearest Auntie." What she said revealed much about her aunt's private life that lay discreetly beneath the public one. "I have a wild, chaotic impulse to go chasing straight out to you, but I know I should probably be only a precious nuisance and you and Mary Smith have such jolly times together that when you have her you don't need anyone else."[68] Marcet herself found a companion that winter, and the suitor, Emmanel Julius, wrote an elaborately stilted letter to Addams asking for Marcet's hand in marriage. Addams blessed the union, although the feminist in her made the argument that Marcet should not take her husband's name, suggesting that they join the two last names. Mary Smith, who was "so much shocked by the proposition," forced Addams to write again withdrawing the appeal.[69] The young couple, however, took the hint and merged their names, becoming Emmanuel and Marcet Haldeman-Julius.

Once away from the pressures of Hull-House and, especially in 1916, the failures of the peace movement, Addams longed to write. From the Antlers Lodge in Colorado Springs, she told Ellery Sedgwick about her literary project. "When I was sent away from Hull-House for a long period of convalescence, I brought with me various notes and unfinished manuscripts."[70] She gave him a fortnight to consider two essays on the Devil Baby at Hull-House, the very pieces she would later use to construct *The Long Road of Woman's Memory.* And Sedgwick responded eagerly to the writer he admired: "It gives me very real satisfaction to print this paper, for it is the Miss Addams about whom no two Americans have a right to think differently."[71] A month later, as the essay came to press, Sedgwick wrote more personally: "I felt guilty. At the time I didn't realize how miserable you had been."[72] And he added earnestly, "To publish 'The Devil Baby at Hull-House' will give me very unusual pleasure." The way out of her dilemma, they both understood, was to write about familiar territory, the closer to Hull-House the better.

In a letter to Marcet, Mary reported on Jane's health: "we walk warily these days."[73] The literary woman, though her handwriting was faint, continued to work. She wanted to avoid contact with the pacifists in Europe. "I have had a relapse here," she informed Schwimmer, "and I am quite convinced it would be folly for me to try to leave the country now. There is nothing 'diplomatic' about this illness, it is unfortunately genuine."[74] No hysteria, no "rest cure," but rather she claimed her time away as "a perfectly defined organic treatment." By the spring, Addams returned to Chicago restored. She accepted the box of red roses sent by President Wilson as he began to line up support for his fall campaign. Ready to deal again with Henry Ford, she traveled to Detroit with Emily Balch for lunch with the Fords, who agreed to continue to support the peace effort in Europe. Harold Ickes hoped for a rapprochement between Teddy Roosevelt and Addams: "I suppose that neither of you would wish to have any publicity in connection with the interview, if it could be brought about, because, of course, the newspapers would twist and distort in order to make a sensational story."[75] Roosevelt failed, however, to change her mind. She intended to support Wilson in the fall campaign, believing that he would work to keep the United States out of the war. "I know I must be a thorn in the flesh to the Progressive Party, and I am really distressed that my convictions won't permit me to march along with my natural comrades," she confided to Ickes.[76]

Jane missed Marcet's wedding in June but managed to march in the suffrage parade during the Republican convention before she and Mary left for their cottage in Hull's Cove. Vigor returned to her handwriting and gumption to her negotiations with editors. "The Devil Baby at Hull-House" had not yet appeared in the *Atlantic Monthly*. "I light heartedly incorporated the material in a book 'The Long Road of Woman's Memory' which the Macmillan Company will bring out in the fall," she announced to Sedgwick who had planned to run the essay in his November issue.[77] "I have stated the dilemma. May I ask you for a suggestion as to the way out?" She jokingly twisted the question, "Is there such a thing as exchanging checks and manuscripts under these painful conditions?" Sedgwick responded in kind: "There shall be no trafficking in your article whatever happens."[78] He agreed to publish the essay in September or

October, ahead of the Macmillan book, and hoped that she would prom-ise him another article for 1917. "Did you think that my letter express-ing my satisfaction with "The Devil-Baby" was not altogether sincere?" He clearly delighted in conversation with her. "Saying just what he thinks, is the best privilege of an editor and the one I prize most. I like your paper enormously."

The literary community surrounded Addams in the summer of 1916. Paul Kellogg, who visited the cottage, wrote: "My four days at Hull's Cove were a real boon to me; and I hope they will be typical of your summer—beginning in fogs and ending in sun splashed waves, and shore and woods."[79] An antiwar essay she published in *Survey* drew the strong praise of Zona Gale. "Oh my dear, when you can keep saying it, and can say it new every time as the Survey article has it, the world has a voice for its dreams."[80] She considered Addams her heart's kindred, as the title of her novel indicated. "The poignancy and *insideness* of this analysis leaves me with a sense of spiritual experiences, *in me,* as I read." Gale saw in Ad-dams's prose "the far look that accompanies the skeptical smile." The So-ciety of Midland Authors, a group that included Gale as well as Edna Fer-ber, Hamlin Garland, Harriet Monroe, James Whitcomb Riley, and Edith Wyatt, invited Jane Addams to join their literary society. "By a general vote your name received the sanction of the Board, and this is intended to car-ry to you notification of such election and a warm welcome to the plea-surable reunions of the Society."[81] She accepted the company of her peers even as she explained that her health kept her in the East. Vachel Lind-say began to correspond with Addams that fall. The Little Theater in Chi-cago performed Lindsay's poetry along with the interpretative dance of Eleanor Daugherty. "She will dance my poems in costume, as I chant them," he explained. He wanted Addams to see the performance and to go to films with him during his visit. "I will talk you to death and create disorder for a radius of ten feet," he playfully wooed her.[82]

Even as her voice resonated in the literary world, it threatened poli-ticians. Her relationship with Ellery Sedgwick at the *Atlantic Monthly* proves the bellwether. Addams and others from the Women's Peace Par-ty sent him a letter for consideration that he decided to hold for thirty days before publishing. As he put his finger into the political wind, he hesitated. "These are such swiftly moving times that even four weeks may change the whole appearance of things," he explained.[83] He then mused about the matter of war and gender. "It is rather shameful to say so, but it would add weight to the discussion (in many people's minds), if readers were commonly to think that the writers were men." Know-ing Addams, he added: "Certainly, there should be no hint as to sex. There is none in the vigor of thought and expression which mark the writers merely as exceptional representatives of their sex, whichever it is." Mired in his own rhetoric, he frankly admitted: "You see, my business is to make people read and consider what I want them to read and consider, and I must be guided by the little I know of human nature." Addams, of course, understood literary cross-dressing. "I quite agree that there is no necessity for indicating the sex of the writers," she pragmatically concurred.[84]

If women could not talk about the war, they could talk about what it means to be women. Addams's *Atlantic Monthly* essay on the Devil Baby drew praise even from Woodrow Wilson: "The pathos and revelation of it all are indeed poignant and I carried away from reading the article what I am sure will be a very permanent impression."[85] And George Brett suggested that *Twenty Years at Hull-House* be placed on the list of required reading for high school students, earning Macmillan a steady twenty-five cents each for its Pocket Book Classic edition. Women writers admired *The Long Road of Woman's Memory.* Harriet Monroe told Addams, "[I]t appeals doubly to both my literary and my social sense."[86] Zona Gale wrote to say, "I think that nothing of all your work which has so moved me, moves me as does *The Long Road of Woman's Memory.*"[87] She, too, was searching for historical continuity and cultural coherence. "The Egyptian chapter touches into those other forms of one unity." Might some knowledge of a larger context, she wondered, prevent the United States from moving into war?

Wilson exposed his hand after winning reelection, and Addams sank into depression. She was living with Mary Smith at 12 West Walton in Chicago and working at Hull-House only a few days a week. She confided to Gale that she doubted her voice held sway over the younger generation. In conversation she quarreled with Paul Kellogg and then sent an apology: "I have been filled with remorse ever since our talk the other morning and have quite concluded that I am not yet fit to be out in the world."[88] She traveled to Philadelphia to rest but escaped to New York to visit Lillian Wald, confiding to her friend: "When I make my confession to Mary, it will be coupled with much gratitude to you for all your good care."[89] Jane Addams, in mind and body, responded to Wilson's public ambivalence over a declaration of war. She knitted baby sweaters and worried about her nephew Stanley's illness and inability, apparently, to support his family. Through Mary, Jane sent money to his family, saying almost nothing about her own relapse into bronchitis. She wrote to Ida Tarbell, who was ill herself: "Certainly I have run away from all my obligations during the last year and am only too conscious of how iron-clad health obligations are."[90] Although depressed, she was not without resources.

Perhaps Louis Lockner's telegram on February 3, acknowledging the fact that the United States would enter the war within days, came as a relief to her. Her energy for public effort returned. The Women's Peace Party collected $11,591 by the first week of February. In a last-ditch effort, she organized a campaign of telegrams to Wilson, pleading for a referendum vote on war in the United States and a joint conference of neutral nations. She helped organize an Emergency Peace Federation mass meeting in Washington, D.C. "How perplexing it all is!" she wrote to Lillian Wald.[91] Mary Smith had retreated to Colorado but only after Addams agreed to meet her in the South and travel together to Florida. "I am being sent away," she complained to Wald, "to get rid of this horrid bronchitis but am allowed to go by way of New York." From New York she traveled to Philadelphia and then to Washington for the rally, and afterward to Baltimore to meet Mary. At the end of February, Addams joined others in sending a telegram to Wilson, protesting the Overman Bill because it "threatens the liberty of speech and activity of the citizens of the United States and is dangerous to Democratic institutions."[92] Three weeks later, she wrote Harriet Thomas news of her life in Oakland, Florida. "We are having wonderful weather here, and I am improving so fast that I cherish hopes of being a normal human being upon my return."[93] As she regained her health, she traveled north to South Carolina and then back to Washington, dismayed by the breakdown of her peace coalition. Carrie Chapman Catt removed her name from the Women's Peace Party, preferring to support the war in the name of National Suffrage, pragmatically focusing on one cause.

"Yesterday morning, given the dark of the day before, I awoke with a stone in my thought," Zona Gale wrote to Addams on April 9, 1917.[94]

"What shall I do? This war breaks my heart," Vachel Lindsay wrote.[95] His champion in Congress was the lone dissenter: "If I had been in Congress I would have voted with Miss [Jeannette Rankin, of Missoula, Montana,] and would have considered it a sufficient reason to say 'I will not vote for war till she does.'"

Louis Lochner took it personally: "It's getting darker and darker, and I am becoming quite discouraged and worn out by the long struggle." He threatened to leave his post and move to Florida to take up farming.

Addams cajoled him: "I do not in least despise raising chickens nor the fact that it takes intelligence to put it through but I am sure you are needed very much just now in the many social movements which are having a hard time."[96]

The entry of the United States into the Great War had a considerable effect on Jane Addams's writing. Ellery Sedgwick had not only printed her work in the past, but had encouraged her to send more articles in the fall of 1916. "I am a very Jew in holding you to your promises, so if I seem too importunate, do not hesitate to snub me," he wrote, thinking himself a witty man in making this slur.[97] He wanted an essay about the political faith of women. Had woman's suffrage, where it already existed in states like Illinois, made any difference in the November 1916 election? Moreover, Sedgwick wanted Addams to suggest ways that women might make a difference in future elections. "I am inclined to believe that women take more interest in municipal than in national politics." He lectured, without a sense of irony, the woman who headed the national Women's Peace Party and had presided over the Women's International Congress at The Hague. He continued to offer his opinion: "It would be natural if they did, for the transition from household to war is easier than the jump from household to nation." Sedgwick seemed unaware of the contradictions in his logic: "Indeed, almost the only conclusion which I have been able to arrive at is the very general one that women incline to pacifism, and that they are not as much interested in foreign politics as men are." Addams declined his offer of an essay until after the war, noting diplomatically that she saw "so much unjustified speculation in regard to the women's vote."[98] She sent him, instead, a talk she had delivered to the Chicago Woman's Club on the efforts of the International Committee of Women for a Permanent Peace. The speech had drawn the ire of the press, and it was cheeky of her to send it to the *Atlantic Monthly* amid the local battle. Irascibility may have kept Addams from despair. She wrote to Sedgwick, "It was so well received by our Jingo press that I venture to send it on for your reading."[99]

His rejection letter of May 9, 1917, silenced her literary voice. After reading the essay and conferring with others, Sedgwick pronounced: "Perhaps it is instinct, rather than judgment, but something there certainly is which tells me that, to review the distressing doubts and hesitations which beset us at the time of crisis, is not helpful nor profitable." And to make the matter worse, he admitted the effectiveness of her appeal. "It has an appreciable effect upon my own present resolution to review once more the devious path of my own convictions, and so it must be with a great mass of people."[100] He delivered the blow by questioning the depth of her thinking. "With much that you say, I agree, and I think it well that, as a nation, we should realize the magnitude of the international task before us, but this article, I think—and I say it with reluctance—does not seem to me likely to effect the result which one has a right to hope from such a paper." His letter acknowledged her power as a writer but denied her intellect as a political thinker.

As she held his letter in her hand, the first real rejection of her as a writer, she must have known how difficult it was going to be for her to speak at all during the war years. The next month, the *New York Times* told the story of her address on "Pacifism and Patriotism in Time of War" to a current events class at the Congregational Church in Evanston, along Chicago's elegant North Shore. "Profound silence followed an address by Miss Jane Addams." Orrin Carter, a member of the Illinois Supreme Court, jumped to challenge her.[101] "'I have been a life long friend of Miss Addams. I have agreed with her on most questions in the past,'" he began. "'That sounds as if you were going to break with me,' interrupted Miss Addams laughing." As his attack continued, she shot back that he should take up the issue of her right to speak with the committee that invited her. The attack echoed in newspapers across the country. What she said that so annoyed the press in 1917 is that the United States ought not create blockades nor implement weaponry that would have the effect of starving civilians in any country. "'The United States owes too much to all nations who have come here to till her broad acres, to allow the women and children of any nation to starve. The United States should tell her allies she is not in this war for the purpose of starving women and children.'" The press maintained that the miseries of war would have the effect of ending the fighting sooner rather than later.

The *Wall Street Journal* editorialized: "Miss Jane Addams furnishes an example of this kind of agitation, unconsciously bringing out the typically illogical position of the pacifist."[102] Her ideas rankled conservative editors in much the same way that they do today. In a harsh review in the *Wall Street Journal* of Jean Bethke Elshtain's *Jane Addams and the Dream of American Democracy* (2002), Christopher Caldwell, a senior editor at the *Weekly Standard*, takes Addams's ideas to task: "At Hull-House, Addams indeed provided a welfare model that was flexible and personalized. But it was not so much an alternative to the bloated modern welfare state as a first step on the road to it."[103] Caldwell scolds Addams for her "jargon-laden" and "run-of-the-mill" and "monolithically humorless" prose, and more so for her "woolly" thinking. It is a mark of the vitality of her thinking and her writing that the *Wall Street Journal*, even today, has such a visceral response.

In 1917, newspapers reported her a casualty of the war itself. The *Cleveland News*, for example, viewed the Evanston speech as the end of her speaking career. "It is saddening to note that the world war has materially damaged the repute of the 'head resident' of Hull House, as it suddenly blighted the political fame of 'the lady from Montana,' who wanted to stand by her country but could not vote for war." Quoting from

"Pacifism and Patriotism in Time of War," the editors concluded with an attack on Addams: "It is an uncommonly silly outburst of pro-German twaddle, it is true, but such stuff is by no means peculiar to the feminine mind. A few males among us have babbled just as inanely." If she found little comfort in the fact that men could, at times, talk as foolishly as women, other papers made even bolder charges. The *St. Paul Pioneer Press* carried the story, adding, "How any loyal American, with the sentences of the President ringing in his ears, could have uttered the seditious balderdash of Miss Addams is past conception."[104]

The strangest charge was reported in the *Atlanta Journal* during the debate over suffrage on the floor of the House of Representatives: "The friends of Miss Addams wrote her that Miss Mildred Rutherford, of Athens, speaking in opposition to the suffrage bill, declared that Miss Addams is pro-German, that she believes in the amalgamation of the races, and that her father was a white slave trafficker."[105] Rutherford had, it seems, connected Addams and *A New Conscience and an Ancient Evil*, but how John Addams became the "cadet" is a mystery. It is a measure of how far the charges went that Addams dignified them with a response: "'The three statements you quote in your letter are absolutely false. I do not hold either opinion. My father was an honorable citizen, a respected state Senator for many years. Deeply regret that Georgia women must encounter a campaign of vituperation.'" Alice Hamilton commiserated, "Well it was detestable of Judge Carter, wasn't it, but men are going to be that way from now one, as long as the war lasts, and please don't let yourself mind it."[106] How to be a villain after having been a saint was her absurd dilemma. "I could slay anyone who hurts you," Hamilton chivalrously joked, "but I do hope you are not letting it hurt." Warning that the blows were only just beginning, she cautioned, "I long to have you develop a sort of protective covering so that they will not hurt you."

Addams tried to publish the "seditious" essay, "Patriotism and Pacifists in War Time," and made plans to escape Chicago for her six weeks of vacation in Bar Harbor. Money for Hull-House projects dwindled during the war amid the turn of public opinion against her. She and Mary stayed with Louise DeKoven Bowen rather than open their cottage at Hull's Cove. The only request for her writing came from *The Seven Arts* but she declined the offer. Macmillan reported, not surprisingly, that her earnings in 1917 came to only $552.20, with *The Long Road of Woman's Memory* selling only 2,725 copies domestically and 99 abroad.

At the nadir of her public life, Jane Addams drew especially close to Mary Smith and their private life. On a visit to Mackinac Island, Jane scribbled a long note to Mary, who had stayed behind to open the cottage: "I am so sorry you have the worry of the sick child and the irate friend," she began.[107] "I do seem to manage to draw all the hardest things to you." We can see the nature of their "marriage" in the letter, full of the intimate language that Addams seemed more comfortable writing than speaking. "I was more or less tongue-tied the day I left. It seemed absurd to tell you how Heavenly good you had been to me month after month." Mary provided income for Addams during their many years together, and Addams used the money to help support members of her family. "I am appalled when I think how much money you have spent on me and how much of everything I have accepted like a greedy thing." Feeling the intimacy that distance can sometimes bring, she confessed: "I am filled with affection for you that I almost understand. I don't know why I write it when I might have said it—but it is a true word."

It was a struggle for Jane to admit how much she depended on Mary, whom she called "my dear fostering mother." The longer she stayed on Mackinac Island, the more she missed her companion: "Your letter from Boston made me quite homesick to be on the other bed."[108] And a few days later, she wrote, "It is hard to be away from you"; and later, "Sometimes I get fearful restless about it!"[109] She admitted growing fond of Alice Hamilton, but asked Mary not to tell Marcet, who was painfully jealous of her aunt's attention to women. "I am feeling so dry and battered that I am not of much use to any body," she lamented to Mary, "but I am always entirely yours."

Addams worked on an essay over the eventful summer of 1917, "Tolstoy and the Russian Soldiers," and published it in the *New Republic*. As she moved to Hull's Cove with Mary in September, Ellery Sedgwick asked permission to republish her two least controversial essays, "The Devil Baby in Hull-House" and "The Unexpected Reactions of a Traveler in Egypt."[110] He followed with an invitation to write something new for the *Atlantic Monthly*. Jane Addams was a tough negotiator, little given to sulking. "The only writing I have in mind at present is something concerning the Russian religious beliefs formulated by Tolstoy as a factor in the present Russian situation," she told him, noting that the *New Republic* had picked up a short version of the essay that she wanted to expand. As for his rejection of her peace essay, she conceded, "I quite agree with your statement that the peace article I sent you was out of date after war was declared." Giving back as good as she got, she added: "It may interest you to see it in pamphlet form."

Sedgwick, wanting nothing controversial, wrote that "the rapidity with which the Russian kaleidoscope changes" made publishing anything on the topic risky. "At present, then, I do not feel that I can take advantage of your offer."[111] She responded that he would need to negotiate with Macmillan on the terms of using her essays from *The Long Road of Woman's Memory*, and he was annoyed when they refused to give him permission to reprint their material. It was only after she interceded for him with Marsh that Macmillan released the Devil Baby section, a negotiation that put Sedgwick in her debt.

During the war years, Addams launched a speaking tour, funded by the U.S. Food Administration, on the subject of the world's food supply and worked hard to stay under the radar of the critical press. She delivered her speech "The World Food Supply—America's Obligation," in many venues in 1918, including El Paso, Pasadena, Sacramento, San Francisco, Palo Alto, Oakland, and Salt Lake City. Her stamina for public speaking belied her maladies and fatigue.

She, too, had the comfort of her family. Marcet visited in the winter of 1918 with her baby daughter Alice, and her letter of thanks reveals a lively cultural life. "It was such a beautiful visit! You can't think how much it all meant to me—being with you, the theatres, the city itself, the warm hospitality and above all the gracious tenderness of everyone and you in particular toward little Alice."[112] Her brother Weber died in March and, saddened as well as relieved, Jane did not go to the hospital to see him. She did listen patiently to her nephew Stanley as he agonized over his responsibility in time of war. Mary Smith underwent two surgeries in 1918, necessitating a long recuperation in Colorado and California.

As they left together for Estes Park, Addams wrote to Winthrop Lane at *Survey*, "Perhaps I can write then."[113] She joked, "I am thinking of putting my pen to paper on the Russian situation. Is not that a bold idea? Can rashness go further?" Her letter reveals a writer back at her task. She apologized to Paul Kellogg for allowing her speech on the food supply to be published in pamphlet form as she was negotiating with him to publish it in *Survey*, the magazine he crafted from *Charities and the Commons*. Her publishing situation at the magazine was a precarious one for a writer mindful of literary autonomy. Kellogg made any subscriber who paid $10 or more a member of his Survey Associates, a group that voted for the board of directors. Addams served as both associate and director and advised Kellogg on the Progressive reforms the magazine promoted. Kellogg was ambitious to establish *Survey Graphic*, an experimental magazine with an engaging visual format that, he hoped, might gain the stature and appeal of the *New Republic* and *The Nation*, and she was a perfect writer for the transition, even as she sought better venues for her writing. She sent her pamphlet to Sedgwick at the *Atlantic Monthly* and Herbert Croly at the *New Republic*, hoping to stir interest in her writing, and then apologized to Kellogg and Lane: "I hope that it is all right and that I am not going back 'on old friends.'"[114]

The literary marketplace seemed to open as the war drew to a close. Croly responded frankly to Addams, "We have been working under great difficulties during the last four or five months owing to the intemperate condition of American public opinion, but I think the worst is over and I am hoping we shall have more leeway for work along the same lines in the future than we have had in the past."[115] He had in mind arguments for international cooperation. Ellery Sedgwick, on his way to Europe to see things firsthand, urged her to wait until his return to send an essay. And as the end of the war was announced in November 1918, Edward Marsh lost little time in writing to Addams, "By all means let me know within a few months if the material you have in mind begins to take shape as a book."[116] Eager to get her next book, he flattered, "I should be much gratified if I could have something for publication next year." Marsh hit the right note when he advised her to continue writing: "I believe the country is coming back to a saner attitude than it has shown of late, and you could help very greatly in this direction."[117]

Addams invited thirty-five guests to a November retreat to raise money for the Women's International League. The gathering was the very bookend of the Henry Street meeting in 1914. Addams rested in the comfort of Lillian Wald's hospitality. "Your room and your fire-place and your apples will be waiting for you," Wald promised.[118] "I will see that you have a quiet place, and luncheon served for you all." In an aside, she joked, "I will punch Mrs. Pinchot to get that money, and any other head that seems to have a pocket-book."

The war left a residuum of loss and resentment. Telegrams and letters poured in from Europe questioning Addams's lethargy during the conflict in responding to the plight of women in Europe. From Copenhagen, Anna Molander fumed, "In order to somewhat lessen your self glorification I now write to tell you that I am a confirmed cripple and you are the one I have to thank for this calamity."[119] Addams became the target because she led the peace movement as the war began and became suspiciously silent as the war proceeded. There was palpable bitterness over her behavior. "But you wanted to keep up your reputation as 'Lady Bountiful,'" Molander charged. Ironically, Addams got hit by critics in the United States for being a friend to radicals in Europe. Senator Archibald D. Stevenson published a list of those Americans who did not help win the war, and, because the list was alphabetically arranged, Jane Addams appeared as the first culprit. Wald sent an angry telegram, urging her to fight back: "ARE YOU TAKING ANY ACTION ON PUBLICATION OF STEVENSON LIST DO NOT MIND

PERSONALLY BUT BELEIVE ACT IRRESPONSIBLE INACCURATE A NATIONAL DIS-
GRACE PLEASE INFORM OUR COMRADES OF YOU OPINOIN AND PROTEST IF
ANY."[120] No doubt Addams preferred the witty response from Paul Jones,
who noted sardonically, "Isn't it a pity that a sense of humor isn't made
one of the qualifications for government office."[121]

Addams's health returned amid the postwar vitriol. She served as a
member of "The Committee of Five" women who supposedly would have
a say in the peace treaty, and she struggled to bring her European colleagues back into the Women's International League. Addams sought
what she called a "new world order" that would promote the League of
Nations and come to rely on mediation rather than armaments for settling disputes. The Women's International League, which had convened
at The Hague in 1915, had long vowed to meet at the close of war. As
Paris was selected for the Peace Conference, the women voted to meet
in Zurich, a neutral city, for their second Peace Congress.

Before the Congress met, Addams made her first trip to the front,
finding the experience invigorating, especially as she visited the trenches. "We are just back from a five day trip through the devastated regions,"
she told Mary who had stayed at home. "It was a wonderful experience
in many ways and I shall always be grateful to have had it."[122] Proximity
to death gave her an exhilarating sense of life, even of her own health.
After visiting the grave of her nephew during a storm, she reported, "I
shall have to give up all pretense of being an invalid for I came through
an awful blizzard . . . on foot for John Linn's grave without taking any cold
or being the least worse for the experience." Alice Hamilton, always a
careful observer and agile writer, described the scene for her family. "We
saw villages pounded to dust and great towns reduced to ruins and miles
and miles of battlefields. One can't possibly imagine it, one has to see it
and even then it is hard to believe."[123] As the two women traveled to
Amien, they spent a cold night snuggled together: "Miss Addams and I
had a single bed in a queer room, but clean," Hamilton reported. "It was
so cold that we didn't mind sleeping together." Hamilton suggested the
reason why the journey was so affecting to women, who know little about
scenes of battle. "As we came back a bitter cold rain began to fall with a
pitiless wind and we toiled on through the sticky mud feeling that we
could imagine pretty well what our men had to endure there." Imagination and empathy allowed them both to feel "like soldiers on leave from
the front."

The Zurich Congress, too, restored Jane Addams's health and vigor.
The large gathering of women returned her to a public stage, a grand
performance for a woman about to turn sixty. Hamilton served as eye-

witness for Mary, giving a precise and intimate portrait of the woman they both indulgently loved. "I do long for you to be here to see J.A. in all her glory, happier I am sure than she has been in five whole years."[124] No reporter or drama critic could have described the scene more knowingly: "This is the opening morning of the Congress. The big room is full of a subdued Babel of many tongues, up on the platform which is charmingly decorated, is the lady surrounded by seven selected women of the different countries and in a few minutes she will make her opening address." As she presided at the Congress and worked to influence Wilson and the leaders who were constructing a retaliatory peace in Europe, her compatriots attacked her at home. The *Chicago Evening Post* published a letter from "An American Citizen not in favor with your high-handed tactics" that viewed the women at Zurich as a suspicious crowd. "Your place is at Chicago, minding your own business, and not mixing with the ENEMY, or trying to tell the Peace Commission how to run things."[125]

Jane Addams had hoped to end 1920 with the Nobel Peace Prize, an award that would vindicate her work during the war and signify the validity of the Women's International League. She wrote to Emily Balch in November that the news had just reached her that Wilson had won the Prize for his work at the end of the war. "I do wish that we could drop the matter," she moaned, and we still hear her disappointment.[126] The book she planned to write for Macmillan would sit for two more years as Addams waited for the public temperature to cool. "I am very much impressed with the fact that our war psychology is in a much earlier stage than that of the other allied countries," she wrote to Anna Garlin Spencer, observing the situation with the detachment of a sociologist, "and that we will have to wait until the present attitude toward movements such as ours is somewhat modified before we can hope for many members."[127]

She delivered a sharply critical lecture at Recital Hall on February 22, 1920, on the topic of "Americanization." Resisting efforts in the press to vilify her, Addams fought back in a letter to Edward S. Beck, editor of the *Chicago Tribune*. "May I protest against the flagrant misrepresentation in the report of my address." The country, she charged, was conducting wholesale raids on immigrants and insisting on senseless deportations, activities that departed from Anglo-Saxon law. In such an atmosphere, immigrants naturally "feel so uncertain as to their rights." The Department of Justice's arrest of four thousand suspected Communists in January 1920 constituted "an attempt to deport a political party." Although the nation panicked over twelve mail bombs sent to U.S. officials, she noted dryly that no one was outraged about the twenty bombs thrown in Chicago "to destroy the homes of colored people or of white men who rented to the Communist Party." Her letter further inflamed her critics. A typical response came from Henry Rowland Curtis, a resident of Oak Park: "If your 'mouthings' were not so ludicrous, or if they emanated from an important source, they would be a stench in the nostrils of all decent people."[128] He regretted that the government had not included Addams on the first "Soviet Ark" of deportations, that a hundred times as many immigrants were not being deported, and that Emma Goldman and Alex Berkman had not been shot for treason. He portrayed Hull-House, having the Devil Baby somehow in his mind, as a "breeder of socialism" and social workers as "parlor" socialists.

In August, Addams and Mary Smith retreated to Colorado Springs for their usual late-summer relaxation. Mary told Florence Kelley, "It has seemed strange to be so far away from the coast of Maine but this has been a most successful 'resort' for us."[129] And with her eye on her companion, she added, "J.A. seems relaxed and more cheerful than she has been for months and I've made a really amazing recovery." Two women in their sixties on holiday may indeed resist giving up their privacy: "We are going home next Sunday and rather dreading it." In a letter that month to Esther Kohn, Mary made fun of pacifist propaganda. "You were awfully good to send us the books and they came at a moment of great need," she confided.[130] "We were reduced to the 'World's Food Supply'"—a clear jab at Jane's essay, "Feed the World and Save the League," that appeared in the *New Republic* that fall. Both women may well have been sick of reading or, for that matter, writing war tracts. "The days are of a rare beauty and the scene grows more enchanting with the changing color," Mary told Kohn. "We shall really hate to leave next week."

The revolution in Russia spawned suspicion in the United States. *The Nation* called the Chicago conviction of ninety-eight members of the International Workers of the World party in 1918 "The Greatest Free Speech Trial of the War." For opposing the war and conscription in spoken or written words only, the members were sentenced to up to twenty years in Leavenworth. Even the new president, Warren G. Harding, wrote privately to Addams about the very idea of the League of Nations: "You can understand why I am reluctant to express myself formally at the present time."[131] Addams asked Albert DeSilver of the National Civil Liberties Bureau not to use her name. At the beginning of 1921, H. S. Latham sent Addams a contract from Macmillan for "A Pacifist in War Time," a title that suggested the autobiographical history she had in mind. As Paul Kellogg pleaded with her to send him something from her book manuscript, she declined: "It is all very transitional now of course."[132] As she dragged her feet, she offered him some hope: "The book languishes but I might send a chapter or two if you want to look them over."

Another ominous aspect of social life in the United States and Europe in the 1920s was racial hatred. Without fully understanding the situation, Jane Addams and Mabel Hyde Kittredge, secretary of the Women's International League for Peace and Freedom (WILPF), wrote to Secretary of State Charles Evans Hughes in the spring of 1921, alerting him to the supposed "military despotism of colored men" in Europe. U.S. newspapers were reporting a sensational story that "colored" French troops, some forty-five thousand men, stationed in Germany, were raping white women. Addams and Kittredge described them as "negroes hardly emerged from barbarism, natives of Madagascar, Algeria, Tunis, and Morocco."[133] The German members of the Women's International League had supposedly complained that the soldiers were raping German women and even boys and that the occupation army demanded white German women perform in brothels for "colored troops." The letter to Hughes claimed that "the many fine colored women of our own nation" likewise abhorred the rape of German women. The organization demanded the withdrawal of "colored" soldiers from Germany.

Mary Church Terrell, the only African American on the board of the Women's International League, was angered by the unsubstantiated report and demanded reconsideration of the charge. "I belong to a race whose women have been the victims of assaults committed upon them by white men and men of all other races," Terrell reminded Addams.[134] "As a rule these men have ruined and wrecked the women of my race with impunity." She conceded that the rape of women in Germany, if it were true, would be as horrible to her as the rape of French women by German soldiers during the war, indeed as horrible as the rape of Haitian women by American soldiers. However, she refused to sign any declaration calling for the removal of troops simply because they were "colored." She suspected that the charges, although widely reported, were false. Carrie Chapman Catt, at her request, conducted an investigation and discovered that no actual complaints had been made within Germany. The story seemed to have been concocted by racists within the United States. "You have always been such a true friend to me," she told Addams, declaring, "I am not narrow. I want to know the truth and do right."

Addams telegraphed Balch a cryptic warning to remove the charges and demands: "FINDING VISES DIFFICULT ALMOST IMPOSSIBLE SORRY WOULD ADVISE GOING WITHOUT."[135] More expansively, she acknowledged in a personal letter to Mary Terrell: "I came to exactly the same conclusion which you have reached that we should protest against the occupation of ene-my territory not against any special troops."[136] She shifted the focus away from racism in America to the issue of military occupation itself. Ter-rell, no doubt, hoped for something more, an apology or at least an ac-knowledgement of culpability.

Escaping from the political heat in America, Addams and Smith sailed on the *Niew Amsterdam* on June 4, 1921, going to Paris and then to Geneva, staying in "two bed rooms with a bath at one of the best ho-tels." They traveled to Vienna, finding it horrible. Mary complained to Esther Kohn that Jane looked frightfully exhausted, apparently from food poisoning. They longed for "a comfortable bed, running water and other vulgar creature comforts."[137] Europe after Armistice was not a glamor-ous or even a commodious place.

As Jane left for Europe with Mary, she told Paul Kellogg that she would release chapters of her book along the route. His telegrams fol-lowed her throughout the journey with the refrain "EAGERLY AWAITING CHAPTER OR ARTICLES FROM YOU SURVEY GRAPHIC." Joking about the cryp-tic genre of the telegram, he quipped, "CONDENSATION IS THE DESPAIR OF COURTESY AND IT DOES PRESENT MY HOPES IF NOT MY EXPECTATION." A week later, he cabled, "BEG YOU SEND SURVEY THREE THOUSAND WORD ARTICLE."[138] She responded two weeks later, "I seem to have nothing suit-able on hand. This last ten days has been my first opportunity to get at my long neglected book."[139] The book she had been composing in vari-ous pieces was still to be assembled in her mind.

"Of course one composes a book out of all the old stuff one has on hand, and for book purposes that makes no difference but it is bad for magazines!"[140] She divulged her writing process, in this letter to Kellogg, as clearly and openly as she did anywhere. *Peace and Bread in Time of War* contains "old stuff" from the *New Republic,* the Kansas City speech that was published in *Survey,* and material she had worked on with Flo-rence Kelley, who had published much of it under her name in *Survey.* By October, Addams was back at Hull-House and telegraphed Kellogg to say that she was sending him her manuscript in a month to give him time to select material for *Survey Graphic.* He responded lightheartedly, "The fact that you have been free and could catch and voice the larger vision made me hungry to have something from your pen in this first number. I am afraid that sentence is chuck full of mixed similes, but I guess my meaning is clear."[141] He cautioned her not to become tied down with other duties at the expense of her writing.

In a postscript to a letter she sent Emily Balch on November 16, she announced, "I got my book off to Macmillan today. I *have* been slow!"[142]

She insisted to Paul Kellogg that the book's publishing must go quickly, ironically, more quickly than he wanted. In a telegram, he flattered her: "PEACE AND BREAD LUMINOUS DISPELLING FOG OF MISREPRESENTATION LIGHTING WAY AHEAD STOP WOULD MEAN GREAT DEAL."[143] He begged her to postpone the book's publication until April, giving him time to publish five installments at $100 a piece in *Survey Graphic*. The same evening, he telegraphed, "ALL RIGHT HAVE WE YOUR PERMISSION GET EXACT PUBLISHING DATE FROM MACMILLAN AND PLAN ACCORDINGLY WHAT IS YOUR CHOICE OF CHAPTERS."[144] And she responded as swiftly, "CERTAINLY SEE MACMILLAN PREFER STRAIGHT CHAPTERS TO SUGGESTED TOPICS."[145] She informed him a week later, as they wrangled over how he would use her material, that she had decided to give the chapters as they were to other magazines. "I have promised articles to the *Christian Century* and one or two other magazines, and this may be a good chance to start fresh!"[146] Maybe she had made such deals, but probably not. She demanded that Kellogg return her manuscripts.

What brought her temper to the boiling point was a letter from H. S. Latham at Macmillan asking her to verify Kellogg's request to stall publication of the book until March or April: "I assume that this meets with your approval."[147] She, of course, had never given Kellogg permission to stall the publication of the book. Latham received her telegram later the same day: "MOST DESIROUS BOOK SHOULD APPEAR PROMPTLY. MATERIAL ALREADY OLD. ABSOLUTELY OPPOSED TO KELLOGG PLAN. AM WRITING."[148] In the longer letter, she insisted that the galley proofs and the page proofs be sent for her approval, reminding him that Macmillan had sent only the galley proofs for her last book. Latham responded that he would try to jam the book through by January.

Her battle with Kellogg over the integrity of a literary voice tells us much about the writer Jane Addams had become. He returned to the bargaining table, noting that Macmillan had not seemed in a rush to publish. In a long, patient, calming letter he explained that he wanted to publish material from the book. In a steady set of exchanges, he worked to edit the book as she resisted his attempts to reshape her narrative. "I think your trying to twist the book into an economic thesis is a great mistake, and will simply give a misleading impression," she upbraided him.[149] She intended her writing to be literary and imaginative history, based on memory and not on issues or, necessarily, on events. "I think it misses the point of the book to abstract food absolutely from the rest." Clearly piqued, she told him she would see him in New York City "if it would be of any use talking about it further." And on that note, she won the argument. He telegraphed simply, "EAGER TO FOLLOW YOUR CHOICE

AS TO CHAPTERS." After the long battle, she asked him to cut the bayoneting story, saying that she was awfully tired of hearing it. And she let him know that she intended to send the final chapter to *Yale Review*, at which point he asked permission to publish it after the book came out.

Kellogg requested a preface that would explain the book to readers, and she tried again to explain what she had in mind: "I was trying to describe what I felt."[150] She had in mind what she called "interpretative art" in the shape of an "autobiographical portrayal" of history. At the end of her labor, she felt queasy, as she always did, about the success of her book. She put the last page proofs in the mail to Macmillan and, that same afternoon, confided to Marcet that she wondered if the book should have ever been written. "A pleasant state of mind to be in after it is finished!" she remarked, and we can hear the release of pressure.[151]

In *Peace and Bread in Time of War* Addams creates a Janus-faced Woodrow Wilson, revealing one visage as he presents his Fourteen Points— many of them borrowed from the Women's International Congress at The Hague. He needed pacifists to ensure his reelection and wooed them with his support of their efforts to end the fighting in Europe as well as his commitment to suffrage. She mocks him as "the philosopher become king" as he appeared to embrace liberal ideas. Then she turns his face around to expose the newly elected president, not pacifist but warrior, as he marches in the preparedness parade in Washington and moves troops to Haiti, Nicaragua, the Virgin Islands, and San Dominican Republic, all efforts to establish a military buffer as clear prelude to a declaration of war, a shift of position that took less than a month to effect in the winter of 1917.

She gives support to her portrait of Wilson and other intellectuals in the United States by speaking through Randolph Bourne, from his article "War and the Intellectuals." He notes, as did she, the "unanimity with which the American intellectuals had thrown their support to the use of war techniques in the crisis," and perhaps more destructively, "the riveting of the war mind upon a hundred million more of the world's people" (61). The swift turn of intellectuals toward war propaganda astonished Jane Addams. Wilson expressed his change of mind in a play with words—"a war to end all wars." She turns the oxymoron over in her mind, working to expose the roughness of its edges. "It is hard for some of us to understand upon what experience this pathetic belief in the regenerative results of war could be founded; but the world had become filled with fine phrases and this one, which afforded comfort to many a young soldier, was taken up and endlessly repeated with an entire absence of the critical spirit" (62). Her words are tough as she damns her generation of intellectuals, and not the masses of people, for the lurch into war.

In deconstructing Wilson's rhetoric, Addams masterfully damns him with his own words. Before the war, as he maneuvered for a powerful place at the peace table, Wilson had advocated neutrality for America, but by January 1917, he had turned away from the pacifists toward engagement as the strategy promising the strongest hand at the table. "What might have happened if President Wilson could have said in January, 1919, what he had said in January, 1917,—'A victor's terms imposed upon the vanquished . . . would leave a sting, a resentment, a bitter memory upon which terms of peace would rest not permanently but only as upon quicksand" (67). And here she has Wilson, as man and as character in her narrative, exposing his twin voices. She removes the question mark and employs an ellipsis to pack language into a single sentence. Addams points out "the paradox that the author of the Fourteen Points returned from Paris, claiming that he had achieved them" (70). The Paris Peace and the League of Nations failed not only to secure a just peace, but more significantly for Addams, failed to stabilize the world enough to avoid the later war. The phrase, "a war to end war," proved little more than political rhetoric.

By 1922, Addams could look back at herself with amusement. "As pacifists were in a certain sense outlaws during the war, our group was no longer in direct communication with the White House" (71). An outlaw need not worry about saving face. She is free, as she discovered such freedom at the end of *The Long Road of Woman's Memory*, to link her early memories to symbolic, even mythic, truth. As she read James George Frazer's *The Golden Bough*, with his image of the Corn Mother and her daughter Demeter and her daughter Persephone, Addams imagined herself as child of the mill, mythic offspring of the Corn Mother. "I was also the daughter, granddaughter and the great granddaughter of millers," she tells her reader, placing her young self into the narrative. "Watching the foaming water my childish mind followed the masses of hard yellow wheat through the processes of grinding and bolting into the piled drifts of white flour and sometimes further into myriad bowls of bread and milk." (76) Covered in white flour, Addams fades into myth, a narrative older than the story of war, back to an ur-story of sustenance. Bread and milk hold an older place in mythology and evolution, she theorizes, than weapons and battle do—a configuration that privileges female nurture over male aggression.

Addams is cautious to give her readers in 1922 no more than they might bear. Her letters record the attacks by the press, calling her foolish and old, but also traitorous and villainous and dangerous to society. "I have just read over some of the newspaper clippings," she confides. "[I]t is easy now to smile at their absurd efforts to give a sinister meaning to two such innocuous words as Fellowship and Reconciliation" (128). The Women's Peace Party office, in an elegant building on Michigan Avenue, drew the fire away from Hull-House itself. "If a bit of mail protruded from the door it was frequently spat upon," she reports, "the door was often befouled in hideous ways." We are left to conjecture how hideous patriotic Americans would dare to be.

The reader begins to see the pattern in her seemingly random remembrance of the past. The emotional and psychological fall from confidence to self-pity turns out to be a fortunate one, as she begins to see the absurdity of her condition. What lifts her to higher ground is her own consciousness, the ability of her mind to look upon itself. "Strangely enough, he [the pacifist] finds it possible to travel from the mire of self-pity straight to the barren hill of self-righteousness and to hate himself equally in both places." (139) A resilient mind can come to see its condition from the very perspective of distance. Her musings move from memory to analysis as she views her situation: "Certainly nothing was clearer than that the individual will was helpless and irrelevant." She places herself in the company of John Stuart Mill in England, Romain Rolland in France, David Starr Jordan in the United States, and Nicholai of Russia. Over her years of intellectual exile, she reread Darwin, along with George Nasmyth, John Hobson, and Lowes Dickenson: "But with or without the help of good books, a hideous sensitiveness remained" (147). In her story, physical illness comes as a result of spiritual alienation as she suddenly finds "every public utterance willfully misconstrued, every attempt at normal relationship repudiated" (148). Clearly the front lines of her battle are in her homeland. Her rebuke sounds alarms for us as readers nearly a century later: "Many people had long supposed liberalism to be freedom to know and to say, not what was popular or convenient or even what was patriotic, but what they held to be true" (182).

Addams shrewdly leaves her readers on a new doorstep, as an expatriate of sorts: "The International Office of our League was established in a charming old house in Geneva." She imaginatively situates her readers in a freer political environment: "It seemed to me that June day of 1921, as I went through its rose-filled garden, that we might be profoundly grateful if our organization was able in any degree to push forward the purposes of the League of Nations and to make its meaning clearer" (245). Miss Addams, comfortably at home in the "very spring of life," forges her anger and despair into the voice of a new female community. "We felt our voices but an infinitesimal strain in the chorus of praise," she declares, as she reasserts her right to speak as a voice from the silence.

5 *Honest Reminiscence*

Red Jane

The United States in the 1920s was not a good place for a liberal intellectual, especially a woman who had supported the Progressive Party and had steadfastly opposed U.S. entry into the Great War. Coupled with those political sins was Addams's support of immigrants, her membership in the American Civil Liberties Union, the National Association for the Advancement of Colored People, and, more so, her guidance of the Women's International League for Peace and Freedom (WILPF) and her association with Hull-House and the settlement movement. Typical of attacks on her politics and, for that matter, on her character came from Lieutenant Joseph J. Hurley in a Sunday evening speech before the Common Cause Forum at Boston's Franklin Union in December 1925. He refused to act as marshal in the Armistice Day Peace Parade because he opposed several of the organizations marching in the parade. He linked the Women's International League with the Fellowship of Reconciliation and, especially, the Fellowship of Youth for Peace as subversive organizations, promoting "pacifism, sovietism and slackerism," perils to "true Americanism" that lurk in the culture and threaten the moral and physical progress of civilization. In choosing his metaphors, he had the women in mind, seeing the groups as "pregnant with evil portent."[1] Hurley voiced a common view of Addams as a "Red" and linked her with WILPF. "As an organization it is a menace to the United States," he ranted. "One of its leading officers is Jane Addams, who has been openly condemned in this country as a dangerous radical." Pacifists were "slackers" because they resisted the use of force.

Jane Addams responded to the reactionary culture at home by spending much of the 1920s abroad with Mary Smith, taking a long tour of the world in 1922 and 1923, exploring Asia, visiting along the route members of the Young Women's Christian Association and building her network of women pacifists who would move very much against the grain in China and Japan and yet fail utterly to halt the brutal invasions that would foster hatreds that continue into the twenty-first century. The China she ventured into was both familiar and unfamiliar. She lectured at South Eastern University in Nanking, Kian-Su Province Educational Association in Shanghai, Nankai College and the Chihil Fishery School in Tientsin, the Provincial Agricultural College in Soochow, and the Girls' School in Kiangsu. Her letters of introduction, as we might imagine, brought her into decidedly Westernized society. She was recognized as a world leader by the International Federation of Settlements, the YWCA, the Women's Christian Temperance Union, the American Association of University Women, the Shanghai Women's Club, the Women's Rights League, and even local Rotary Clubs. Westerners living in China embraced her, inviting her to speak to women's groups and to join them at garden parties. Her tour included the Summer Palace, Tiananmen Square and the Imperial City, and the Western Hills Temple.

There is nothing extraordinary in such a tour for a woman of her day or of ours. What was different, perhaps, was her insistence on visiting factories to see the condition of workers; at a silk weaving factory, she saw children under ten years of age working twelve to fourteen hours a day. More dramatically, she encountered bandits on her way to visit the grave of Confucius, and the newspapers reported her bravery in showing her face to the robbers, a maneuver that supposedly scared them off. She ended her trip with a month-long stay in Peking, where she was upset in a rickshaw, suffering pain in her arm and along her side. The accident uncovered a cancerous tumor that led to a mastectomy, a surgery that she delayed having until she reached a hospital in Tokyo. A month after her return to the United States, the hospital collapsed in a cataclysmic earthquake that killed thousands of people and devastated the very ground she had toured.

Although eight years elapsed between the publishing of *Peace and Bread in Time of War* and her next book, *The Second Twenty Years at Hull-House*, Addams continued to write, publishing letters, speeches, reviews, and introductions, scattered pieces that she would later cobble together. In the summer of 1924 from Hull's Cove in Bar Harbor, she used illness as her excuse for not sending Paul Kellogg an article for the *Survey Graphic* number on the theme of war and peace. "I am just a trifle glad of the excuse for my failure," she wrote.[2] She balked at the task, yet again, of putting her pacifism into words, knowing that the nation had little patience with pacifists, even less with immigrants. "I have covered endless sheets of paper with notes but I do not really like any of them," she admitted. It may well have seemed futile to her that summer as she received news of the massacre of hundreds of thousands in Greece, refugees from Armenia.

Her own life that summer absorbed her attention. She encouraged WILPF to meet in Washington in May 1924 and organized what had become its traditional Summer School in Chicago. And then she retreated to Hull's Cove, where she worked with Emily Balch to square financial accounts after the Fourth International Congress, including the $4,015.75 in the First Trust and Savings Bank, money that WILPF collected from the Congress and the Summer School. By August, she wrote to Hannah Clothier Hull that the women at Hull's Cove were enjoying their summer retreat. "We have had one glorious day after another on this beautiful island," she declared during the "wonderful summer."[3] A fog descended over the island, giving the landscape a lovely subdued coloring, one that Addams delighted in as she and Mary lingered through the early fall before returning to Chicago.

She supported Robert LaFollette in his doomed campaign for president in 1924, writing a note for the *New Republic* on why she preferred him, and she watched with the satisfaction of a suffragist as five women ran for Congress from Pennsylvania. The question for women in the mid-1920s was what effect, if any, their vote had made. The truth is that women, who had united on the single issue of suffrage, were agreeing on little else after the passage of the amendment. The example that nettled Jane Addams was the splintering of the Council on Women, an international group headed by Carrie Chapman Catt that relied on funds from various women's organizations, including the Daughters of the American Revolution, a reactionary crowd who considered Addams a traitor because of her pacifism and her interest in the Bolsheviks. Lucia Ames Mead told Alice Hamilton, who told Jane Addams, "[T]he D.A.R.s and Daughters of 1812 are refusing to give any money to the coming meeting of the Council so long as the W.I.L. remains in it."[4] Carrie Chapman Catt's Council planned to meet in the DAR hall, and even the use of space became an issue. Addams recommended to the Women's International League board that they withdraw from the council as a "magnanimous" gesture, one that would free Catt to raise money.

Her letters in December show her working through difficulties as she stood very near the center of the storm. She talked privately with Catt about the political mess as she publicly moved away from the National Council on Women. "I think [Catt] felt she could get certain women to come in who would otherwise be frightened off," she wrote to Hannah Hull, "and she is probably right."[5] She explained the situation: "The National League of Women Voters asked me to come to represent them and at first I was inclined to accept the invitation but Grace Abbott sent me a newspaper clipping from Washington showing that Mrs. Potts and all the rest were waiting to attack them if they had any chance." Addams shrewdly concluded. "[I]t seemed to me better that I should not be there, and I wrote to Miss Sherman declining the appointment." Rather unsentimentally, she backed away, allowing women's organizations to unite without rubbing shoulders with pacifists who had taken truly radical positions. Catt presided over the Conference on the Cause and Cure of War in January 1925, sending a delegation to the U.S. Senate to lobby in favor of the World Court. Both women supported the Court as well as the League of Nations, but Catt publicly distanced herself from Addams, as they had privately agreed would be the best course of action. The *New York Herald Tribune* reported: "Mrs. Catt declared she had no sympathy with the policies of the International League for Peace and Freedom. She paid a high personal tribute, however, to Miss Jane Addams."[6] Catt traced her involvement, along with Addams, to the American Peace Party in 1915, but claimed that she had been expelled from the group as America entered the war because she supported Wilson's declaration.

"[Mrs. Catt] isn't a big woman, none of the absolute suffragists are, they never had a chance to get broad,"[7] Hamilton soothed in a letter to Addams. She argued that Catt had settled too early with the DAR and, as a result, the Conference on the Cause and Cure of War lacked teeth. Addams wrote to Catt after the event, still bristling from the newspaper accounts that WILPF had expelled Catt. The truth was the New York City branch of WILPF was the culprit, not the organization as a whole. "So please do not hold this against us any longer; will you?" she pleaded, adding in irritation: "I am sure you are too familiar with false reports of things pertaining to your own work."[8] And then she wrote to Hull, "Mrs. Catt is usually so careful I cannot understand why she would have said that particular thing about being expelled unless the situation left a rankle behind and broke out quite unexpectedly to herself." To calm her own rankling, she laughed, "However, I am not a psychiatrist!"[9]

The battle of women over the issue of peace played itself out in private and public; indeed, in Washington, then as now, the two converged. Attacks on WILPF members included gossip about the sexual lives of its members, young women who lived in Washington away from their mothers and were thus vulnerable, supposedly, to the promiscuity of urban life. "I believe Washington is in a very unhealthy state of mind," Hannah Hull reported to her women friends.[10] "Some business women who live there seem to have sex relations on the brain," she observed, "and try to judge everybody in these terms." One young woman in WILPF became the victim of gossip in a tale that claimed she was wrecking a marriage and was being blackmailed as a result. Hull advised her to tell "Mother," and her mother advised her not to flee the scandal.

As women squabbled in public, Jane Addams drew closer to women in her private sphere. Lillian Wald learned from Mary that she planned to visit Mexico with Jane during the winter months, escaping from the cold of Chicago and the chill of life in the United States. She fished for an invitation to join the two women, although she knew that Mary preferred to travel alone with Jane. "Suggest this softly," Lillian wrote to Jane, "and lowly to Mary who may think two's company and three's more or so the old adage insists."[11] Mary and Jane left Chicago on March 1st and traveled for four weeks on a working holiday, and indeed Lillian joined them on March 9. She became wretchedly ill from eating a tomato, and ironically Mary cared for her while Jane continued to travel (the condition worsened and required extensive cutting in a surgery to free her intestines). All three women suffered that winter from various maladies. After Lillian's surgery, Mary commiserated by detailing her own ailments: "I am scratched from head to toe for 'protein test' with the result that I must henceforth be clothed in linen and paper with a minimum of wool."[12] She joked about the absurdity of her condition, a wealthy woman with allergies of all sorts, some of them literal and others metaphoric. "Silk, cotton and furs are clearly not for me. I am inclined to trust in Providence and let nature do its worst though Dr. Koessler daily mutters, 'what for do you make all these expensive tests and then do nothing.'" Jane suffered from tonsillitis and remained under Dr. Herrick's care; bronchitis and influenza plagued her as they did many of her generation. Her nephew Stanley wrote a Mother's Day letter that, no doubt, eased the burden of aging: "Legally and sentimentally and practically, you have been my 'Mother' for some thirty-four years, so I am writing to you."[13]

"Do not give up Maine this summer. We are getting too old to work all the time," Addams wrote to Florence Kelley in May.[14] By work, she meant the duties of Hull-House and, once she left Chicago, she spent much of her time writing and reading, especially biography, that summer. She composed a reminiscence of Teddy Roosevelt, a story about their drive together on a cold day when, finding her hatless, he shed his own hat in courtesy to her. She relaxed into reading William Allen White's biography of Woodrow Wilson, writing to congratulate him: "It seems to me by far the best estimate of him which has been made."[15] She looked on as Louise DeKoven Bowen completed her book *Growing Up with a City* and played the role of literary agent, securing the publication of the first two chapters in the *Atlantic*, even as she managed to string Kellogg along at *Survey Graphic* as a backup. Kellogg wooed them both: "It is quite understandable that Mrs. Bowen should strike for the Atlantic audience and its aura."[16] As he began to negotiate for other segments of the book, Addams warned her friend about his penchant for reworking books to suit his purpose.

In a much stickier literary negotiation, she supported the publication of an English translation of Aletta Jacobs's memoirs, a commitment that would stretch out for years as she sought a suitable venue. She joined forces in the effort with Carrie Chapman Catt and Margaret Sanger. Addams, too, endorsed a book of letters from European intellectuals, including Romain Rolland, H. G. Wells, Bertrand Russell, and Albert Einstein. She wrote the brief reminiscence "My Dear Romain Rolland" for the festschrift *Liber Amicorum Romain Rolland*. And she found herself cast as the subject of a Ph.D. thesis that studied American leaders, a project assigned to Margaret Dunn by Charles Merriam for a series he saw as his pet project. In April 1925, Leonard and Virginia Woolf published *The Story of the League of Nations Told for Young People* at the Hogarth Press. Kathleen Innes wrote the book to narrate the history of the Women's International League and to stimulate interest in pacifism among the young, who had little memory of the Great War and much to gain in avoiding a second world war.

Something Very Erratic

Speaking as Virginia Woolf in *The Second Twenty Years at Hull-House* (1930), Jane Addams defined reality as "'something very erratic and very undependable, sometimes it seems to dwell in shapes too far away from us to discern what their nature is, nevertheless whatever it touches, it fixes and makes permanent'" (81). She had been reading Woolf's books as they appeared in the 1920s and, no doubt, liked *Mrs. Dalloway* and, perhaps, *Orlando*. The words that lodged in her memory came from *A Room of One's Own*, the perspicacious lecture to young women on the course of female literary history. Near the end of the essay, Woolf jokes about the irony that she is about to be utterly conventional and reflects on her motives. "There runs through these comments and discursions the conviction—or is it the instinct?—that good books are desirable and that good writers, even if they show every variety of human depravity, are still good human beings."[17] In earnest about the philosophical usefulness of the literary life, Woolf attempts to define reality for the would-be writer:

> What is meant by "reality"? It would seem to be something very erratic, very undependable—now to be found in a dusty road, now in a scrap of newspaper in the street, now in a daffodil in the sun. It lights up a group in a room and stamps some casual saying. It overwhelms one walking home beneath the stars and makes the silent world more real than the world of speech—and then there it is again in an omnibus in the uproar of Picadilly. Sometimes, too, it seems to dwell in shapes too far away for us to discern what their nature is. But whatever it touches, it fixes and makes permanent. That is what remains over when the skin of the day has been cast into the hedge; that is what is left of past time and of our loves and hates. Now the writer, as I think, has the chance to live more than other people in the presence of this reality. (110)

The metaphors resonated with Jane Addams, who used such images in her own writing. In memory, she elided the middle passage, moving from "very erratic and very undependable" to "whatever it touches, it fixes and makes permanent." Once dressed as Woolf, Addams felt perfectly comfortable—as she always did—speaking in the cadence of her own voice. The idea remained fixed in her mind and resurfaced a year later in the title of her next book, *The Excellent Becomes the Permanent* (1932).

The mind lives in a world of myriad impressions, Woolf had lectured writers in 1910, and a brave writer records the impressions, though they are erratic, trusting in the vision, however indiscernible. "Life is not a series of gig lamps symmetrically arranged; life is a luminous halo, a semi-transparent envelope surrounding us from the beginning of consciousness to the end," she insisted, giving writers permission to break away from traditional modes of representation.[18] She built her literary theory on the work of psychologists, including William James, who in *The Principles of Psychology* (1890) conceived of the mind as the "stream of thought, of consciousness, or of subjective life." Struggling with metaphor, James noted that psychology examines a pail full of water from the stream but ignores the waters flowing around it, the "halo or penumbra that surrounds and escorts it."[19]

When Jane Addams presented social and political history as what she called "honest reminiscence" in *The Second Twenty Years*, she echoed both James and Woolf. A writer ought to think herself free to record seemingly disconnected impressions, images, and narratives that flow through her mind, confident that what emerges will be an accurate accounting of experience. "There are certain days which remain in our memories," Addams begins her chapter on women, "because we then seem to have broken through into that reality which ever lies beneath the outward appearance" (80). The scene is her travel on the Danube to Budapest on a summer day in 1913, and she makes sense of the moment by using Woolf's description of reality. The linking of scene and sensibility is literal, and yet Addams uses the river trip to philosophize about the nature of the mind itself and the usefulness of a metaphor like stream of consciousness. Her book is punctuated by scenes of shifting consciousness. As a mature female observer, she reminds us of no one more than Mrs. Dalloway, the heroine of Woolf's 1925 novel: "She sliced like a knife through everything; at the same time was outside, looking on."[20]

Jane Addams promises the steady gaze of all her years. Women of a certain age often yearn for a return of youth or, at least, some rough proximity to the springtime of life. Shining a harsh light on her generation, she exposes its wrinkles: "In fact, the young people themselves in moments of exasperation have been known to say that many of the follies of which they are accused in cabarets and other frivolous places are really affected by older people who, equipped with the foolish clothing and the brilliant complexions of the young, are dancing and drinking to an extent that fills the actual young with dismay, and that most unfairly discredits the coming generation" (2). As her contemporaries revel in the callow gaiety of 1920s America, Addams steps into the persona of the mature onlooker. "Even if we, the elderly, have nothing to report but sordid compromises, nothing to offer but a disconcerting acknowledgment that life has marked us with its slow stain, it is still better to define our position," she pledges her readers. "With all our errors thick upon us, we may at least be entitled to the comfort of Plato's intimation that truth itself may be discovered by honest reminiscence" (6). We hear the echo of the motto, "Free from the world's slow stain," in the promise of nature at the Bowen Country Club, and we see her figure, thick with age as well as error. Her account of life in the United States before and after the Great War carries, too, the shadow of the stock market crash and her prophetic gaze into the future of the Depression years and the inevitable resurgence of war that will come after her death.

If one were to read only a single book by Jane Addams, *The Second Twenty Years* would be a good choice for its conversational style, its associative logic, and its relaxed musings. As she had confided to Paul Kellogg about *Peace and Bread*, a book is cobbled together from scraps of material: "Of course one composes a book out of all the old stuff one has on hand."[21] Eight years separate the two books, years that Addams spent more in travel than in writing, and as she worked on new essays, she looked over her "old stuff," culling paragraphs, letters, readings, and essays. The book is an assemblage of narratives, observations, and arguments. It is as though Addams is free to write the way she always tended. She moves into rhetorical costume easily, slipping into her own clothes and dressing, at times cross-dressing, in those of others, talking in one breath as Jane Addams and, in the next, as a Halsted neighbor or as a philosopher or a scholar. Rarely does she stop to identify the sources of the quotes she liberally uses; only four times does she bother to footnote and in two of those cites herself. The book is full of voices from the street, the academy, from her friends, and, at times, her enemies, and we understand that no editor in 1929 could force a scholarly work out of her.

Writing as a mature woman has its advantages. Woolf wrote in March 1929 in an essay entitled "Women's Fiction" that women no longer need "squint askance" at the world through the eyes of men. A woman's style of writing, the way she arranges words on the page and the ease she feels in abandoning established patterns, may differ markedly from male literary genres. When a woman comes to write, "she will find that she is perpetually wishing to alter the established values—to make serious what appears insignificant to a man, and trivial what is to him important."[22] We think of the early run-ins between Addams and Richard Ely, for example, and his lectures about the rules of academic writing, even as she imagined other modes of expression. "And for that, of course," Woolf tells us, "[a woman writer] will be criticized; for the critic of the opposite sex will be genuinely puzzled and surprised by an attempt to alter the current scale of values, and will see in it not merely a difference of view, but a view that is weak, or trivial, or sentimental, because it differs from his own." The inclination of later editors to pull Addams's books apart and reposition the pieces under various themes comes from a misunderstanding of their essential shape.

Woolf talked, too, about the changing course of female thought. "The change which has turned the English woman from a nondescript influence, fluctuating and vague, to a voter, a wage-earner, a responsible citizen, has given her both in her life and in her art a turn towards the impersonal," she observes. "Her relations now are not only emotional; they are intellectual, they are political." Woolf looks to future women writers who will take on the philosophical questions of human destiny and the meaning of life. With time and books and space, the female writer will move into the realm of art. "From this it is a short step to the practice of the sophisticated arts," Woolf tell us, "hitherto so little practiced by women—to the writing of essays and criticism, of history and biography." Had she been looking in the direction of American writers, she might have used the literary art of Jane Addams as illustration. She had been practicing the art of the essay since her days at Rockford Female Seminary and was, in 1929, continuing to imagine the art of the historian and social critic, and she would in her final act as a writer experiment with biography.

In *The Second Twenty Years* Addams reviews the Progressive efforts to ameliorate conditions in the United States and, much in the spirit of modernism, concedes, "I cannot tell just when we began to have a sense of futility" (20). The issues before the reformers are not all that different from those before us still: a living wage, safety and health on the job, affordable housing, and worker's compensation and other benefits, including health insurance. Looking back with the experience of age, Addams sets her credo, ominously, in the past tense; "I believed that peace was not merely an absence of war but the nature of human life." Folding the history of the World War into the history of labor reform, she notes dryly that 15,000 industrial deaths would amount to the killing of every adult male in a city of 75,000 people. Echoing her theme in *The Long Road of Woman's Memory*, she tempers her earlier optimism: "I came to believe that 'the ancient kindliness which sat beside the cradle of the race,' cannot assert itself in our generation against the waste of life in warfare" (37). She claims, "At moments we believed that we were witnessing a new pioneering of the human spirit," even as she admits defeat. "But why write longer of these glowing plans which have long since been abandoned?" (42). The question becomes a central one in the book. Why, indeed?

Jane Addams watched the decline of her causes during the decade of the 1920s. In a capitalist economy perhaps no clearer sign can be found than payment for labor. The Russell Sage Foundation, in a study of professional salaries, traced the pay of social workers from 1914, when income of $800 per year matched that of elementary teachers, to 1925, when income stagnated at $1,500 per year, $300 less than elementary teachers earned. The flat pattern of compensation reflected the public's turn away from settlement work as laudable service. The United States expressed continued xenophobia in the Immigrant Acts of 1922, 1924, and 1928, all laws that limited entry into the country and expelled anyone who looked suspicious. Rosika Schwimmer found herself scooped into the net as she applied for citizenship. At the very end of consideration, she refused to pledge that she would be willing to take up arms to defend the country in case of attack, an omission that Hurley and others referred to as a "Slacker's Oath." Of course, a pacifist would indeed refrain from bearing arms. As the law was designed to do, she was scheduled for deportation.

In the summer of 1926, Addams sought another escape from the United States and in March traveled with Mary Smith to the West Indies. As she planned her trip, Paul Kellogg asked about her literary work: "It has been sometime since I have pressed for an article from you." He beckoned: "[Y]ou have understood, I hope, that we are always eager for them."[23] Kellogg diplomatically claimed that he had been hesitating for some time only because more prestigious periodicals were eager for her work. The truth is, of course, that no one had been very interested in material that went against the grain of popular thought. He proceeded cautiously: "Yet it seems to me there is a great hungriness among folk who are up to their elbows in work for their communities, and who would prize word from you at this time." Social work, he suggested, might still be open to her as a permissible topic, and she sent him her essay "How Much Social Work Can a Community Afford?" More forcefully, he urged her to take up the fear of Bolshevism: "Would it be possible for you to write on that during the early summer so that we could print the article in the fall? We would prize it." And he flattered her that no writer would be more courageous. But how could she write about Russia and pacifism, given the vitriol of American culture? She chose an oblique angle by taking up a project that Aylmer Maude offered in April 1926 for her to write an introduction to Tolstoy's *What Then Must We Do?* What better way to blend her efforts as a social worker, a pacifist, and a writer than by coupling herself, yet again, with Tolstoy, not to recall the story of her awkwardness at the riverbank but to reestablish her link to Russian thought before the Bolsheviks descended? "I am quite sure that anything you may write about it will be very acceptable," Maude assured her, pleased to have Jane Addams in a series of new editions that included introductions by H. G. Wells, H. Granville-Barker, and Gilbert Murray.[24]

As Jane and Mary traveled to Dublin in August for the WILPF congress, they wandered through the Irish countryside, a diversion that struck the two women very differently. "Achill seemed to me quite thrilling," Mary Smith enthused in a letter to Ida Lovett, "darker, sadder and wilder than anything we've seen."[25] The two women walked out across the grassy causeway and over white dunes to the sea, where they read "noblest works of literature while perched on rocks or sitting on the garden benches." The pastoral interlude charmed Mary as much as it disquieted Jane, who itched to be with people. And Mary conceded, "J. A. did not like it at all and was relieved to return to the comparative gaiety of Mallaramy."

The rest before the strain of the Women's International League may well have stalled the heart attack that Addams suffered as she arrived back in England. Aletta Jacobs, a blunt woman, wrote a condolence that was more an admonishment: "That is bad news I received this morning of you. A heart-attack in England after your wonderfull work in Dublin."[26] She chided her for putting in such long days, from nine in the morning until late into the evening, with side trips for social gatherings during the midday hour, which was supposedly scheduled for rest. Jacobs was avuncular—if we might borrow the adjective—in pointing out that her activity "is too much for a young and strong person and should it not be too much for a lady who is on the wrong side of 50." Lying in bed, Addams probably laughed at the line, knowing the frustrations on the wrong side of fifty. Oh, to be fifty again . . . even sixty.

The angina sent her into a long convalescence, one that her doctors agreed she might spend in Geneva if she stayed in a hotel with an elevator and if she rested in bed much of the time. Her planned trip to Germany was cancelled in favor of the rest necessary to endure the ocean crossing on September 16, 1926. It is true that Jane Addams never cared much for rest.

After returning to Chicago, her doctor advised her to live with Mary Smith in the family house on Walton Street and to avoid the activity of Hull-House. She fussed with her *Survey* article, admitting to Kellogg that she was frustrated and disappointed in her own writing. She fired a telegram: "VERY MUCH DISLIKE ARTICLE IN PRESENT FORM CAN SEND CORRECTED COPY IF YOU CAN USE NOW OR LATER EVEN WILLING TO PAY FOR SETTING IT UP AGAIN."[27] Kellogg published her piece on settlement work and dropped part of a speech she had given in Cleveland into his issue on peace, although the writing projects satisfied neither writer nor editor that fall.

Recovering from a heart attack is no easy matter for a woman supposedly tangled in seditious activities. Traveling from Evanston, Illinois, to the equally conservative Grand Rapids, Michigan, Helen Palmer Dawes (Mrs. Rufus C. Dawes), chairman of the international relations committee of the National Federation of Women's Clubs, launched an attack on the ailing Jane Addams in celebration, ironically, of Armistice Day. Oddly, Dawes herself advocated curbing natural behavior, bending warlike behavior into peaceful action, and yet she drew a hard line between her activities and those of the Women's International League with its Communist loyalties. "'I speak so freely of this,' said Mrs. Dawes, 'because Miss Addams herself does not conceal the fact that she does not believe in our ideas of American loyalty.'"[28] The story ran nationwide, making its way into the *New York Times,* having the effect of keeping alive the DAR charge that Addams was a "Red."

Even closer to home, Captain Ferre Watkins, commander of the Illinois department of the American Legion, accused Addams of having advocated stripping the uniforms from West Point cadets in her speech against compulsory military service. Warming to his own rhetoric, the commander attacked Hull-House itself as a rallying post for radicals and communists and linked their activities to an international plot to destroy civilization. Through a lawyer, Charles S. Cutting, the residents of Hull-House drafted a response to what they saw as "the utterly silly and puerile" charges of Watkins, countering that Hull-House was in truth a meeting place for free speech. The editors at *The Progressive* were even blunter: "The reason that many people long ago began to revolt against the patriotic firebrands who see an anarchist, communist or bolshevist in every American citizen who has a political opinion that has not been rubber-stamped by the conventional boob-intellect may be found in such charges as those recently voiced by one Capt. Ferre Watkins, commander of the Illinois American Legion, that 'Hull House is a rallying point of every radical and communist movement in Chicago.'"[29] Her colleagues in the peace movement urged her to charge the Legion and the DAR with libel.

"It seems to me however so desirable to drop the whole matter that I should deprecate prolonging the publicity which has been much exaggerated on both sides," she responded.[30] Reading the fresh attacks, her friend Albert Kennedy wrote that he hoped she had developed thick skin. To cheer her, he told "the story of the old fish wife, who, when remonstrated with for skinning eels alive, said that they had become accustomed to it."[31]

Caroline Bartlett Crane, a founder of the Peoples' Church in Kalamazoo, Michigan, is typical of Addams's supporters, even during these dark years. "I am moved to express to you my love and loyalty and my belief that you are the greatest woman of your generation," she enthused.[32] Crane had studied theology at the University of Chicago and established herself as an investigator of urban pollution, conducting studies of many cities in the country, reporting on the quality of water, the efficiency of sewers, and—most famously—on the contamination of slaughterhouses. By 1925, Crane turned her mind to the problem of home ownership among the working class and spearheaded the design of an orderly and substantial Cape Cod cottage that Kalamazooans built for entry to a 1925 contest, "Better Homes in America," a competition organized by Herbert Hoover, then secretary of commerce. The house won the competition among fifteen hundred entries, and Crane put her literary skill to work on *Everyman's House,* the story of the project and her musings about the ideal of home ownership as a counter to bolshevism in America.[33] After all, how much time would a workingman have for subversive activity after laboring all day to pay his mortgage? Even as she joined popular reform projects, like this one, she remembered the early work of social settlements. "I have not met you in years," Crane reminded Addams of their first encounter in 1906, adding the astonishing claim, "but there is scarcely one day in which I do not think of you."

By January 1927 the public attacks on Jane Addams looked even more like caricature. Charles Norman Fay claimed that Jane Addams "stands for everything Bolshevist, except perhaps murder and robbery"—it is the "perhaps" that perks our ear. He labored long with typewriter, pencil, and ruler to construct a "spider-web" of conspicuous radicals and organizations that had supposedly infiltrated the United States.[34] At the top of his chart of culprits, by virtue of his alphabetical ordering, was Jane Addams, and from her name Fay drew lines to various organizations listed across the page, ranking them by color. The Women's International League for Peace and Freedom, for example, was "yellow," demarcating its pacifism and its supposed link to Germany. Addams's allegiance to the LaFollette-Wheeler campaign was "pink" in its Progressive leanings. The ACLU was "red radical," an outright communist organization. The activities of the American Federation of Labor were "red and part-red," while the League of Women Voters was merely "rose-colored" because of its link to educational and religious institutions. Not surprisingly, the American government itself was implicated in the tendency of Congress and the Department of Labor to listen to subversives such as Addams. The web, familiar as it seems to us today, continued to circulate among the reactionary fringe in Illinois, resurfacing in a variant version in *The Red Network,* a book written and privately published by Elizabeth Kirkpatrick Dilling in the 1930s.

Addams instinctively took a step back, giving others room to defend her. By January 20, 1927, President Coolidge and Chicago Mayor William Dever organized a dinner in her honor at the Furniture Mart, a venue that allowed fifteen hundred supporters to be seated. "For many years she has been the target of vituperation from those frightened super-patriots whose conception of citizenship is summed up in vocal flag-waving," an announcement proclaimed.[35] She was haled as the "first citizen" of Chicago at the celebration that marked a turn in public opinion.

The vindication caught the eye of editors. Paul Hutchinson, the managing editor of *Christian Century,* wrote in February that he would like, more than anything else, to have an article by the first of April; Paul

Kellogg wanted something for his "Fascist Number" of *Survey Graphic*; and W. H. Murray, editor of the religious book department at Macmillan, wrote that he would be delighted to have any work by her on religion. Hull-House residents had been associated with religious groups from its beginnings in 1889. Eleanor J. Stebner traces the relationship between settlement work and spirituality in *The Women of Hull House: A Study in Spirituality, Vocation, and Friendship* (1997), linking the Social Gospel movement and other religious traditions to Addams and claiming Hull-House as a "quasi-spiritual community."[36] Making a tie between her writing and religious affiliation, however, irritated Addams. Murray's request caused stress between Addams and Latham, who would have to apologize later for putting Murray on her trail. The collection of memorial addresses, *The Excellent Becomes the Permanent*, would be published through Macmillan's religion department in 1932, and she would complain loudly that the promotion of the book was inadequate.

The book project that absorbed her time in 1927 was the saga of her years at Hull-House. "It seems to us that the time is ripe to stir up a little fresh enthusiasm for TWENTY YEARS AT HULL HOUSE," Latham wrote on May 20, 1927, knowing that summer was her season for literary work.[37] Pressuring her on money, he asked her to accept 10 percent in royalties and a one-time payment of $250 for all rights to place the new edition in the cheaper Modern Reader's Series. He argued that the book, not to say its author, was old and therefore "the more difficult and the more costly it is to keep it alive." Reminding a woman of her age, however, may not be a way to win her. Addams suggested that they wait until 1929 and retitle the book "Twice Twenty Years at Hull-House."[38] At his offer of 10 percent and a flat rate for a pocket version, she balked, writing him curtly, "As you recall when you published the book in the Macmillan's Pocket American and English Classics, I gave up all my royalties and perhaps I tend to regard that as my share in the direction of popularizing books." Jane Addams could be a daunting agent and Latham agreed to 15 percent on the new book, a collection of bits and pieces of her writing over two decades.

By May, Addams was shuttling between Hull-House and its booth at the World's Fair in Chicago, marking "The Century of Progress." Although she was celebrated in Chicago, she remained a suspicious character in other parts of the country. Carrie Chapman Catt reported on DAR activities in California, especially the spreading of anti-Addams propaganda in a slander pamphlet, *The Common Enemy*. "You and Mrs. Kelley stand at the top of the list of those most decidedly sat upon," Catt joked, even as she pressed Addams to answer questions that she hoped to use, together with her lawyer, to respond to the DAR in the *Woman Citizen*.[39] In a letter to Emily Balch, Addams reflected, "I sometimes think we are very foolish to do anything about it." And in her response to Catt, she returned the joke—"Hoping I am not boring you to extinction"—as she responded in her nearly illegible hand to every question.[40] In her response, Catt spoke in a prickly voice, again disavowing her allegiance to WILPF, even as she defended the group against the charges of being a communist organization of slackers. Florence Kelley later wrote that the time had come "when there must be a libel suit to stop this endless and ever more wide-spread sewage."[41] Addams declined but added that Kelley might go it alone.

In the late summer as they returned to Bar Harbor, Jane and Mary threw open the house to family, especially all the children, and to friends. The women knitted sweaters and indulged in a thoroughly domestic life. Addams read Ben Lindsay's book *The Companionate Marriage* and ironically confessed to him that she had not agreed with his basic principle even as she read the book. Yet at Hull's Cove, a truly successful companionate marriage proceeded. A typical social event that summer, among the well-heeled summer residents of Bar Harbor, was an evening at the home of Mr. and Mrs. Walter G. Ladd to see a demonstration of how to dye textiles, accompanied by Alabama plantation stories and songs by the Hampton Quartette, a social occasion to taste a representation of the slave culture of the Old South.

In the background was the national, even international, drama of the Sacco and Vanzetti trial. Addams forcefully opposed the execution of Sacco and Vanzetti, seeing herself, much as Emile Zola had seen himself in the Dreyfus case, as the moral voice in a benighted country. To President Calvin Coolidge at his vacation home in Rapid City, South Dakota, Addams telegraphed, "THOSE OF US LONG DEVOTED TO THE AMERICANIZATION OF FOREIGN-BORN CITIZENS BELIEVE THAT CLEMANCY IN THE SACCO-VANZETTI CASE WOULD AFFORD A GREAT OPPORTUNITY FOR THE HEALING OF WOUNDS AND FOR A REAL RECONCILIATION BETWEEN ANGLOSAXONS AND LATIN PEOPLES."[42] She urged him to intercede with the governor of Massachusetts to commute the death penalty, and she used the Dreyfus case as the model. Addams was surprised by the failure of all efforts and certainly dismayed at the execution. That summer, too, she was asked to sign a petition urging general amnesty for Flemish nationalists arrested during the Great War, a petition signed by John Galsworthy, the president of PEN, H. G. Wells, and Leonard Woolf, among many other political and intellectual kin.

She worked during the fall on the Tolstoy introduction she had promised Aylmer Maude and delivered the manuscript by the end of January in spite of a rugged case of influenza during her usual winter escape from Chicago to the milder climate of Colorado. Mary Smith wrote to Florence Kelley, "Jane is much better and has had a little food. She even feels like being propped up to read and is taking an interest in life."[43] Although ill, Addams tried to help Rosika Schwimmer, who complained she was a "woman without a country," expatriated from Europe for her love of democracy and, ironically, ousted from the United States because of her pacifism. Aletta Jacobs also reemerged that winter, and Addams negotiated along with Catt and Sanger to get her book manuscript away from Thomas and Adele Seltzer. The summer months included a long stay at the Hotel La Plaza at Carmel by the Sea, where Mary and Jane invited her nephew, Stanley Linn, and his wife, Myra, and all their children to visit. She managed, even among family guests, to write a hurried preface to Abraham Epstein's *The Challenge of the Aged.*

The professional heart of her activities that summer took place in Honolulu, where she presided over the Pan-Pacific Women's Association Conference for six days in August, attending receptions and teas and basking in the warmth of the occasion. In letters to friends, Mary Smith reported that the weather was hot and the conference boring. She seemed, however, indulgently proud of Jane's popularity and vitality.

The Republican National Committee invited Addams to the nomination of Herbert Hoover, and he chatted with her by phone, securing her support for his fall campaign. She had worked with him during the war on food distribution and would remain loyal to him in both his campaigns for president. Lillian Wald supported Al Smith, as did Addams's Progressive friends Harold Ickes and Paul Kellogg, who opposed, among other things, the building of Hoover Dam. The year included work in the American Civil Liberties Union (ACLU), a group that steered her somewhat wrong on the issue of war protesters. In a collective letter to Herbert Hoover, the group urged amnesty for fifteen hundred men and women convicted of antiwar speech during the Great War. "Now ten long years after the war, is not the time ripe, Mr. President, to clear the record of war prosecutions for opinions, to release these men and women from continuing punishment, and to restore to them their rights as citizens."[44] The list of those supporting amnesty included "Jane Addams, writer, social worker, Chicago, Ill., Henry Sloane Coffin, Clergyman, author, New York City," and "John Dewey, Professor of Law, Columbia Univ.," along with "Mary E. Woolley, President, Mt. Holyoke College," and "Lillian D. Wald, social worker, New York City."[45] Addams followed up with a letter to

Hoover, asking him to intercede. The letter he sent back, marked "*Confidential,*" tried to clear the air. After investigating the ACLU accusations, he reported to Addams that only 750 people had been convicted of anti-war activities during the war; that only 206 remained in jail by March 4, 1921; and that the last 33 had been released on August 31, 1923.[46] Both Hoover and Addams may have been confused over the meaning of the phrase "clear the record." The ACLU sought restoration of citizenship rights, not merely release from jail. Addams apologized to Hoover for sending him what seemed to have been inaccurate material. (It is worth noting that Franklin Roosevelt later fully pardoned the whole group of war protesters, allowing them to function as full citizens once more.)

What catches our eye is the phrase "Jane Addams, writer, social worker, Chicago, Ill.," with its deft transposition of identifiers, writer first and social worker second. We see her at her task in 1929 as she labored to find the time and energy to write *The Second Twenty Years at Hull-House.* Mary Smith contracted a bad case of bronchitis that made its way to Jane Addams, who found herself so ill that Alice Hamilton withheld her mail. The two women escaped the cold of Chicago as soon as they were able to travel by train to Tucson, Arizona. Once away from Hull-House, as she always did, Addams turned her mind to writing.

"[S]he labors on a new book in which she is sunk at the moment,"[47] Mary reported to Lillian. The relaxation of her body spurred the activity of her mind. "She is writing quite briskly and reading very little—but convalescing most successfully." Her goal was to publish the book to coincide with the fortieth anniversary of Hull-House in September 1929. "I am out here trying to make a beginning on the "Second Twenty Years at Hull House," Addams wrote to Paul Kellogg in February. "I am continually needing more material than I brought with me."[48] The Bull Moose campaign had grown foggy over time, and she asked him to send her copies of the planks of the Progressive Party platform. "I would never believe that I could forget them, but I am obliged to confess I am very vague about them now." The book emerged from vague memories and yellowed documents. Paul Kellogg responded, "I am not at all sure it is a bad thing for you to be writing it when you are away from published materials."[49] As a savvy editor, he urged her to follow her instincts as a writer: "You will get less of documentary quotation, and more of the spirit of Hull House and its mysteries." A month later, she returned his materials, after having written "Five Years Effort toward Social Justice." She sent along, too, her impression: "I suspect that you will be disappointed in the chapter, as I certainly am. I suppose that it is the experiences of the war which makes it all seem so remote."[50] He was, perhaps, the one person she could fully confide in as she worked on the narrative.

By the end of March, Addams completed a working draft of the book and turned her mind to peddling the manuscript. She explained to Kellogg that Macmillan wanted the material by the first of August, and he complained that he would have little time to prepare a serialization in *Survey* prior to the publication of the book. He asked her for rough carbons of the chapters, and he planned to cut the eight thousand words in half. The negotiation began with his request to publish "A Decade of Prohibition" and "Twenty Years of Delinquency in Chicago," selecting them by their titles alone. He hoped to begin with her introduction, "After Sixty-Five," in a one-page spread in *Survey Graphic*. Kellogg acknowledged that anything she might place in a more prestigious magazine, the *Atlantic* for example, would be beyond his grasp, but he worked hard to secure as much material as possible for *Survey*.

He described *Twenty Years at Hull-House* and *The Second Twenty Years* as volumes which, "like prisms, have caught the life and colors, as well as the shadows, of life in the American community" and again urged her to set the publication of the book back to 1930 in order to allow him time to publish installments and get the heart of the book out to twenty-five thousand readers as a spearhead to the book's emergence. For five or six articles, he offered $1,000. Addams resisted postponing the book past January 1930 because she wanted publication to coincide roughly with the anniversary of Hull-House. Kellogg coaxed her into an extension: "After all if you are reviewing the twenty years it is scarcely thinkable that you are doing it diary fashion, with the last entry on the last day; rather that you are looking back over the decades in perspective, and may be permitted to stand off a bit from the closing year and day in putting your final stamp on the period."[51] His appeal was the perfect balance between flattery and truth. She sent him one long chapter instead of three and announced that she was inclined to send the prohibition chapter to the *Atlantic* "to offset some of the nonsense which in my opinion has recently appeared there!"[52]

In the dance between the two, Kellogg moved his foot forward as she moved hers back. On reading the longer chapter, his declared, "I do want it, and the others."[53] Choosing his words carefully, he told her: "No, your writing has not lost its cunning; nor the informing mind that guides it. And I am not disappointed. I shall look forward eagerly for the other two chapters." And she relaxed, sending Kellogg long chapters, explaining that she always wrote more than she finally used; and he encouraged her with the observation that at times the old materials were woven deftly together with the new into patterns that illuminated the whole work.

He admired her fluid style of writing, the associative logic of her long narrative, the flow that Virginia Woolf thought a modern writer ought to record, rather loosely and comfortably. "In this chapter on immigrants, it is as if you went from room to room of the subject, flooding each in turn with a lamp in your hands," Kellogg wrote.[54] He liked the way she put "several strands together into a skein, which your readers might apprehend and visualize." As an editor, however, he urged her to make a clear, firmer statement than she intended. "At least you should know the impression it made on me—a luminous play from room to room without a clear structural picture of your house." He got it right; that was precisely the kind of book she was writing. Sensing her desire to protect her creation, Kellogg wrote delicately on the issue of cutting the manuscript, "I know that you would feel happier dealing with your own children."[55] By the end of their negotiation, Addams came to agree with Kellogg that the book publication ought to be pushed back well into 1930 to allow time for *Survey* to run installments, and time for her to revise in Bar Harbor during her usual summer writing season.

In the leisurely and perceptive book that emerged, Addams was conscious of her art, musing on the power of fiction, drama, music, painting, sculpture, even film to transport an audience and to transform its understanding of the human condition. Addams uses terms like "arena" and "pageant" to describe the world she imagines. In the background is Walt Whitman, who lamented the irony in American culture that people too often follow leaders who have very little concern for their welfare. The characters in her narrative range from Virginia Woolf to H. G. Wells, including intellectuals who were among Addams's closest friends—Florence Kelley, John Dewey, Paul Kellogg, Alice Hamilton—and others more remote—Albert Einstein, Thomas Edison, Mahatma Gandhi. At one moment, she assumes the voice of Hegel in asserting that the state "is the realization of the moral idea" (89). At the next moment, she is dressed as an old woman from Wisconsin, seated in her automobile, schooling her son in the history of the rugged pioneer woman: "'Who can better vote on the needs of this great country than a woman like that'" (92). And moving even closer to Whitman's common folk, she speaks through the voice of an illiterate woman, who declares, "'Of course I am going to vote the way my man told me to,'" even as she makes its clear to Addams that she wants to support a local contagious disease hospital (93). On the common road, mingling with philosophers and peasants,

Addams claims knowledge beyond that found merely in books and universities. The intellectual must press real flesh.

Looking back on her experiences in *The Second Twenty Years*, she softens the memory with writing we might associate with experimental fiction. "My first actual impression of the war came one beautiful morning in August when a huge German liner, to our amazement suddenly appeared at the bottom of a hill on the Island of Mount Desert upon which our cottage was built" (117–18). A German invasion of America! Her letters at the time do not record the appearance of the ship, but the image of intrusion, the public and political war invading the private and domestic shores of Bar Harbor, is meant to startle complacent readers. Later in the book, she narrates an epiphany as she travels to the Geneva headquarters of the Women's International League for Peace and Freedom. "There comes to me in Switzerland more than anywhere else those glimpses of what Plato calls the 'eternal patterns,'" she confides. "Suddenly and unexpectedly it becomes visible before one's eyes" (148). In talking about the strident rejection of immigrants in the wake of the war, she writes, "We have learned that life is never logical and apparently not even reasonable, at least a surface reasonableness is often misleading as to the profounder trends underneath" (271). To read events, we must admit to our blindness. Not content with a mere backward glance, Addams creates a montage of images.

Although much of the book rehearses old themes—the frustrations of the Progressive Party, the unflappable energy of the suffrage movement, the failures of pacifism—Addams takes up contemporary causes, commenting along the way about the efficacy of efforts to ameliorate the human condition. She argues that nineteenth-century women's clubs "might be made a great apparatus for the evocation of cultural life" (94). Talking with the elevator boy and then with her colleague Mary McDowell, Addams ends the discussion in the voice of an unidentified club woman who makes the argument for organizations like the Women's International League: "'[D]iscussions of international relations are more popular than papers on the poets of the seventeenth century'" (99). More over, women, free of male conventions, "may enable the average citizen to escape from the deadening effects of worn-out conventional phrases, which so largely dominate political life" (109). Her example, Jeannette Rankin, links suffrage and pacifism as Addams reminds readers that it was the representative from Wyoming who stood before her male peers on April 5, 1917, to declare, "'I want to stand by my country—but I cannot vote for war'" (109). She adds, with chagrin, that twelve years later (and nine years after the suffrage amendment) all eight female representatives voted with their male colleagues for a strong national defense. Addams fears that perhaps "women in politics thus far have been too conventional, too afraid to differ with the men, too ill at ease to trust their own judgments, too skeptical of the wisdom of the humble to incorporate the needs of simple women into the ordering of political life" (109–10).

She mocks the timidity of her profession in the 1920s: "We are quite willing to work hard at the abolition of toothache, but not willing to discuss social theory, and if a powerful newspaper called the effort Bolshevistic, so filled with terror have certain words become, that doubtless a few social workers would be found to say: 'We don't really approve of dental clinics; and, of course, we do not extend their services to adults who might be radicals; we are only experimenting with baby teeth'" (156). The woman of seventy, looking out on the second and third generations of social workers, sees all their flaws.

Among the youthful generation, the children and grandchildren of Halsted neighbors, Jane Addams witnesses a considerable change, one she finds surprising and, certainly, ironic. What catches her eye is the "spirit of conformity in matters of opinion among young people especially among college students" (189). The children of immigrants are more likely to go to college than the children of American citizens and are mindful of the advantages of assimilation. "They are anxious to appear as if their families had lived in America much longer than they have and to conform so carefully that no one will suspect their recent coming" (189). They live in an age that holds anyone newly arrived under suspicion and especially reviles those who, because of race or social class, cannot find a way to blend into the bland patterns of the American middle class.

Other modern issues in the book may seem surprising, given Addams's age and inclinations. She goes after Sigmund Freud in delightful fury, charging that "the Freudian theories as to dangers of repression were seized upon by agencies of publicity, by half-baked lecturers and by writers on the new psychology and finally interpreted by reckless youth as a warning against self-control" (192). Freud's theory put relationships like the one she had with Mary Rozet Smith under the microscope. In answering the question about her sense of duty and her knowledge and experience with sexuality, the very question that Allen Davis once put to Alice Hamilton, Addams slips the noose. The young have it wrong, she asserts, in assuming that an old maid is "narrow and unhappy and, above all, hopelessly embittered." Instead of speaking directly, she moves into the voice of Emily Greene Balch, her younger colleague from Wellesley College, who responds with a question: "'Is it compatible with the modern theories about sex that two generations of professionally trained women lived, without vows or outward safeguards, completely celibate lives with no sense of its being difficult or of being misunderstood?'" (197). Good question—one we continue as scholars to ponder.

Amid an odd pastiche of images of the Bowen Country Club, Addams tells us more about her relationship with Mary Smith than she does anywhere in the public eye. "For me personally there is connected with the club, an association with two of my most enduring friendships; with Mary Rozet Smith, with whom I have studied, traveled and lived throughout all the years of Hull House," she openly acknowledges. The other friendship is with Louise DeKoven Bowen, the benefactress of the country club itself. She returns to Mary, however, to say that the two of them feel secure in Bowen's cottage at the country club: "Miss Smith and myself occupy it not so much in the capacity of guests as of those who are at home— in that definition of a home as a place where they have to take you in," she adds with Robert Frost's "Death of a Hired Man" in her mind (352).

The Second Twenty Years covers new ground in its scrutiny of the contemporary world of the 1920s. In her community, made up largely of southern Europeans, a square mile was home to 400 saloons; in 1911 Chicago's 328 dance halls entertained 86,000 people, most of them teenagers, on Saturday nights. The social reform movement to ban alcohol initially had its intended effect of improving the standard of living of the poor and working class, but bootlegging ended family stability and, by seeding the growth of a criminal class, had the unintended effect of forcing the newly prosperous immigrants out of the city. Addams does not deliver a temperance lecture but, surprisingly, uses the change in the Halsted neighborhood to tell colorful tales of corruption in the mode of a Zola novel. Sicilians in Chicago, she confides, "have an unsavory reputation for desperate measures in connection with bootlegging" (242). She observes that the culprit in gang warfare is "big business." Chicago is the conduit between the stills of Canada and the market in the United States, much as Miami is a major site today in the exchange of drugs. The children of the streets, then as now, are attracted by the glamour of the trade. "It is as if this adventurous spirit were transferred from the wild west into the city streets," Addams explains, as she links bootlegging to roadhouses, prostitution, banditry, and the automobile on the prairie around Chicago, open land that shelters illicit conduct (247).

As a bloody illustration, she recounts the Valentine's Day Massacre on February 14, 1929, and suggests the corruption of the police in a subsequent incident when they gunned down four gangsters who were escaping, "the automobile landing in the ditch when the dead hands of the driver dropped from the wheel" (250–51). She weaves together police reports, newspaper accounts, urban legends, and rumors. The Chicago police are players in vice as much as Capone and Moran. What fascinates her is the urge to move beyond the boundaries of supposedly civilized society. Youth, she observes, "looks for a method with which it may defy the conventions and startle its elders" (253). There are times when Addams's imagination gets far out in front of her experience, and the reader stops at a line like: "Many flappers are afraid to drive with men who carry hip flasks" (253). One wonders how many flappers Jane Addams knew and, more to the point, how many of them would have come clean to her about their encounters with men who carry hip flasks.

Addams moves toward a long consideration of art in a section that reminds us of the early chapters of *The Spirit of Youth*. With Whitman's "Leaves of Grass" in mind, his invocation of both body and soul, she writes: "It may be the withdrawal into the country after a week of leisure and uproar, it may be the opportunity to read in leisurely fashion, to invite one's soul and to speak easily of the deeper issues of life and death, but I think that the peculiar charm of this chapter upon recreation in relation to the arts, is the sense of being basically at ease which can come only when the play instinct is reduced to relaxation and developed in an understanding atmosphere" (352). The linking of recreation—the play of the body—and the imagination—the play of the mind—is at the core of her thinking about art. And she couples that aesthetic idea with her sense of the moral society: "The patriotism of the modern state must be based not upon a consciousness of homogeneity but upon a respect for variation, not upon inherited memory but upon trained imagination" (367). It is our minds, engaged in play and in art, that may save us as a culture. It is fair to say that Addams, over the twenty years between 1910 and 1930, came to see art and the possibilities of the imagination as hopefully as she had society and the possibilities of the intellect in her relative youth. In remembering the publishing of five Hull-House songs, she gives us another version of her credo (again in the past tense): "We believed that all the songs in this collection fulfilled the highest mission in music, first in giving expression to the type of emotional experience which quickly tends to get beyond words, and second in affording an escape from the unnecessary disorder of actual life, into the wider region of the spirit which, under the laws of a great art, may be filled with an austere beauty and peace" (375). This penultimate chapter, written from honest reminiscence, links her to Virginia Woolf as the two women pondered the role of the writer in the modern world.

Black Thursday

The stock market crash on what came to be known as Black Thursday, October 24, 1929, happened almost without notice in the letters Jane Addams was writing. It took time for word to spread but, more so, for word to settle into minds busy with other thoughts. Certainly, no one seemed to understand the dire repercussions, the long slow decline in fortunes and increase in misfortunes. Addams was working on magazine installments of *The Second Twenty Years* for Paul and Arthur Kellogg and lamented, "[I]t is very difficult to write here and I am not sure that I can get the manuscript ready before Spring."[56] Paul Kellogg sent her a long letter on October 24 encouraging her to continue writing because the book promised to refresh thinking about social work, a profession that was languishing by the end of the 1920s. As writers often do, she explained to her editor that she was finding absolutely no time to write and then announced, "It is probable that I shall have to go away from late Winter and early Spring and try to get it ready."[57]

Addams arranged for a luncheon at the Bowen Country Club, reserving a special train car from Northwestern Station at 10:32 on Sunday, October 19. The week following the market crash, the Midland Authors held a dinner at the Fortnightly Club to honor John Dewey with Addams as the only female scheduled to speak, the others being male professors. She never made it to the dinner, and Dewey wrote, "[T]here is no one in the world whom I would have so much desired to be present and speak."[58] Addams broke her arm in an accident, spent much of the next month in the hospital, and found herself in much the same mood as the country by the end of the fall. Her hope was to gather strength enough to travel to New York City for the meeting of the National Federation of Settlements on December 7 and 8.

The first ripple in her correspondence of the economic collapse came in a December letter from Madeleine Doty, secretary of WILPF, who acknowledged the arrival of a check Addams had sent her. "It will be a big help in tiding me over this rather difficult financial time," Doty explained.[59] Hull-House investments were tied to the stock market and, by year's end, the effect was more than a ripple. Writing to Julius Rosenwald, a member of the Hull-House board of trustees and a major contributor to the private institution, Louise DeKoven Bowen and Addams explained: "You will remember when at your request we sold approximately $100,000 worth of bonds bearing 5% interest and invested in Sears, Roebuck & Company stock, you guaranteed that at the end of five years, if the stock was not worth what we paid for it you would make up the difference, and you also guaranteed that we would receive yearly 5% on our investment."[60] Looking hard at the books at the end of 1929, the women discovered that they could not pay their bills, owing to the decline in stock value, especially that of United States Gypsum Company, but also because of Sears. It is the Sears investment that they hoped to recoup from Rosenwald. Hull-House received cash dividends of $1,250 that year and sold stock dividends amounting to $2,926.33, providing $4,176.33 of the expected $5,000 shortfall in their budget for the year. They hoped to recover from Rosenwald the difference of $823.67. Had it not been for the crash in the stock market, they pointed out that Hull-House would not need the cash, and then they added a sharp rebuke of his investment advice: "[T]hese unpleasant collapses are, to my mind, just why an organization like Hull-House should not own stock."[61] Rosenwald swallowed the criticism and sent the shortfall.

Traveling to Tucson, Arizona, in the winter of 1930, Jane and Mary took up residence at the El Conquistador Hotel. By March, Ellen Starr wrote to tell Jane that she had an abscess on her spine, requiring surgery, and asked her long-time friend for help. Mary sent a letter to Lillian Wald that tells us much about the relationships as all the women grew frailer. She commiserated with Lillian, who had returned to the maelstrom of New York in the early days of the Depression, and she thanked her for sending a novel by Virginia Woolf—probably *Mrs. Dalloway* or possibly *Orlando*. Then Mary unloaded: "Did I write you that J. A. was starting for Chicago, on account of Miss Starr's operation when all the doctors on the case telegraphed her not to come?"[62] The surgery revealed the abscess was benign and yet Jane hurried through her work on *The Second Twenty Years* so that she could be free to go. Mary complained about her own ailments, especially the asthma that failed to respond to the warm, dry climate of Arizona: "Almost everyone seems to feel that I may not be able to swing open the simple house at Hull's Cove," she lamented, "and I don't know. It is clear that I can't travel." Yet Mary hoped to convince Jane that the cottage would work out for them during the summer months. She wanted the isolated intimacy. The battle over her energy and Jane's duties toward her and toward Ellen was one familiar to Lillian. Mary continued, "This suggestion does not meet with general favor, however, and I am still very feeble when it comes to carrying my point. I think J. A. is nobly intending to support my tottering steps, or more accurately, my wheezing breaths wherever they may be directed." The two women were a good match, Mary knowing instinctively how to get her way even as Jane seemed in charge.

As it turned out, Jane stayed in Tucson that spring, working slowly on *The Second Twenty Years.* She was especially unhappy with her chapter on the women's movement and admitted to Paul Kellogg that she had developed a distaste for the essay in its magazine form and planned a radical revision for the book. After a month of writing during the summer, Addams completed her final chapters, one on the arts and the last one, perhaps clumsily attached, on current events. Kellogg found it difficult to cut her "well welded" chapter on the arts to magazine size, or so he claimed. What he wanted was another essay altogether on "patriotism of the modern state," one that would argue for variation of thought and attention to the imagination.[63] After the long weaving together of materials for the book itself, Addams continued to feel that somehow the manuscript had failed. In September, she wrote to Henrietta Barnett, the wife of the late Canon Barnett, "I will send you a book in the course of time although I am afraid it is not a very interesting one."[64]

No Wisdom Comes at Seventy

Addams celebrated twin birthdays in 1930, one for Hull-House and the other for herself. On May 9, 1930, Hull-House celebrated its fortieth anniversary, having moved the party back eight months from the actual birth date of September 14, 1889. The bigger social and political event, however, was the marking of Jane Addams's seventieth birthday. United Press invited her to respond to eleven questions that would be circulated to reporters, a daunting task at any age. By telegram, she disclaimed: "NO SPECIAL WISDOM COMES AT SEVENTY CAN BE SECURED ONLY THROUGH ADAPTATION TO CHANGING WORLD STOP IMPOSSIBLE TO REPLY TO ELEVEN QUESTIONS IN SO SHORT A SPACE."[65] She pointed out that women's achievements include schooling politicians on health and humanitarian issues, securing for their families a higher standard of living, crafting legislation for insurance against unemployment, working for disarmament and the World Court in the spirit of international comity and good will. No sentimental romantic, she added, "CHANGING STANDARDS ALTHOUGH EASILY MISINTERPRETED DO NOT NECESSARILY AFFECT BASIC MORALITY."

As to the more personal question of why Miss Addams of Hull-House would mark her seventieth birthday at Hull's Cove and not at Hull-House, she explained, "MY FRIEND MISS SMITH AND MYSELF FOR EIGHTEEN YEARS HAVE HAD A COTTAGE AT HULL'S COVE." Longtime friends, the Morgenthaus of Bar Harbor, had organized a private birthday luncheon in her honor. The Associated Press reported that millionaires, diplomats, university presidents, young politicians, and social scientists paid tribute to Jane Addams at the party. John D. Rockefeller Jr. called Addams "Christ-like," and others, including Henry Morgenthau, Robert M. Hutchins, Arthur Henderson, and Richard C. Cabot praised her accomplishments. The celebration in Bar Harbor marked her socially, perhaps more than chronologically.

In November 1930, Ellen Starr, who was moving to the East to live in a sanitarium, asked Jane to dismantle her Chicago apartment. Old and frail as she was, Jane went to the apartment herself to sort through Ellen's papers, divide up furniture, distribute books to friends, and close out the household. "I'm not dead yet!" Ellen joked, ordering her to "rent the stuff as if it were yours" but to leave some things "get-at-able."[66] The old and honorable dishes, Ellen conceded, were used up, and she gave them to Jane, except for a beautiful Mexican plate and another fancy one she had always liked. The Italian art Ellen planned to hang on to a bit longer. She was clearly charmed by the personal attention, and Jane seemed utterly at ease managing yet another household. Alice Hamilton, watching from a cool-eyed distance, said she was foolish to do chores for Ellen. "Why you should do chores like closing Miss Starr's flat, I do not see," she scolded. "If only you would keep yourself for things that really count."[67]

Age has a way, perhaps, of rounding rough edges in relationships. Carrie Chapman Catt, who had organized the National Committee on the Cause and Cure of War without including Addams on her speakers' list, wrote to her in November 1930 to send a check for $100 as a donation to WILPF. She had deserted the pacifists at the beginning of the war in the hope of securing women's suffrage at its close and had been successful in her strategy. The $100 may well have been guilt money. Catt explained that she was much surprised by an Achievement Award from the *Pictorial Review* in 1930. "I am at this moment the possessor of $5,000 I never expected to receive," she announced "and this afternoon I am giving it all away."[68] Addams acknowledged it as a generous act in the face of the Depression.

The Second Twenty Years appeared that November, prompting Louise Bowen to write, "I liked it immensely. I think it is one of the most interesting ones you have ever written."[69] Julia Lathrop (who would become the central figure of Addams's last book) thanked her for a copy of the book. "I trust we shall all see the Nobel award to you *soon*. It would have come long since if Wisdom were in the saddle," she quipped.[70] Latham wrote to send her royalty check for 1930, a little chagrined by the meager amount but warm in his affection for a writer who had earned a good deal of money for Macmillan over the years. Within the month, he wrote again to say that her new book was selling well in a dull year and to suggest another writing project. Alice Hamilton had mentioned to him the idea of a book of social prophecy, perhaps entitled "The Next Fifty Years." "That strikes me as a bully idea," he coaxed. "May I not send you a contract for such a book, understanding fully that you would take your time for its completion and that we would in no way press you for it?"[71] She did not feel prophetic at seventy and nothing came of the book idea.

Some rough edges simply never dull. Rosika Schwimmer read *The Second Twenty Years*, paying close attention to the story of the women's delegation in 1915. Irritated still with Addams's impulse to use old material and her inclination to fictionalize, Schwimmer reminded her sharply that Alice Hamilton had accompanied Addams to Europe after the congress at The Hague, not as a delegate but merely as a friend. One might argue that no good deed goes unpunished and, perhaps, that thought crossed Addams's mind as she worked to mollify her long-time colleague. She responded in the conciliatory tone she often used in her letters to difficult people: "I am very sorry I made the same mistake the second time." Then she tried to explain her literary genre: "I suppose I was not trying to give an historic account but merely my impressions of those post war years."[72] Her claim to poetic license did little to soothe the pacifist.

"Your Aunt Jane is lying and writing in a steam heated room which she keeps at about 90," Mary Smith playfully reported to Myra Lynn in the spring of 1931.[73] The eccentricities of her companion seemed not to ruffle her. "She is really remarkably well and has been writing with great spirit and energy!" The frailties of age showed in the winter months as Jane moved again to Tucson in the company of Mary and Louise, all three women "afoot" in the warm climate. Addams turned quite naturally to her writing project, this one *The Excellent Becomes the Permanent*, the title coming from her reading of Virginia Woolf. The new book was to be a collection of old pieces of writing, eulogies, memorials, and dedications that she had delivered over the years for friends and relatives of friends.

That year, Jane Addams was back in style. As an international figure, she appeared on various lists beside Sigmund Freud in Austria, H. G. Wells in England, Albert Einstein and Thomas Mann in Germany, Mahatma Gandhi in India, and John Dewey and Upton Sinclair in the United States. The University of Chicago awarded her an honorary Doctor of Law degree. Of her days as a suspicious character, she wrote in private letters that they made her skeptical but not cynical. "I was threatened with every dire fate that could befall a human being," she confided to Marcet.[74] Her visceral response to the supposed danger was not to take precautions, and the truth was that nothing ever happened. "The man who indulges in threats possesses a curious temperament, which no longer frightens me," she admitted in old age. She still had her critics, truly vicious ones in the 1930s, but their caviling came in response to the rise of her reputation as a thinker and a writer.

In another sign of Addams's return from political and literary exile, Charles A. Beard wrote in January 1931 to invite her participation on a collaborative book on the idea of progress. He wanted her to write the chapter on social reconstruction, considering the outstanding achievements in her field and probing the striking problems ahead. Beard placed Addams alongside the scientist Robert Millikan, the judge Dwight W. Morrow, the educational philosopher John Dewey, and other leaders in their professions. As she sat in the sauna that winter, one of the pieces of writing she worked on was "The Process of Social Transformation" for Beard's edited book, *A Century of Progress* (1932).[75] He promised $750 for that piece, and Macmillan sent $250 for delivery of the manuscript of *The Second Twenty Years*. That spring she turned her attention again to the James family, writing a review of the biography *Charles W. Eliot*, written by William's son, Henry James Jr.

The United States was a dangerous place for many people in the 1930s. Even as she rested and wrote in Tucson, she followed events in the outside world. Theodore Dreiser sent her an urgent letter in June 1931, detailing the national scandal in Scottsboro, Alabama. "The charge was rape," he told her. "But the charge was an afterthought. The boys—Negroes, fourteen to twenty years of age—were arrested for stealing a ride on a freight train. The white girls, in overalls, were also found 'hoboing' on this train."[76] He had it right that the young women were coaxed into the accusations by a sheriff looking for a reason to lynch the young men. Dreiser's postscript asked for money to fund the National Committee for the Defense of Political Prisoners: "The Scottsboro case is our immediate issue in our fight against the present epidemic of racial, industrial, and political persecutions in our country." He invited Addams to join him and Lincoln Steffens, Burton Rascoe, John Dos Passos, and Suzanne LaFollette.

W. E. B. Du Bois, a long-time colleague, invited Addams to write for the twentieth annual children's number of the *Crisis*. "I am writing to ask if you would not send us a little message to American Negro children?"[77] Requesting a manuscript of five hundred words by the first of September, he made the case for its significance: "I know the burdens put upon you but I do think that such a word from you would do a world of good!" Esther Henshaw responded from Hull-House, asking Du Bois for permission to hold the letter until September, when Addams planned to return from her summer trip to New England, where she was under orders to rest. He tried again in September, requesting something by the first of October to mark the twenty-first anniversary of the magazine. She finally responded to the request, not with an article but with a complement, the politician in Addams ever at work: "I have read [the *Crisis*] through the twenty-one years of its existence, and am happy to congratulate the editor and the staff upon their able achievement." She added in the postscript that she had only just received his letter and that she regretted writing such a brief response, but "I need not assure you it is genuine."[78] In the November issue of the *Crisis*, her statement of support for the magazine appeared in the column, "What Our Readers Say."[79]

Addams was a significant public character in her old age. In 1931, Bryn Mawr acknowledged her with a $5,000 award recognizing her "eminent achievement." Helen Keller interviewed her as part of a series of the most distinguished people for *Good Housekeeping*. A young woman, Lillie Peck, proposed writing a joint volume, and Addams responded favorably to the possibility of collaborative work even as she reported: "My writing took quite another direction this winter."[80] A weird six-page letter arrived in June 1931 listing Addams's sins in editing, typesetting, and proofreading from Louis N. Feidel, who took it upon himself to inform her and the staff at Macmillan of their errors in *The Second Twenty Years at Hull-House*. The Disarmament Campaign Committee of WILPF organized a radio address from station WMAQ in Chicago on Celebrate Goodwill Day. In her nearly illegible hand, Addams scribbled across the schedule: "Stupid mistake missed radio hour."[81]

Will Durant wrote her that summer, full of philosophical doubt. "What is the meaning or worth of human life?" he asked, the daunting question much on her mind that year.[82] To her, the excellence of human endeavor offered an answer. She spent the summer months in Bar Harbor, reworking her material on Tolstoy and connecting it to the economic efforts of Gandhi. Publishing the essay she wrote, however, was not easy. As distinguished as Addams had become, editors avoided any volatile political issue. She sent the article to Ellery Sedgwick in October and then to the *Pictorial Review*, and finally found a place at the *Christian Century* in November.[83]

Paul Kellogg reviewed *The Second Twenty Years* together with Lincoln Steffens's *Autobiography* for the *Yale Review* in the fall of 1931. He argues that both writers belong in the "curricula of the 1930's."[84] Understanding and articulating the gestalt of modern life is something Kellogg thought that Addams did by virtue of her feminine nature or instinct. Steffens had to learn how, or so Kellogg suggests, using that as a reason for spending much of the review on the man rather than the woman. Kellogg proclaims: "The German universities corrected that trait in him to some extent, he says, but especially was it his knocking up against all manner of men with his inveterate inquisitiveness, and his prying into their shells; crooks and cops; bosses, presidents, premiers, dynamiters, timber-magnates, railroad presidents, artists, bankers—everyone but women." What is utterly clear from the review is that Kellogg was pleased to be a man in the company of men, especially "dynamiters." In his mind, women had another role to play in the modern world: "More especially, we get luminous intuition into nascent forces that stir the common life, forces which may mold the new America quite as much, or more, than the formulas for its ordering." The female mind, much like the female body, functions as a life force beneath the more palpable events of the world. A woman might be "luminous" but not explosive. We wonder what went through Addams's mind as she read the review.

The Depression hit hard in 1931 as the hope for any immediate reversal dimmed. The men at the University of Chicago Press wrote that summer about its publishing, finally, of Aletta Jacobs's memoir as a Social Service Monograph. Money was tight, and Edith Abbott asked Addams to pay "the funds of its issue."[85] The book could not be born without her money, and Jane continued to care for her colleague as she continued to tend many friends and relatives. Most people thought the crash of the stock market would be short-term, but signs suggested that the collapse would last a long time. Julius Rosenwald, whose accountants kept a close eye on funds he gave to Hull-House, offered $250,000 in the fall for the relief of the unemployed in Chicago. Kellogg wrote Addams to enlist her help in the "Remember '93" issue of *Survey* magazine. The idea was to compare the economic conditions of the 1930s to those of the 1890s: "An article which, while it would sound some of the depths and shadows of that time, would none the less bring out how in spite of it, or because of it, there were beginnings of affirmative endeavors which [crossed out: we are] came to count for the common welfare."[86] What he wanted, in his heavy-handed way, was an argument for the pendulum theory. Addams wrote "Social Consequences of Business Depressions," publishing it as a pamphlet through the University of Chicago Press and in *Survey* in January 1932.

The Depression in the United States was part of a global economic spasm that had military reverberations. In the late 1920s, WILPF had hoped to organize a "Mission to China," an effort to organize Chinese women as pacifists even as their country suffered civil war. By 1930 as reports of the famine in China reached two million dead with another two million in jeopardy, the American Red Cross, surprisingly, decided to take no action. Yella Hertzka wrote to Addams from Geneva that the Women's International League would also abandon the effort, blaming the Chinese people for the failure of assistance. Salving her conscience, Hertzka explained to Addams that famines were "quite a different thing when they recur owing to the neglect of arrangements which would be of permanent value," like the building of roads to transport food. "The Chinese for centuries have not undertaken the improvements in transportation that are necessary to prevent the perpetual recurrences of famine."[87] In May, Amy Wu, a fledgling member of the Women's International League, wrote to her colleagues in the West that pacifism was doomed.[88] The Japanese invasion of China was brutal and relentless. "The cry is now for war and admittedly drastic and futile, the consensus of opinion is that it is better to die fighting than to placidly give in to Japanese in this way." Wu did not see help coming from the League of Nations either: "The League is really a huge joke." Chiang Kai-shek had left Nanking, and Chang Hsüeh-liang, the controller of Manchuria, had fled the invasion, leaving Chinese citizens to face the slaughter unprotected by an army. Given the attacks against women in the conflict, especially rape and dismemberment, it would be hard to imagine what women might have done to avoid the war, much less to avoid being its vulnerable victims. Ida Tarbell wrote that she hoped Addams was "not too torn by the Far Eastern Tragedy."[89]

In October, Latham agreed to publish her manuscript, "The Excellent Becomes the Permanent," with a monetary hesitation: "It is a very unusual and in our opinion distinguished piece of work. At the same time, it is a work for which we are afraid the public will be limited, and in these days, when all publics are limited so far as books are concerned, this is a more than ordinarily serious matter."[90] The upshot of the deal was that Macmillan would pay only 10 percent on the first 1,000 copies (15 percent after that) but only after the books had in fact sold. As an afterthought, Latham quizzed her about the title itself, an awkward and nearly unrecognizable literary allusion to Woolf: "It is a good title for those who are in the know, so to speak, but I am not sure it's as popular a title as we might find." Addams responded that she was willing to compromise by agreeing to wait for her money but she wanted the full 15 percent: "I dislike the feeling of 'demotion.'"[91] Latham agreed to pay the 15 percent but suggested marketing the book through Macmillan's religious books department, an agreement that would cause both of them consternation later. As for the title, she told him she would think about renaming it as she convalesced from an attack of bronchitis.

In the days before antibiotics, bronchitis was often fatal, especially to an old woman. In closing the letter to Latham, Jane Addams made a joke worthy of Mark Twain. "In case of my demise in the hospital, it would sell the books, would it not, because of its particular theme?"

Addams traveled to Washington, D.C., in October with Mary Smith and Alice Hamilton to present a disarmament petition to President Hoover and to attend a mass meeting. The women went on to New York City and visited Ellen Starr. Addams's bronchitis came on in the city as she accepted the $5,000 Achievement Award given by the *Pictorial Review*, the same award that Carrie Chapman Catt had collected the year before. Her hospitalization forced her to cancel her scheduled nationwide radio address over NBC on Tuesday, October 20, although she hoped to be well enough to speak on Saturday, October 24, on "Social Consequences of Business Depressions," using the same material she planned to publish the next year.[92] She managed to give the address, even as she made plans for surgery at Johns Hopkins Hospital.

The Borderland between Life and Death

In the fall of 1931 as Jane Addams readied herself for surgery and the possibility of death, she paid close attention to the financial details of her life. She asked Macmillan for an accounting of her royalties; they sent $3,757.59 along with the contract for *The Excellent Becomes the Permanent*. She signed it. As she placed the essays together in the book, she appended her chapter on Egypt from *The Long Road of Woman's Memory*, no doubt thinking that the graceful essay on perception and history might serve well as an obituary. She sent Paul Kellogg the manuscript "Social Consequences of Business Depressions" for publication in *Survey*; she sent it "as is," confessing, "I am not up to writing."[93] She sent her beleaguered essay "Tolstoy and Gandhi" to the *Christian Century*.

A poignant record of her sense of responsibility in the face of death comes in a long letter to Ellen Gates Starr: "Before I go to the hospital, I am transferring to the Hull-House Association, for a so-called Pension Fund, twelve thousand dollars, which at five percent should bring in six hundred dollars a year, or fifty dollars a month; and I am putting a paper into the Hull-House strong box, with this, stating that I wish the $50 a month to go to you as long as you live, and that after that it will be a part of the general fund of Hull-House."[94] The additional $50 a month would insure Ellen an income of $250 a month, enough to pay for her to live at the Suffern Sanitarium. Nothing in the letter calls attention to Addams and her own ailments. She ended rather matter-of-factly: "Naturally I am planning to come back from the hospital, and then everything will go along as usual, but I am writing this in case I do not come back." The X-rays had been done and she lay in bed waiting for the surgery.

On December 8, 1931, the news arrived—at literally the eleventh hour—that the Nobel Committee had awarded the Peace Prize to Jane Addams and Nicholas Murray Butler, the president of Columbia University. The $46,350 prize was to be split in half. She was chagrined that the Peace Prize had come to her personally rather than to the Women's International League for Peace and Freedom, but that may have been a cover for the irritation that Butler, who had supported the U.S. effort in the Great War, was equally laudable. Butler telegraphed, in gentlemanly fashion, to say how honored he was to be in her company. Telegrams poured in from Chicago, across the country and, as the news disseminated, from around the world. Alfred E. Smith, who had not managed to get Addams's vote, congratulated her as the first American woman to be recognized: "IT IS ESPECIALLY A CAUSE FOR CONGRATULATIONS WHEN A WOMAN'S NAME IS ADDED TO THE DISTINGUISHED COMPANY."[95] Grace Abbott voiced the feminist response: "I WISH NICK MIGHT HAVE BEEN ELIMINATED."[96] Julia Lathrop joked, "SHE SHOULD HAVE HAD WHOLE LOAF."[97] W. E. B. Du Bois made the same joke a different way, pointing out that "HALF A LOAF OF RECOGNITION IS SOMETHING."[98] Paul Kellogg registered the pacifist's irritation: "THOSE NOBEL PEOPLE HAVE BEEN BLIND SO LONG THAT IT IS EVER SO GOOD TO LEARN BY THE PAPERS THAT THEY HAVE ONE EYE OPEN AT LAST."[99] Walter Lippmann, the editor at the time of the *New York Herald Tribune*, articulated the vindication that pacifists felt for the years of vilification: "You have stood, through fair weather and foul, for the elementary spirit of peace, and in the long run there could be no doubt that your teachings will be vindicated."[100]

By 1932, the Depression had dug into the fortunes of most people, the wealthy along with the poor. Mary explained to Jane's nephew Stanley that she was staying with Louise while Jane was in the hospital because she did not have the money to stay elsewhere: "I can no longer afford hotels and the like."[101] Typical of appeals from people far less fortunate was a letter that arrived in December from Margaret Cole, who pressed Jane Addams for cash: "I need $250 very very badly because I know if I don't get it, it will mean the means of breaking up me dear little home."[102] She had read of Addams's good fortune with the Nobel committee and hoped for a loan, even sending along the name of her bank.

The real medical emergency for Addams was not the much-talked-about bronchitis but rather a lump in her abdomen that suggested a return of the cancer removed earlier in Tokyo from her breast. Medical wisdom had it that once cancer had been detected, it was largely a question of time before its return. The surgery took place on December 12 to remove what turned out to be not cancer but a benign cyst on her ovary. Surgery, however benign the cyst, was an ordeal, then as now, for a woman over seventy. During the operation, her blood pressure dropped dramatically, and, after she awoke, she suffered from nausea brought on by the anesthetic as well as the surgery itself. The pain in her abdomen was excruciating, in spite of the fact that morphine was available to her. She suffered horrid gas pains, common after abdominal surgery, and problems with her blood pressure. Doctors injected her with glucose in the veins to nourish her. The staff kept her in isolation to prevent infection. They allowed her no activity, not even the reading of telegrams. A nurse cared for her day and night, and even a week after surgery, she remained too weak to raise her head. Mary Smith sat with her day after day in the hospital, and Clara Landsberg read aloud to her by the hour. Mary wrote a newsy letter at the end of December: "I simply have to write you collectively for your Aunt Jane is so popular that a large part of the population of the U.S.A. has been moved to write to her or send her flowers or a present and to thank them all (or worse still to tell them there is nothing left of the Nobel Award for their pressing needs) is some stunt. It leaves me little time to gossip."[103]

Rosika Schwimmer, ever in the middle of the news, announced in the January 1932 issue of the *World Tomorrow* that Jane Addams had given the money from the Nobel Peace Prize to the Women's International League for Peace and Freedom. That was not quite true. The Nobel committee sent her $16,480.55 in January, depositing the full amount into her account at the Continental Illinois Bank and Trust Company. Addams divided up the money, giving $15,000 to WILPF, $3,000 for the May congress planned for Grenoble, and $12,000 to be invested in an endowment at 5 percent. She placed $500 in her own account and paid herself back for the *Pictorial Review* award money she had already given to WILPF. As usual, she sent money to her nephew Stanley, and she made plans to travel south with Mary, who was exhausted from asthma. Mary admitted to friends that with a return of Jane's energy, she found herself in "complete sloth."

The truth was that the women of their generation, born during the Civil War and educated in the 1880s, were in their seventies frail indeed. Arthur Kellogg and Zona Gale organized a special issue of *Survey Graphic* in February 1932 on the women of Hull-House, not the ills of the flesh but the gifts of their spirit, complete with photographs, including Florence

Kelley in the Germantown Hospital, Grace Abbott in Colorado, and Ellen Gates Starr in a sanitarium. Jane Addams wrote to the failing Florence Kelley in February 1932, "Mary Smith and I talk of you so often and our hearts are filled with a great desire to see you oftener during this long term at the hospital, but not yet as long as one I had years ago with my spine!"[104] The women yearned to be together and took solace in the act of writing letters. She ended, "With dearest love to you dearest of old friends." Quite possibly Kelley never read the letter. Lillian Wald wrote to Addams and Smith on February 20 that she had gone to see Florence Kelley and found that her mind seemed to be wandering. She called the doctor and Kelley died on Wednesday morning. Her body, dressed and laid out for viewing, looked young to Wald, maybe thirty-five (the very age of youth to women in their seventies). The body in repose looked peaceful and quiet, Wald assured her friends, and no one spoke of religion or of life beyond the earthly one. Kelley had asked to be cremated and to have her ashes scattered near the grave of her daughter.

Gale visited Hull-House as she put together the issue of *Survey Graphic* on the effort of women to create social work. "It was a joy to see you," she wrote after her return to Wisconsin, "and it was something more: a kind of energy."[105] The issue, "Great Ladies of Halsted Street," appeared in the March 1932 *Survey Graphic*.

As Addams was completing the story of her second twenty years at Hull-House, she sorted through essays and speeches, looking for the makings of *The Excellent Becomes the Permanent*. In writing an introduction that would yoke these earlier essays and speeches together, Addams considered changing patterns of religious belief. Noting that her generation had abandoned Victorian ideals without having gotten very far in constructing new ones, she puzzled over the modern recompense: "But when we deplore that our assurance is less and that we are but scantily compensated by our larger tolerance, we forget that adaptation is always taking place in every field and that the modern world in its flux and complexity, the current temper with its disillusionment and bafflement, is naturally seeking its own adjustment" (5). The question, of course, was what secular adjustment might allow for an assurance of immortality? Addams dedicated the book to her long-time friend Alice Hamilton because the two women, one a moralist and the other a scientist, sought meaning "in the very borderland between life and death."

Jane Addams was herself a woman of precarious health and certain doom. Looking backward to William James, she notes that some people manage to live by ideals in such an authentic way that for "a transfigured few" actual experience may shine even more brilliantly than "the incandescence of man's imagination." Such experience may embody a secular vision of salvation, even in the face of "the awe-inspiring presence of death, in the midst of wreckage and grim suffering." Addams has in mind the experiences of her many friends and colleagues and, perhaps more so, her own wrecks and suffering. To her collection of memorials, she appends her personal essay, placing herself in company with the dead.

The book eulogizes six women, including Mary's mother, Sarah Rozet Smith, and five men, a child, and Addams herself. The design of the book allowed Addams to end with her own most provocative essay on memory, imagination, and the possibilities of art, a reprise of her trip to Egypt that she had published once as an essay and again as the ending of *The Long Road of Woman's Memory*. Her life as a writer might well have ended with *The Excellent Becomes the Permanent*, a backward glance that took very little literary effort to arrange in 1932 and, especially, to publish, coming out as it did just after the Nobel Prize Committee had finally turned to her.

By March the book was out, beautifully printed but little understood, especially by L. H. Titterton, the editor of the religious book department at Macmillan. It grated on her that he was the editor and that her book was classified as a study of religion. Addams rebuked him in a letter that contained a clipping from the *New York Times*, one that advertised the book by listing the names of those eulogized in the essays: "It seems to be a great mistake not to emphasize the theme of the book rather than the personalities who illustrate it."[106] Not content that the man understood how to sell the book, Addams rewrote the advertising copy for him: "The book attempts, through various personalities who have been connected with Hull-House, to answer the reiterated question: 'What is your attitude toward the future life?'" The book was having a hard time in the press, a hard time, that is to say, getting any press. Addams took Latham to task: "Of course The New York Times—almost the only lay publication on your list—had a very interesting review, but I cannot imagine Zion's Herald or The Christian Endeavor World stimulating its sale!"[107] She lay the blame for the book's failure on Titterton and the religious books department. She scolded Latham, telling him that dozens of people had been calling her directly to find out about the book. Not surprisingly, Latham agreed to buy ads in the *New Republic* and *Survey Graphic* and sent a long list of places where he claimed Macmillan had already advertised the book and urged her to keep him informed.

Jane Addams pressed on that spring, even as colleagues and friends died around her. Vachel Lindsay's death prompted her to write a brief remembrance of "Chinese Nightingale" and "General Booth Enters Heaven." "For days the impression remained with his hearers that poetry was at last restored to its legitimate place, and we all, both native and immigrant, realized for the first time what solace the earliest poets might have brought to their hearers, so often hard pressed by life."[108] She returned to her life at Hull-House, although she gave up the trip to Oslo to accept the Peace Prize with Butler, cancelled plans to attend the Conference of Social Workers in Philadelphia, and let her colleagues know that she would not be able to travel to Grenoble for the Women's International Congress. Julia Lathrop worked to organize a memorial for Florence Kelley, but news arrived on April 16 that Lathrop herself was dead. Ellen Starr commiserated, "It was the way she entirely curbed a tendency she had earlier to use her brilliant wit in any way that might hurt! You could feel her do it. It was lovely, so genuinely kindly."[109] Ellen wrote frankly about mortality: "We don't know much about it. The four of us, all on the verge. May you be the last." Addams continued work on a memorial for both Kelley and Lathrop but found few people who were able to attend.

Around her, too, Addams saw the defeat of many efforts. Herbert Hoover enlisted Addams's support for his fall campaign. Fatigued by the hard job of guiding the country through the Depression, he ran for reelection in 1932. And although one would think, with the benefit of hindsight, that Addams would have welcomed Franklin Delano Roosevelt to office, she did in fact vote for Hoover and worked on a peace plank in the Republican platform. She remained loyal to the man who had done good work during the Great War to feed its victims, even as he failed in his role as president. Julius Rosenwald died in 1932, and as the auditors made their way through his accounts, they discovered that the Depression had hit him as well. His estate was $10,185,000 in debt, and, as a result of the debts, the employees of Sears lost $7,825,000 from the Employee's Aid Fund. Addams pragmatically approved an offer from the estate to accept $23,750 to use toward the purchase of Sears stock at half price. As with Hull-House, the Women's International League threatened to break apart without the guiding mind of Jane Addams and without the very presence of her body. The women in Britain, often uncomfortable with WILPF, threatened to withdraw from the organization. She looked at the problem as a disagreement among family members but conceded to Kathleen Courtney, "Perhaps it takes more moral energy than any of us possess to compose this situation."[110]

Mary and Jane retreated from the public world in the summer of 1932, traveling first to Hadlyme, Connecticut, to visit Alice Hamilton and Ellen Starr, and then to Bar Harbor. "It is very beautiful here and it seems homelike and familiar to be back again," she confided to her friend Hannah

Clothier Hull.[111] The homecoming was bittersweet for the two women, who were in the process of selling their cottage at Hull's Cove. They managed to find a buyer and sold the house in September. Addams explained the monetary exigency to her niece, Mary Addams Hulbert: "It has been difficult to give up such a beautiful spot in this most beautiful weather but after all 'the depression' loss makes *itself* felt—We leave here Sept. 30th."[112]

It was probably the pressure of money that drove Jane Addams to the lecture circuit in the fall of 1932. Her October schedule, one that reportedly shocked her doctor, included speeches in Philadelphia and New York City. She negotiated for hotels and days that would accommodate her admittedly frail health. On October 22, 1932, as she accepted an honorary law degree from Swarthmore, she criticized her compatriots. "The national self-righteousness of the American people is often honestly disguised as patriotism," she reproached her audience. "It is really, however, part of that adolescent self-assertion, sometimes crudely expressed in sheer boasting, which the United States has never quite outgrown."[113] Her words resonate today. Gandhi commiserated in a letter from Poona: "My inner being tells me that spiritual unity can only be attained by resisting with our whole soul the modern fake life."[114] And his words resonate, as well.

Addams ended *The Excellent Becomes the Permanent* with her essay on Egypt and Cedarville not only because she had run out of energy to write something new, but also because she had come to understand, even more clearly, the marks that cataclysmic events leave on human consciousness. Very near the end of life, Jane Addams finds solace in honest reminiscence.

6 Writing a Life

"I need money," James Weber Linn wrote his famous Aunt Jane in February 1933 during the especially lean year of the Depression. He had written a novel but needed more income than it was likely to earn him. Looking around for his next writing project, he mulled the idea of a biography, one that would feature the life of his controversial aunt. To his eye, she was an attractive literary commodity. "I look on the biography as a big job, which will take at least a couple of years."[1] The Nobel committee and the Roosevelt White House had acknowledged her work for world peace and social welfare, and her nephew, an entrepreneur somewhat in the tradition of his grandfather John Addams, believed her reputation and celebrity might be turned into the money he very much needed. "My idea is that I should first go carefully over all your records —books, letters, clippings, etc.—and not only make notes but outline the book; and then when I get it thus outlined, in talks with you I can get the details and the personality to make it rich and vital, as it should be." The book promised to earn him acclaim as a biographer and further establish her as a significant voice in the modern world. "You think of yourself as merely an intelligent and sympathetic and hardworking woman who has had the good fortune to increase the world's interest in social understanding, perhaps, to some small extent," he appealed to her modesty. And then he good-naturedly engaged her ego: "No doubt Tolstoi thought of himself in the same way." The juxtaposition must have pleased her. "But Tolstoi was a voice, and you have been a voice." It is that voice that Linn hoped to record.

The economic strain of the Depression united nephew and aunt. "I am also a professional, 56 years old, writing to a woman of distinction about a book that must be of value, might be of high importance, and if rightly done will incidentally bring in royalties enough to help both Hull House and your more or less dependent family." He boasted that they might earn together as much as $100,000, "if I'm the man to do it."

Houghton Mifflin wanted the deal but cautioned about the book's length and price. Ferris Greenslet conceded that the authorized life of Miss Addams would prove to be an important biographical publication but warned Linn not to write a long book. If he were to write the proposed 200,000 words, the book would cost $5.00, and few people would be willing to pay the price. But if he could hold the length to 160,000, the book could be priced at a more affordable $3.50. Getting down to business, Greenslet advised: "I have an idea that Miss Addams was a woman of action rather than of many epistulary words. If that is true, you wouldn't need to print many actual documents and I should suppose that a story of her life, even in great detail, could be told within 160,000 well chosen words, not forgetting that the biographic art like Michael Angelo's is 'the purgation of superfluities.'"[2] The burden of brevity, then as now, constrains biographers.

Linn was not the first writer to think about telling the story of Jane Addams. Emil Ludwig, who billed himself as "Biographer of the Great," had written an article in the 1920s, "The Greatest Living Americans," in which he placed Addams together with John D. Rockefeller, Thomas Edison, and Orville Wright. "Now, the art of telling the life-story of a human being is possible only if there exist for the portrayer abundant documents—like stones for the building of a house," he theorized, making the case for the significance of his own work. If the person were still living, of course, the problem of collecting and analyzing the stones could be problematic. For that reason, Ludwig selected the "greatest" Americans on the basis of personal contact. His ego was a strong one, and he enhanced his own status by proximity to the "great" figures he condescended to include on his short list. "*Jane Addams* looks like Goodness personified," he began the supposedly revealing portrait.[3] Using a broad brush, he added: "In the epoch in which the Rockefellers are uniting all their imagination and energies in order to heap together money and make a power of it, the Addams' are assembling all the strength of their hearts and their head to collect money and transmute it into human happiness." His portrait was fairly typical of the sentimental treatment she received during her lifetime and even later.

In the spring of 1933, Edward Wagenknecht sent Jane Addams a chapter about her from his book, *Eve in Modern Dress*—the title itself appealed to her. He included a letter on the nature of biography: "These papers are all 'psychographs'; they exemplify, on a reduced scale, the technique I have already employed in 'The Man Charles Dickens' (Houghton Mifflin, 1929) and 'Jenny Lind' (Houghton Mifflin, 1931)."[4] Wagenknecht used scientific jargon with a good deal of confidence although he was skeptical about biography as merchandise during the Depression years: "[I]t may be judged advisable to wait until after business picks up (if it ever does)." In his fifth chapter, he applies his 'psychograph' to her, curiously blending science and sentiment. "Jane Addams may seem somewhat out of place in a book of famous women artists. Yet she has, I think, a strong claim herself to be considered the greatest artist of them all." His point is that Addams was foremost among female artists because she found "life itself more interesting than any reflection of it" and, therefore, rejected "the purely aesthetic impulse," making of her life a work of art. He concludes, much in the mood of the day, by claiming that if America is to be saved, "it will not be her battleships that will save her," but good women like Jane Addams. The guise of scientific detachment did little to conceal Wagenknecht's own romanticism.

Winifred Wise wrote to Jane Addams to enlist her help in writing another type of biography. "I want very much to write a book for older girls about you and about your work for I believe that adolescent girls with their high ideals are very much interested in social work and especially in you, Miss Addams."[5] As with Linn, Wise wanted to schedule interviews and to read Addams's letters and other Hull-House papers to cull material for her narrative. "It is inevitable that someone should write a book about you, Miss Addams," she argued. "Would you not prefer to have this done under your direct supervision?" Wise used discretion in promising to take readers only through Addams's girlhood and young womanhood, the years that would serve as a model of female behavior. Her interview questions would probe only that early life: "What I would ask of you in interviews would be personal little anecdotes of your girlhood and young womanhood, such anecdotes as may seem trivial to you but are priceless to a biographer." She proposed the title "Kind Heart— The Story of Jane Addams" in the Junior Literary Guild series published by Rand McNally.

During the long winter of 1933, Jane and Mary planned to travel to Arizona with Louise DeKoven Bowen and her daughter, a young woman who enjoyed playing golf every day. Life was brutal for those enduring the cold weather in Chicago and, more so, the chilly economy. Addams wrote to Margaret Dreier Robins that she yearned to stay at Hull-House, where "one has a sense of at least 'standing by' if only to hear the stories of the unemployed. It has been like a disaster of flood, fire or earthquake, this universal wiping out of resources."[6] Addams confided to her niece Esther Linn Hulbert that Bowen was paying for expenses "door-to-door" or they would not have been able to afford the travel to the Southwest.[7] Mary had a bad case of bronchitis and needed to escape the rough weather to convalesce. Once in Arizona, she donned a stiff brace to relieve the pain in her back, probably caused by osteoporosis, and began sleeping on boards and taking large doses of calcium. After they arrived in Arizona, Jane continued to feel the pressure of money, as she explained to Marcet, "I am afraid that I cannot pay my March bills without your checks which I can easily understand might have been delayed by the bank."[8]

The women rested in the salubrious climate and watched from the Biltmore Hotel as Adolf Hitler arrested Jewish merchants in Germany. "The green of the golf course is very refreshing to the eye," Addams wrote to Ida Lovett, confessing that she was homesick and filled with guilt because of the indulgent, idle life she was living.[9] To Eva White, she confided, "[I] am feeling very much like a deserter from the battlefield."[10] As the honorary chair of WILPF, she petitioned Roosevelt to support disarmament and looked on as younger women, Alice Hamilton and Clara Landsberg, traveled to Germany to protest the discharge of Jewish doctors. Later that spring Michael Williams released an appeal to Addams and other world leaders to support the International Emergency Committee for the Emigration of German Jews and German Christians of Jewish Descent: "Between two and three hundred thousand young Jewish men and women are absolutely deprived of any hope of a future commensurate with the common rights and opportunities of human beings in a civilized state. The older Jews must live out their broken lives as best they may deprived of all the rights of citizens (save in a few exceptional cases) and stigmatized as a race to whom the German nation, so long as its present appalling dictatorship dominates its conduct, has no place within its polity."[11] The message was ominous.

Alice Hamilton wrote from Munich in June that "little that is clear-cut emerges from my notes, only impressions" and "that this whole thing is a mixture of black and white and one must try to see the white, but it is sometimes hard."[12] Germany was demoralized, she observed, by the lack of religious unity, the degeneration of art, the lack of respect for thrift, sobriety, and hard work. The Nazis seemed to be altering the country overnight. "Laws are passed daily, dealing with just such things, and there is no opposition. It will be interesting to see what comes out of it all. Certainly it is a demonstration of what Government control can do; for there is no field of life that does not come under it." The irony for Hamil-

ton, and no doubt for Addams, was the danger of unfettered and unques-
tioned social reform. Hamilton continued to voice her ambivalence,
pointing out in her hard-eyed way that Roosevelt could not credibly take
a stand against Hitler: "[C]ertainly President Roosevelt could not make
a formal protest any more than Germany could formally protest against
the last Maryland lynching."[13] What is more, she complained that pro-
Nazi speakers were being harassed in the United States. Her point was
that in a democracy free speech granted everyone the right to be heard,
and yet we can still hear in her voice anti-Semitic and racist tones. "I wish
somebody could make the Jews behave better. This interference with free
speech if the speaker is a Nazi is so bad. And in New York the Jewish and
Negro doctors have just forced a Nazi doctor out of a hospital position
in Harlem, exactly as the Brown Shirts do in Germany."[14] The problem
for democracy, then and now, was how to balance free speech and fair play.
Addams called for religious comity in a national radio address on July 23,
1933, protesting the treatment of Jews in Germany after Women's International League member Camille Drevet, who would become a member
of Comité de Vigilance des Intellectuals Anti-Fascistes, was ousted from
the country because she was Jewish. The green calm surrounding the
Biltmore Hotel was deceptive indeed.

Addams returned to Chicago in the spring, active in the Century of
Progress, an exposition meant to be an unambiguous celebration of reforms in the United States. Addams helped to create the social service
exhibit and raised $5,000 from Carnegie for the construction of a peace
exhibit. Her stamina was remarkable in her seventy-third year; she gave
lectures every other day at the exposition, inviting Eleanor Roosevelt, a
woman Lillian Wald described as "a real person," to speak that summer.
Addams was dismayed with audiences at the Century of Progress because
they—especially the young—seemed to know little about social settlements. Alvin Johnson asked her to write a section on settlements for his
Encyclopedia of Social Science, and she agreed, sensing her duty to school
the younger generation in the work she had been doing all her life. *Encyclopedia Britannica* asked her to craft a statement defining, even, the
term "bread line." She was chagrined to find her long efforts consigned
to encyclopedia entries.

The family claim continued during the Depression years in spite of
Addams's age and frail health. Her instinct with her relatives was always
to soothe them. Letters to nieces and nephews were chatty, never calling attention to professional chores or to the discomforts and misfortunes
of aging. Her nephew Stanley complained that his wife Myra had taken
a teaching job in 1933 for a salary of $1,500 a year, a job that required her

to live away from him. "Frankly, I would like to support the family and have Myra just teach enough to satisfy her longing but not enough to gum up the family life too much," he whined, utterly lacking a sense of irony. He was, after all, writing to a woman who designed social work as a profession for women.[15] Addams answered the letter in her patient way, explaining that she could continue to afford the $100 per month she had always sent him and his family, but because of the hard economic times, the monthly stipend would deplete the capital she had squirreled away for his children's education. Although it made her heart ache, she advised any member of the family to take any job offered. "I myself earn almost no money now altho I have a good course of lectures at Bryn Mawr College in Oct. that will help out this year," she explained, adding a rare personal aside: "My doctor won't permit much lecturing and there I am!"[16] Putting perhaps the most hopeful face on the economic disaster, she told Stanley that he would later be able to tell his grandchildren about the hard times he had endured.

On Jane's seventy-third birthday—the last birthday they would celebrate together—Mary wrote the most revealing letter that has survived. "You know that you have made my life—all its meaning and color have come from you," she confided. "I bless you for it and wish I could ever show you how much I care."[17] They had been well mated through their forty years of marriage and joked good-naturedly about their dependence on each other. "I succeed in scolding you roundly for the most part, like the irascible mothers who beat their darlings when they narrowly escape being run over." Her birthday wish was that life would be gayer in 1934. A month later, however, the two women were sick again with bronchitis and lived in what Hamilton called a house full of invalids.

The winter of 1934, as it turned out, proved the saddest in Jane Addams's adult life. On February 13, Mary sat down to write a series of short letters to friends and family, giving them the details of a severe heart attack that Jane had suffered. "Miss Addams had a rather severe heart attack last Friday," Mary reported to Charles Ewing, although she assured him, most hopefully, that the patient was behaving well. "She is a very docile patient, perhaps because she feels too languid and exhausted to make any effort."[18] More urgently, she telegraphed Stanley about his aunt's dire condition. Her letter writing done at the end of the long and fatiguing day, she went to bed exhausted herself, full of foreboding. She assumed that the woman who had given her life "all its meaning and color" lay dying.

For eight long days, the letters fell strangely silent. On February 21, Emily Balch sent the first note—of condolence, not to Mary but to Jane:

"It does not seem possible that lovely spirit is no longer embodied among us."[19] Letters and telegrams began arriving, dozens of them, the first ones terse and sad, the later ones more expansive, all acknowledging the great loss that Addams had suffered. Dorothy Detzer expressed what many of her friends were thinking: "SO DEEPLY SORRY. I KNOW THE GRIEF THAT IS YOURS—ONE WANTS TO SHARE YET NOT INTRUDE."[20] Jane Addams, such a vital public woman, was intensely private about her own life. In a long letter, Ellen Starr remembered Mary as "perfect of her pattern, and such a lovely pattern!" Acknowledging the long marriage, she added tenderly, "Often I had thought that one of you would have to finish the journey without the other."[21] What no one expected was that Jane Addams would finish the journey alone.

Eleanor Smith wrote the official account of what had happened on February 13. Mary had been suffering from a bad cold and went to bed to take care of herself, and no one in the household thought that her illness was serious. Her temperature rose to 102 degrees as she lay in bed under a doctor's care for two days, when they discovered her bronchitis had turned into pneumonia. Still the medical attention was on Jane's heart, not Mary's. "Neither Dr. Britton nor Dr. Herrick, who were in daily attendance, were anxious as to the outcome, for her heart was strong, but the asthma made her breathing difficult."[22] On Wednesday morning, not a week after Jane's heart attack, the doctors noted that the pneumonia had spread through Mary's right lung. She grew gravely ill by midnight: "Her pulse and respiration became more rapid; her temperature dropped several degrees." By the next morning, she rallied, only to relapse and die suddenly at two o'clock that afternoon. Jane, near death herself, did not see Mary before she died, and she remained alone through the next days as Mary's body, washed and dressed, lay "just naturally" on the couch in the back drawing room. From all outward appearances, Jane Addams took the shock well; certainly she was little given to burdening others with her grief.

Addams's last year revived her energy in surprising ways. Northern Trust Company wrote to her as they settled Mary Rozet Smith's estate. Jane had, over the course of their long years together, received $250 a month from Mary, money that she had redistributed to her family and friends. The money left to her, given the financial difficulties of the 1930s, would earn only $208.33 per month. From other monies left her, Jane sent $500 to Myra and $250 to Stanley and offered to help them purchase a new car, no doubt to allow the couple to visit each other more frequently, as they lived apart because of the distance between their jobs. The car talk masked the real problems with the marriage. Myra confided to her

Aunt Jane that she was "lonely and comfortless in the graceless life" that they lived.[23] Addams wrote to James Weber Linn that she doubted Stanley had tried seriously to work out the problems and conceded that Myra would have to return to her job for another year.[24] Among Addams's duties, regardless of her health, was the parenting of her sisters' children— none of whom came to her bedside after the heart attack and Mary's death.

As she recovered her health, Addams spent fourteen weeks in bed at Mary Smith's house on Walton Street. By the end of March, she was sitting up, visiting with friends, signing letters, and making plans for travel. She told Grace Abbott that she still suffered from a cold and was being kept in bed "much to [her] disgust."[25] Alice Hamilton stayed with her as both friend and doctor, and they kept the "nice old house" open until May. As strength allowed, Jane sorted through Mary's belongings, emptying the big house of its furniture, sending things to their friends. Completing her task by June, she took the train to Hadlyme, Connecticut, to spend the summer months with Alice.

Hadlyme was a tranquil and lovely spot. Addams wrote several letters that summer describing the setting and its effect on her. To Ida Lovett, she confided, "I am settled down into a very delightful room here and my heart is doing very well. I think, altho a bruised spirit heals slowly."[26] Along with loneliness, Addams suffered the vagaries of age: stiffness, slowness, and fatigue. She enjoyed the visits of old friends, especially Lillian Wald, to whom she confided: "Mary's dear friends seem the greatest consolation I have but that as you know is only part of my pleasure in being with you."[27] She wrote to many friends that summer, sending photographs of Hamilton's house and inviting them all to visit. Addams gave the route to Allen Winthrop: "Hadlyme is on all the Socony Road Maps but the post office is at the upper end of the village and looks farther away from the Conn. River than it [the village] really is."[28] She advised him to look for a sign near Chester posting directions to the Hadlyme Ferry, which would take him across the Connecticut River and land him right in front of Hamilton's house.

From her bed, Addams joined all sorts of organizations in 1934. She accepted a position on the board of the National Committee for Immigration Welfare. She served as chairman of the Illinois Committee on Old Age Pensions. Eleanor Roosevelt asked her to serve as vice-chairman in the Women's Crusades of 1934 on the National Citizens Committee for the Mobilization for Human Needs. The Women's International League for Peace and Freedom organized a Zurich Congress in 1934, and Addams was anxious to travel to see her friends, who struggled to keep the organization together. The British women were balking because of the situ-

ation in India; they wanted unilateral control of the issue. Addams organized the sending of the Women's International League papers to Swarthmore College for what would become its Peace Collection and lamented
to Grace Abbott in August that she "would be bitterly disappointed if the
WIL were disbanded and think we have really no right to do it unless it
comes to the very worst."[29] Albert Einstein sought her support of Karl
von Ossietzky's nomination for the Nobel Peace Prize as Ossietzky was
"languishing in a Nazi concentration camp because of his pacifist beliefs."[30] She responded that she would send her recommendation, and he
was awarded the Prize in 1935.

Hull-House always ran roughly when she was not somehow in
charge. Even from her bed in Connecticut, she read letters from people
who wanted to live at the settlement, and she continued to have a hand
in making selections. In 1934, she accepted Zona Gale's daughter as a new
resident but confided to Alma Birmingham, "I am sure that I will confer
in all of them and if I do not we'll never tell."[31] She instructed Birmingham to send her the correspondence whenever it seemed "too heavy or
bewildering." Knowing how institutions work, she added, "It is always
hard to make the old residents work in summer and I suppose we have
fallen in the way of imposing a little on the new ones." She negotiated
money troubles in the Hull-House kitchen and the Coffee House.

Away from the daily burdens of Hull-House, Addams turned, as was
her habit, to writing. What was to be her last book, *My Friend, Julia Lathrop,* would use her moral imagination in a new way. In a letter to the
Nation, she announced that she was seeking Lathrop's personal letters
and reported her joy to Grace Abbott as the first ones arrived: "Lillian
Wald gave me some fine letters."[32] Perhaps because biography was a new
genre for her or, more simply, because she felt the weight of old age,
Addams decided to collaborate with Grace Abbott on the project. "I have
been going over the material you sent me with the liveliest interest," she
acknowledged as they began their work together.[33] Addams liked the idea
of a two-volume biography, one that would allow her to write the parts
she remembered and to assign Abbott the parts she knew little about,
especially Lathrop's work at the Children's Bureau in Washington. "I seem
a little hazy about it in the first place, and in the second it will be very
difficult for me to say anything that might seem to detract from L. D. W.'s
[Lillian Wald's] part in it." The design of the biography left Addams free
to talk about the beginnings of Lathrop's life and her work at Hull-House
and then to skip to the end of the story. It was an odd design, at best, one
that accommodated Jane Addams more than anyone. Even with the plan

in place, the task went slowly: "I have not yet gotten any 'start'—but hope that it may come! At any rate I promise to work on it."

Spurred by the pressure of time, Addams announced to Abbott in July 1934, "For the first time yesterday afternoon I seemed to get a little glimpse of what might be done."[34] She explained to friends that by collaborating with Grace Abbott she had figured out a way to write about Julia Lathrop and, even then, her memory of the early years in Illinois and at Rockford failed her. She wrote to Graham Taylor about the problem: "I have begun and find great dearth of material on her early life."[35] She requested letters or other papers and promised Taylor to have them copied and returned safely to him. "I am of course no end grateful for any illuminating incidents or stories about her," she confessed.

Addams found herself in precisely the situation of her own biographers Linn and Wise—How to build a story of a life? She considered the nature of biographical narrative, admitting to friends that she was not much interested in talking about children and, in fact, doubted their significance to the story of a woman's life. She believed, however, that ancestors play an important role in shaping a life and asked Maud E. Lavery, in the editorial office of the *Social Service Review* at the University of Chicago, to send material for the book, including dictionary entries on John Lothropp (1584–1653), letters written by him, a copy of his will, and a memoir by John Lathrop from the collections of the Massachusetts Historical Society.[36] With these documents in hand, Addams reported, "I have started at last and have 25 pages!" The length of the manuscript was continually in her mind, perhaps because her final days were so precious. "I will probably change it everlastingly!" she joked with a hint of gallows humor.

She wrote to James Weber Linn that summer as both colleague and subject. "The Julia Lathrop MSS is going very well, altho my pace is slow. I am anxious to show it to you."[37] The truth is that she managed to get everyone around her working on the book. She reported to Grace Abbott by September that she had written 120 pages of a working draft. Alice Hamilton served as a secretary of sorts, indulgently following orders. In a long letter asking Maud Lavery to research a series of questions about Lathrop's life, Hamilton ends with a laugh: "Miss Addams tells me to end this letter in my own person, so I will do so, with the hope that these various requests will not give you much trouble."[38] Information was scarce. Addams read what Julia Lathrop had written about Florence Kelley together with sixteen letters that she had written to Kelley herself. Private papers proved much harder to find than public material. Addams marked the letters for use—one on the death of Kelley's daughter Margaret, one on Lathrop's first bout with the Illinois legislature, one about the attacks of the DAR, and another about Kelley's illness.

Working on the biography took all her literary energy. During the summer, Carrie Chapman Catt invited Addams to write an essay on the psychological effects of war, one that would serve as the closing chapter of a book of essays she was editing based on her conference the Cause and Cure of War. Addams wanted to be included in the book—still irritated that she had not been invited to the meeting itself—although she hardly had the energy to devote to the task of composing the piece. She asked Hamilton to help her but their essay stalled, prompting Addams to ask Emily Balch to gather responses from European women who had suffered through the Great War. Addams offered to pay for all Balch's expenses, warning that the deadline was only three months away. She knew the request was a long shot. "But that perhaps is whistling to keep up the courage," she joked.[39]

As Addams prepared to leave Connecticut in September, she wrote to Lucia Ames Mead, "I am very much better and go back to Chicago on October 1, almost restored." Her last long summer in New England had a strong effect on her: "I am really yeilding to the charm of New England this year more than I ever did before."[40] She visited Ellen Starr before her return and found her much healthier than she expected. The journey back home went smoothly and she settled into Louise Bowen's house, hoping to work at Hull-House for three hours every day. Addams kept her office hours every day for a week but discovered that she simply did not have the energy for work, explaining to Wald that she was planning to cut down to three hours every other day. Though she felt the fatigue of age, her spirits remained high. "Everything is going on there quite cheerfully and of course is booming as all settlements are with the added help from EEP and other such alphabets." She was pleased with the news that the WILPF Congress had gone reasonably well.

"This summer I have really written a lot on our book," she reported to Grace Abbott, "and I am anxious to have you see its drift and tone."[41] As she returned Florence Kelley's letters to Nicholas, a son they called Ko, she talked about the way the book was turning out: "We are discovering it is unexpectedly difficult to find sufficient illustrations of Julia Lathrop's wit and wisdom, which all her friends remember with such vividness."[42] Ko wrote to tell her that the Kelley children wanted someone to write the story of their mother's life and urged her to take on the project; and Addams found herself thinking about a next book. The Lathrop children read the manuscript of their mother's biography and took

Addams to task for passages that the children thought were "not in good taste, or not necessary for purely background." They were relieved to have the opportunity to censor the manuscript, and Addams, for her part, seemed utterly unruffled, seeing the cuts as minor ones and, no doubt, believing that the children ought to have the right to make changes if they felt uncomfortable with the narrative she constructed. "I was very glad to make the few changes," she wrote to Grace Abbott.[43]

Jane Addams, in her seventies and very near the end of her life, told the story of her friend Julia Lathrop in a conversational voice, acknowledging that she did not know much about the middle of the story and suggesting that her familiarity with the beginning and end of a productive public life might suffice. Anyone reading the book, then or now, can feel the autobiographical urge as she openly admits, "I have found it difficult to avoid relating my own memories." Julia Lathrop's story overlapped with her own early life in rural Illinois so much so that the biography strained to stay on track. A reviewer for the *Boston Evening Transcript* expected "to find this book the chronicle of a friendship, offering intimate side-lights on personality that only a friend is qualified to give."[44] What Addams offered, however, was the outer shell of Lathrop's life. "In this respect the book is disappointing, for Miss Addams has written with an almost New England restraint"—the reviewer sensed the reticence of a woman who, after all, was comfortable living on the coast of Maine.

The biography tells us much about Jane Addams the writer. Her mind was full of memories in her last months of life, and her final experiment with writing reveals an able imagination and a vital intellect. In this book, as in her others, she casts herself as a listener, an honest transmitter of other voices. What sets the book apart is Addams's willingness to let the voices speak for themselves. She had collected letters, fragments, and memories from friends and acquaintances, each remembering Julia Lathrop. In writing the book, she embedded passages from the written accounts without transmuting them into her voice as she had done in earlier books. Perhaps she lacked the energy to dress in rhetorical costume. The narrative moves back and forth, and she acknowledges the tendency of memory and imagination to get things wrong by insisting on "a consistency which facts do not justify" (49). Having said that, Addams makes a claim that reminds us of Virginia Woolf: "[T]he estimate of [Julia Lathrop's] character never changed and I could dip in anywhere to illustrate her disinterested virtue." The book moves forward by such dippings.

The asides of a self-conscious writer interrupt the narrative flow. Addams reminds readers, for example, that Julia Lathrop "concerns us more than the social implications of her early surroundings however important to later life the conditions in childhood may be" (33). Here she weighs two seemingly contradictory ideas she believes to be true: social conditions have the power to shape individual fate and yet individuals have more significance than events. At times in the book, her observations seem utterly offhand as memory asserts itself: "It is curious that I have always remembered that sunrise" (54). Often the anecdotes from Lathrop's life are really about Addams herself. In one scene, she casts herself as a fledgling writer being urged on by Julia Lathrop, who admonishes her, "Don't cave in, J. A., this is our chance to give the public the pure milk of the word!" (56) And Addams ends the scene in self-mockery, calling her early book "a fine Victorian example of rose water for the plague'" (57).

Her last literary negotiations were prickly ones, both with Paul Kellogg at *Survey Graphic* and H. S. Latham at Macmillan. She began a lengthy negotiation to sell her manuscript to both men, the bargain she had always sought with publishers. Even at the end of her life, she had energy left to play one last hand. Kellogg read her manuscript at the beginning of October and wrote to her right away. "You made Miss Lathrop live through those pages," he complimented her as he asked permission to publish material from the book in two or three essays for *Survey Graphic*. The situation with Macmillan was tricky because the company had suffered financially in the Depression. Latham wrote to say that the press would negotiate with her for the remaining copies of *Peace and Bread in Time of War*, the one of all her books to go out of print during her lifetime. She wanted to buy the remaining shells of the book (for $50) and to send them to Swarthmore College as part of the Peace Collection. "It is the only book I have ever written which is going out of print," Addams confessed to Emily Cooper Johnson, "and the experience may be good for me!"[45] She still had a healthy sense of irony. Another problem she faced with Macmillan was the one Linn faced with Houghton Mifflin. "We think a full length volume would probably have a better chance than two dealing with Miss Lathrop," Latham cautioned.[46] The deal came down to money—any long biography, especially one that required two volumes, would mean a high price. Although eager to get the manuscript, Latham faced the prospect of another project that might not pay for itself. Both he and Addams seem chastened by the market.

Carrie Chapman Catt looked warily at the market, too, as she assembled the final chapters for her book on peace. Dorothy Canfield Fisher had agreed to write the book's conclusion. The women all knew that the American reading public had little patience for pacifism pure and simple. Catt was pleased in December by the arrival of Addams's chapter on the psychology of peace. Ever a truth teller, Catt praised Addams for sending an "exceedingly neat and tidy" manuscript and sternly pronounced, "[Y]our chapter is excellent, whether you know it or not."[47] And then Catt, understanding the limitations of their topic and perhaps the very quality of the writing, conceded, "It is not an immortal book."

Her nephew continued to write his biography of her, one that they hoped would be immortal. Addams had the dual tasks of managing the biographies being written both by her and about her, and she occasionally misplaced documents, an irritating consequence of writing from life. She had loaned Winifred Wise materials to use as she narrated Addams's early years, papers that James Linn needed to read in order to finish his version of the story. Apparently Wise had already returned the two volumes of letters that Addams had written during her first trip to Europe, when she had traveled on the boat with Henry James, along with the Rockford valedictory address, "Cassandra." When Addams wrote to her that winter requesting the return of the documents, Wise wrote to say that she no longer had them. "Enclosed are the only things I have from you— a school paper and several valentines which I had held thinking they might provide illustrative material for the book I have written."[48] The fragments of Addams's writing had become more valuable as her life closed, especially as material for those who would tell and retell her story.

As the cold winter months began in 1935, Addams advised her nephew to get his appointments set up with her before she left Chicago with Louise Bowen to return to the Biltmore Hotel in Arizona surrounded by the green golf course. Once she arrived in Arizona, Addams read Linn's manuscript and offered criticism any biographer would welcome. She pointed out what she considered to be errors in fact. The Addams family had purchased their land from William Penn, she explained, using material she had gleaned from research. She had asked the genealogist Henry Ferris to track down the details of the Addams family history in Pennsylvania, especially the claim that a Richard Addams had come to America along with William Penn on the ship *Welcome* in 1682, a valiant story that turned out not to be true. She told Linn that although the family patriarch Robert Adams liked what Penn had to say about handling the Indians, the Adams/Addams family never became Quakers. Her father, John Addams, had not even been a professing Christian and had never belonged to a church. Moreover, he had not been a pacifist.

It nettled her that Linn had overstated the family theology and, perhaps more so, that he had inflated the family wealth. Here her math strangely failed her. "On page 3, you have made the estate too large," she told him. "My share was [crossed out: only] one-sixth of [crossed out: the estate of] between 65,000 and $70,000." That would place her inheritance at $11,000 or more. Maybe her calculation was simply fuzzy or perhaps she chafed at the idea that anyone would know the details of her private finances. "I think I should call it $4,000 instead of $7,000," she insisted, no doubt baffling her nephew. Another sensitive detail was the difference in age between her parents; the first Mrs. Addams was in truth five years older than her husband. Page by page she scrutinized the manuscript, pointing out errors of fact or interpretation. She offered pictures of herself as a child for him to study and bindings made by Ellen Starr of her written work. "It seems a very promising start," she encouraged him even as she warned about carelessness.[49]

In Arizona she herself was writing without interruption. By March 1, 1935, Addams could report having written 220 pages at 250 words per page, as she calculated 55,000 words in all. She finished chapter five and wrote to tell Grace Abbott that she was sending a list of chapters to Paul Kellogg. "He is always inclined to over-edit," she warned.[50] As she sent the full manuscript to Macmillan, she announced to Ida Lovett: "J. Lathrop book is coming to an end so far as my part is concerned—I hope to get it off in a few days and then to write more letters."[51] She sent her part of the Lathrop book to Abbott on March 4. With the seeming restoration of her health, Addams was able to travel to the University of California, Berkeley, to receive an honorary law degree on March 23.

The woman most on her mind was Mary Smith. Louise Bowen planned a memorial for Mary at the Bowen Country Club in May, where the Hull-House women would officially rename the Music Cottage in Mary's honor. "I want to write something for it, but find it almost impossible to detach myself sufficiently to do it," Addams confided to Lillian Wald.[52] She worked on a dedication speech, completing six pages that she would never finish.

In struggling with the speech, she reread the letters Mary Smith had saved over the forty years they spent together. "I have been going over a box full of letters of mine to Mary Smith," she wrote to her nephew, as she considered what to show him and what to destroy.[53] The letters brought back a strong sense of the past, one that Addams wanted to keep private. In her books, she had always told the story of her life in a stylized way, weaving the tale of the girl from Cedarville into the many tales of migrants who settled in the Hull-House neighborhood. The letters to Mary Smith, however, recorded and reflected on the most intimate relationship of her life, one that Jane Addams thought had no place in a biography.

"Mary quite filled a drawer of her desk—all sorts of notes," she wrote Linn, telling him perhaps more than she understood. It is one thing to be an author and quite another to be the subject. That afternoon Jane

Addams was both. She had needed letters as she wrote her biography of Julia Lathrop, and she complained to friends that she had considerable trouble finding personal documents. The lack of material, she lamented, made it difficult to bring Lathrop to life. Yet after writing the manuscript, she had agreed that Julia Lathrop's children ought to have the right to purge anything they found too private for the reading public to see. And in her own case, she felt utterly free to destroy the very letters that may have clarified the nature of her "Boston marriage" to Mary Smith.

"I am destroying a good many and sending others," she wrote frankly to her biographer. Then she added a baffling aside: "Not that you will want to use them, I hope, but will give you a certain 'feel' of the 1890s etc. Among those I am destroying are the purely family ones—of her family or mine—but I am sending a few on to you that you may want to read first—Please 'read & destroy.'" It is incredible for us, looking back from the twenty-first century, to imagine why a biographer would make such a demand. The "purely family" information, the stuff of story telling, seemed to her mind outside the realm of biography! As a woman born in the nineteenth century, she thought the story ought to stop at the door, revealing a public life but not a private one. Three days later, she reported to Linn that she had destroyed one half to two-thirds of the letters she had written to Mary Smith, finding them "much too intimate to be used."[54] She was especially sensitive to "undue impression of money" in the letters and told him again that she wanted all the letters destroyed.

It was an odd moment, one biographer admitting to another that she was destroying the very information he would need to do his work, and even then advising him to destroy the material she had spared. Any Addams biographer who followed would be grateful to Linn (certainly I am) for not following her orders to purge even the letter she was writing to him.

In the spring of 1935, the Roosevelt White House, mindful of Addams's age and frailty, was eager to celebrate her career as they worked to fold her ideas into their social welfare program. Hannah Clothier Hull played the part of go-between as arrangements were made for a luncheon in Washington. Addams joked good-naturedly: "A party at the White House would be quite nice if Mrs. Roosevelt wanted it, but I suspect they ought to be rather careful about 'Pacifists' even now."[55] The celebration dinner was scheduled for May, a time when Addams hoped to be able to travel. She intended, in fact, to live in New England that summer and to begin work on the Florence Kelley book, one she planned to write together with Alice Hamilton.

She planned to be in Washington in the spring anyway because the Women's International League was marking its twentieth anniversary at a dinner honoring her at the Willard Hotel. Mary Moss Wellborn had the responsibility of organizing the dinner and took a good deal of heat from the honoree. What grated on Addams was news that the speakers were being asked to keep their remarks brief. She joked to Hannah Clothier Hull, "I will have a 'heart attack' if such wild propositions continue."[56] To Wellborn herself, Addams was more caustic: "[I]s not a minute and a half much too short a time to give to a speaker who has anything to say?"[57] Addams was pleased to find Edna St. Vincent Millay and Eleanor Roosevelt on the guest list but continued to agonize over those who might have been excluded. As late as April 3, she wrote to Hannah Hull, "I dreamed last night that the Com had forgotten Mde R. Schwimmer—Of course we won't do that will we!"[58] They sent off the forgotten invitation. Anxiety dreams are ubiquitous, of course, and this one gives us a sense of what she wrestled with at night.

Latham wrote in March that Macmillan agreed to take the proposed two-volume biography of Julia Lathrop. Only thirteen chapters of the manuscript seemed to him ready for the press; chapters fourteen and fifteen still needed work. He offered her 10 percent on the first 2,500 copies sold, but 15 percent on the next 2,500, and 25 percent on the next 2,500 should the book continue to sell. After she agreed, James Putnam sent her the contract, giving her until June 1 to revise the last chapters. She signed and returned the contract. Grace Abbott wrote to tell her that *Social Service Review* had decided to publish two chapters from the biography—"Julia Lathrop and Outdoor Relief in Chicago, 1893–94" would be published in March and "Julia Lathrop's Services to the State of Illinois" would follow in June.

The last sustained argument of Jane Addams's life had to do with her writing. She asked Paul Kellogg what he wanted of the remaining manuscript for publication in *Survey Graphic* before the book appeared. "As the week-end was crowded, I was up with the lark this morning and read your last chapters by a wood fire in the grate at Henry Street," he began his letter of response.[59] Complimenting her on the hard work a biography calls for, he asked her permission to try his hand at recombining sections of the book to recreate magazine-style articles, five installments that would begin in June. All along, she insisted that he take or reject the book chapter by chapter without editing the text. Through all the years of their relationship as author and editor, she and Kellogg fought over who would control her prose. With the Julia Lathrop manuscript, he hit a nerve that was already sore. It may be, too, that the writer fought back so tenaciously because she was at the very edge of exhaustion. Kellogg, as he had requested, reworked sections of the book, carving out articles that he wanted to publish and sending his version of her biography on April 29, the day before she was scheduled to leave for Washington.

"I hardly know what to say about this Ms., which came this morning," Addams cautiously began the letter.[60] "I should like very much to return it with my O.K. but I really feel too uncomfortable about it. It does not seem to be quite fair to the book that you have dropped entirely all the biographical features." Jane Addams rarely wrote long letters, but this one continued, even in its typed form, onto the second page, and her anger mounted as she put her case against Kellogg into words. She explained that she intended to work on the revised manuscript for Macmillan as soon as she returned from Washington and acknowledged that she had agreed to let him try his hand at editing the manuscript for use in *Survey.* "It never occurred to me that you would go through the entire book beginning with the Preface and leaving out the biographical setting. I do not believe I can stand for it as it is," she declared. Addams reminded him of the trouble they had had working together on the last book, *The Second Twenty Years at Hull-House,* and explained that she had not imagined they would arrive at the same impasse.

"Perhaps I would better say what then seemed to me to be true that you were constantly trying to say what you think would be a good thing for me to say and not what I really was trying to say although it may easily have been an inferior thing." Jane Addams made the author's claim for the integrity of her writing. Her voice was never clearer as she demanded her right to speak through her work, even as she accepted her writing, flaws and all.

Less than an hour later, Addams took the train for Washington. Waiting for her as she arrived was a telegram from Paul Kellogg, conceding at once "ENTIRELY ALL RIGHT. WILL FOLLOW YOUR WISHES."[61]

The Roosevelts held a reception in her honor at the White House, but Addams did not have the stamina for two events in one day. She asked that her press conference be a small one, not the grand one planned. The big event of the day was the dinner in the evening to celebrate the twentieth anniversary of the Women's International League. Twelve hundred people attended the dinner, including Eleanor Roosevelt, who was allotted her minute and a half: "When the day comes when difficulties are faced and settled without resorting to the type of waste which war has always meant, we shall look back in this country upon the leadership you have given us, Miss Addams, and be grateful for having had you living among us."[62] The next day, Addams found the energy to take part in an international radio program on peace.

Ethel Dewey sent out the official account of what happened after

Addams returned to Chicago, "She seemed very well on her return from Washington, but after leaving here last Tuesday evening, (the fourteenth), she was taken with severe pain in her right side [later accounts mark the left side]. A surgeon, Dr. Arthur Curtis, was called in last Friday, and he decided to operate the next morning [May 18]. The pain was caused by Abdominal adhesions, the result of an operation in 1931."[63] Dewey claimed that the operation had been a success, Addams's heart and blood pressure were stable, and they all hoped for a steady recovery. The truth was that the surgeon discovered an intestinal malignancy, a situation that put any chance of recovery out of the question.

Before her surgery, Jane Addams, mindful of the June deadline, revised the final chapters of the Julia Lathrop biography for Macmillan, working to shape them into a graceful text. On May 10, she turned her attention to Paul Kellogg. "I have meant to write you ever since I came home as the letter I sent before I left was written in such haste I knew not what unfair thing I may have said," she wrote in her usual conciliatory voice.[64] She reported that she had removed the chapter on the League of Women Voters and had sent it to Grace Abbott to become part of the other volume. As it stood, her manuscript was tighter—five thousand words shorter—and, she hoped, more coherent. She thanked him for his support of the Washington dinner, noting that *Survey* had identified more closely with pacifists over the years than the *Nation* had ever had the courage to do. "I hope that you and Helen Hall can drive up to see us in Hadlyme, Conn., this summer," she added hopefully. "It is an easy drive from New York and we have a beautiful site on the Connecticut River." She went into surgery on May 18, perhaps with the summer months of recovery in her mind.

After the operation, when everyone around her fought against gloom, Jane Addams wrote her last letter, one about her literary work. She confided to Grace Abbott that she regretted not stopping the biography at Lathrop's appointment to the Children's Bureau, marking clearly the part of the life that she best remembered. The last two chapters continued to bother her, even after she had merged them into an awkward conclusion. From the looks of it, she had found the stamina to cut and paste the comments of others, but not to write anything new. "I don't like to stop the book on the note of her death . . . so I have put in just a page or two of the tributes which have to do with her earlier years."[65] Closure is never easy for a writer, and the irony of her struggle with death must have been palpable. Addams signed the letter, "Hastily—Jane Addams." Hastily at the end, perhaps especially at the end.

Among her papers is an urgent telegram from Paul Kellogg to Alice

Hamilton that arrived at Passavant Hospital at 11:23 on the morning of May 21 as Jane Addams lay feverish and scarcely conscious. She would live for three more hours. "IF YOU CAN GIVE THE MESSAGE PLEASE ASSURE MISS ADDAMS THAT NOTHING SHE SAID WAS UNFAIR THAT I ENTIRELY UN- DERSTOOD AND FULLY ACCEPTED HER JUDGMENT BUT DEFERRED ANSWER- ING UNTIL I COULD SEND HER THE SECTIONS OF HER LUMINOUS MANUSCRIPT IN LINE WITH HER WISHES STOP IT WAS DEAR OF HER TO WRITE STOP WITH AFFECTIONATE GREETINGS AND HOPE."[66] The message of vindication, whether she heard it or not, is a fitting way to end a writer's life.

NOTES

Introduction: The Moral Imagination

1. Paley, *Just as I Thought,* 169. In a chapter that explains Paley's desire to be both political and literary, she describes her journey to meet Christa Wolf in East Berlin, before the Wall came down between the two Germanies, because she wanted to talk with this "pacifist feminist" who had written *The Quest for Christa T.* and *Patterns of Childhood.* "What interested me was the woman, the writer who had a passionate commitment to literature and believed at the same time that she had to have a working relationship with society—and a responsibility as well" (208). I find the same commitment to literature and society in Addams.

2. Lasch, *The Social Thought of Jane Addams,* xxvi. Jane Addams readers have been a popular way to reconsider her writing but, as this collection does, they repackage her books in ways that destroy their literary shapeliness by interrupting the narrative and the flow from thought to thought. Lasch divides her work into chapters of his own making: "The Snare of Preparation"; "The City"; "Reform, Political and Social"; "Democracy and Education"; and "Peace." Under "Peace," for example, he excerpts pages 3–5, then 7–19 and jumps to 23–27 from *Newer Ideals of Peace,* and places them together with pages 132–51 and 173–77 from a book written fifteen years later, *Peace and Bread in Time of War,* ending this section with a brief essay written ten years after that, "How to Build a Peace Program." Lasch, much as he admired Jane Addams as a public figure, had little regard for her as a writer in control of her material. It is true that she often cobbled together pieces of her own writing as she wrote final drafts for her books, but in this assembling of material, she was in charge.

3. Douglas, *Jane Addams, A Centennial Reader,* xix. This collection also reshuffles Addams's writing, creating seven chapters: "Social Work," "Position of Women," "Child Welfare," "The Arts," "Trade Unions and Labor," "Civil Liberties," and "International Peace," introduced by a leader in each field. Note the emphasis given her work, here inflecting feminist issues, in the Women's International League for Peace and Freedom that spearheaded the retrieval project. Jean Bethke Elshtain has, likewise, rearranged Addams's writing for a collection that accompanies her new biography and provides her readers with texts she considers significant to her portrait. *The Jane Addams Reader* divides the work into sections labeled "'The Snare of Preparation' and the Creation of Vocation"; "Justice and Amelioration—Finding Democracy's Middle Way"; "'Woman's Remembering Heart': Bread-Giving, Peace-Making, and Sympathy as Political Forces"; and "Culture, Character, and the Power of Memory."

4. Ibid., Hall, 4.

5. Ibid., Montagu, 100.

6. Davis, *American Heroine: The Life and Legend of Jane Addams,* 159. Davis, more than any scholar of the twentieth century, revived interest in Addams as a person, although I would argue that in humanizing her, he underrated her as a writer, often

misunderstanding her use of imaginative, mythic, fictional, and poetic techniques to appeal to her readers. She was more conscious of her style, I think, and more emotionally distanced from her persona than Davis gives her credit for being.

7. Deegan, *Jane Addams and the Men of the Chicago School, 1892–1918*, 8. Deegan reopens the relationship between Addams and the male professors at the University of Chicago and keenly hopes to establish Addams's influence over these men and the female contribution to the conception of sociology as a discipline. Deegan has little familiarity with the literary world, calling George Bernard Shaw, to give one example, George E. Shaw (see page 254).

8. Elshtain, *The Nation* (12 February 2001). In her book *Jane Addams and the Dream of American Democracy*, Elshtain focuses on Addams as a woman who served the public: "Addams was adamant throughout her life that Hull-House should offer shelter from the storm and a new way of being in the world. It was a place of civic education, a spirited enterprise that served as a vehicle for the creation of community and the sustaining of identities. Indeed, the central role Hull-House played in generating identity is the hallmark of its mission" (153). The service of the intellect to the community is what Elshtain means when she calls Addams a "public intellectual."

9. Monroe, Review of *Democracy and Social Ethics*, JAPP 11-22.

10. Linn, *Jane Addams: A Biography*, 17. As Linn tells the story from his perspective as a boy and a young man, the portrait is convincing; he acquaints us with the woman he knew from personal contact. However, Linn, as is the case with other biographers, wanders away from the private woman and becomes overwhelmed with detail in his attempts to tell the story of her public life, knowledge that did not come firsthand.

11. Stevens, *The Collected Poems*, 9.

12. Parini, "2 Distinct Approaches to Biography, with Bellow and Updike as Subjects," B14.

13. Davis, *American Heroine*, 109.

14. See Heilbrun, *Writing a Women's Life*, especially the discussion of Jill Conway and Jane Addams, 24–25.

15. Bryan, Introduction, *The Jane Addams Papers: A Comprehensive Guide*, 1. Scholars are fortunate indeed to have these eyes to direct them to materials from so many different places.

16. Addams, *Twenty Years at Hull-House*, 7. All page numbers from the books of Jane Addams will follow the pagination of first editions and will be placed parenthetically in the text. For a list of first editions, see her publications at the beginning of the bibliography.

17. Panofsky, *Studies in Iconography: Humanistic Themes in the Art of the Renaissance*, 7.

18. Stead, *If Christ Came to Chicago!*, 11, also 412 and 419.

19. Cook, "Female Support Networks and Political Activism: Lillian Wald, Crystal Eastman, Emma Goldman," 43–61. Cook insists that scholars look again at relationships between women at the turn of the last century, using Jane Addams and Mary Smith and the women of Hull-House to argue for homosocial if not homosexual modes of living. The letters between Addams and Smith (most of the surviving letters are those from Addams to Smith) characterize their relationship as a marriage; clearly they loved and cared for each other over the forty years they were together. See also Smith-Rosenberg, "The Female World of Love and Ritual: Relations between Women in Nineteenth-Century America," and for a study of an earlier period, see Nancy F. Cott, *The Bonds of Womanhood: "Woman's Sphere" in New England, 1780–1835*.

20. Elshtain, *Jane Addams and the Dream of American Democracy*, 117.

21. Kathryn Kish Sklar, "Who Founded Hull House?"

22. Jane Addams to Alice Addams Haldeman, 23 February 1893, JAPP 2-1388.

23. Jane Addams to Mary Rozet Smith, 27 June 1900, JAPP 3-1597.

24. Lasch, *The Social Thought of Jane Addams*, xiv.

25. Davis, *American Heroine*, 18.

26. The Harvard edition includes a useful introduction by Anne Firor Scott, an admirer of Jane Addams's work and her writing. She notes that Addams was successful in adopting the point of view of workers: "She identified herself so well with the servant girl that she often gave the impression that she had been a maid" (liii).

27. Dickens, *Hard Times*, 308.

28. See Bakhtin, *The Dialogic Imagination: Four Essays by M. M. Bakhtin*. In the essay "Discourse in the Novel," Bakhtin defines the novel as a literary genre: "The novel can be defined as a diversity of social speech types (sometimes even diversity of languages) and a diversity of individual voices, artistically organized" (262).

29. William James to Jane Addams, 17 September 1902, JAPP 4-444.

30. William James to Jane Addams, 12 February 1907, JAPP 5-63.

31. William James to Jane Addams, 13 December 1909, JAPP 5-963.

Chapter 1: Three Journeys

1. James, *The Portrait of a Lady*, 9.

2. Jane Addams to Alice Addams Haldeman, 27 August 1883, JAPP 1-1148.

3. Jane Addams to Alice Addams, 7 January 1869, JAPP 1-0115.

4. Linn, *Jane Addams*, 29. Linn's biography includes insider stories. In this portrait of the family, I am relying, too, on what she said herself, as well as on what Allen Davis has to say about conflicting accounts.

5. Ibid., 39.

6. Jane Addams to Alice Addams, 15 January 1870, JAPP 1-133.

7. Jane Addams to Vallie Beck, 21 March 1877, JAPP 1-210.

8. Jane Addams to Vallie Beck, 30 March 1876, JAPP 1-179.

9. Jane Addams to Alice Addams Haldeman, 12 March 1871, JAPP 1-143.

10. Jane Addams to Vallie Beck, 1 May 1876, JAPP 1-189.

11. Jane Addams to Vallie Beck, 21 March, 1877, JAPP 1-211.

12. Jane Addams to Vallie Beck, 30 May 1877, JAPP 1-227.

13. Jane Addams, Diary 1875–1883, JAPP 28-1482 through 28-1735.

14. Addams, "Home Items."

15. Also from June 1879; the version in the magazine differs from the diary account only in that she cleans up the sentence structure, learning the task, if not the art, of editing.

16. Jane Addams, Editorial.

17. Vallie Beck to Jane Addams, 6 December 1877, JAPP 1-276; and Ida May Carey to Jane Addams, 5 December 1877, JAPP 1-272.

18. Linn, *Jane Addams*, 47.

19. Ibid., 48.

20. Appears in diary, 3–4 July and 8–14 July 1875, and reappears as essay in 1880 or 1881, JAPP 46-90.

21. Addams, JAPP 46-90.

22. Addams, JAPP 45-1808.

23. Addams, JAPP 45-1705, and for drafts, see 45-1697 and 45-1754.

24. Catherine Dorr to Jane Addams, 23 May 1881, JAPP 1-639.

25. Helen Harrington to Jane Addams, 23 July 1881, JAPP 1-680; and 17 August 1881, JAPP 1-695.

26. Martha Thomas to Jane Addams, 21 August 1881, JAPP 1-719. Thomas will not marry Mr. D. (whoever he was) but rather Mr. Greene.

27. Linn, *Jane Addams*, 50.

28. Jane Addams to John Addams, 8 May 1881, JAPP 1-621.

29. Rollin Salisbury to Jane Addams, 11 June 1881, JAPP 1-659.

30. Jane Addams to Ellen Gates Starr, 29 January 1880, JAPP 1-473 through 1-476.

31. Diliberto, *A Useful Woman*, 82. She gives a convincing narrative of the vacation and the death.

32. Jane Addams to Ellen Starr, 3 September 1881, JAPP 1-762. For her inheritance, see Davis, *American Heroine*, 31. He uses figures recorded on 5 January 1885 at the Stephenson County Courthouse, Freeport, Illinois.

33. Lewis, *The Jameses: A Family Narrative*, 170.

34. Linn, *Jane Addams*, 77.

35. Jane Addams, "Five Sunday Mornings in England," 21 pages, (ca. 1884–85), JAPP 4-404 to 4-425.

36. Jane Addams, "Three Days on the Mediterranean Subjectively Related," JAPP 46-441 to 46-447.

37. Jane Addams to Anna Haldeman, 23 October 1885, JAPP 2-124.

38. In *Philanthropy and Social Progress*, 12–13.

39. Addams, "Claim on the College Woman," 59.

40. Addams, "The College Woman and Christianity."

41. Jane Addams to Laura Addams, 25 April 1888, JAPP 2-935.

42. Jane Addams to Sarah Hostetter, 24 April 1888, JAPP 2-930.

43. Jane Addams to Anna Haldeman Addams, 27 April 1888, JAPP 2-939.

44. Troyat, *Tolstoy*, 167. See also, Leo Tolstoy, *My Confession*, 18.

45. Tolstoy, *My Confession*, 76.

46. Ibid., 94.

47. In *Philanthropy and Social Progress*, 29.

48. In the view of Mary Jo Deegan in her book, *Jane Addams and the Men of the Chicago School, 1892–1918*, Albion Small and his male colleagues built a department and indeed an academic discipline on "self-interest, competition, and the exclusion of women and children from topics of study and interest." Until 1928, when W. F. Ogburn joined the staff at the University of Chicago, collecting quantitative data was "women's work" and thus statistical sociology adopted its methods from the work of women at Hull-House as they gathered data for *Hull-House Maps and Papers*. They put together maps and taxonomies from information gleaned from observation, interviews and ethnographies. Rivka Shpak Lissak in her study, *Pluralism & Progressives: Hull House and the New Immigrants, 1890–1919*, notes that Hull-House contributed to the Chicago School of Sociology theory the idea of "natural areas." The settlement promoted social interaction and, in the process, caused the complementary disintegration of ethnic neighborhoods: "Americanization was considered a necessary condition for mobility."

49. Davis, *American Heroine*, 128.

50. Conway in "Women Reformers and American Culture, 1870–1930," gets bogged down in a rigid conception of gender difference and criticizes Addams for not using male discourse. Scientific thought, Conway seems not to understand, blends intuition and reason, hunches and experiments.

51. Jane Addams to Katharine Coman, 7 December 1891, JAPP 2-1283.

52. Jane Addams to Mary Rozet Smith, 4 September 1895, JAPP 2-1754.

53. William Dean Howells, "Shaw's Criticism of Tolstoy," in Shaw, *Selected Letters,* 5, 378–79.

54. George Bernard Shaw to Lytton Strachey, 20 March 1904, *Selected Letters,* 5, 90.

55. Maude, *The Life of Tolstoy,* II, 530. Pages number will be cited in the text.

56. Maude, "A Talk with Miss Jane Addams and Leo Tolstoy."

57. Aylmer Maude to Jane Addams, 16 October 1896, JAPP 3-468; her letter to Maude only exists in his edited version of it in *The Life of Tolstoy.*

58. Jane Addams to Alice Addams Haldeman, April 1885, JAPP 2-042.

59. Jane Addams to Alice Addams Haldeman, 13 September 1885, JAPP 2-114.

60. Jane Addams to Alice Addams Haldeman, 23 September 1886, JAPP 2-316.

61. Tolstoy, *What Is to Be Done?* 237.

62. Addams, "Count Tolstoy," and "Tolstoy's Theory of Life."

63. Addams, Introduction, *What Then Must We Do?,* vii.

Chapter 2: Finding a Voice

1. Addams, "Cassandra," JAPP 46-267, 46-319, 46-337.

2. Ruskin, "Of Queens' Gardens," 111–22. Tolstoy, whose *What to Do?* (1882) Addams read in 1888, echoed Ruskin's call to women to save men from their proclivities: "Women, mothers of the wealthy classes, the salvation of men of our world from the evils from which it suffers, is in your hands!"

3. Elshtain, *Jane Addams and the Dream of American Democracy,* 254.

4. Bakhtin, *The Dialogic Imagination,* 343. "It is not a free appropriation and assimilation of the word itself that authoritative discourse seeks to elicit from us; rather, it demands our unconditional allegiance. Therefore authoritative discourse permits no play with the context framing it, no play with its borders, no gradual and flexible transitions, no spontaneously creative stylizing variants on it." Addams wanted the authority to speak but sought a method that would escape the brittle quality of the traditional social tract.

5. Devine, *Charities.*

6. Review, *Post,* JAPP 11-0012.

7. See Davis, *American Heroine,* 112–14. Davis also notes that no journal would publish her criticism of Pullman. The *Forum, North American Review, Century,* and *Atlantic Monthly* all turned her down because she dared to suggest that he was wrong.

8. "A Voter," Letter to Jane Addams, 17 January 1898, JAPP 3-0937.

9. Edwin Seligman to Jane Addams, 26 April 1902, JAPP 4-0348.

10. Oliver Wendell Holmes to Richard Ely, 10 July 1906, JAPP 4-1408.

11. Jane Addams to Richard Ely, 10 January 1901, JAPP 4-0001.

12. Richard Ely to Jane Addams, 11 January 1901, JAPP 4-0004.

13. Jane Addams to Richard Ely, 18 May 1901, JAPP 4-0110.

14. Clarence Darrow to Jane Addams, 11 September 1901, JAPP 4-0207.

15. William Stead to Jane Addams, 12 October 1901, JAPP 4-0218.

16. Jane Addams to Florence Kelley, July 1901, JAPP 4-0152 and 0153.

17. Jane Addams to Richard Ely, 11 November 1901, JAPP 4-0228.

18. Richard Ely to Jane Addams, 28 January 1902, JAPP 4-0262.

19. Jane Addams to William Vaughn Moody, 9 February 1901, JAPP 4-0024.

20. J. David Thompson to Jane Addams, 4 April 1902, JAPP 4-0303.

21. Anita McCormick Blaine to Jane Addams, 17 April 1902, JAPP 4-0345.

22. Jane Addams to Mary Rozet Smith, 3 May 1902, JAPP 4-0373.

23. Aylmer Maude, Review of *Democracy and Social Ethics, The Whim* (2 December 1902), JAPP 11-197.

24. William Dean Howells to Jane Addams, 9 April 1902, JAPP 4-324.

25. William Dean Howells to Jane Addams, 26 October 1899, JAPP 3-1458.

26. Jane Addams to Mary Rozet Smith, 6 April 1902, JAPP 4-0308.

27. Jane Addams to Mary Rozet Smith, 8 April 1902, JAPP 4-0319.

28. Jane Addams to Mary Rozet Smith, 11 April 1902, JAPP 4-0330 and 4-0335.

29. Henry Ward to Jane Addams, 4 May 1902, JAPP 4-0377.

30. Jane Addams to Mary Rozet Smith, 19 May 1902, JAPP 4-0382.

31. Jane Addams to Mary Rozet Smith, 26 May 1902, JAPP 4-0391.

32. William Kent to Jane Addams, 19 May 1902, JAPP 4-0387.

33. Vida Scutter to Jane Addams, 13 June 1902, JAPP 4-0402.

34. William S. Booth to Jane Addams, 11 October 1902, JAPP 4-0459.

35. George Brett to Jane Addams, 29 October 1902, JAPP 4-0464; and Richard Ely to Jane Addams, 24 November 1902, JAPP 4-0478.

36. Jane Addams to Richard Ely, 27 November 1902, JAPP 4-0480.

37. Jane Addams to George Brett, 2 January 1903, JAPP 4-0510.

38. Jane Addams to Richard Watson Gilder, 6 April 1903, JAPP 4-580.

39. Jane Addams to Raymond Robbins, 24 June 1903, JAPP 4-0627.

40. Jane Addams to Mary Rozet Smith, 4 August 1904, JAPP 4-0891.

41. Richard Ely to Jane Addams, 7 November 1904, JAPP 4-0970.

42. Jane Addams to Richard Ely, 9 November 1904, JAPP 4-0971.

43. Jane Addams to Richard Ely, 24 December 1904, JAPP 4-1007.

44. William Hard to Jane Addams, 15 January 1905, JAPP 4-1028.

45. Jane Addams to W. E. B. Du Bois, 28 April 1905, JAPP 4-1056.

46. The book was published by Doubleday, Page & Company in 1906.

47. Walter Hines Page to Jane Addams, 8 November 1905, JAPP 4-1174.

48. Jane Addams to Richard Ely, 20 November 1905, JAPP 4-1178.

49. Mrs. M to Jane Addams, 20 March 1906, JAPP 4-1299.

50. Angelique Kilmer to Jane Addams, 30 March 1906, JAPP 4-1306.

51. Jessie Goldner to Jane Addams, 28 February 1906, JAPP 4-1270.

52. Robert Adger Bowen to Jane Addams, 27 February 1906, JAPP 4-1268.

53. Edward Bok to Jane Addams, 17 March 1906, JAPP 4-1295.

54. Jane Addams to Walter Hines Page, 10 April 1906, JAPP 4-1327.

55. Jane Addams to Julia Lathrop, 22 March 1906, JAPP 4-1300.

56. Jane Addams to Richard Ely, 14 August 1906, JAPP 4-1423.

57. Jane Addams to Richard Ely, 5 September 1906, JAPP 4-1434.

58. Richard Ely to Jane Addams, 10 October 1906, JAPP 4-1473.

59. Richard Ely to Jane Addams, 13 October 1906, JAPP 4-1475.

60. This paragraph continues from Ely's letter on October 13. She responded on October 15, 1906, JAPP 4-1478.

61. Jane Addams to George Brett, 12 December 1906, JAPP 4-1516.

62. George Brett to Jane Addams, 14 December 1906, JAPP 4-1520.

63. Jane Addams to Julia Lathrop, 12 February 1907, JAPP 5-0060.

64. William James to Jane Addams, 24 January 1907, JAPP 5-0029.

65. Jane Addams to Mary Rozet Smith, 29 October 1898, JAPP 3-1191. In the last decade of the nineteenth century in Chicago, no woman held more social power in Chicago than Bertha Palmer, buttressed as she was by Potter Palmer's money.

66. Liberty Tracts, no. 1. Chicago: Central Anti-Imperial League, 1899, JAPP 46-898.

67. See Davis, *American Heroine*, 140–41. Davis discusses James's question: "But how decide conflicts?" That root question about aggression led him to contemplate the tendency in human beings as in other animals to settle disputes through physical force, what seemed to be an instinct for war. If the human mind might overcome the

tendencies of the body, he wondered, how might human aggression be redirected? "Find some innocent way out, Examples: savage virtues preserved by athletics." Davis uses James's diary to prove that James was thinking about finding an equivalent for the warring instinct before Addams did and that her work was, therefore, derivative.

68. *Friends' Intelligencer* 51 (9 January 1904), 30, JAPP 4-1234.

69. Jane Addams to Mary Rozet Smith, 5 October 1904, JAPP 4-0934.

70. William James, "The Moral Equivalent of War."

71. Levine, *Jane Addams and the Liberal Tradition*, 95.

72. Davis, *American Heroine*, 140.

73. Menand, *The Metaphysical Club: A Story of Ideas in America*, 313.

74. Reviews of her book can be found among her papers. They consist of clippings from Henry Romeike, Inc., New York. See *Transcript*, n.d., JAPP 11-207 and *Examiner*, 2 February 1907, JAPP 11-208.

75. Florence Kelley, *National Consumers' League*, n.d., JAPP 11-0201.

76. Francis Hackett, 2 February 1907, JAPP 11-0209.

77. See JAPP 11-217.

78. *New York Tribune*, JAPP 11-0218, and *Nation*, 14 March 1907, JAPP 11-0231.

79. George Herbert Meade, *The American Journal of Sociology*, JAPP 11-0311.

80. Jane Addams to Richard Ely, 9 October 1906, JAPP 4-1475.

81. Lewis, *The Jameses: A Family Narrative.*

82. Addams, *Newer Ideals of Peace*, 11. Page numbers will be cited in the text.

83. Hobhouse, *Democracy and Reaction*, xxvii.

84. Royce, *The Spirit of Modern Philosophy*, 275.

85. Morley, *On Compromise*, 212–13.

86. Andrew Ross, who looks at twenty-first-century Chicago from the perspective of the "green" movement, sees the situation in precisely the way Jane Addams saw it. In "The Social Claim on Urban Ecology," he points out that "green criticism" has its roots in the Chicago School of the 1920s; he might have looked more closely at what Jane Addams was struggling to articulate in the very first years of the century. Today, we devote attention to the obvious physical needs of the city environment, including "green spaces, green architectural design, human-scale neighborhood planning, traffic mitigation, pedestrian-friendly development, waste management, and energy efficiency," Ross explains. The Progressives in Chicago at the turn into the twentieth century had such ideas in mind as well. But, more so, they had in mind subtler green issues. Ross continues to ask the question: "[S]houldn't a green outlook on urbanism include attention to the redistribution of wealth, de facto racial desegregation, extension of community board power, safeguarding of public services and education, reforms of political decision-making at city, state, and federal levels, and the like?" These are precisely the issues Addams had in mind as "newer ideals."

87. Addams got to know Boaz in 1922; she later exchanged letters with him about the Nobel Peace Prize in 1933, both arguing that it should go to "ousted German" scientists or pacifists, most of whom were Jews being persecuted by the Nazis.

88. Florence Kelley to Jane Addams, 23 January 1907, JAPP 5-0025.

89. Richard Ely to Jane Addams, 30 January 1907, JAPP 5-0042.

90. Margaret Dreier Robins to Jane Addams, 18 February 1907, JAPP 5-0071.

91. Kate Kimball to Jane Addams, 19 February 1907, JAPP 5-0074.

92. H. J. Pinkett to Jane Addams, 12 May 1908, JAPP 5-0425.

93. W. E. B. Du Bois to Jane Addams, 19 May 1908, JAPP 5-0448.

94. W. E. B. Du Bois to Jane Addams, 2 June 1908, JAPP 5-0466.

95. James Keeley to Jane Addams, 29 March 1907, JAPP 5-0094.

96. Norman Hapgood to Jane Addams, 30 January 1908, JAPP 5-0315.

97. Edward Marsh to Jane Addams, 25 May 1907, JAPP 5-0151.

98. Robert Adger Brown to Jane Addams, 27 September 1907, JAPP 5-0235.

99. Jane Addams to Alice, 14 August 1908, JAPP 5-0520.

100. Edward Marsh to Jane Addams, 23 February 1909, JAPP 5-0710.

101. Jane Addams to Edward Marsh, 25 February 1909, JAPP 5-0711.

102. Edward Marsh to Jane Addams, 2 March 1909, JAPP 5-0716.

103. Edward Bok to Jane Addams, 25 May 1909, JAPP 5-0801.

104. Ahnebrink, *The Beginnings of Naturalism in American Fiction.*

105. Emile Zola, "Le Roman Experimental," 180.

106. Ibid., 181.

107. Carla Cappetti looks closely at the connection between the literature of sociology and literary naturalism in her book *Writing Chicago.* She groups Addams with what she calls "proto- and neo-sociologists," among them Hamlin Garland, Henry B. Fuller, Theodore Dreiser, Clarence S. Darrow, Hutchins Hapgood, Robert Herrick, Carl Sandburg, Vachel Lindsay, Edgar Lee Masters, Ben Hecht, W. R. Burnett, Floyd Dell, Meyer Levin, and William Attaway, all writers that she situates in Chicago. The Second City was for Cappetti the "mecca of modern journalism and newspaper humor, the home of a great deal of early American literary realism, and arguably the birthplace of American urban literature"(7). In her configuration, humanistic sociology traces its lineage back to literature, the work of the moral imagination creating stories about urban life. The Hull-House neighborhood, known as Moonshine Valley or the Bloody Nineteenth, a port of entry for Polish, Italian, Irish, Russian, Greek, Mexican, Lithuanian, Bohemian, Croatian, African American, and Jewish immigrants, served as "the true center of the modern city" although, ironically, even James T. Farrell moved out as soon as he could afford it. Cappetti notes that Chicago's sociologists dwelled on the immigrant community as a slum, an expression of urban pathology.

108. Groos, *The Play of Man,* 352.

109. *The Show World,* 3 August 1907, JAPP 12-395.

110. Wharton, *The Letters of Edith Wharton,* 140.

111. Jane Addams, Banquet Address for Mrs. Humphrey Ward, July 1908, JAPP 5-0485.

112. Margaret Deland to Jane Addams, 8 March 1906, JAPP 4-1283.

113. Upton Sinclair to Jane Addams, 29 May 1905, JAPP 4-1070.

114. Upton Sinclair to Jane Addams, 29 July 1922, JAPP 14-1727; and 16 August 1922, JAPP 14-1796.

115. Jane Addams to Upton Sinclair, 17 August 1922, JAPP 14-1797.

116. Theodore Dreiser to James E. West, 5 July 1910, JAPP 5-1214.

117. Theodore Dreiser to Jane Addams, June 1931, JAPP 22-0559.

118. Norris, *The Pit: A Story of Chicago,* 73.

119. Her portrait of the urban vortex in *Twenty Years at Hull-House* sounds downright Norrisonian: "Thus the average human youth, 'with all the sweetness of the common dawn,' is flung into the vortex of individual life wherein the everyday tragedy escapes us save one of them become conspicuously unfortunate" (382).

Chapter 3: Public and Private

1. Jane Addams to Ida Tarbell, 23 August 1909, JAPP 5-0863.

2. Jane Addams to Alice Addams Haldeman, 14 September 1909, JAPP 5-0869.

3. Tarbell, *The History of the Standard Oil Company,* II, 292.

4. Ida Tarbell to Jane Addams, 2 April 1908, JAPP 5-0363.

5. Ida Tarbell to Jane Addams, 17 October 1908, JAPP 5-0567.

6. Jane Addams to Ida Tarbell, 31 October 1908, JAPP 5-0585.

7. John S. Phillips to Ida Tarbell, attached to Ida Tarbell Letter to Jane Addams, 7 May 1908, JAPP 5-0403.

8. B.F., "Letter to the Editor," *Evening Post* (29 May 1908), JAPP 5-0483.

9. Walter Hines Page to Jane Addams, 13 August 1908, JAPP 5-0518.

10. Walter Hines Page to Jane Addams, 14 September 1908, JAPP 5-0538.

11. George Brett to Jane Addams, 27 May 1909, JAPP 5-0805.

12. Jane Addams to Mary Rozet Smith, 11 June 1909, JAPP 5-0820.

13. Jane Addams to Mary Rozet Smith, 20 June 1909, JAPP 5-0834.

14. Walter Hines Page to Jane Addams, 16 September 1909, JAPP 5-0877.

15. Elizabeth Jordan to Jane Addams, 3 November 1909, JAPP 5-0901.

16. Ida Tarbell to Jane Addams, 4 November 1909, JAPP 5-0906.

17. Thomas Crowell to Jane Addams, 19 March 1906, JAPP 4-1297.

18. Thomas Y. Crowell & Company to Jane Addams, 27 February, JAPP 5-0076.

19. Richard Ely to Jane Addams, 31 December 1910, JAPP 5-1444.

20. Jane Addams to Elizabeth Jordan, 20 May 1907, JAPP 5-0146.

21. W. A. Bradley, *Bookman* (January 1911), JAPP Addendum 11-0718, found on Reel 82.

22. Francis Hackett, "Book of the Week," *The Chicago Evening Post* (25 November 1910), JAPP Addendum 11-0600.

23. *The Sociological Review,* April 1911, JAPP Addendum 11-0802.

24. White, *The American Magazine,* 70.

25. Tarbell, "The American Woman," 722.

26. William James, *Journal of Sociology,* JAPP 5-0976.

27. Vida Scutter to Jane Addams, 13 November 1909, JAPP 5-0929.

28. Florence Converse to Jane Addams, 22 February 1910, JAPP 5-1037.

29. Jane Addams to Mary Rozet Smith, 13 March 1910, JAPP 5-1066.

30. Princess Alice, consort of Alexander, Prince of Teck, to Jane Addams, 10 July 1910, JAPP 5-1220.

31. Jane Addams to Clara Landsberg, 7 August 1910, JAPP 5-1241.

32. Jane Addams to Graham Taylor, 4 September 1910, JAPP 5-1266.

33. Jane Addams to Graham Taylor, 4 September 1910, JAPP 5-1266.

34. Jane Addams to Florence Kelley, 23 September 1910, JAPP 5-1283) and to Clara Landsberg, 26 September 1910, JAPP 5-1285.

35. Jane Addams to George Brett, 24 October 1910, JAPP 5-1308.

36. Edward Marsh to Jane Addams, 30 November 1910, JAPP 5-1357.

37. Jane Addams to Mary Rozet Smith, 8 November 1910, JAPP 5-1318.

38. Robert Woods to Jane Addams, 8 December 1910, JAPP 5-1388.

39. Edward Marsh to Jane Addams, 3 January 1911, JAPP 6-0024.

40. Jane Addams to Mary Rozet Smith, February 1911, JAPP 6-0070.

41. Jane Addams to Mary Rozet Smith, 7 February 1911, JAPP 6-0087.

42. George Brett to Jane Addams, 7 October 1910, JAPP 5-1298.

43. Jane Addams to George Brett, 2 November 1910, JAPP 5-1308.

44. Edward Marsh to Jane Addams, 30 November 1910, JAPP 5-1357.

45. George Brett to Jane Addams, 4 January 1911, JAPP 6-0027.

46. Jane Addams to George Brett, 13 January 1911, JAPP 6-0047.

47. Tebbel, "The New Publishers Arrive," 307.

48. Jane Addams to Anita McCormick Blane, 3 February 1911, JAPP 6-0078.

49. George Brett to Jane Addams, 13 April 1911, JAPP 6-0224.

50. Jane Addams to George Brett, 17 April 1911, JAPP 6-0233.

51. James Taylor to Jane Addams, 15 May 1911, JAPP 6-0313.

52. Jane Addams to Lillian Wald, 3 May 1911, JAPP 6-0284; Jane Addams to Katharine Coman, 27 May 1911, JAPP 6-0332; and Jane Addams to Grace Abbott, 28 July 1911, JAPP 6-0380.

53. Jane Addams to Edward Marsh, 31 July 1911, JAPP 6-0386.

54. George Brett to Jane Addams, 2 August 1911, JAPP 6-0391.

55. Samuel S. McClure to Jane Addams, 8 August 1911, JAPP 6-0401.

56. Samuel S. McClure to Jane Addams, 15 August 1911, JAPP 6-0418.

57. Edward Marsh to Jane Addams, 17 August 1911, JAPP 6-0423.

58. Jane Addams to Samuel S. McClure, [ca. 28 August 1911], JAPP 6-0438.

59. Samuel S. McClure to Jane Addams, 1 September 1911, JAPP 6-0439.

60. Jane Addams to Lillian Wald, 11 August 1911, JAPP 6-0403.

61. Alice Hamilton to Jane Addams, 14 August 1911, JAPP 6-0408.

62. Jane Addams to Mary Rozet Smith, 24 August 1911, JAPP 6-0430.

63. Jane Addams to Alice Haldeman, 19 February 1912, JAPP 6-825.

64. Jane Addams to Mary Rozet Smith, 21 February 1912, JAPP 6-831. Addams does not make time for reading other novels. She asks Little, Brown not to send *Farmstead Quarries*, for example; see Jane Addams to Little, Brown, and Company, 8 November 1910, JAPP 5-1317.

65. Lingeman, *Theodore Dreiser: An American Journey*, 15. Lingeman focuses on Theodore's life but intersperses information on the Dreiser sisters throughout the biography. *Sister Carrie* creates a fictional tale about Emma. (Lingeman, 48.)

66. Dedrick, "Our Sister of the Street," 107.

67. Ibid., 107.

68. Peiss, *Cheap Amusements: Working Women and Leisure in Turn-of-the-Century New York*. Also her essay, "'Charity Girls,' and City Pleasures: Historical Notes on Working-Class Sexuality, 1880–1920." And see Kneeland, *Commercialized Prostitution in New York City*.

69. See Barry, *The Prostitution of Sexuality*, 91–113. Barry argues with Walkowitz, "Male Vice and Female Virtue: Feminism and the Politics of Prostitution in Nineteenth-Century Britain," 420–33. For a contemporary account, see Butler, *Personal Reminiscences of a Great Crusader*, 221.

70. Police Department of the City of Boston, *A Record of the Enforcement of the Laws against Sexual Immorality since December 1, 1907 as contained in the information relating thereto embodied in the reports to the Governor of Massachusetts made annually by the Police Commissioner for the City of Boston*, 23.

71. Billington-Grieg, "The Truth about Sexual Slavery," quoted in Barry, *The Prostitution of Sexuality*, 117. Stange, *Personal Property: Wives, White Slaves, and the Market in Women*, 5. Stange agrees: "In truth, the existence of white slavery was repeated disproved by well-publicized investigations."

72. Quoted in Barry, 117.

73. Goldman, "The Traffic in Women," *Anarchism and Other Essays*, 184.

74. The Vice Commission of Chicago, *The Social Evil in Chicago*.

75. Wilson, *Chinatown Quest*. See also Barry, 118.

76. Weeks, *Sex, Politics and Society: The Regulation of Sexuality since 1800*.

77. Stallybrass and White, *The Politics and Poetics of Transgression*, 171–80. See especially the chapter "Bourgeois Hysteria and the Carnivalesque."

78. Connelly, *The Response to Prostitution in the Progressive Era*, 22. Connelly reads the white slave narrative as a jeremiad, a lament over the loss of agrarian values and an admission of guilt, a stage necessary for the acceptance of the social changes already evident in the twentieth-century city.

79. Davis, *American Heroine*, 182.

80. Stange, *Personal Property: Wives, White Slaves, and the Market in Women*, 137.

81. Lippmann, *A Preface to Politics*, 78.

82. Davis, *American Heroine*, 183.

83. Gilman, *The Living of Charlotte Perkins Gilman: An Autobiography*, 184–85. For a longer discussion of the literary relationship between Addams and Gilman, see Beer and Joslin, "Diseases of the Body Politic: White Slavery in Jane Addams' *A New Conscience and an Ancient Evil* and Selected Short Stories by Charlotte Perkins Gilman."

84. Ibid., 229.

85. Gilman, *Women and Economics*, 95.

86. "His Mother" features a woman detective catching her own son in the act of becoming a white slaver. "He locked the door as he brought her in; he laid the helpless form down on his bed, standing a moment with a sneering smile." To his consternation, the eyes he encounters are the gray eyes of his mother, who turns her own son over to the police. Gilman is fascinated with sex as a social and biological force, yet the heavy hand of the sociologist flattens the power of the fiction, Janet Beer concludes.

87. James L. W. West in reconstructing the manuscript of 1901–2 and placing it against a fair copy of the 1911 version reveals how thoroughly Hitchcock eviscerated the novel, changing or removing sixteen thousand words from the manuscript before he would publish it. See James L. W. West III, "The Composition of *Jennie Gerhardt*," 441.

88. Ewen, *Immigrant Women in the Land of Dollars: Life and Culture on the Lower East Side, 1890–1925*, 268.

89. Charlotte Howett Lansey to Jane Addams, 27 January 1912, JAPP 6-798.

90. Phoebe Willets to Jane Addams, 11 July 1912, JAPP 6-1114.

91. Phoebe Willets to Jane Addams, 17 July 1912, JAPP 6-1128.

92. Charles N. Sawyer to Jane Addams, 19 March 1912, JAPP 6-879.

93. H. H. Herbst to Jane Addams, 20 January 1912, JAPP 6-0779.

94. B. A. Behrend to Jane Addams, 22 May 1912, JAPP 6-1006.

95. Theodore Roosevelt to Jane Addams, 31 October 1912, JAPP 6-512.

96. Colored Woman's Civic Club to Jane Addams, 6/7 August 1912, JAPP 6-1205.

97. J. F. Ransom to Jane Addams, 6 August 1912, JAPP 6-1209.

98. W. M. Trotter to Jane Addams, 6–7 August 1912, JAPP 6-1210.

99. P. C. Allen to Jane Addams, 6 August 1912, JAPP 6-1196.

100. Hamlin Garland to Jane Addams, 9 August 1912, JAPP 6-1270.

101. Wallace Thayer, *Buffalo Reality*, n.d., JAPP 6-1404.

102. Jane Addams, "Speech of Jane Addams Seconding the Nomination of Theodore Roosevelt," JAPP 7-0084.

103. Theodore Roosevelt to Jane Addams, 8 August 1912, JAPP 6-1252.

104. Theodore Roosevelt to Jane Addams, 9 August 1912, JAPP 6-1275.

105. *New York Times* to Jane Addams, 8 August 1912, JAPP 6-1250.

106. Jane Addams to Lillian Wald, 15 August 1912, JAPP 6-1376.

107. Mary McDowell to Jane Addams, 16 August 1912, JAPP 6-1391.

108. Anna Howard Shaw to Jane Addams, 16 August 1912, JAPP 6-1405.

109. Jane Addams, *New York Times*, 15 August 1912.

110. Theodore Roosevelt to Jane Addams, 16 August 1912, JAPP 6-1400.

111. Edward Bok to Jane Addams, 1 September 1912, JAPP 7-0009.

112. Edward Bok to Jane Addams, 4 September 1912, JAPP 7-0034.

113. Virgil W. McNitt to Jane Addams, 21 September 1912, JAPP 7-0123.

114. "Philanthropy and Politics" [September-October 1912], JAPP 47-0488.

115. "The Progressive Party and Organized Labor," [September 1912], JAPP 47-0491.

116. "The Progressive Party and Woman Suffrage," [September 1912], JAPP 47-0498.

117. "The Steps by which I Became a Progressive" [September-October 1912], JAPP 47-0505.

118. "The Progressive Party and Social Legislation," September 18 [1912], JAPP 47-0523.

119. Jenkin Lloyd Jones to Jane Addams, 10 October 1912, JAPP 7-0236.

120. Norman Hapgood to Jane Addams, 23 September 1912, JAPP 7-0126.

121. "The Progressive Party and the Negro," *Crisis* 5 (November 1912), JAPP 47-0604.

122. Jane Addams to Sophonisba Breckinridge, 5 September 1912, JAPP 7-0051.

123. Edward Bok to Jane Addams, 27 September 1912, JAPP 7-0140.

124. "The Progressive's Dilemma: The New Party," an article that appeared in *The American Magazine* just before the election, JAPP 47-0607.

125. Jane Addams to Alice Addams Haldeman, 14 October 1912, JAPP 7-0247.

126. Theodore Roosevelt to Jane Addams, 5 November 1912, JAPP 7-0374.

127. Jane Addams to Theodore Roosevelt, 20 November 1912, JAPP 7-0441.

128. George Brett to Jane Addams, 23 October 1912, JAPP 7-0304.

129. Jane Addams to George Brett, 6 November 1912, JAPP 7-0375.

130. Jane Addams to Robert Underwood Johnson, 6 November 1912, JAPP 7-0378.

131. Jane Addams to Robert Underwood Johnson, 10 December 1912, JAPP 7-0528.

132. Ida Tarbell to Jane Addams, 26 November 1912, JAPP 7-0467; and Ida Tarbell to Jane Addams, 3 December 1912, JAPP 7-0511.

133. Gifford Pinchot to Jane Addams, 10 January 1913, JAPP 7-0666.

134. Edward Bok to Jane Addams, 3 December 1912, JAPP 7-0497.

135. Edward Bok to Jane Addams, 9 December 1912, JAPP 7-0526.

136. Edward Bok to Jane Addams, 22 January 1913, JAPP 7-0719.

137. Mary Rozet Smith to Esther Kohn, 1 March 1913, JAPP 7-0784.

138. Jane Addams to Helen Culver, 11 April 1913, JAPP 7-0815.

139. May Childs Nerney to Jane Addams, 4 August 1913, JAPP 7-1024; and Jane Addams to Anita McCormick Blaine, 7 August 1913, JAPP 7-1025.

140. Blanche Wright to Jane Addams, 18 October 1913, JAPP 7-1144.

141. Edward Bok to Jane Addams, 15 September 1913, JAPP 7-1073.

142. George Brett to Jane Addams, 24 September 1913, JAPP 7-1089.

143. Norman Hapgood to Jane Addams, 26 September 1913, JAPP 7-1090.

144. Jane Addams to Albert Beveridge, 1914, JAPP

145. Edward Bok to Jane Addams, 9 January 1914, JAPP 7-1296.

146. Edward Bok to Jane Addams, 11 March 1914, JAPP.

147. Jane Addams, "Need a Woman over Fifty Feel Old?" *Ladies' Home Journal* (October 1914), JAPP 47-1067.

148. Polacheck, *I Came a Stranger: The Story of a Hull-House Girl*, 67.

149. Jane Addams to Lillian Wald, 3 July 1914, JAPP 7-1542.

Chapter 4: Telling a War Story

1. Gale, *Heart's Kindred*, 75. Page numbers will be cited in the text.

2. Jane Addams to Zona Gale, 29 July 1915, JAPP 8-1230.

3. Jane Addams to Zona Gale, 3 August 1915, JAPP 8-1267.

4. Rosika Schwimmer to Jane Addams, 17 August 1914, JAPP 7-1568.

5. Jane Addams to Paul Kellogg, [ca. 15 September] [1914], JAPP 7-1587.

6. Lillian Wald [for Jane Addams] to Emily Greene Balch, 22 September 1914, JAPP 7-1601; a list of names of those invited is attached to the letter of invitation.

7. [Jane Addams] to Sarah Hostetter, 10 October 1914, JAPP 7-1630.

8. Jane Addams to Mary Rozet Smith, 16 October 1914, JAPP 7-1642.

9. Jane Addams to Mrs. Desha [Madeline] Breckenridge, 30 November 1914, JAPP 7-1728.

10. Carrie Chapman Catt to Jane Addams, [December] [1914], JAPP 7-1731.

11. Jane Addams to David Starr Jordan, 8 December 1914, JAPP 7-1744.

12. Jane Addams to Rosika Schwimmer, 11 December 1914, JAPP 7-1756.

13. Jane Addams to Carrie Chapman Catt, 14 December 1914, JAPP 7-1764.

14. Carrie Chapman Catt to Jane Addams, 16 December 1914, JAPP 7-1772.

15. Jane Addams to Carrie Chapman Catt, 21 December 1914, JAPP 7-1796.

16. Richard Ely to Jane Addams, 11 September 1914, JAPP 7-1758.

17. Rosika Schwimmer to Jane Addams, 1 January 1915, JAPP 8-0016.

18. Antoinette Funk to Jane Addams, 29 March 1915, JAPP 8-0559.

19. Rosika Schwimmer to Jane Addams, 1 January 1915, JAPP 8-0016.

20. Carrie Chapman Catt to Jane Addams, 4 January 1915, JAPP 8-0044.

21. Jane Addams to Rosika Schwimmer, 6 January 1915, JAPP 8-0052.

22. Rosika Schwimmer to Jane Addams, 19 January 1915, JAPP 8-0126.

23. George W. Nasmyth to Jane Addams, 15 January 1915, JAPP 8-0088.

24. Carrie Chapman Catt to Jane Addams, 16 January 1915, JAPP 8-0094.

25. Rosika Schwimmer to Jane Addams, 16 February 1915, JAPP 8-0332.

26. Women's Peace Party, JAPP 8-0257.

27. Jane Addams to Lyra D. Trueblood, 21 January 1915, JAPP 8-0140.

28. [Jane Addams] to Mrs. Christian D. Hemmick, 2 February 1915, JAPP 8-0249.

29. Jane Addams to Mary Rozet Smith, 4 March 1915, JAPP 8-0406.

30. Edward Bok to Jane Addams, 18 March 1915, JAPP 8-0488.

31. Lillian Wald to Jane Addams, 25 March 1915, JAPP 8-0531.

32. Jane Addams to [Lillian Wald], 26 March 1915, JAPP 8-0537.

33. Jane Addams to Ray Stannard Baker, 26 March 1915, JAPP 8-0532.

34. Jane Addams to Emily Balch, 26 March 1915, JAPP 8-0533.

35. Mary Rozet Smith to Lillian Wald, 31 March [1915], JAPP 8-0615.

36. Jane Addams to Lillian Wald, 6 April 1915, JAPP 8-0681.

37. Jane Addams to Mary Rozet Smith, 22 April 1915, JAPP 8-0754.

38. [Alice Hamilton] to Mary Rozet Smith, 22 April 1915, JAPP 8-0763.

39. JAPP 8-0763.

40. Jane Addams, "Carnegie Hall Address," JAPP 47-1180.

41. Stanislas d'Halewyn to Jane Addams, 10 July 1915, JAPP 8-1139.

42. Elizabeth Glendower Evans to Jane Addams, 22 July 1915, JAPP 8-1186.

43. [Mary H. Page to Jane Addams, ca. 1 April] [1915], including translation of a letter from P. Fossé, 1 April 1915, on French conditions at the front, JAPP 8-0637.

44. Jane Addams to Paul Kellogg, 27 July 1915, JAPP 8-1219.

45. Jane Addams to Marcet Haldeman, 3 October 1915, JAPP 9-0003.

46. Jane Addams to Marcet Haldeman, 10 October 1915, JAPP 9-0074.

47. Jane Addams to Julia Grace Wales, 1 November 1915, JAPP 9-0214.

48. Katharine Coman to Jane Addams, 1 January 1913, JAPP 7-0637.

49. Buell, *Writing for an Endangered World: Literature, Culture, and Environment in the U.S. and Beyond,* 9. Buell also notes that Addams admired Bates's lesbian sonnets in *Yellow Clover,* 77–111, prompting her to write congratulating Bates for defining "a new type of friendship," 272, note 38. See also Jane Addams to Katharine Bates, 9 May 1922, JAPP 14-1402, a letter upon the death of Coman.

50. Katharine Coman to Jane Addams, [1910] [ca. 29 December], fragment, JAPP 5-1432.

51. Katharine Coman to Jane Addams, 17 November 1911, JAPP 6-0563.

52. Katharine Coman to Jane Addams, 1 January 1913, JAPP 7-0637.

53. Coman, *Economic Beginnings of the Far West: How We Won the Land beyond the Mississippi*, I, viii. Page numbers will be cited in the text.

54. Jane Addams to Katharine Coman, 25 January 1913, JAPP 7-0723.

55. Jane Addams to Katharine Coman, 23 March 1913, JAPP 7-0798.

56. Mary Lynn McCree Bryan assumes that the essay was written in February 1914, but the letter from Sedgwick to Addams on 3 July 1913, JAPP 7-0914, refers to her essay, which will be published as "The Unexpected Reactions of a Traveler in Egypt," *Atlantic Monthly* 113 (February 1914), 178–86.

57. Addams, "The Unexpected Reactions of a Traveler in Egypt," JAPP 47-0928.

58. Ellery Sedgwick to Jane Addams, 23 February 1916, JAPP 9-1070.

59. Vachel Lindsay to Jane Addams, 29 October 1916, JAPP 10-0174.

60. Gale, "The United States and the Artist," 109.

61. Zona Gale, Review of *Peace and Bread in Time of War*, enclosed with letter, Zona Gale to Jane Addams, 6 April [1922], JAPP 14-1221

62. Elizabeth P. Dowling to McMullin, 14 September 1915, JAPP 8-1490.

63. Edwin G. Pipp to Jane Addams, 18 November 1915, JAPP 9-0331.

64. Anna Garlin Spencer to Jane Addams, 29 November 1915, JAPP 9-0482.

65. Alice Hamilton [for Jane Addams] to Rosika Schwimmer, 2 December 1915, JAPP 9-0513.

66. Louis P. Lochner to Jane Addams, 26 January 1916, JAPP 9-0885.

67. Rosika Schwimmer to Jane Addams, 26 January 1916, JAPP 9-0893.

68. Marcet Haldeman to Jane Addams, 3 February 1916, JAPP 9-0961.

69. Jane Addams to Marcet Haldeman, 16 April 1916, JAPP 9-1293.

70. Jane Addams to Ellery Sedgwick, 12 February 1916, JAPP 9-1001.

71. Ellery Sedgwick to Jane Addams, 29 February 1916, JAPP 9-1097.

72. Ellery Sedgwick to Jane Addams, 15 March 1916, JAPP 9-1204.

73. Mary Rozet Smith to Marcet Haldeman, 15 February 1916, JAPP 9-1020.

74. Jane Addams to Rosika Schwimmer, 18 February 1916, JAPP 9-1039.

75. Harold Ickes to Jane Addams, 15 April 1916, JAPP 9-1291.

76. Jane Addams to Harold Ickes, 1 May 1916, JAPP 9-1356.

77. Jane Addams to Ellery Sedgwick, 7 July 1916, JAPP 9-1532.

78. Ellery Sedgwick to Jane Addams, 10 July 1916, JAPP 9-1547.

79. Paul Kellogg to Jane Addams, 13 September 1916, JAPP 10-0032.

80. Zona Gale to Jane Addams, [September] [1916], JAPP 10-0002.

81. Edwin Belmer, Secretary, to Jane Addams, 17 October 1916, JAPP 10-0117.

82. Vachel Lindsay to Jane Addams, 29 October 1916, JAPP 10-0174.

83. Ellery Sedgwick to Jane Addams, 13 September 1916, JAPP 10-0032.

84. Jane Addams to Ellery Sedgwick, 16 September 1916, JAPP 10-0046.

85. Woodrow Wilson to Jane Addams, 17 October 1916, JAPP 10-0120.

86. Harriet Monroe, 22 December 1916, JAPP 10-0444.

87. Zona Gale to Jane Addams, 4 January 1917, JAPP 10-0513.

88. Jane Addams to Paul Kellogg, 14 January 1917, JAPP 10-0557.

89. Jane Addams to Lillian Wald, 14 January 1917, JAPP 10-0562.

90. Jane Addams to Ida Tarbell, 30 January 1917, JAPP 10-0684.

91. Jane Addams to Lillian Wald, 13 February 1917, JAPP 10-0814.

92. Jane Addams *et al.* to Woodrow Wilson, 21 February 1917, JAPP 10-0868.

93. Jane Addams to [Harriet Thomas], 16 March 1917, JAPP 10-0954.

94. Zona Gale to Jane Addams, [9 April 1917], JAPP 10-1052.

95. Nicholas Vachel Lindsay to Jane Addams, 9 April 1917, JAPP 10-1054.

96. Jane Addams to Louis Lochner, 2 May 1917, JAPP 10-1158.

97. Ellery Sedgwick to Jane Addams, 15 November 1916, JAPP 10-0274.

98. Christina Wolbrecht, University of Notre Dame, and Kevin Corder, Western Michigan University, are currently working on a collaborative project, supported by the National Science Foundation, on women's voting behavior and its impact on the American political system in the period immediately following the granting of women's suffrage in 1920. Using a Bayesian approach to ecological inference, they are estimating men's and women's turnout in seven sample states. From their statistical study, they have found little difference between male and female patterns of voting in the 1920 election. Wolbrecht and Corder won the Carrie Chapman Catt Prize for Research on Women and Politics in 2001.

99. Jane Addams to Ellery Sedgwick, 1 May 1917, JAPP 10-1157.

100. Ellery Sedgwick to Jane Addams, 9 May 1917, JAPP 10-1218.

101. "Jane Addams told Pacifism Is Unwise," *New York Times* (12 June 1917), JAPP 10-1362.

102. "Review and Outlook: Starvation and War," *Wall Street Journal* (12 June 1917), JAPP 10-1390.

103. Caldwell, "BOOKSHELF: An Early Advocate of Welfare—and a Moralist Too."

104. "They Should Disavow It," *St. Paul Pioneer Press* (12 June 1917), JAPP 10-1396.

105. "Miss Addams Denies Charges Made Against Her Before Committee," *Atlanta Journal* (9 August 1917), 4, JAPP 11-0060.

106. Alice Hamilton to Jane Addams, 13 June 1917, JAPP 10-1406.

107. Jane Addams to Mary Rozet Smith, 25 August 1917, JAPP 11-0143.

108. Jane Addams to [Mary Rozet Smith], 27 August 1917, JAPP 11-0150.

109. Jane Addams to Mary Rozet Smith, 2 September 1917, JAPP 11-0201.

110. Ellery Sedgwick to Jane Addams, 18 September 1917, JAPP 11-0249.

111. Ellery Sedgwick to Jane Addams, [October ?] [1917], fragment, JAPP 11-0304.

112. Marcet Haldeman-Julius to Jane Addams, [January 1918], JAPP 11-0575.

113. Jane Addams to Winthrop O. Lane, 10 July 1918, JAPP 11-1081.

114. Jane Addams to Winthrop Lane, 5 October 1918, JAPP 11-1181.

115. Herbert Croly to Jane Addams, 26 July 1918, JAPP 11-1103.

116. Edward C. Marsh to Jane Addams, 18 November 1918, JAPP 11-1274.

117. Edward C. Marsh to Jane Addams, 29 January 1919, JAPP 12-0107, and 5 February 1919, JAPP 12-0124.

118. Lillian Wald to Jane Addams, 6 November 1918, JAPP 11-1232.

119. Anna Molander to Jane Addams, 17 November 1918, JAPP 11-1261.

120. Lillian Wald to Jane Addams, 25 January 1919, JAPP 12-0079.

121. Paul Jones to Jane Addams, 29 January 1919, JAPP 12-0106.

122. Jane Addams to Mary Rozet Smith, 1 May 1919, JAPP 12-347.

123. Alice Hamilton to Hamilton Family, May 1919, JAPP 12-0350.

124. Alice Hamilton to Mary Rozet Smith, 12 May 1919, JAPP 12-365.

125. *Chicago Evening Post* (20 May 1919), JAPP 12-0397.

126. Jane Addams to Emily Greene Balch, 27 November 1919, JAPP 12-0978.

127. Jane Addams to Anna Garlin Spencer, 2 December 1919, JAPP 12-1006.

128. Henry Rowland Curtis to Jane Addams, 23 February 1920, JAPP 12-1383.

129. Mary Rozet Smith to Florence Kelley, 8 September 1920, JAPP 13-0396.

130. Mary Rozet Smith to Esther Loeb Kohn, 11 September [1920], JAPP 13-0403.

131. Warren G. Harding to Jane Addams, 20 February 1921, JAPP 13-1029.

132. Jane Addams to Paul Kellogg, 28 February 1921, JAPP 13-1050.

133. [Jane Addams] and [Mabel Hyde Kittredge] to Charles Evans Hughes, 5 March 1921, JAPP 13-1079.

134. Mary Church Terrell to Jane Addams, 18 March 1921, JAPP 13-1230.
135. Jane Addams to Emily Greene Balch, [23?] March 1921, JAPP 13-1234.
136. Jane Addams to Mary Church Terrell, 29 March 1921, JAPP 13-1247.
137. Mary Rozet Smith to Esther Loeb Kohn, 22 August 1921, JAPP 14-0121.
138. Paul Kellogg to Jane Addams, 15 August 1921, JAPP 14-0074.
139. Jane Addams to Paul Kellogg, 2 September 1921, JAPP 14-0165.
140. Jane Addams to Paul Kellogg, [16] November 1921, JAPP 14-464.
141. Paul Kellogg to Jane Addams, 11 October 1921, JAPP 14-0277.
142. Jane Addams to Emily Greene Balch, 16 November 1921, JAPP 14-0462.
143. Paul Kellogg to Jane Addams, 21 November 1921, JAPP 14-0489.
144. Paul Kellogg to Jane Addams, 21 November 1921, JAPP 14-0490.
145. Jane Addams to Paul Kellogg, 22 November 1921, JAPP 14-0492.
146. Jane Addams to Paul Kellogg, 28 November 1921, JAPP 14-0516.
147. H. S. Latham to Jane Addams, [ca. 2 December] [1921], copy, JAPP 14-0554.
148. Jane Addams to H. S. Latham, 2 December 1921, JAPP 14-0554.
149. Jane Addams to Paul Kellogg, 6 December 1921, JAPP 14-0590.
150. Jane Addams to Paul Kellogg, 6 January 1922, JAPP 14-0788.
151. Jane Addams to Marcet Haldeman-Julius, 18 January 1922, JAPP 14-0827.

Chapter 5: Honest Reminiscence

1. For reports of the attack, see the following letters and articles from the *Boston Herald:* "Peace Societies Deny 'Red' Ties," "Hurley Replies to Critics of Speech," and "Parade Bodies in League with Soviet, Says Hurley," JAPP 17-1311, 17-1312, and 17-1313.
2. Jane Addams to Paul Kellogg, 30 July 1924, JAPP 16-0968.
3. Jane Addams to Hannah Cothier Hull, August 1924, JAPP 16-1022.
4. Alice Hamilton to Jane Addams, December 1924, JAPP 16-1473.
5. Jane Addams to Hannah Clothier Hull, 10 December 1924, JAPP 16-1526.
6. Emma Bugbee, "Women Invade Senate to Help World Court," *New York Herald Tribune* (22 January 1925), JAPP 16-1773.
7. Alice Hamilton to Jane Addams, 24 January 1925, JAPP 16-1775.
8. Jane Addams to Carrie Chapman Catt, 28 January 1925, JAPP 16-1793.
9. Jane Addams to Hannah Clothier Hull, 31 January 1925, JAPP 16-1804.
10. Hannah Clothier Hull to Miss Addams, Dr. Hamilton, Miss Doty, Mrs. White, and Mrs. Taussig, 6 May 1925, JAPP 17-0412.
11. Lillian D. Wald to Jane Addams, 17 February 1925, JAPP 17-0093.
12. Mary Rozet Smith to Lillian D. Wald, 25 April 1925, JAPP 17-0376.
13. Stanley R. Linn to Jane Addams, 10 May 1925, JAPP 17-0428.
14. Jane Addams to Florence Kelley, 11 May 1925, JAPP 17-0434.
15. Jane Addams to William Allen White, 22 July 1925, JAPP 17-0743.
16. Paul Kellogg to Jane Addams, 13 November 1925, JAPP 17-1099.
17. Woolf, *A Room of One's Own,* 109–10.
18. Woolf, "Modern Fiction," 123.
19. James, *The Principles of Psychology,* 245–55.
20. Woolf, *Mrs. Dalloway,* 8.
21. Paul Kellogg to Jane Addams, 16 November 1921, JAPP 14-464.
22. Woolf, "Women and Fiction."
23. Paul Kellogg to Jane Addams, 5 April 1926, JAPP 17-1671.
24. Aylmer Maude to Jane Addams, 16 April 1926, JAPP 17-1774.

25. Mary Rozet Smith to Ida Lovett, 1 August 1926, JAPP 18-0420.

26. Aletta H. Jacobs to Jane Addams, 19 August 1926, JAPP 18-0502.

27. Jane Addams to Paul Kellogg, 26 October 1926, JAPP 18-0661.

28. For a report of the speech, see "Mrs. Dawes Scores Peace Society in Armistice Day Talk," JAPP 18-0740.

29. To follow the attacks and counterattacks, see "Hull House Residents Protest," JAPP 18-0747; "More or Less Personal," *The Progressive* (1 December 1926), JAPP 18-0749; and "Charges Absurd Says Jane Addams," JAPP 18-0755.

30. Jane Addams to Women's Peace Union, 14 November 1926, JAPP 18-0741.

31. Albert J. Kennedy to Jane Addams, 12 November 1926, JAPP 18-0728.

32. Caroline Bartlett Crane to Jane Addams, 27 November 1926, JAPP 18-0798.

33. Crane, *Everyman's House.* For a discussion of the reformer's life and career, see Rickard, *A Just Verdict: The Life of Caroline Bartlett Crane,* especially pages 245–46.

34. For a copy of the chart, see "The Spider-Web," compiled and printed by Chas. Norman Fay, Cambridge, Massachusetts, JAPP 18-1192.

35. See "Jane Addams," JAPP 18-1063, and "Pres. Coolidge Lauds Jane Addams," JAPP 18-1242.

36. Stebner, *The Women of Hull House: A Study in Spirituality, Vocation, and Friendship,* 186.

37. H. S. Latham to Jane Addams, 20 May 1927, JAPP 18-1788.

38. Jane Addams to H. S. Latham, 27 May 1927, JAPP 18-1791.

39. Carrie Chapman Catt to Jane Addams, 26 May 1927, JAPP 18-1824.

40. Jane Addams to Emily Balch, 31 May 1927, JAPP 18-1858; and Jane Addams to Carrie Chapman Catt, 2 June 1927, JAPP 19-0015.

41. Florence Kelley to Jane Addams, 20 July 1927, JAPP 19-0248.

42. Jane Addams to Calvin Coolidge, ca. 9 August 1927, JAPP 19-0356.

43. Mary Rozet Smith to Florence Kelley, 15 January 1928, JAPP 19-1178.

44. Jane Addams et al. to Herbert Hoover, 21 November 1928, JAPP 20-0535.

45. ACLU to Herbert Hoover, 21 November 1928, JAPP 20-0535.

46. Herbert Hoover to Jane Addams, 29 August 1929, JAPP 20-1413.

47. Mary Rozet Smith to Lillian Wald, 2 March 1929, JAPP 20-0872.

48. Jane Addams to Paul Kellogg, 4 February 1929, JAPP 20-0782.

49. Paul Kellogg to Jane Addams, 9 February 1929, JAPP 20-0811.

50. Jane Addams to Paul Kellogg, 6 March 1929, JAPP 20-0887.

51. Paul Kellogg to Jane Addams, 9 May 1929, JAPP 20-1094.

52. Jane Addams to Paul Kellogg, 10 May 1929, JAPP 20-1101.

53. Paul Kellogg to Jane Addams, 14 May 1929, JAPP 20-1105.

54. Paul Kellogg to Jane Addams, 21 May 1929, JAPP 20-1134.

55. Paul Kellogg to Jane Addams, 25 May 1929, JAPP 20-1150.

56. Jane Addams to Arthur Kellogg, 15 October 1929, JAPP 20-1553.

57. Jane Addams to Paul Kellogg, 28 October 1929, JAPP 20-1606.

58. John Dewey to Jane Addams, 26 October 1929, JAPP 20-1601.

59. Madeleine Z. Doty to Jane Addams, 2 December 1929, JAPP 20-1757.

60. Jane Addams to Julius Rosenwald, 23 December 1929, JAPP 20-1853.

61. Lousie DeKoven Bowen [for Jane Addams] to Julius Rosenwald, 23 December 1929, JAPP 20-1853.

62. Mary Rozet Smith to Lillian Wald, 5 March 1930, JAPP 21-0342.

63. Paul Kellogg to Jane Addams, 27 August 1930, JAPP 21-0810.

64. Jane Addams to Henrietta Barnett, 18 September 1930, JAPP 21-1071.

65. Jane Addams to United Press, 4 September 1930, JAPP 21-0852.

66. Ellen Gates Starr to Jane Addams, 5 November 1930, JAPP 21-1265.

67. Alice Hamilton to Jane Addams, 27 November 1930, JAPP 21-1372.
68. Carrie Chapman Catt to Jane Addams, 6 November 1930, JAPP 21-1279.
69. Louise DeKoven Bowen to Jane Addams, 21 November 1930, JAPP 21-1337.
70. Julia Lathrop to Jane Addams, 21 November 1930, JAPP 21-1339.
71. H. S. Latham to Jane Addams, 23 December 1930, JAPP 21-1523.
72. Jane Addams to Rosika Schwimmer, 13 April 1931, JAPP 22-0334.
73. Mary Rozet Smith to Myra R. Linn, 1 March 1931, JAPP 21-0263.
74. Jane Addams to Marcet Haldemann-Julius, 11 December 1930, JAPP 21-1451.
75. Charles Beard, ed., *A Century of Progress.*
76. Theodore Dreiser to Friend [Jane Addams], June 1931, JAPP 22-0559.
77. W. E. B. Du Bois to Jane Addams, 7 August 1931, JAPP 22-0773.
78. Jane Addams to W. E. B. Du Bois, 30 September 1931, JAPP 22-1011.
79. Addams, "What Our Readers Say."
80. Jane Addams to Lillie M. Peck, 28 April 1931, JAPP 22-0387.
81. Mabel Vernon to Jane Addams, ca. 17 May 1931, JAPP 22-0523.
82. Will Durant to Jane Addams, 15 June 1931, JAPP 22-0602.
83. Addams, "Tolstoy and Gandhi."
84. Paul Underwood Kellogg, review of *The Second Twenty Years at Hull-House* by Jane Addams and the *Autobiography* of Lincoln Steffens, draft, JAPP 22-0981.
85. Edith Abbott to Jane Addams, 31 August 1931, JAPP 22-0905.
86. Paul Kellogg to Jane Addams, 8 October 1931, JAPP 22-1034.
87. Yella Hertzka to Jane Addams, 3 March 1930, JAPP 21-0330.
88. Amy Wu to Hannah Clothier Hull, May 1930, JAPP 23-0631.
89. Ida Tarbell to Jane Addams, 15 October 1931, JAPP 22-1054.
90. H. S. Latham to Jane Addams, 17 October 1931, JAPP 22-1062.
91. Jane Addams to H. S. Latham, 26 October 1931, JAPP 22-1063.
92. See Press Release, National Broadcasting Company, October 1931, JAPP 22-1068.
93. Jane Addams to Paul Underwood Kellogg, 19 November 1931, JAPP 22-1234.
94. Jane Addams to Ellen Gates Starr, 2 November 1931, JAPP 22-2256.
95. Alfred E. Smith to Jane Addams, 12 December 1931, JAPP 22-1606.
96. Grace Abbott to Jane Addams, 10 December 1931, JAPP 22-1334.
97. Julia Lathrop to Jane Addams, Alice Hamilton, and Mary Rozet Smith, 11 December 1931, JAPP 22-1496.
98. W. E. B. Du Bois to Jane Addams, 11 January 1932, JAPP 23-0511.
98. Paul Kellogg to Jane Addams, 10 December 1931, JAPP 22-1391.
100. Walter Lippmann to Jane Addams, 14 December 1931, JAPP 22-1717.
101. Mary Rozet Smith to Stanley Linn, 13 December 1931, JAPP 22-1674.
102. Margaret Cole to Jane Addams, 14 December 1931, JAPP 22-1691.
103. Mary Rozet Smith to the Linns, 27 December 1931, JAPP 23-0300.
104. Jane Addams to Florence Kelley, 15 February 1932, JAPP 23-0752.
105. Zona Gale to Jane Addams, 23 February 1932, JAPP 23-0802.
106. Jane Addams to L. H. Titterton, March 1932, JAPP 23-0846.
107. Jane Addams to H. S. Latham, 26 April 1932, JAPP 23-1185.
108. Jane Addams, JAPP 23-1050.
109. Ellen Gates Starr to Jane Addams, 19 April 1932, JAPP 23-1148.
110. Jane Addams to Kathleen Courtney, 15 August 1932, JAPP 24-0047.
111. Jane Addams to Hannah Clothier Hull, 11 August 1932, JAPP 24-0035.
112. Jane Addams to Mary Addams Hulbert, 23 September 1932, JAPP 24-0190.
113. "Jane Addams Hits National Boasting," *New York Times*, JAPP 24-0328.
114. Mahatma Gandhi to Jane Addams, 7 October 1932, JAPP 24-0236.

Chapter 6: Writing a Life

1. James Weber Linn to Jane Addams, 13 February 1933, JAPP 24-0868.
2. Ferris Greenslet to James Weber Linn, 11 April 1933, JAPP 24-1068.
3. Emil Ludwig, "The Greatest Living Americans," *The Red Book Magazine*, JAPP 19-1369.
4. Edward Wagenknecht to Jane Addams, 10 April 1933, JAPP 24-1049.
5. Winifred Wise to Jane Addams, 2 May 1933, JAPP 24-1132.
6. Jane Addams to Margaret Dreier Robins, 20 February 1933, JAPP 24-0885.
7. Jane Addams to Esther Linn Hulbert, 23 February 1933, JAPP 24-0894.
8. Jane Addams to Marcet Haldeman-Julius, [March?] [1933], JAPP 24-0903.
9. Jane Addams to Ida Lovett, 10 March 1933, JAPP 24-0945.
10. Jane Addams to Eva Whiting White, 27 March 1933, JAPP 24-1001.
11. Michael Williams to Jane Addams, May 1933, JAPP 24-1123.
12. Alice Hamilton to Jane Addams, 2 June 1933, JAPP 24-1250.
13. Alice Hamilton to Jane Addams, 26 October 1933, JAPP 25-0323.
14. Alice Hamilton to Jane Addams, 24 November 1933, JAPP 25-0445.
15. Stanley Linn to Jane Addams, 27 August 1933, JAPP 25-0084.
16. Jane Addams to Stanley Linn, 31 August 1933, JAPP 25-0112.
17. Mary Rozet Smith to Jane Addams, 3 September 1933, JAPP 25-0125.
18. Mary Rozet Smith [for Jane Addams] to Charles Hull Ewing, 13 February 1934, JAPP 25-0759.
19. Emily Balch to Jane Addams, 21 February 1934, JAPP 25-0788.
20. Dorothy Detzer to Jane Addams, ca. 21 February 1934, JAPP 25-0794.
21. Ellen Gates Starr to Jane Addams, 23 February 1934, JAPP 25-0850.
22. Eleanor Smith to Unknown, ca. 27 February 1934, fragment, JAPP 25-0913.
23. Myra Linn to Jane Addams, 4 July 1934, JAPP 26-002.
24. Jane Addams to James Weber Linn, 15 July 1934, JAPP 26-0035.
25. Jane Addams to Grace Abbott, 30 March 1934, JAPP 25-1125.
26. Jane Addams to Ida Lovett, 28 June 1934, JAPP 25-1423.
27. Jane Addams to Lillian Wald, 8 July 1934, JAPP 26-0020.
28. Jane Addams to Allen Winthrop, 30 July 1934, JAPP 26-0072.
29. Jane Addams to Grace Abbott, 7 August 1934, JAPP 26-0100.
30. Albert Einstein to Jane Addams, 12 October 1934, JAPP 26-0378.
31. Jane Addams to Alma Birmingham, 29 June 1934, JAPP 25-1426.
32. Jane Addams to Grace Abbott, ca. 28 June 1934, JAPP 25-1415.
33. Jane Addams to Grace Abbott, 27 July 1934, JAPP 26-0062.
34. Jane Addams to Grace Abbott, 30 July 1934, JAPP 26-0071.
35. Jane Addams to Graham Taylor, 9 August 1934, JAPP 26-0106.
36. Maud E. Lavery to Jane Addams, 9 August 1934, JAPP 26-0107.
37. Jane Addams to James Weber Linn, 26 August 1934, JAPP 26-0166.
38. Alice Hamilton [for Jane Addams] to Maud E. Lavery, 31 August 1934, JAPP 26-0185.
39. Jane Addams to Emily Balch, 28 August 1934, JAPP 26-0174.
40. Jane Addams to Lucia Ames Mead, 15 September 1934, JAPP 26-0249. This letter was a gift to me from Harrison Hayford.
41. Jane Addams to Grace Abbott, 1 October 1934, JAPP 26-0336.
42. Jane Addams to Nicholas "Ko" Kelley, 1 October 1934, JAPP 26-0337.
43. Jane Addams to Grace Abbott, 29 October 1934, JAPP 26-0452.
44. "Jane Addam's Good Friend and Jane Addams," *Boston Evening Transcript Book Review*, JAPP 4-0079.

45. Jane Addams to Emily Cooper Johnson, 14 January 1935, JAPP 26-0886.
46. H. S. Latham to Jane Addams, 28 November 1934, JAPP 26-0567.
47. Carrie Chapman Catt to Jane Addams, 10 December 1934, JAPP 26-0647.
48. Winifred E. Wise to Jane Addams, 15 January 1935, JAPP 26-0893.
49. Jane Addams to James Weber Linn, 2 February 1934, JAPP 26-0977.
50. Jane Addams to Grace Abbott, 21 January 1935, JAPP 26-0936.
51. Jane Addams to Ida Lovett, 12 February 1935, JAPP 26-1011.
52. Jane Addams to Lillian Wald, 25 February 1935, JAPP 26-1077.
53. Jane Addams to James Weber Linn, 5 March 1935, JAPP 26-1128.
54. Jane Addams to James Weber Linn, 8 March 1935, JAPP 26-1137.
55. Jane Addams to Hannah Clothier Hull, 30 October 1934, JAPP 26-0456.
56. Jane Addams to Hannah Clothier Hull, 12 March 1935, JAPP 26-1156.
57. Jane Addams to Mary Moss Wellborn, 12 March 1935, JAPP 26-1158.
58. Jane Addams to Hannah Clothier Hull, 3 April 1935, JAPP 26-1280.
59. Paul Kellogg to Jane Addams, 8 April 1935, JAPP 26-1301.
60. Jane Addams to Paul Kellogg, 30 April 1935, JAPP 26-1440.
61. Paul Kellogg to Jane Addams, 2 May 1935, JAPP 26-1498.
62. Linn, *Jane Addams: A Biography*, 415.
63. Ethel Dewey [for Jane Addams], 19 May 1935, JAPP 26-1561.
64. Jane Addams to Paul Kellogg, 10 May 1935, JAPP 26-1536.
65. Jane Addams to Grace Abbott, 20 May 1935, JAPP 26-1564.
66. Paul Kellogg to Alice Hamilton, 21 May 1935, JAPP 26-1583.

BIBLIOGRAPHY

Writings of Jane Addams

PAPERS

All letters and manuscripts used in this book can be found in *The Jane Addams Papers Project* (JAPP), eighty-two reels of microfilm that comprise an edition of her papers, both personal and professional, and papers associated with Hull-House. All citations from the microfilm collection are cited in endnotes by reel number and frame. Mary Lynn McCree Bryan directed the editing of the microfilm project together with Nancy Slote, the associate director, and Maree de Angury, the assistant to the editor. They also designed *The Jane Addams Papers: A Comprehensive Guide*, a thoroughly reliable and impressively detailed map of the microfilm collection. From this collection, Bryan, Barbara Bair, and de Angury have published the first volume of material from the microfilm archive, *The Selected Papers of Jane Addams, Volume I, Preparing to Lead, 1860–81*. All of these sources have been vital to my writing this biography. The project, in both its microfilm and book versions, offers scholars a considerable and dependable source of information on Addams, other writers, and social workers, as well as on Hull-House, sister institutions, and other community, national, and international organizations.

BOOKS

Jane Addams wrote ten books and collaborated on three book projects. The University of Illinois Press is in the process of reissuing Addams's books with new introductions. For this biography, I have used first editions for my research, and pagination, noted parenthetically in the text, follows these editions. The following is a chronological list of her books and those she wrote and edited with other people:

Philanthropy and Social Progress: Seven Essays by Miss Jane Addams, Robert A. Woods, Father J. O. S. Huntington, Professor Franklin H. Giddings, and Bernard Bosanquet. Edited by Henry C. Adams. New York: Thomas Y. Crowell, 1893.

Hull-House Maps and Papers: A Presentation of Nationalities and Wages in a Congested District of Chicago, together with Comments and Essays on

Problems Growing Out of the Social Conditions. Edited by Jane Addams and Florence Kelley. New York: Thomas Y. Crowell, 1895.

Democracy and Social Ethics. Citizen's Library Series. New York: Macmillan, 1902.

The Newer Ideals of Peace, Citizen's Library Series. New York: Macmillan, 1907.

The Spirit of Youth and the City Streets. New York: Macmillan, 1909.

Twenty Years at Hull-House. New York: Macmillan, 1910.

A New Conscience and an Ancient Evil. New York: Macmillan, 1912.

Jane Addams, Emily Greene Balch, and Alice Hamilton. *Women at The Hague.* New York: Macmillan, 1915.

The Long Road of Woman's Memory. New York: Macmillan, 1916.

Peace and Bread in Time of War. New York: Macmillan, 1922.

The Second Twenty Years at Hull-House. New York: Macmillan, 1930.

The Excellent Becomes the Permanent. New York: Macmillan, 1932.

My Friend, Julia Lathrop. New York: Macmillan, 1935.

ESSAYS

Jane Addams wrote hundreds of essays and speeches that are included in *The Jane Addams Papers Project,* many of which are cited in footnotes by their JAPP reel and frame number. The following is a list of essays that I have cited by publication:

"Claim on the College Woman," *Rockford Collegian* 23 (June 1895): 59–63.

"The College Woman and Christianity," *Independent* 53 (8 August 1901): 1852–55.

"Count Tolstoy," *Chautauqua Assembly Herald* 27 (11 July 1902): 5, 7.

Editorial, *Rockford Seminary Magazine* 9 (March 1881): 88–89.

"Home Items," *Rockford Seminary Magazine* 7 (June 1879): 161.

Introduction to *What Then Must We Do?,* translated by Aylmer and Louise Maude (1882; translated London: Oxford University Press, 1934), vii.

"The Objective Value of a Social Settlement" and "The Subjective Necessity for Social Settlements." In *Philanthropy and Social Progress,* edited by Henry C. Adams, 1–56. New York: Thomas Crowell, 1893; reprint, Freeport, New York: Books for Library Press, 1969.

"Three Days on the Mediterranean Subjectively Related," *Rockford Seminary Magazine* 14 (January 1886): 11–17.

"Tolstoy and Gandhi," *Christian Century* 48 (25 November 1931): 1485–88.

"Tolstoy's Theory of Life," *Chautauqua Assembly Herald* 27 (14 July 1902): 2–3.

"The Unexpected Reactions of a Traveler in Egypt," *Atlantic Monthly* 113 (February 1914): 178–86.

"What Our Readers Say," *Crisis* 40 (November 1931): 382.

Works Cited

Ahnebrink, Lars. *The Beginnings of Naturalism in American Fiction: A Study of the Works of Hamlin Garland, Stephen Crane, and Frank Norris, with Special References to Some European Influence, 1891–1903.* Cambridge, Massachusetts: Harvard University Press, 1950.

Bakhtin, Mikhail. *The Dialogic Imagination.* Edited by Michael Holquist, translated by Caryl Emerson and Michael Holquist. Austin: University of Texas Press, 1981.

Barry, Kathleen. *The Prostitution of Sexuality.* New York: New York University Press, 1995.

Bates, Katharine. *Yellow Clover.* New York: Dutton, 1922.

Beard, Charles, ed. *A Century of Progress.* New York: Harpers, 1933.

Beer, Janet, and Katherine Joslin. "Diseases of the Body Politic: White Slavery in Jane Addams' *A New Conscience and an Ancient Evil* and Selected Short Stories by Charlotte Perkins Gilman," *Journal of American Studies* Special Issue: "Women in America," 33 Part I (April 1999): 1–18.

Bennett, Michael, and David W. Teague. *The Nature of Cities: Ecocriticism and Urban Environments.* Tucson: University of Arizona Press, 1999.

Bowen, Louise de Koven. *Open Windows.* Chicago: Ralph Fletcher Seymour, 1946.

Bremmer, Robert H. *American Philanthropy.* Chicago History of American Civilization Series, edited by Daniel J. Boorstin. Chicago: University of Chicago Press, 1960.

Brown, Victoria Bissell, *The Education of Jane Addams.* Philadelphia: University of Pennsylvania Press, 2003.

Bryan, Mary Lynn McCree, ed., with Nancy Slote and Maree de Angury. *The Jane Addms Papers: A Comprehensive Guide.* Bloomington: Indiana University Press, 1996.

Bryan, Mary Lynn McCree, Barbara Bair, and Maree de Angury, eds. *The Selected Papers of Jane Addams, Volume I, Preparing to Lead, 1860–81.* Urbana and Chicago: University of Illinois Press, 2003.

Buell, Lawrence. *Writing for an Endangered World: Literature, Culture, and Environment in the U.S. and Beyond.* Cambridge, Massachusetts: Harvard University Press, 2001.

Butler, Josephine. *Personal Reminiscences of a Great Crusader.* 1911; reprint, Westport, Connecticut: Hyperion, 1976.

Caldwell, Christopher. "BOOKSHELF: An Early Advocate of Welfare—and a Moralist Too," *The Wall Street Journal* (2 January 2002): A16.

Cappetti, Carla. *Writing Chicago: Modernism, Ethnography, and the Novel.* The Social Foundations of Aesthetic Forms Series. Edited by Jonathan Arac. New York: Columbia University Press, 1993.

Chambers, Clarke, and Paul U. Kellogg. *The Survey: Voices for Social Welfare and Social Justice.* Minneapolis: University of Minnesota Press, 1971.

Connelly, Mark. *The Response to Prostitution in the Progressive Era.* Chapel Hill: University of North Carolina Press, 1980.

Coman, Katharine. *Economic Beginnings of the Far West: How We Won the Land beyond the Mississippi.* New York: Macmillan, 1912.

Commons, John R. *Races and Immigrants in America.* New York: Macmillan, 1907; reprint, New York: Augustus M. Kelley, 1967.

Conway, Jill. "Jane Addams: An American Heroine," *Daedalus* 93:2 (spring 1964): 761–780.

———. "Women Reformers and American Culture, 1870–1930," *Journal of Social History* 5:2 (winter 1971–72): 166–77.

Cook, Blanche Wiesen. "Female Support Networks and Political Activism: Lillian Wald, Crystal, Emma Goldman," *Chrysalis* 3 (1977): 43–61.

Cott, Nancy F. *The Bonds of Womanhood: "Woman's Sphere" in New England, 1780–1835.* New Haven: Yale University Press, 1977.

Crane, Caroline Bartlett. *Everyman's House.* Garden City, New York: Doubleday, Page & Company, 1925.

Crane, Stephen. *Maggie: A Girl of the Streets (A Story of New York).* Edited by Kevin J. Hayes. Bedford Cultural Edition. 1893; reprint, Boston: Bedford/St. Martin's, 1999.

Cronin, William. *Nature's Metropolis: Chicago and the Great West.* New York: Norton, 1991.

Davis, Allen F. *American Heroine: The Life and Legend of Jane Addams.* New York: Oxford University Press, 1965.

Dedrick, Florence Mabel. "Our Sister of the Street." In *Fighting the Traffic in Young Girls or The War on the White Slave Trade,* edited by Ernest A. Bell, 107. Chicago: G. S. Ball, 1910.

Deegan, Mary Jo. *Jane Addams and the Men of the Chicago School, 1892–1918.* New Brunswick and Oxford: Transaction Books, 1988.

Dewey, John. *The Public and Its Problems.* 1927; reprint, Chicago: Swallow, 1954.

———. *Theory of the Moral Life.* Introduced by Arnold Isenberg. 1908; reprint, New York: Holt, Rinehart and Winston, 1967.

Dickens, Charles. *Hard Times.* London, 1854; reprint, New York: Penguin, 1969.

Diliberto, Gioia. *A Useful Woman: The Early Life of Jane Addams.* New York: Scribner, 1999.

Douglas, William O. Introduction to *Jane Addams, A Centennial Reader.* Edited by Emily Cooper Johnson, xix. New York: Macmillan, 1960.

Douglass, Frederick. *The Oxford Frederick Douglass Reader.* Edited by William L. Andrews. New York and Oxford: Oxford University Press, 1996.

Drake, St. Clair, and Horace R. Cayton. *Black Metropolis: A Study of Negro Life in a Northern City.* Revised with introductions by Richard Wright and E. C. Hughes. 1945; reprint, New York: Harcourt, Brace & World, 1962.

Dreiser, Theodore. *Jennie Gerhardt.* Edited by James L. W. West III. 1911; reprint, Philadelphia: University of Pennsylvania Press, 1992.

———. *Sister Carrie.* Edited by Donald Pizer. 1900; reprint, New York: Norton, 1970.

Du Bois, W. E. B. *The Oxford W. E. B. Du Bois Reader.* Edited by Eric J. Sundquist. New York and Oxford: Oxford University Press, 1996.

Eliot, George. *The Essays of George Eliot.* Edited by Thomas Pinney. New York: Columbia University Press, 1963.

Elshtain, Jean Bethke. "The Future of the Public Intellectual: A Forum." *The Nation,* 12 February 2001. http://www.thenation.com.

———. *Jane Addams and the Dream of American Democracy.* New York: Basic Books, 2002.

———, ed. *The Jane Addams Reader.* New York: Basic Books, 2002.

Ely, Richard T. *The Ground under Our Feet: An Autobiography.* New York: Macmillan, 1938.

———. *Socialism: An Examination of Its Nature, Its Strength and Its Weakness, with Suggestions for Social Reform.* New York: Thomas Y. Crowell, 1894.

Ewen, Elizabeth. *Immigrant Women in the Land of Dollars: Life and Culture on the Lower East Side, 1890–1925.* New York: Monthly Review Press, 1985.

Farrell, John C. *Beloved Lady: A History of Jane Addams' Ideas on Reform and Peace.* Baltimore: Johns Hopkins University Press, 1967.

Gale, Zona. *Friendship Village.* New York: Macmillan, 1908.

———. *Heart's Kindred.* New York: Macmillan, 1915.

———. *Portage, Wisconsin, and Other Essays.* New York: Alfred A. Knopf, 1928.

Gilbert, Miriam. *Jane Addams: World Neighbor.* Makers of America Series. New York: Abingdon Press, 1960.

Gilman, Charlotte Perkins. *The Living of Charlotte Perkins Gilman.* 1935; reprint, New York: Harper Colophon, 1975.

———. *Women and Economics: A Study of the Economic Relations between Men and Women as a Factor in Social Evolution.* Boston: Small, Maynard, 1898.

Goldman, Emma. "The Traffic in Women." In *Anarchism and Other Essays,* 184. 1910; reprint, Port Washington, New York: Kennikat Press, 1969.

Groos, Karl. *The Play of Man.* Translated by Elizabeth L. Baldwin. 1901; reprint, New York: Appleton, 1912.

Hamilton, Alice. *Exploring the Dangerous Trades: The Autobiography of Alice Hamilton, M.D.* Boston: Little, Brown, 1943.

Heilbrun, Carolyn G. *Writing a Women's Life.* New York: Norton, 1988.

Hobhouse, L. T. *Democracy and Reaction.* Edited by P. F. Clarke. London: T. Fisher Unwin, 1904; reprint, Brighton, Sussex: Harvester, 1972.

Howells, William Dean. *Criticism and Fiction.* New York: Harper and Brothers, 1891.

Jackson, Shannon. *Lines of Activity: Performance, Historiography, Hull-House Domesticity.* Ann Arbor: University of Michigan Press, 2000.

James, Henry. *The Complete Notebooks of Henry James: The Authoritative and Definitive Edition.* Edited by Leon Edel and Lyall H. Powers. New York and Oxford: Oxford University Press, 1987.

————. *The Letters of Henry James.* Volume 2. Edited by Leon Edel. New York: Scribner's, 1920.

————. *Portrait of a Lady.* 1880; reprint, New York: Norton, 1975.

James, William. "The Moral Equivalent of War." In *The Writings of William James,* edited by John J. McDermott, 660–71. New York: Random House, 1967.

————. *Pragmatism and Four Essays from* The Meaning of Truth. 1907 and 1909; reprint, New York: New American Library, 1974.

————. *The Principles of Psychology.* New York: Holt, 1890.

————. *The Varieties of Religious Experience.* Introduced by Reinhold Niebuhr. 1902; reprint, New York: Collier Books, 1961.

————. *The Writings of William James.* Edited by John J. McDermott. New York: Random House, 1967.

Johnson, Mary Ann, ed., and Wallace Kirkland, photographer. *The Many Faces of Hull-House.* Urbana and Chicago: University of Illinois Press, 1989.

Joslin, Katherine. "Jane Addams as Naturalist: Turning the Theory Inside Out." In *Twisted from the Ordinary: Essays on American Literary Naturalism,* edited by Mary Papke, 276–88. Tennessee Studies in Literature, volume 40. Chattanooga: University of Tennessee Press, 2002.

————. "Literary Cross-Dressing: Jane Addams Finds Her Voice in *Democracy and Social Ethics.*" In *Femme de conscience: Aspects du feminisime americain (1848–1875),* edited by Susan Goodman and Daniel Royot, 217–38. Paris: Presses de la Sorbonne Nouvelle, 1994.

————. "Slum Angels: The White Slave Narrative in Theodore Dreiser's *Jennie Gerhardt.*" In *Women, Migration, and Movement,* edited by Susan Roberson, 106–20. Columbia: University of Missouri Press, 1998.

Kelley, Florence. "The Sweating-System." In *Hull-House Maps and Papers,* edited by Jane Addams and Florence Kelley, 27–48. Boston: Thomas Y. Crowell, 1895.

Kelley, Florence, and Alzina Stevens. "Wage-Earning Children." In *Hull-House Maps and Papers,* edited by Jane Addams and Florence Kelley, 49–78. Boston: Thomas Y. Crowell, 1895.

Kerber, Linda K. "Can a Woman Be an Individual?: The Discourse of Self-Reliance." In *Toward an Intellectual History of Women,* 200–23. Chapel Hill: University of North Carolina Press, 1997.

Kneeland, George. *Commercialized Prostitution in New York City.* New York: Century, 1913.

Lasch, Christopher. *The New Radicalism in America: 1889–1963.* New York: Vintage Books, 1967.

————, ed. *The Social Thought of Jane Addams.* The American Heritage Series. Edited by Leonard W. Levy and Alfred Young. Indianapolis and New York: Bobbs-Merrill, 1965.

Levine, Daniel. *Jane Addams and the Liberal Tradition.* Madison: State Historical Society of Wisconsin, 1971.

Lewis, R. W. B. *The Jameses: A Family Narrative.* New York: Farrar, Straus, and Giroux, 1991.

Lingeman, Richard. *Theodore Dreiser: An American Journey.* Abridged edition. New York: John Wiley and Sons, 1993.

Linn, James Weber. *Jane Addams: A Biography.* New York and London: D. Appleton-Century, 1938.

Lippmann, Walter. *A Preface to Politics.* New York: Macmillan, 1933.

Lissak, Rivka Shpak. *Pluralism and Progressives: Hull House and the New Immigrants, 1889–1919.* Chicago and London: University of Chicago Press, 1989.

Lloyd, Henry Demarest. *Wealth against Commonwealth.* New York: Harper and Brothers, 1894.

Maude, Aylmer. *The Life of Tolstoy.* Vol. 2. New York: Dodd, Mead, and Company, 1910.

———. "A Talk with Miss Jane Addams and Leo Tolstoy," *The Humane Review* (June 1902): 203–18.

Menand, Louis. *The Metaphysical Club: A Story of Ideas in America.* New York: Farrar, Straus, and Giroux, 2001.

Moers, Ellen. *Literary Women: The Great Writers.* 1963; reprint, Garden City, New York: Anchor Press/Doubleday, 1977.

Monroe, Harriet. Review of *Democracy and Social Ethics* by Jane Addams. *Chicago American* (19 April 1902): n.p.

Morley, John. *On Compromise.* London: Macmillan, 1917.

Norris, Frank. *The Pit: A Story of Chicago.* Edited by Joseph R McElrath Jr. and Gwendolyn Jones. 1903; reprint, New York: Penguin, 1994.

Paley, Grace. *Just as I Thought.* New York: Farrar, Straus, and Giroux, 1998.

Panofsky, Erwin. *Studies in Iconography: Humanistic Themes in the Art of the Renaissance.* 1939; reprint, New York: Harper and Row, 1972.

Parini, Jay. "2 Distinct Approaches to Biography, with Bellow and Updike as the Subjects," *The Chronicle of Higher Education* (3 November 2000): B14–17.

Peiss, Kathy. "'Charity Girls,' and City Pleasures: Historical Notes on Working-Class Sexuality, 1880–1920." In *Passion and Power: Sexuality in History,* edited by Kathy Peiss and Christina Simmons, 57–69. Philadelphia: Temple University Press, 1989.

———. *Cheap Amusements: Working Women and Leisure in Turn-of-the-Century New York.* Philadelphia: Temple University Press, 1986.

Polacheck, Hilda Satt. *I Came a Stranger: The Story of a Hull-House Girl.* Edited by Denna J. Polacheck Epstein. Urbana and Chicago: University of Illinois Press, 1989.

Police Department of the City of Boston. *A Record of the Enforcement of the Laws against Sexual Immorality since December 1, 1907 as contained in the information relating thereto embodied in the reports to the Governor of Massachusetts made annually by the Police Commissioner for the City of Boston.* Boston: Boston Printing Department, 1907.

Polikoff, Barbara Garland. *With One Bold Act: The Story of Jane Addams.* Chicago: Boswell Books, 1999.

Rickard, O'Ryan. *A Just Verdict: The Life of Caroline Bartlett Crane.* Kalamazoo, Michigan: New Issues Press, 1994.

Riis, Jacob. *How the Other Half Lives: Studies among the Tenements of New York.* 1890; reprint, New York: Dover, 1971.

Roberson, Susan L., ed. *Women, America, and Movement: Narratives of Relocation.* Columbia: University of Missouri Press, 1998.

Romero, Lora. *Home Fronts: Domesticity and Its Critics in the Antebellum United States.* Durham and London: Duke University Press, 1997.

Ross, Andrew. "The Social Claim on Urban Ecology." In *The Nature of Cities: Ecocriticism and Urban Environments,* edited by Michael Bennett and David W. Teague, 15–32. Tucson: University of Arizona Press, 1999.

Rossi, Alice, ed. *The Feminist Papers:From Adams to de Beauvoir.* New York: Columbia University Press, 1973.

Royce, Josiah. *The Spirit of Modern Philosophy.* Boston: Houghton, Mifflin, 1901.

Ruskin, John. "Of Queens' Gardens." In *The Works of John Ruskin,* edited by E. T. Cook and Alexander Wedderburn, 111–22. London: George Allen, 1903–12.

Schneirov, Richard. *Labor and Urban Politics: Class Conflicts and the Origins of Modern Liberalism in Chicago, 1864–97.* Urbana and Chicago: University of Illinois Press, 1998.

Schreiner, Olive. *Woman and Labor.* New York: Frederick A. Strokes, 1911.

Scott, Anne Firor. Introduction to *Democracy and Social Ethics,* by Jane Addams. Cambridge, Massachusetts: Harvard University Press, 1964.

Shaw, George Bernard. *Essays in Fabian Socialism.* London: Constable, 1932.

Sinclair, Upton. *The Jungle.* 1906; reprint, New York: Penguin, 1986.

Sklar, Kathryn Kish. *Florence Kelley & the Nation's Work: The Rise of Women's Political Culture, 1830–1900.* New Haven and London: Yale University Press, 1995.

———. "Who Founded Hull House?" In *Lady Bountiful Revisited: Women, Philanthropy, and Power,* edited by Kathleen McCarthy, 94–118. New Brunswick: Rutgers University Press, 1990.

Smith, Carl S. *Chicago and the American Literary Imagination, 1880–1920.* Chicago and London: University of Chicago Press, 1984.

Smith-Rosenberg, Carol. "The Female World of Love and Ritual: Relations between Women in Nineteenth-Century America," *Signs* 1 (1975): 1–29.

Stallybrass, Peter, and Allon White. *The Politics and Poetics of Transgression.* Ithaca, New York: Cornell University Press, 1986.

Stange, Margit. *Personal Property: Wives, White Slaves, and the Market in Women.* Baltimore and London: Johns Hopkins University Press, 1998.

Stead, William T. *If Christ Came to Chicago.* 1894; reprint, Evanston, Illinois: Chicago Historical Bookworks, 1990.

Stebner, Eleanor J. *The Women of Hull House: A Study in Spirituality, Vocation, and Friendship.* Albany: State University of New York Press, 1997.

Stevens, Wallace. *The Collected Poems.* New York: Knopf, 1976.

Tarbell, Ida. *All in the Day's Work.* New York: Macmillan, 1939.

———. "The American Woman." *The American Magazine* 69:6 (April 1910): 722.

———. *The History of the Standard Oil Company.* New York: Macmillan, 1904.

Tebbel, John. "The New Publishers Arrive." In *A History of Book Publishing in the United States,* vol. II, part 3, 307–93. New York: R. R. Bowker Company, [1972]–1981.

Tims, Margaret. *Jane Addams of Hull-House.* London: Allen and Unwin, 1961.

Tobin, Beth Fowkes. *Superintending the Poor: Charitable Ladies and Paternal Landlords in British Fiction, 1770–1860.* New Haven: Yale University Press, 1993.

Tolstoy, Leo. *My Confession.* 1882; reprint, New York, 1887.

———. *What Then Must We Do?* Translated by Alymer and Louise Maude. London: Oxford University Press, 1934.

Trolander, Judith Ann. *Professionalism and Social Change: From the Settlement House Movement to Neighborhood Centers, 1886 to the Present.* New York: Columbia University Press, 1987.

Troyat, Henri. *Tolstoy.* Translated by Nancy Amphoux. Garden City, New York: Doubleday, 1967.

The Vice Commission of Chicago. *The Social Evil in Chicago.* Chicago: Gunthorp-Warren Printing Company, 1911.

Wald, Lillian. *The House on Henry Street.* New York: Henry Holt, 1915.

Walkowitz, Judith R. "Male Vice and Female Virtue: Feminism and the Politics of Prostitution in Nineteenth-Century Britain." In *Powers of Desire: The Politics of Sexuality,* edited by Ann Snitow, Christine Stansell, and Sharon Thompson, 420–33. New York: Monthly Review Press, 1983.

Weber, Adna Ferrin. *The Growth of Cities in the Nineteenth Century: A Study in Statistics.* New York: Macmillan, 1899; reprint, Ithaca: Cornell University Press, 1963.

Weeks, Jeffery. *Sex, Politics and Society: The Regulation of Sexuality since 1800.* London: Longman, 1981.

West, James L. W., III. "The Composition of *Jennie Gerhardt.*" In *Jennie Gerhardt,* edited by Thomas P. Riggio, James L. W. West III, and Lee Ann Draud, 421–60. Philadelphia: University of Pennsylvania Press, 1992.

Wharton, Edith. *The Letters of Edith Wharton.* Edited by R. W. B Lewis and Nancy Lewis. New York: Scribners, 1988.

———. *A Son at the Front.* New York: Scribner's, 1922.

Wiebe, Robert H. *The Search for Order, 1877–1920.* New York: Hill and Wang, 1967.

Wilcox, Delos F. *The American City: A Problem in Democracy.* Citizen's Library Series. New York: Macmillan, 1904.

Wilson, Carol Green. *Chinatown Quest.* San Francisco: California Historical Society, 1974.

Wilson, Christopher P. *The Labor of Words: Literary Professionalism in the Progressive Era.* Athens: University of Georgia Press, 1985.

Wilson, Margaret Gibbons. *The American Woman in Transition: The Urban Influence, 1870–1920.* Westport, Connecticut: Greenwood Press, 1979.

Woolf, Virginia. "Modern Fiction." In *The Common Reader,* 184–95. London and New York: Harcourt, Brace & World, 1925.

———. *Mrs. Dalloway.* 1925; reprint, San Diego: Harcourt Brace Jovanovich, 1981.

———. *A Room of One's Own.* London: Harcourt Brace Jovanovich, 1929.

———. "Women and Fiction," *The Forum* (March 1929). In *Women and Writing,* edited by Michele Barrett, 43–52. San Diego, New York, and London: Harcourt Brace Jovanovich, 1979.

Zola, Emile. *L'Assommoir.* 1876; translated by Leonard Tancock, London: Penguin, 1970.

———. "Le Roman Experimental." In *Le Roman experimental,* Paris, 1880. Translated in *Documents of Modern Literary Realism,* edited by George J. Becker, 162–96. Princeton: Princeton University Press, 1963.

INDEX

Adams, Henry, 60, 106

Adams, Henry C.: *Philanthropy and Social Progress* (editor), 44

Abbott, Edith, 233

Abbott, Grace: as advisor and friend, 205; collaboration on *My Friend, Julia Lathrop*, 249, 250–53, 256–60; health of, 238; views on Nobel Prize, 236

Addams, Anna Haldeman (stepmother), 8, 21–22

Addams, Jane: aging of, 228–29; appearance of, 28, 112: awards and honors, 75, 215, 230, 232, 235, 256; books (*see under specific titles*); campaigning, 140–41; caring for friends, 233, 235–36, 246–47; as character in novel, 149–50; charisma of, 28–29; criticism of her politics and pacifism, 69, 12, 135, 178, 188–93, 194–95, 200–201, 202–7, 213, 215, 216–17; death of, 261; destruction of correspondence, 256–57; diaries of, 25–35, 51–52; earnings of, 70, 73–74, 78, 79, 92–93, 105, 118–20, 137, 143–44, 243, 189, 216, 235, 237, 241; education of, 8, 23–25, 36–37; essays (*see under specific titles*); handwriting, 38, 183; and Hull-House, 5, 43; humor of, 71–72, 139, 158–59, 166, 217, 235, 257–58; and hysteria, 35–37; as icon, 10–12, 150; illness and health of, 114, 115, 166, 183, 185–86, 193, 203–4, 213, 218, 226, 234–37, 238–39, 247–48; inheritance of, 36, 54–55, 255–56; literary reputation of, 5, 13, 89–93; and "marriage" to Mary

Rozet Smith, 11, 47–48, 72, 75, 116, 120, 146, 150, 153, 189–90, 213, 223–24, 256–57; Nobel Peace Prize, 5, 229, 236–37; as pacifist and president of WILPF, 5, 155–62, 183; poetry of, 29–30, 48; political philosophy of, 135, 140; rejection letter, 187–88; religious belief of, 35; response to her own writing, 70, 74, 79–80, 199, 258–61; as "saint," 10–12; search for profession, 44; and sexual attraction, 11, 27–29, 34, 39; Smith College story, 26; social class, 71–72, 120; social ethics of, 62; social work, 5, 11, 211; and travel, 19, 35, 37–39, 40–42, 47–55, 69, 78, 92, 114, 118, 140, 143, 169–71, 182, 186, 193, 195, 197, 203, 206, 217, 240–41; and writer's block, 74, 115; and writing process, 73, 197–98, 209–10; and writing schedule, 104–5, 114–15, 120–21, 172, 182, 203–4, 212, 219, 230–31, 250, 256; writing style of, 2, 4–5, 15, 45, 59, 174–75, 176, 178, 191–92

Addams, John Huy (father): achievements of, 7; death of, 35

Addams, John Weber. *See* Addams, Weber

Addams, Martha (sister), 22

Addams, Sarah Alice. *See* Haldeman, Alice Addams

Addams, Sarah Weber (mother), 7, 21

Addams, Weber (brother): death of, 191; education of, 22; and mental illness, 115

Adler, Felix, 152

Alcott, Bronson, 30

Dunn, Margaret, 207
Durant, William J., 232

Edison, Thomas A., 152, 221, 243
Egypt trip, 173, 176–77
Einstein, Albert, 207, 221, 230, 250
Eliot, George (Aurore Dupin), 29
Eliot, T. S., 178
Elshtain, Jean Bethke: *Jane Addams and the Dream of American Democracy*, 3, 11–12, 60, 188; *Jane Addams Reader*, 263n3; views on Jane Addams as public intellectual, 264n8
Ely, Richard T.: as editor of *Hull-House Maps and Papers*, 46; as editor of *Newer Ideals of Peace*, 68, 69–70; as literary "godfather" to Jane Addams, 73, 75, 76, 102–3, 108, 155; views on writing style, 78–79, 210
Emergency Peace Federation, 186
Emerson, Ralph Waldo, 13, 62, 169
environmentalism, 86–87, 142–43
Epstein, Abraham: *Challenge of the Aged* (preface by Jane Addams), 218
Esenwein, Joseph (*Lippincott's Monthly Magazine*), 91
Euripides, 158, 172, 175
Evans, Augusta, 29
Evans, Elizabeth, 165
Everett, Edward, 29
Ewen, Elizabeth: *Immigrant Women in the Land of Dollars*, 130
Ewing, Charles H., 247
Excellent Becomes the Permanent, The (Jane Addams): contract and earnings of, 239; editing of, 239; literary discussion of, 14, 208, 239, 241; writing of, 238–39
"experimental moralist," 100–101, 103

fairy tales, 109–10
Farrell, James T., 6, 270n107
Farrell, John C., *Beloved Lady*, 12
Fay, Charles Norman, 215
Federation of Women's Clubs, 72

"Feed the World and Save the League" (Jane Addams), 195
Fellowship of Reconciliation, 202
Fellowship of Youth for Peace, 202
Feidel, Louis N., 232
Ferber, Edna, 184
Ferdinand, Franz, 150–51
Ferris, Henry, 255
Fields, James T., 117
Fisher, Dorothy Canfield, 254
"Fifteen Years at Hull-House" (Jane Addams), 77
First World War, 8, 11–12, 82. *See also* Great War; World War
"Five Sunday Mornings in England" (Jane Addams), 38
"Five Years of Effort toward Social Justice" (Jane Addams), 219
Ford, Henry, 179–82, 183
Ford Peace Ship, 180–82
Fossé, P., 165–66
Franklin, Benjamin, 10, 106
Frazer: *The Golden Bough*, 200
Freeman, Mary Wilkins, 106
Free Society. See Isaaks, Abraham
Freud, Sigmund, 223–24, 230
Frost, Robert, 224
Fuller, Henry Blake, 97
Fuller, Margaret, 29, 106–7
Funk, Antoinette, 156

Gale, Zona: as campaigner, 140; "Great Ladies of Halsted Street," 237–38; *Heart's Kindred*, 149–50, 156, 166; as literary "god daughter" of Jane Addams, 178–79, 184; view of *Long Road of Woman's Memory*, 185; view of war, 186; as writer, 111, 147
Galsworthy, John: 7, 118, 217
Garfield, James R., 79
Garland, Hamlin, 6, 134, 147, 184
Gavrilo, Princip, 150
Ghandhi, Mahatma, 221, 230, 241
Gibson, Mary Wilson: *The American Woman in Transition*, 61
Gilbert, Miriam: *Jane Addams, World Neighbor*, 12

186, 238; views on Eleanor
Roosevelt, 246; views on Ellen
Gates Starr, 227; views on Mary
Rozet Smith, 249
Walkins, Ferre (Captain), 214
Walkowitz, Judith: *City of Dreadful
Delight,* 123
Wall Street Journal. See Caldwell,
Christopher
"War against War" campaign, 154
Ward, Mary (Mrs. Humphrey Ward),
49, 95–96, 103, 109, 147
warring instinct, 80–81
Waugh, Catharine, 30
Webb, Beatrice Potter, 7, 49
Webb, Sidney J., 7, 49
Weber, Adna Ferrin: *The Growth of
Cities in the Nineteenth Century,*
86
Weeks, Jeffrey, 125
Wells, H. G.: as character in Jane Add-
ams's writing, 221; as intellectual,
7, 207, 230; as pacifist, 82, 212, 217;
visit to Hull-House, 78
Wells-Barnett, Ida: *The Red Record,* 6,
91, 98. *See also* race relations
Wharton, Edith, 6, 37, 95, 106, 147
White, Allon: *The Politics and Poet-
ics of Transgression,* 125
White, Eva, 245
White, William Allen, 111, 207
white slavery, 99–100, 121–28, 174
Whitman, Walt, 5, 85, 221, 225
Wilcox, Delos: *The American City,* 86
Williams, Corinne, 28–29, 31–32
Williams, Michael, 245
Wilson, Woodrow: as candidate for
president, 141, 183; as character in
Jane Addams's writing, 199–200;
and Nobel Peace Prize, 1920, 194;
relationship with Jane Addams,
185; views on war and peace, 151–
52, 156, 185–86, 199–200

Winthrop, Allen, 249
Wise, Winifred E.: *Jane Addams of
Hull-House,* 244, 251, 255
Wolbrecht, Christina, 277n98
Wolf, Christa, 263n1
Women at The Hague (Jane Addams,
Emily Balch, and Alice Hamilton):
editing of, 163, 166; literary discus-
sion of, 14, 162–67; writing of, 163,
166–67
Women's International League for
Peace and Freedom: Jane Addams as
president 12, 202, 222, 237, 240; at-
tacks on, 215; congresses, 163–64,
179, 193–94, 240, 249–50, 257–59
Women's Peace Party, 157–58, 184,
186, 201
Woods, Robert, 115–16
Woolf, Leonard, 207, 217
Woolf, Virginia: as character in Jane
Addams's writing, 207–8, 225; and
Hogarth Press, 207; influence on
Jane Addams's writing, 7, 175, 221,
227, 230, 253; "Women's Fiction,"
210–11
Woolley, Mary E., 218
Wordsworth, William, 45, 96, 170
"World Food Supply—America's Obli-
gation, The" (Jane Addams), 191
World War, 150–51, 211. *See also* First
World War; Great War
Wright, Blanche, 144
Wright, Orville, 243
Wright, Richard, 6, 93–94
Wu, Amy, 234
Wyatt, Edith F., 184

Yeats, William Butler, 172
Young, Ella Flagg, 147

Zola, Emile: Dreyfus case, 217;
L'Assommoir, 98–99; literary naturalism, 93, 96, 101, 147, 224

KATHERINE JOSLIN is a professor of English and director of the program in American studies at Western Michigan University. She is coeditor of *American Feminism: Key Source Documents, 1848–1920* (2003) and *Wretched Exotic: Essays on Edith Wharton in Europe* (1996), and is the author of *Edith Wharton* (1991) and numerous essays.

The University of Illinois Press
is a founding member of the
Association of American University Presses.

University of Illinois Press
1325 South Oak Street
Champaign, IL 61820-6903
www.press.uillinois.edu